PRAISE FOR *THE LINUX COMMAND LINE*

"I can honestly say I have found THE beginner's guide to Linux."
—LINUX JOURNAL

"Anyone who reads this book and makes use of the examples provided will not be able to avoid becoming a Unix command line pro by the time they've hit the end of the book."
—ITWORLD

"The most approachable tome on the subject."
—LINUX MAGAZINE

"If you're new to the command line, there is definitely a lot that you can learn from this book."
—UBUNTU MUSINGS

"This is exactly what a Linux beginner needs to get up to speed quickly. The book goes beyond simply walking through all of the command line utilities, and ventures into the realm of theory and how things work together."
—NICHOLAS C. ZAKAS, WEB SOFTWARE ENGINEER AND AUTHOR

"This is the best introduction to the command line I have read."
—BEGINLINUX.COM

"There is so much information contained within this book [that] you're almost guaranteed to learn something. I did."
—THE LINUX BLOG

"The best single source of Linux command line instruction available."
—ECOMMERCE DEVELOPER

THE LINUX COMMAND LINE

A Complete Introduction

by William E. Shotts, Jr.

no starch press

San Francisco

THE LINUX COMMAND LINE. Copyright © 2012 by William E. Shotts, Jr.

Eleventh printing

19 18 17   11 12 13

ISBN-10: 1-59327-389-4
ISBN-13: 978-1-59327-389-7

Publisher: William Pollock
Production Editor: Serena Yang
Cover Design: Octopod Studios
Developmental Editor: Keith Fancher
Technical Reviewer: Therese Bao
Copyeditor: Ward Webber
Compositors: Serena Yang and Alison Law
Proofreader: Paula L. Fleming

For information on bulk sales, distributors, or translations, please contact No Starch Press, Inc. directly:

No Starch Press, Inc.
245 8th Street, San Francisco, CA 94103
phone: 1.415.863.9900; info@nostarch.com; www.nostarch.com

Library of Congress Cataloging-in-Publication Data

Shotts, William E.
 The Linux command line: a complete introduction / William E. Shotts, Jr.
     p. cm.
 Includes index.
 ISBN-13: 978-1-59327-389-7 (pbk.)
 ISBN-10: 1-59327-389-4 (pbk.)
 1. Linux. 2. Scripting Languages (Computer science) 3. Operating systems (Computers) I. Title.
 QA76.76.O63S5556 2011
 005.4'32--dc23

                                    2011029198

To Karen

BRIEF CONTENTS

PART 4: WRITING SHELL SCRIPTS

CONTENTS IN DETAIL

PART 1
LEARNING THE SHELL

12
A GENTLE INTRODUCTION TO VI

13
CUSTOMIZING THE PROMPT

PART 3
COMMON TASKS AND ESSENTIAL TOOLS

14
PACKAGE MANAGEMENT

15
STORAGE MEDIA

20
TEXT PROCESSING

233

21
FORMATTING OUTPUT 267

22
PRINTING 285

23
COMPILING PROGRAMS 297

PART 4
WRITING SHELL SCRIPTS

35
ARRAYS

36
EXOTICA

ACKNOWLEDGMENTS

I want to thank the following people who helped make
this book possible.

First, the people who inspired me: Jenny Watson, Acquisitions Editor
at Wiley Publishing, originally suggested that I write a shell-scripting book.
Though Wiley didn't accept my proposal, it became the basis of this book.
John C. Dvorak, noted columnist and pundit, gave great advice. In an
episode of his video podcast, "Cranky Geeks," Mr. Dvorak described the
process of writing: "Hell. Write 200 words a day and in a year, you have a
novel." This tip led me to write a page a day until I had a book. Dmitri
Popov wrote an article in *Free Software Magazine* titled "Creating a book template with Writer," which inspired me to use OpenOffice.org Writer for
composing the text. As it turned out, it worked wonderfully.

Next, the volunteers who helped me produce the original, freely dis-
tributable version of this book (available at LinuxCommand.org): Mark
Polesky performed an extraordinary review and test of the text. Jesse Becker,
Tomasz Chrzczonowicz, Michael Levin, and Spence Miner also tested and
reviewed portions of the text. Karen M. Shotts contributed a lot of hours
editing my original manuscript.

Next, the good folks at No Starch Press who worked long and hard making the commercial version of my book: Serena Yang, Production Manager; Keith Fancher, my editor; and the rest of the No Starch Press staff.

And lastly, the readers of LinuxCommand.org, who have sent me so many kind emails. Their encouragement gave me the idea that I was really on to something!

INTRODUCTION

I want to tell you a story. No, not the story of how, in 1991, Linus Torvalds wrote the first version of the Linux kernel. You can read that story in lots of Linux books. Nor am I going to tell you the story of how, some years earlier, Richard Stallman began the GNU Project to create a free Unix-like operating system. That's an important story too, but most other Linux books have that one, as well. No, I want to tell you the story of how you can take back control of your computer.

When I began working with computers as a college student in the late 1970s, there was a revolution going on. The invention of the microprocessor had made it possible for ordinary people like you and me to actually own a computer. It's hard for many people today to imagine what the world was like when only big business and big government ran all the computers. Let's just say you couldn't get much done.

Today, the world is very different. Computers are everywhere, from tiny wristwatches to giant data centers to everything in between. In addition to ubiquitous computers, we also have a ubiquitous network connecting them together. This has created a wondrous new age of personal empowerment and creative freedom, but over the last couple of decades something else has been happening. A single giant corporation has been imposing its control over most of the world's computers and deciding what you can and cannot do with them. Fortunately, people from all over the world are doing something about it. They are fighting to maintain control of their computers by writing their own software. They are building Linux.

Many people speak of "freedom" with regard to Linux, but I don't think most people know what this freedom really means. Freedom is the power to decide what your computer does, and the only way to have this freedom is to know what your computer is doing. Freedom is a computer that is without secrets, one where everything can be known if you care enough to find out.

Why Use the Command Line?

Have you ever noticed in the movies when the "super hacker"—you know, the guy who can break into the ultra-secure military computer in under 30 seconds—sits down at the computer, he never touches a mouse? It's because movie makers realize that we, as human beings, instinctively know the only way to really get anything done on a computer is by typing on a keyboard.

Most computer users today are familiar with only the *graphical user interface (GUI)* and have been taught by vendors and pundits that the *command line interface (CLI)* is a terrifying thing of the past. This is unfortunate, because a good command line interface is a marvelously expressive way of communicating with a computer in much the same way the written word is for human beings. It's been said that "graphical user interfaces make easy tasks easy, while command line interfaces make difficult tasks possible," and this is still very true today.

Since Linux is modeled after the Unix family of operating systems, it shares the same rich heritage of command line tools as Unix. Unix came into prominence during the early 1980s (although it was first developed a decade earlier), before the widespread adoption of the graphical user interface and, as a result, developed an extensive command line interface instead. In fact, one of the strongest reasons early adopters of Linux chose it over, say, Windows NT was the powerful command line interface, which made the "difficult tasks possible."

What This Book Is About

This book is a broad overview of "living" on the Linux command line. Unlike some books that concentrate on just a single program, such as the shell program, bash, this book will try to convey how to get along with the command line interface in a larger sense. How does it all work? What can it do? What's the best way to use it?

This is not a book about Linux system administration. While any serious discussion of the command line will invariably lead to system administration topics, this book touches on only a few administration issues. It will, however, prepare the reader for additional study by providing a solid foundation in the use of the command line, an essential tool for any serious system administration task.

This book is very Linux-centric. Many other books try to broaden their appeal by including other platforms, such as generic Unix and Mac OS X. In doing so, they "water down" their content to feature only general topics. This book, on the other hand, covers only contemporary Linux distributions. Ninety-five percent of the content is useful for users of other Unix-like systems, but this book is highly targeted at the modern Linux command line user.

Who Should Read This Book

This book is for new Linux users who have migrated from other platforms. Most likely you are a "power user" of some version of Microsoft Windows. Perhaps your boss has told you to administer a Linux server, or maybe you're just a desktop user who is tired of all the security problems and want to give Linux a try. That's fine. All are welcome here.

That being said, there is no shortcut to Linux enlightenment. Learning the command line is challenging and takes real effort. It's not that it's so hard, but rather it's so *vast*. The average Linux system has literally *thousands* of programs you can employ on the command line. Consider yourself warned: Learning the command line is not a casual endeavor.

On the other hand, learning the Linux command line is extremely rewarding. If you think you're a "power user" now, just wait. You don't know what real power is—yet. And, unlike many other computer skills, knowledge of the command line is long lasting. The skills learned today will still be useful 10 years from now. The command line has survived the test of time.

It is also assumed that you have no programming experience—not to worry. We'll start you down that path as well.

What's in This Book

This material is presented in a carefully chosen sequence, much as though a tutor were sitting next to you, guiding you along. Many authors treat this material in a "systematic" fashion, which makes sense from a writer's perspective but can be very confusing to new users.

Another goal is to acquaint you with the Unix way of thinking, which is different from the Windows way of thinking. Along the way, we'll go on a few side trips to help you understand why certain things work the way they do and how they got that way. Linux is not just a piece of software; it's also a small part of the larger Unix culture, which has its own language and history. I might throw in a rant or two, as well.

This book is divided into four parts, each covering some aspect of the command line experience:

- **Part 1: Learning the Shell** starts our exploration of the basic language of the command line, including such things as the structure of commands, filesystem navigation, command line editing, and finding help and documentation for commands.

- **Part 2: Configuration and the Environment** covers editing configuration files that control the computer's operation from the command line.

- **Part 3: Common Tasks and Essential Tools** explores many of the ordinary tasks that are commonly performed from the command line. Unix-like operating systems, such as Linux, contain many "classic" command-line programs that are used to perform powerful operations on data.

- **Part 4: Writing Shell Scripts** introduces shell programming, an admittedly rudimentary, but easy to learn, technique for automating many common computing tasks. By learning shell programming, you will become familiar with concepts that can be applied to many other programming languages.

How to Read This Book

Start at the beginning of the book and follow it to the end. It isn't written as a reference work; it's really more like a story with a beginning, a middle, and an end.

Prerequisites

To use this book, all you will need is a working Linux installation. You can get this in one of two ways:

- **Install Linux on a (not so new) computer.** It doesn't matter which distribution you choose, though most people today start out with Ubuntu, Fedora, or OpenSUSE. If in doubt, try Ubuntu first. Installing a modern Linux distribution can be ridiculously easy or ridiculously difficult, depending on your hardware. I suggest a desktop computer that is a couple of years old and has at least 256MB of RAM and 6GB of free hard disk space. Avoid laptops and wireless networks if at all possible, as these are often more difficult to get working.

- **Use a live CD.** One of the cool things you can do with many Linux distributions is run them directly from a CD-ROM without installing them at all. Just go into your BIOS setup, set your computer to "Boot from CDROM," insert the live CD, and reboot.. Using a live CD is a great way to test a computer for Linux compatibility prior to installation. The disadvantage of using a live CD is that it may be very slow compared to having Linux installed on your hard drive. Both Ubuntu and Fedora (among others) have live CD versions.

Note: *Regardless of how you install Linux, you will need to have occasional superuser (i.e., administrative) privileges to carry out the lessons in this book.*

After you have a working installation, start reading and follow along with your own computer. Most of the material in this book is "hands on," so sit down and get typing!

WHY I DON'T CALL IT "GNU/LINUX"

In some quarters, it's politically correct to call the Linux operating system the "GNU/Linux operating system." The problem with "Linux" is that there is no completely correct way to name it because it was written by many different people in a vast, distributed development effort. Technically speaking, Linux is the name of the operating system's kernel, nothing more. The kernel is very important, of course, since it makes the operating system go, but it's not enough to form a complete operating system.

Enter Richard Stallman, the genius-philosopher who founded the Free Software movement, started the Free Software Foundation, formed the GNU Project, wrote the first version of the GNU C Compiler (GCC), created the GNU General Public License (the GPL), etc., etc. He *insists* that you call it "GNU/Linux" to properly reflect the contributions of the GNU Project. While the GNU Project predates the Linux kernel and the project's contributions are extremely deserving of recognition, placing them in the name is unfair to everyone else who made significant contributions. Besides, I think "Linux/GNU" would be more technically accurate since the kernel boots first and everything else runs on top of it.

In popular usage, "Linux" refers to the kernel and all the other free and open source software found in the typical Linux distribution—that is, the entire Linux ecosystem, not just the GNU components. The operating system marketplace seems to prefer one-word names such as DOS, Windows, Solaris, Irix, AIX. I have chosen to use the popular format. If, however, you prefer to use "GNU/Linux" instead, please perform a mental search and replace while reading this book. I won't mind.

PART 1

LEARNING THE SHELL

1

WHAT IS THE SHELL?

When we speak of the command line, we are really referring to the shell. The *shell* is a program that takes keyboard commands and passes them to the operating system to carry out. Almost all Linux distributions supply a shell program from the GNU Project called bash. The name *bash* is an acronym for *Bourne Again Shell,* a reference to the fact that bash is an enhanced replacement for sh, the original Unix shell program written by Steve Bourne.

Terminal Emulators

When using a graphical user interface, we need another program called a *terminal emulator* to interact with the shell. If we look through our desktop menus, we will probably find one. KDE uses konsole and GNOME uses gnome-terminal, though it's likely called simply "terminal" on our menu. A number of other terminal emulators are available for Linux, but they all do basically the same thing: give us access to the shell. You will probably develop a preference for one or another based on the number of bells and whistles it has.

Your First Keystrokes

So let's get started. Launch the terminal emulator! Once it comes up, you should see something like this:

```
[me@linuxbox ~]$
```

This is called a *shell prompt,* and it appears whenever the shell is ready to accept input. While it may vary in appearance somewhat, depending on the distribution, it will usually include your *username@machinename,* followed by the current working directory (more about that in a little bit) and a dollar sign.

If the last character of the prompt is a hash mark (#) rather than a dollar sign, the terminal session has *superuser* privileges. This means that either we are logged in as the root user or we've selected a terminal emulator that provides superuser (administrative) privileges.

Assuming that things are good so far, let's try some typing. Enter some gibberish at the prompt like so:

```
[me@linuxbox ~]$ kaekfjaeifj
```

Since this command makes no sense, the shell tells us so and gives us another chance:

```
bash: kaekfjaeifj: command not found
[me@linuxbox ~]$
```

Command History

If we press the up-arrow key, we see that the previous command kaekfjaeifj reappears after the prompt. This is called *command history.* Most Linux distributions remember the last 500 commands by default. Press the down-arrow key, and the previous command disappears.

Cursor Movement

Recall the previous command with the up-arrow key again. Now try the left- and right-arrow keys. See how we can position the cursor anywhere on the command line? This makes editing commands easy.

Try Some Simple Commands

Now that we have learned to type, let's try a few simple commands. The first one is date. This command displays the current time and date:

```
[me@linuxbox ~]$ date
Thu Oct 25 13:51:54 EDT 2012
```

A related command is cal, which, by default, displays a calendar of the current month:

```
[me@linuxbox ~]$ cal
     October 2012
Su Mo Tu We Th Fr Sa
    1  2  3  4  5  6
 7  8  9 10 11 12 13
14 15 16 17 18 19 20
21 22 23 24 25 26 27
28 29 30 31
```

To see the current amount of free space on your disk drives, enter **df**:

```
[me@linuxbox ~]$ df
Filesystem          1K-blocks      Used Available Use% Mounted on
/dev/sda2           15115452    5012392   9949716  34% /
/dev/sda5           59631908   26545424  30008432  47% /home
/dev/sda1             147764      17370    122765  13% /boot
tmpfs                 256856          0    256856   0% /dev/shm
```

Likewise, to display the amount of free memory, enter the **free** command:

```
[me@linuxbox ~]$ free
             total       used       free     shared    buffers     cached
Mem:        513712     503976       9736          0       5312     122916
-/+ buffers/cache: 375748     137964
Swap:      1052248     104712     947536
```

Ending a Terminal Session

We can end a terminal session by either closing the terminal emulator window or entering the exit command at the shell prompt:

```
[me@linuxbox ~]$ exit
```

THE CONSOLE BEHIND THE CURTAIN

Even if we have no terminal emulator running, several terminal sessions continue to run behind the graphical desktop. Called *virtual terminals* or *virtual consoles*, these sessions can be accessed on most Linux distributions by pressing CTRL-ALT-F1 through CTRL-ALT-F6 on most systems. When a session is accessed, it presents a login prompt into which we can enter our username and password. To switch from one virtual console to another, press ALT and F1–F6. To return to the graphical desktop, press ALT-F7.

2

NAVIGATION

The first thing we need to learn (besides just typing) is how to navigate the filesystem on our Linux system. In this chapter we will introduce the following commands:

- pwd—Print name of current working directory.
- cd—Change directory.
- ls—List directory contents.

Understanding the Filesystem Tree

Like Windows, a Unix-like operating system such as Linux organizes its files in what is called a *hierarchical directory structure*. This means that they are organized in a tree-like pattern of directories (sometimes called folders in other systems), which may contain files and other directories. The first directory in the filesystem is called the *root directory*. The root directory contains files and subdirectories, which contain more files and subdirectories, and so on.

Note that unlike Windows, which has a separate filesystem tree for each storage device, Unix-like systems such as Linux always have a single filesystem tree, regardless of how many drives or storage devices are attached to the computer. Storage devices are attached (or more correctly, *mounted*) at various points on the tree according to the whims of the *system administrator*, the person (or persons) responsible for the maintenance of the system.

The Current Working Directory

Most of us are probably familiar with a graphical file manager, which represents the filesystem tree, as in Figure 2-1. Notice that the tree is usually shown upended, that is, with the root at the top and the various branches descending below.

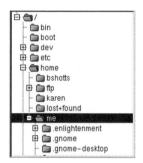

However, the command line has no pictures, so to navigate the filesystem tree, we need to think of it in a different way.

Imagine that the filesystem is a maze shaped like an upside-down tree and we are able to stand in the middle of it. At any given time, we are inside a single directory and we can see the files contained in the directory and the pathway to the directory above us (called the *parent directory*) and any sub-directories below us. The directory we are standing in is called the *current working directory*. To display the current working directory, we use the pwd (print working directory) command:

Figure 2-1: Filesystem tree as shown by a graphical file manager

```
[me@linuxbox ~]$ pwd
/home/me
```

When we first log in to our system (or start a terminal emulator session), our current working directory is set to our *home directory*. Each user account is given its own home directory, which is the only place the user is allowed to write files when operating as a regular user.

Listing the Contents of a Directory

To list the files and directories in the current working directory, we use the ls command:

```
[me@linuxbox ~]$ ls
Desktop  Documents  Music  Pictures  Public  Templates  Videos
```

Actually, we can use the ls command to list the contents of any directory, not just the current working directory, and it can do many other fun things as well. We'll spend more time with ls in Chapter 3.

Changing the Current Working Directory

To change your working directory (where we are standing in our tree-shaped maze) we use the cd command: Type **cd** followed by the pathname of the desired working directory. A *pathname* is the route we take along the branches of the tree to get to the directory we want. Pathnames can be specified in one of two ways, as absolute pathnames or as relative pathnames. Let's deal with absolute pathnames first.

Absolute Pathnames

An *absolute pathname* begins with the root directory and follows the tree branch by branch until the path to the desired directory or file is completed. For example, there is a directory on your system in which most of your system's programs are installed. The pathname of that directory is */usr/bin*. This means from the root directory (represented by the leading slash in the pathname) there is a directory called *usr* that contains a directory called *bin*.

```
[me@linuxbox ~]$ cd /usr/bin
[me@linuxbox bin]$ pwd
/usr/bin
[me@linuxbox bin]$ ls

...Listing of many, many files ...
```

Now we can see that we have changed the current working directory to */usr/bin* and that it is full of files. Notice how the shell prompt has changed? As a convenience, it is usually set up to automatically display the name of the working directory.

Relative Pathnames

Where an absolute pathname starts from the root directory and leads to its destination, a *relative pathname* starts from the working directory. To do this, it uses a couple of special symbols to represent relative positions in the file-system tree. These special symbols are . (dot) and .. (dot dot).

The . symbol refers to the working directory and the .. symbol refers to the working directory's parent directory. Here is how it works. Let's change the working directory to */usr/bin* again:

```
[me@linuxbox ~]$ cd /usr/bin
[me@linuxbox bin]$ pwd
/usr/bin
```

Okay, now let's say that we wanted to change the working directory to the parent of */usr/bin*, which is */usr*. We could do that two different ways, either with an absolute pathname:

```
[me@linuxbox bin]$ cd /usr
[me@linuxbox usr]$ pwd
/usr
```

or with a relative pathname:

```
[me@linuxbox bin]$ cd ..
[me@linuxbox usr]$ pwd
/usr
```

Two different methods produce identical results. Which one should we use? The one that requires the least typing!

Likewise, we can change the working directory from */usr* to */usr/bin* in two different ways, either by using an absolute pathname:

```
[me@linuxbox usr]$ cd /usr/bin
[me@linuxbox bin]$ pwd
/usr/bin
```

or with a relative pathname:

```
[me@linuxbox usr]$ cd ./bin
[me@linuxbox bin]$ pwd
/usr/bin
```

Now, there is something important that I must point out here. In almost all cases, you can omit the ./ because it is implied. Typing

```
[me@linuxbox usr]$ cd bin
```

does the same thing. In general, if you do not specify a pathname to something, the working directory will be assumed.

Some Helpful Shortcuts

In Table 2-1 we see some useful ways the current working directory can be quickly changed.

Table 2-1: cd Shortcuts

Shortcut	Result
cd	Changes the working directory to your home directory.
cd -	Changes the working directory to the previous working directory.
cd ~*username*	Changes the working directory to the home directory of *username*. For example, cd ~bob changes the directory to the home directory of user *bob*.

IMPORTANT FACTS ABOUT FILENAMES

- Filenames that begin with a period character are hidden. This only means that ls will not list them unless you say ls -a. When your account was created, several hidden files were placed in your home directory to configure things for your account. Later on we will take a closer look at some of those files to see how you can customize your environment. In addition, some applications place their configuration and settings files in your home directory as hidden files.

- Filenames and commands in Linux, as in Unix, are case sensitive. The filenames *File1* and *file1* refer to different files.

- Linux has no concept of a "file extension" like some other operating systems. You may name files any way you like. The contents and/or purpose of a file is determined by other means. Although Unix-like operating systems don't use file extensions to determine the contents/purpose of files, some application programs do.

- Though Linux supports long filenames that may contain embedded spaces and punctuation characters, limit the punctuation characters in the names of files you create to period, dash (hyphen), and underscore. *Most importantly, do not embed spaces in filenames.* Embedding spaces in filenames will make many command line tasks more difficult, as we will discover in Chapter 7. If you want to represent spaces between words in a filename, use underscore characters. You will thank yourself later.

3

EXPLORING THE SYSTEM

Now that we know how to move around the filesystem, it's time for a guided tour of our Linux system. Before we start, however, we're going to learn some more commands that will be useful along the way:

- ls—List directory contents.
- file—Determine file type.
- less—View file contents.

More Fun with ls

ls is probably the most used command and for good reason. With it, we can see directory contents and determine a variety of important file and directory attributes. As we have seen, we can simply enter ls to see a list of files and subdirectories contained in the current working directory:

```
[me@linuxbox ~]$ ls
Desktop  Documents  Music  Pictures  Public  Templates  Videos
```

Besides the current working directory, we can specify the directory to list, like so:

```
me@linuxbox ~]$ ls /usr
bin  games    kerberos  libexec  sbin   src
etc  include  lib       local    share  tmp
```

or even specify multiple directories. In this example we will list both the user's home directory (symbolized by the ~ character) and the */usr* directory:

```
[me@linuxbox ~]$ ls ~ /usr
/home/me:
Desktop  Documents  Music  Pictures  Public  Templates  Videos
/usr:
bin  games    kerberos  libexec  sbin   src
etc  include  lib       local    share  tmp
```

We can also change the format of the output to reveal more detail:

```
[me@linuxbox ~]$ ls -l
total 56
drwxrwxr-x 2 me me 4096 2012-10-26 17:20 Desktop
drwxrwxr-x 2 me me 4096 2012-10-26 17:20 Documents
drwxrwxr-x 2 me me 4096 2012-10-26 17:20 Music
drwxrwxr-x 2 me me 4096 2012-10-26 17:20 Pictures
drwxrwxr-x 2 me me 4096 2012-10-26 17:20 Public
drwxrwxr-x 2 me me 4096 2012-10-26 17:20 Templates
drwxrwxr-x 2 me me 4096 2012-10-26 17:20 Videos
```

By adding -l to the command, we changed the output to the long format.

Options and Arguments

This brings us to a very important point about how most commands work. Commands are often followed by one or more *options* that modify their behavior and, further, by one or more *arguments*, the items upon which the command acts. So most commands look something like this:

```
command -options arguments
```

Most commands use options consisting of a single character preceded by a dash, such as -l. But many commands, including those from the GNU Project, also support *long options*, consisting of a word preceded by two dashes. Also, many commands allow multiple short options to be strung together. In this example, the ls command is given two options, the l option to produce long format output, and the t option to sort the result by the file's modification time:

```
[me@linuxbox ~]$ ls -lt
```

We'll add the long option --reverse to reverse the order of the sort:

```
[me@linuxbox ~]$ ls -lt --reverse
```

The ls command has a large number of possible options. The most common are listed in Table 3-1.

Table 3-1: Common ls Options

Option	Long Option	Description
-a	--all	List all files, even those with names that begin with a period, which are normally not listed (i.e., hidden).
-d	--directory	Ordinarily, if a directory is specified, ls will list the contents of the directory, not the directory itself. Use this option in conjunction with the -l option to see details about the directory rather than its contents.
-F	--classify	This option will append an indicator character to the end of each listed name (for example, a forward slash if the name is a directory).
-h	--human-readable	In long format listings, display file sizes in human-readable format rather than in bytes.
-l		Display results in long format.
-r	--reverse	Display the results in reverse order. Normally, ls displays its results in ascending alphabetical order.
-S		Sort results by file size.
-t		Sort by modification time.

A Longer Look at Long Format

As we saw before, the -l option causes ls to display its results in long format. This format contains a great deal of useful information. Here is the Examples directory from an Ubuntu system:

```
-rw-r--r-- 1 root root 3576296 2012-04-03 11:05 Experience ubuntu.ogg
-rw-r--r-- 1 root root 1186219 2012-04-03 11:05 kubuntu-leaflet.png
-rw-r--r-- 1 root root   47584 2012-04-03 11:05 logo-Edubuntu.png
-rw-r--r-- 1 root root   44355 2012-04-03 11:05 logo-Kubuntu.png
-rw-r--r-- 1 root root   34391 2012-04-03 11:05 logo-Ubuntu.png
-rw-r--r-- 1 root root   32059 2012-04-03 11:05 oo-cd-cover.odf
-rw-r--r-- 1 root root  159744 2012-04-03 11:05 oo-derivatives.doc
-rw-r--r-- 1 root root   27837 2012-04-03 11:05 oo-maxwell.odt
-rw-r--r-- 1 root root   98816 2012-04-03 11:05 oo-trig.xls
```

```
-rw-r--r-- 1 root root   453764 2012-04-03 11:05 oo-welcome.odt
-rw-r--r-- 1 root root   358374 2012-04-03 11:05 ubuntu Sax.ogg
```

Let's look at the different fields from one of the files and examine their meanings in Table 3-2.

Table 3-2: ls Long Listing Fields

Field	Meaning
-rw-r--r--	Access rights to the file. The first character indicates the type of file. Among the different types, a leading dash means a regular file, while a d indicates a directory. The next three characters are the access rights for the file's owner, the next three are for members of the file's group, and the final three are for everyone else. The full meaning of this is discussed in Chapter 9.
1	File's number of hard links. See the discussion of links at the end of this chapter.
root	The user name of the file's owner.
root	The name of the group that owns the file.
32059	Size of the file in bytes.
2012-04-03 11:05	Date and time of the file's last modification.
oo-cd-cover.odf	Name of the file.

Determining a File's Type with file

As we explore the system, it will be useful to know what files contain. To do this, we will use the file command to determine a file's type. As we discussed earlier, filenames in Linux are not required to reflect a file's contents. For example, while a filename like *picture.jpg* would normally be expected to contain a JPEG compressed image, it is not required to in Linux. We can invoke the file command this way:

file *filename*

When invoked, the file command will print a brief description of the file's contents. For example:

```
[me@linuxbox ~]$ file picture.jpg
picture.jpg: JPEG image data, JFIF standard 1.01
```

There are many kinds of files. In fact, one of the common ideas in Unix-like operating systems such as Linux is that "everything is a file." As we proceed with our lessons, we will see just how true that statement is.

While many of the files on your system are familiar, for example MP3 and JPEG files, many kinds are a little less obvious, and a few are quite strange.

Viewing File Contents with less

The less command is a program to view text files. Throughout our Linux system, there are many files that contain human-readable text. The less program provides a convenient way to examine them.

Why would we want to examine text files? Because many of the files that contain system settings (called *configuration files*) are stored in this format, being able to read them gives us insight about how the system works. In addition, many of the actual programs that the system uses (called *scripts*) are stored in this format. In later chapters, we will learn how to edit text files in order to modify system settings and write our own scripts, but for now we will just look at their contents.

WHAT IS "TEXT"?

There are many ways to represent information on a computer. All methods involve defining a relationship between the information and some numbers that will be used to represent it. Computers, after all, understand only numbers, and all data is converted to numeric representation.

Some of these representation systems are very complex (such as compressed video files), while others are rather simple. One of the earliest and simplest is called *ASCII text*. ASCII (pronounced "As-Key") is short for American Standard Code for Information Interchange. This simple encoding scheme was first used on Teletype machines.

Text is a simple one-to-one mapping of characters to numbers. It is very compact. Fifty characters of text translate to fifty bytes of data. It is not the same as text in a word processor document such as one created by Microsoft Word or OpenOffice.org Writer. Those files, in contrast to simple ASCII text, contain many non-text elements that are used to describe their structure and formatting. Plain ASCII text files contain only the characters themselves and a few rudimentary control codes like tabs, carriage returns, and linefeeds.

Throughout a Linux system, many files are stored in text format, and many Linux tools work with text files. Even Windows recognizes the importance of this format. The well-known Notepad program is an editor for plain ASCII text files.

The less command is used like this:

```
less filename
```

Once started, the less program allows you to scroll forward and backward through a text file. For example, to examine the file that defines all the system's user accounts, enter the following command:

```
[me@linuxbox ~]$ less /etc/passwd
```

Once the less program starts, we can view the contents of the file. If the file is longer than one page, we can scroll up and down. To exit less, press the Q key.

Table 3-3 lists the most common keyboard commands used by less.

Table 3-3: less Commands

Command	Action
PAGE UP or b	Scroll back one page.
PAGE DOWN or Spacebar	Scroll forward one page.
Up Arrow	Scroll up one line.
Down Arrow	Scroll down one line.
G	Move to the end of the text file.
1G or g	Move to the beginning of the text file.
/characters	Search forward to the next occurrence of characters.
n	Search for the next occurrence of the previous search.
h	Display help screen.
q	Quit less.

LESS IS MORE

The less program was designed as an improved replacement of an earlier Unix program called more. Its name is a play on the phrase "less is more"—a motto of modernist architects and designers.

less falls into the class of programs called *pagers*, programs that allow the easy viewing of long text documents in a page-by-page manner. Whereas the more program could only page forward, the less program allows paging both forward and backward and has many other features as well.

A Guided Tour

The filesystem layout on your Linux system is much like that found on other Unix-like systems. The design is actually specified in a published standard called the *Linux Filesystem Hierarchy Standard.* Not all Linux distributions conform to the standard exactly, but most come pretty close.

Next, we are going to wander around the filesystem ourselves to see what makes our Linux system tick. This will give you a chance to practice your navigation skills. One of the things we will discover is that many of the interesting files are in plain, human-readable text. As we go about our tour, try the following:

1. cd into a given directory.

2. List the directory contents with ls -l.

3. If you see an interesting file, determine its contents with file.

4. If it looks as if it might be text, try viewing it with less.

Note: *Remember the copy-and-paste trick! If you are using a mouse, you can double-click a filename to copy it and middle-click to paste it into commands.*

As we wander around, don't be afraid to look at stuff. Regular users are largely prohibited from messing things up. That's the system administrator's job! If a command complains about something, just move on to something else. Spend some time looking around. The system is ours to explore. Remember, in Linux, there are no secrets!

Table 3-4 lists just a few of the directories we can explore. Feel free to try more!

Table 3-4: Directories Found on Linux Systems

Directory	Comments
/	The root directory, where everything begins.
/bin	Contains binaries (programs) that must be present for the system to boot and run.
/boot	Contains the Linux kernel, initial RAM disk image (for drivers needed at boot time), and the boot loader. Interesting files: • /boot/grub/grub.conf or menu.lst, which are used to configure the boot loader • /boot/vmlinuz, the Linux kernel

(continued)

Table 3-4 (*continued*)

Directory	Comments
/dev	This is a special directory that contains *device nodes*. "Everything is a file" also applies to devices. Here is where the kernel maintains a list of all the devices it understands.
/etc	The */etc* directory contains all of the system-wide configuration files. It also contains a collection of shell scripts that start each of the system services at boot time. Everything in this directory should be readable text. Interesting files: While everything in */etc* is interesting, here are some of my all-time favorites: • */etc/crontab*, a file that defines when automated jobs will run • */etc/fstab*, a table of storage devices and their associated mount points • */etc/passwd*, a list of the user accounts
/home	In normal configurations, each user is given a directory in */home*. Ordinary users can write files only in their home directories. This limitation protects the system from errant user activity.
/lib	Contains shared library files used by the core system programs. These are similar to DLLs in Windows.
/lost+found	Each formatted partition or device using a Linux filesystem, such as ext3, will have this directory. It is used in the case of a partial recovery from a filesystem corruption event. Unless something really bad has happened to your system, this directory will remain empty.
/media	On modern Linux systems the */media* directory will contain the mount points for removable media such as USB drives, CD-ROMs, etc. that are mounted automatically at insertion.
/mnt	On older Linux systems, the */mnt* directory contains mount points for removable devices that have been mounted manually.
/opt	The */opt* directory is used to install "optional" software. This is mainly used to hold commercial software products that may be installed on your system.

Table 3-4 (continued)

Directory	Comments
/proc	The /proc directory is special. It's not a real filesystem in the sense of files stored on your hard drive. Rather, it is a virtual filesystem maintained by the Linux kernel. The "files" it contains are peepholes into the kernel itself. The files are readable and will give you a picture of how the kernel sees your computer.
/root	This is the home directory for the root account.
/sbin	This directory contains "system" binaries. These are programs that perform vital system tasks that are generally reserved for the superuser.
/tmp	The /tmp directory is intended for storage of temporary, transient files created by various programs. Some configurations cause this directory to be emptied each time the system is rebooted.
/usr	The /usr directory tree is likely the largest one on a Linux system. It contains all the programs and support files used by regular users.
/usr/bin	/usr/bin contains the executable programs installed by your Linux distribution. It is not uncommon for this directory to hold thousands of programs.
/usr/lib	The shared libraries for the programs in /usr/bin.
/usr/local	The /usr/local tree is where programs that are not included with your distribution but are intended for system-wide use are installed. Programs compiled from source code are normally installed in /usr/local/bin. On a newly installed Linux system, this tree exists, but it will be empty until the system administrator puts something in it.
/usr/sbin	Contains more system administration programs.
/usr/share	/usr/share contains all the shared data used by programs in /usr/bin. This includes things like default configuration files, icons, screen backgrounds, sound files, etc.
/usr/share/doc	Most packages installed on the system will include some kind of documentation. In /usr/share/doc, we will find documentation files organized by package.

(continued)

Table 3-4 (continued)

Directory	Comments
/var	With the exception of /tmp and /home, the directories we have looked at so far remain relatively static; that is, their contents don't change. The /var directory tree is where data that is likely to change is stored. Various databases, spool files, user mail, etc. are located here.
/var/log	/var/log contains log files, records of various system activity. These are very important and should be monitored from time to time. The most useful one is /var/log/messages. Note that for security reasons on some systems, you must be the superuser to view log files.

Symbolic Links

As we look around, we are likely to see a directory listing with an entry like this:

```
lrwxrwxrwx 1 root root   11 2012-08-11 07:34 libc.so.6 -> libc-2.6.so
```

Notice how the first letter of the listing is l and the entry seems to have two filenames? This is a special kind of a file called a *symbolic link* (also known as a *soft link* or *symlink*). In most Unix-like systems it is possible to have a file referenced by multiple names. While the value of this may not be obvious now, it is really a useful feature.

Picture this scenario: A program requires the use of a shared resource of some kind contained in a file named *foo*, but *foo* has frequent version changes. It would be good to include the version number in the filename so the administrator or other interested party could see what version of *foo* is installed. This presents a problem. If we change the name of the shared resource, we have to track down every program that might use it and change it to look for a new resource name every time a new version of the resource is installed. That doesn't sound like fun at all.

Here is where symbolic links save the day. Let's say we install version 2.6 of *foo*, which has the filename *foo-2.6*, and then create a symbolic link simply called *foo* that points to *foo-2.6*. This means that when a program opens the file *foo*, it is actually opening the file *foo-2.6*. Now everybody is happy. The programs that rely on *foo* can find it, and we can still see what actual version is installed. When it is time to upgrade to *foo-2.7*, we just add the file to our system, delete the symbolic link *foo*, and create a new one that points to the new version. Not only does this solve the problem of the version upgrade, but it also allows us to keep both versions on our machine. Imagine that *foo-2.7* has a bug (damn those developers!) and we need to revert to the old version. Again, we just delete the symbolic link pointing to the new version and create a new symbolic link pointing to the old version.

The directory listing above (from the */lib* directory of a Fedora system) shows a symbolic link called *libc.so.6* that points to a shared library file called *libc-2.6.so*. This means that programs looking for *libc.so.6* will actually get the file *libc-2.6.so*. We will learn how to create symbolic links in the next chapter.

HARD LINKS

While we are on the subject of links, we need to mention that there is a second type of link called a *hard link*. Hard links also allow files to have multiple names, but they do it in a different way. We'll talk more about the differences between symbolic and hard links in the next chapter.

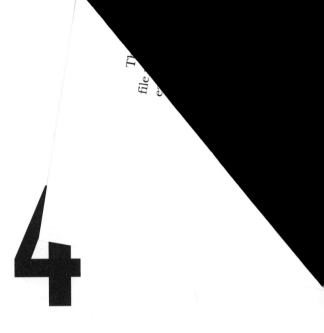

4

MANIPULATING FILES AND DIRECTORIES

At this point, we are ready for some real work! This chapter will introduce the following commands:

- cp—Copy files and directories.
- mv—Move/rename files and directories.
- mkdir—Create directories.
- rm—Remove files and directories.
- ln—Create hard and symbolic links.

These five commands are among the most frequently used Linux commands. They are used for manipulating both files and directories.

Now, to be frank, some of the tasks performed by these commands are more easily done with a graphical file manager. With a file manager, we can drag and drop a file from one directory to another, cut and paste files, delete files, and so on. So why use these old command-line programs?

The answer is power and flexibility. While it is easy to perform simple file manipulations with a graphical file manager, complicated tasks can be easier with the command-line programs. For example, how could we copy all the HTML files from one directory to another—but only those that do not exist in the destination directory or are newer than the versions in the destination directory? Pretty hard with a file manager. Pretty easy with the command line:

```
cp -u *.html destination
```

Wildcards

Before we begin using our commands, we need to talk about the shell feature that makes these commands so powerful. Because the shell uses filenames so much, it provides special characters to help you rapidly specify groups of filenames. These special characters are called *wildcards*. Using wildcards (also known as *globbing*) allows you to select filenames based on patterns of characters. Table 4-1 lists the wildcards and what they select.

Table 4-1: Wildcards

Wildcard	Matches
*	Any characters
?	Any single character
[*characters*]	Any character that is a member of the set *characters*
[!*characters*]	Any character that is not a member of the set *characters*
[[:*class*:]]	Any character that is a member of the specified *class*

Table 4-2 lists the most commonly used character classes.

Table 4-2: Commonly Used Character Classes

Character Class	Matches
[:alnum:]	Any alphanumeric character
[:alpha:]	Any alphabetic character
[:digit:]	Any numeral
[:lower:]	Any lowercase letter
[:upper:]	Any uppercase letter

Using wildcards makes it possible to construct very sophisticated selection criteria for filenames. Table 4-3 lists some examples of patterns and what they match.

Table 4-3: Wildcard Examples

Pattern	Matches
*	All files
g*	Any file beginning with *g*
b*.txt	Any file beginning with *b* followed by any characters and ending with *.txt*
Data???	Any file beginning with *Data* followed by exactly three characters
[abc]*	Any file beginning with either *a*, *b*, or *c*
BACKUP.[0-9][0-9][0-9]	Any file beginning with *BACKUP.* followed by exactly three numerals
[[:upper:]]*	Any file beginning with an uppercase letter
[![:digit:]]*	Any file not beginning with a numeral
*[[:lower:]123]	Any file ending with a lowercase letter or the numerals *1*, *2*, or *3*

Wildcards can be used with any command that accepts filenames as arguments, but we'll talk more about that in Chapter 7.

CHARACTER RANGES

If you are coming from another Unix-like environment or have been reading some other books on this subject, you may have encountered the [A-Z] or the [a-z] character range notations. These are traditional Unix notations and worked in older versions of Linux as well. They can still work, but you have to be very careful with them because they will not produce the expected results unless properly configured. For now, you should avoid using them and use character classes instead.

mkdir—Create Directories

The mkdir command is used to create directories. It works like this:

    mkdir directory...

A note on notation: In this book, when three periods follow an argument
in the description of a command (as above), it means that the argument can
be repeated; thus, in this case,

    mkdir dir1

would create a single directory named *dir1*, while

    mkdir dir1 dir2 dir3

would create three directories named *dir1*, *dir2*, and *dir3*.

cp—Copy Files and Directories

The cp command copies files or directories. It can be used two different ways:

    cp item1 item2

to copy the single file or directory *item1* to file or directory *item2* and:

    cp item... directory

to copy multiple items (either files or directories) into a directory.

Tables 4-4 and 4-5 list some of the commonly used options (the short option and the equivalent long option) for cp.

Table 4-4: cp Options

Option	Meaning
-a, --archive	Copy the files and directories and all of their attributes, including ownerships and permissions. Normally, copies take on the default attributes of the user performing the copy.
-i, --interactive	Before overwriting an existing file, prompt the user for confirmation. If this option is not specified, cp will silently overwrite files.
-r, --recursive	Recursively copy directories and their contents. This option (or the -a option) is required when copying directories.
-u, --update	When copying files from one directory to another, copy only files that either don't exist or are newer than the existing corresponding files in the destination directory.
-v, --verbose	Display informative messages as the copy is performed.

Table 4-5: cp Examples

Command	Results
cp file1 file2	Copy *file1* to *file2*. If *file2* exists, it is overwritten with the contents of *file1*. If *file2* does not exist, it is created.
cp -i file1 file2	Same as above, except that if *file2* exists, the user is prompted before it is overwritten.
cp file1 file2 dir1	Copy *file1* and *file2* into directory *dir1*. *dir1* must already exist.
cp dir1/* dir2	Using a wildcard, all the files in *dir1* are copied into *dir2*. *dir2* must already exist.
cp -r dir1 dir2	Copy directory *dir1* (and its contents) to directory *dir2*. If directory *dir2* does not exist, it is created and will contain the same contents as directory *dir1*.

mv—Move and Rename Files

The mv command performs both file moving and file renaming, depending on how it is used. In either case, the original filename no longer exists after the operation. mv is used in much the same way as cp:

    mv item1 item2

to move or rename file or directory *item1* to *item2* or

    mv item... directory

to move one or more items from one directory to another.

mv shares many of the same options as cp, as shown in Tables 4-6 and 4-7.

Table 4-6: mv Options

Option	Meaning
-i, --interactive	Before overwriting an existing file, prompt the user for confirmation. If this option is not specified, mv will silently overwrite files.
-u, --update	When moving files from one directory to another, move only files that either don't exist in the destination directory or are newer than the existing corresponding files in the destination directory.
-v, --verbose	Display informative messages as the move is performed.

Table 4-7: mv Examples

Command	Results
mv file1 file2	Move *file1* to *file2*. If *file2* exists, it is overwritten with the contents of *file1*. If *file2* does not exist, it is created. In either case, *file1* ceases to exist.
mv -i file1 file2	Same as above, except that if *file2* exists, the user is prompted before it is overwritten.
mv file1 file2 dir1	Move *file1* and *file2* into directory *dir1*. *dir1* must already exist.
mv dir1 dir2	Move directory *dir1* (and its contents) into directory *dir2*. If directory *dir2* does not exist, create directory *dir2*, move the contents of directory *dir1* into *dir2*, and delete directory *dir1*.

rm—Remove Files and Directories

The rm command is used to remove (delete) files and directories, like this:

    rm item...

where *item* is the name of one or more files or directories.

> ## BE CAREFUL WITH RM!
>
> Unix-like operating systems such as Linux do not have an undelete command. Once you delete something with rm, it's gone. Linux assumes you're smart and you know what you're doing.
>
> Be particularly careful with wildcards. Consider this classic example. Let's say you want to delete just the HTML files in a directory. To do this, you type:
>
>   rm *.html
>
> which is correct, but if you accidentally place a space between the * and the .html like so:
>
>   rm * .html
>
> the rm command will delete all the files in the directory and then complain that there is no file called *.html*.
>
> **Here is a useful tip:** Whenever you use wildcards with rm (besides carefully checking your typing!), test the wildcard first with ls. This will let you see the files that will be deleted. Then press the up arrow key to recall the command and replace the ls with rm.

Tables 4-8 and 4-9 list some of the common options for rm.

Table 4-8: rm Options

Option	Meaning
-i, --interactive	Before deleting an existing file, prompt the user for confirmation. If this option is not specified, rm will silently delete files.
-r, --recursive	Recursively delete directories. This means that if a directory being deleted has subdirectories, delete them too. To delete a directory, this option must be specified.
-f, --force	Ignore nonexistent files and do not prompt. This overrides the --interactive option.
-v, --verbose	Display informative messages as the deletion is performed.

Table 4-9: rm Examples

Command	Results
rm file1	Delete *file1* silently.
rm -i file1	Before deleting *file1*, prompt the user for confirmation.
rm -r file1 dir1	Delete *file1* and *dir1* and its contents.
rm -rf file1 dir1	Same as above, except that if either *file1* or *dir1* does not exist, rm will continue silently.

ln—Create Links

The ln command is used to create either hard or symbolic links. It is used in one of two ways:

    ln *file link*

to create a hard link and

    ln -s *item link*

to create a symbolic link where *item* is either a file or a directory.

Hard Links

Hard links are the original Unix way of creating links; symbolic links are more modern. By default, every file has a single hard link that gives the file its name. When we create a hard link, we create an additional directory entry for a file. Hard links have two important limitations:

- A hard link cannot reference a file outside its own filesystem. This means a link cannot reference a file that is not on the same disk partition as the link itself.

- A hard link cannot reference a directory.

A hard link is indistinguishable from the file itself. Unlike a directory list containing a symbolic link, a directory list containing a hard link shows no special indication of the link. When a hard link is deleted, the link is removed, but the contents of the file itself continue to exist (that is, its space is not deallocated) until all links to the file are deleted.

It is important to be aware of hard links because you might encounter them from time to time, but modern practice prefers symbolic links, which we will cover next.

Symbolic Links

Symbolic links were created to overcome the limitations of hard links. Symbolic links work by creating a special type of file that contains a text pointer to the referenced file or directory. In this regard they operate in much the same way as a Windows shortcut, though of course they predate the Windows feature by many years. ;-)

A file pointed to by a symbolic link and the symbolic link itself are largely indistinguishable from one another. For example, if you write something to the symbolic link, the referenced file is also written to. However, when you delete a symbolic link, only the link is deleted, not the file itself. If the file is deleted before the symbolic link, the link will continue to exist but will point to nothing. In this case, the link is said to be *broken*. In many implementations, the ls command will display broken links in a distinguishing color, such as red, to reveal their presence.

The concept of links can seem confusing, but hang in there. We're going to try all this stuff and it will, hopefully, become clear.

Let's Build a Playground

Since we are going to do some real file manipulation, let's build a safe place to "play" with our file manipulation commands. First we need a directory to work in. We'll create one in our home directory and call it *playground*.

Creating Directories

The mkdir command is used to create a directory. To create our *playground* directory, we will first make sure we are in our home directory and then create the new directory:

```
[me@linuxbox ~]$ cd
[me@linuxbox ~]$ mkdir playground
```

To make *playground* a little more interesting, let's create a couple of directories inside it called *dir1* and *dir2*. To do this, we will change our current working directory to *playground* and execute another mkdir:

```
[me@linuxbox ~]$ cd playground
[me@linuxbox playground]$ mkdir dir1 dir2
```

Notice that the mkdir command will accept multiple arguments, allowing us to create both directories with a single command.

Copying Files

Next, let's get some data into our playground. We'll do this by copying a file. Using the cp command, we'll copy the *passwd* file from the */etc* directory to the current working directory.

```
[me@linuxbox playground]$ cp /etc/passwd .
```

Notice how we used the shorthand for the current working directory, the single trailing period. So now if we perform an ls, we will see our file:

```
[me@linuxbox playground]$ ls -l
total 12
drwxrwxr-x 2 me   me 4096 2012-01-10 16:40 dir1
drwxrwxr-x 2 me   me 4096 2012-01-10 16:40 dir2
-rw-r--r-- 1 me   me 1650 2012-01-10 16:07 passwd
```

Now, just for fun, let's repeat the copy using the -v option (verbose) to see what it does:

```
[me@linuxbox playground]$ cp -v /etc/passwd .
`/etc/passwd' -> `./passwd'
```

The cp command performed the copy again, but this time it displayed a concise message indicating what operation it was performing. Notice that cp overwrote the first copy without any warning. Again, this is a case of cp assuming that you know what you're doing. To get a warning, we'll include the -i (interactive) option:

```
[me@linuxbox playground]$ cp -i /etc/passwd .
cp: overwrite `./passwd'?
```

Responding to the prompt by entering a y will cause the file to be over-written; any other character (for example, n) will cause cp to leave the file alone.

Moving and Renaming Files

Now, the name *passwd* doesn't seem very playful and this is a playground, so let's change it to something else:

```
[me@linuxbox playground]$ mv passwd fun
```

Let's pass the fun around a little by moving our renamed file to each of the directories and back again:

```
[me@linuxbox playground]$ mv fun dir1
```

moves it first to directory *dir1*. Then

```
[me@linuxbox playground]$ mv dir1/fun dir2
```

moves it from *dir1* to *dir2*. Then

```
[me@linuxbox playground]$ mv dir2/fun .
```

finally brings it back to the current working directory. Next, let's see the effect of mv on directories. First we will move our data file into *dir1* again:

```
[me@linuxbox playground]$ mv fun dir1
```

and then move *dir1* into *dir2* and confirm it with ls:

```
[me@linuxbox playground]$ mv dir1 dir2
[me@linuxbox playground]$ ls -l dir2
total 4
drwxrwxr-x 2 me   me    4096 2012-01-11 06:06 dir1
[me@linuxbox playground]$ ls -l dir2/dir1
total 4
-rw-r--r-- 1 me   me    1650 2012-01-10 16:33 fun
```

Note that because *dir2* already existed, mv moved *dir1* into *dir2*. If *dir2* had not existed, mv would have renamed *dir1* to *dir2*. Lastly, let's put everything back:

```
[me@linuxbox playground]$ mv dir2/dir1 .
[me@linuxbox playground]$ mv dir1/fun .
```

Creating Hard Links

Now we'll try some links. First the hard links: We'll create some links to our data file like so:

```
[me@linuxbox playground]$ ln fun fun-hard
[me@linuxbox playground]$ ln fun dir1/fun-hard
[me@linuxbox playground]$ ln fun dir2/fun-hard
```

So now we have four instances of the file *fun*. Let's take a look at our *playground* directory:

```
[me@linuxbox playground]$ ls -l
total 16
drwxrwxr-x 2 me   me    4096 2012-01-14 16:17 dir1
drwxrwxr-x 2 me   me    4096 2012-01-14 16:17 dir2
-rw-r--r-- 4 me   me    1650 2012-01-10 16:33 fun
-rw-r--r-- 4 me   me    1650 2012-01-10 16:33 fun-hard
```

One thing you notice is that the second field in the listing for *fun* and *fun-hard* both contain a *4*, which is the number of hard links that now exist for the file. You'll remember that a file will always have at least one link because the file's name is created by a link. So, how do we know that *fun* and *fun-hard* are, in fact, the same file? In this case, ls is not very helpful. While we can see that *fun* and *fun-hard* are both the same size (field 5), our listing provides no way to be sure they are the same file. To solve this problem, we're going to have to dig a little deeper.

When thinking about hard links, it is helpful to imagine that files are made up of two parts: the data part containing the file's contents and the name part, which holds the file's name. When we create hard links, we are actually creating additional name parts that all refer to the same data part. The system assigns a chain of disk blocks to what is called an *inode*, which is then associated with the name part. Each hard link therefore refers to a specific inode containing the file's contents.

The ls command has a way to reveal this information. It is invoked with the -i option:

```
[me@linuxbox playground]$ ls -li
total 16
12353539 drwxrwxr-x 2 me     me     4096 2012-01-14 16:17 dir1
12353540 drwxrwxr-x 2 me     me     4096 2012-01-14 16:17 dir2
12353538 -rw-r--r-- 4 me     me     1650 2012-01-10 16:33 fun
12353538 -rw-r--r-- 4 me     me     1650 2012-01-10 16:33 fun-hard
```

In this version of the listing, the first field is the inode number, and as we can see, both *fun* and *fun-hard* share the same inode number, which confirms they are the same file.

Creating Symbolic Links

Symbolic links were created to overcome the two disadvantages of hard links: Hard links cannot span physical devices, and hard links cannot reference directories, only files. Symbolic links are a special type of file that contains a text pointer to the target file or directory.

Creating symbolic links is similar to creating hard links:

```
[me@linuxbox playground]$ ln -s fun fun-sym
[me@linuxbox playground]$ ln -s ../fun dir1/fun-sym
[me@linuxbox playground]$ ln -s ../fun dir2/fun-sym
```

The first example is pretty straightforward: We simply add the -s option to create a symbolic link rather than a hard link. But what about the next two? Remember, when we create a symbolic link, we are creating a text description of where the target file is relative to the symbolic link. It's easier to see if we look at the ls output:

```
[me@linuxbox playground]$ ls -l dir1
total 4
-rw-r--r-- 4 me     me     1650 2012-01-10 16:33 fun-hard
lrwxrwxrwx 1 me     me        6 2012-01-15 15:17 fun-sym -> ../fun
```

The listing for *fun-sym* in *dir1* shows that it is a symbolic link by the leading l in the first field and the fact that it points to *../fun*, which is correct. Relative to the location of *fun-sym*, *fun* is in the directory above it. Notice too, that the length of the symbolic link file is 6, the number of characters in the string ../fun rather than the length of the file to which it is pointing.

When creating symbolic links, you can use either absolute pathnames, like this:

```
[me@linuxbox playground]$ ln -s /home/me/playground/fun dir1/fun-sym
```

or relative pathnames, as we did in our earlier example. Using relative pathnames is more desirable because it allows a directory containing symbolic links to be renamed and/or moved without breaking the links.

In addition to regular files, symbolic links can also reference directories:

```
[me@linuxbox playground]$ ln -s dir1 dir1-sym
[me@linuxbox playground]$ ls -l
total 16
drwxrwxr-x 2 me    me    4096 2012-01-15 15:17 dir1
lrwxrwxrwx 1 me    me       4 2012-01-16 14:45 dir1-sym -> dir1
drwxrwxr-x 2 me    me    4096 2012-01-15 15:17 dir2
-rw-r--r-- 4 me    me    1650 2012-01-10 16:33 fun
-rw-r--r-- 4 me    me    1650 2012-01-10 16:33 fun-hard
lrwxrwxrwx 1 me    me       3 2012-01-15 15:15 fun-sym -> fun
```

Removing Files and Directories

As we covered earlier, the rm command is used to delete files and directories. We are going to use it to clean up our playground a little bit. First, let's delete one of our hard links:

```
[me@linuxbox playground]$ rm fun-hard
[me@linuxbox playground]$ ls -l
total 12
drwxrwxr-x 2 me    me    4096 2012-01-15 15:17 dir1
lrwxrwxrwx 1 me    me       4 2012-01-16 14:45 dir1-sym -> dir1
drwxrwxr-x 2 me    me    4096 2012-01-15 15:17 dir2
-rw-r--r-- 3 me    me    1650 2012-01-10 16:33 fun
lrwxrwxrwx 1 me    me       3 2012-01-15 15:15 fun-sym -> fun
```

That worked as expected. The file *fun-hard* is gone and the link count shown for *fun* is reduced from four to three, as indicated in the second field of the directory listing. Next, we'll delete the file *fun*, and just for enjoyment, we'll include the -i option to show what that does:

```
[me@linuxbox playground]$ rm -i fun
rm: remove regular file `fun'?
```

Enter y at the prompt, and the file is deleted. But let's look at the output of ls now. Notice what happened to *fun-sym*? Since it's a symbolic link pointing to a now nonexistent file, the link is *broken*:

```
[me@linuxbox playground]$ ls -l
total 8
drwxrwxr-x 2 me    me    4096 2012-01-15 15:17 dir1
lrwxrwxrwx 1 me    me       4 2012-01-16 14:45 dir1-sym -> dir1
drwxrwxr-x 2 me    me    4096 2012-01-15 15:17 dir2
lrwxrwxrwx 1 me    me       3 2012-01-15 15:15 fun-sym -> fun
```

Most Linux distributions configure ls to display broken links. On a Fedora box, broken links are displayed in blinking red text! The presence of a broken link is not in and of itself dangerous, but it is rather messy. If we try to use a broken link, we will see this:

```
[me@linuxbox playground]$ less fun-sym
fun-sym: No such file or directory
```

Let's clean up a little. We'll delete the symbolic links:

```
[me@linuxbox playground]$ rm fun-sym dir1-sym
[me@linuxbox playground]$ ls -l
total 8
drwxrwxr-x 2 me    me    4096 2012-01-15 15:17 dir1
drwxrwxr-x 2 me    me    4096 2012-01-15 15:17 dir2
```

One thing to remember about symbolic links is that most file operations are carried out on the link's target, not the link itself. However, rm is an exception. When you delete a link, it is the link that is deleted, not the target.

Finally, we will remove our *playground*. To do this, we will return to our home directory and use rm with the recursive option (-r) to delete *playground* and all of its contents, including its subdirectories:

```
[me@linuxbox playground]$ cd
[me@linuxbox ~]$ rm -r playground
```

CREATING SYMLINKS WITH THE GUI

The file managers in both GNOME and KDE provide an easy and automatic method of creating symbolic links. With GNOME, holding the CTRL and SHIFT keys while dragging a file will create a link rather than copying (or moving) the file. In KDE, a small menu appears whenever a file is dropped, offering a choice of copying, moving, or linking the file.

Final Note

We've covered a lot of ground here, and the information may take a while to fully sink in. Perform the playground exercise over and over until it makes sense. It is important to get a good understanding of basic file manipulation commands and wildcards. Feel free to expand on the playground exercise by adding more files and directories, using wildcards to specify files for various operations. The concept of links may be a little confusing at first, but take the time to learn how they work. They can be a real lifesaver.

5

WORKING WITH COMMANDS

Up to this point, we have seen a series of mysterious commands, each with its own mysterious options and arguments. In this chapter, we will attempt to remove some of that mystery and even create some of our own commands. The commands introduced in this chapter are these:

- type—Indicate how a command name is interpreted.
- which—Display which executable program will be executed.
- man—Display a command's manual page.
- apropos—Display a list of appropriate commands.
- info—Display a command's info entry.
- whatis—Display a very brief description of a command.
- alias—Create an alias for a command.

What Exactly Are Commands?

A command can be one of four things:

- **An executable program** like all those files we saw in */usr/bin*. Within this category, programs can be *compiled binaries,* such as programs written in C and C++, or programs written in *scripting languages,* such as the shell, Perl, Python, Ruby, and so on.

- **A command built into the shell itself.** bash supports a number of commands internally called *shell builtins.* The cd command, for example, is a shell builtin.

- **A shell function.** *Shell functions* are miniature shell scripts incorporated into the *environment.* We will cover configuring the environment and writing shell functions in later chapters, but for now just be aware that they exist.

- **An alias.** An *alias* is a command that we can define ourselves, built from other commands.

Identifying Commands

It is often useful to know exactly which of the four kinds of commands is being used, and Linux provides a couple of ways to find out.

type—Display a Command's Type

The type command is a shell builtin that displays the kind of command the shell will execute, given a particular command name. It works like this:

    type command

where *command* is the name of the command you want to examine. Here are some examples:

```
[me@linuxbox ~]$ type type
type is a shell builtin
[me@linuxbox ~]$ type ls
ls is aliased to `ls --color=tty'
[me@linuxbox ~]$ type cp
cp is /bin/cp
```

Here we see the results for three different commands. Notice that the ls command (taken from a Fedora system) is actually an alias for the ls command with the --color=tty option added. Now we know why the output from ls is displayed in color!

which—Display an Executable's Location

Sometimes more than one version of an executable program is installed on a system. While this is not very common on desktop systems, it's not unusual on large servers. To determine the exact location of a given executable, the which command is used:

```
[me@linuxbox ~]$ which ls
/bin/ls
```

which works only for executable programs, not builtins or aliases that are substitutes for actual executable programs. When we try to use which on a shell builtin (for example, cd), we get either no response or an error message:

```
[me@linuxbox ~]$ which cd
/usr/bin/which: no cd in (/opt/jre1.6.0_03/bin:/usr/lib/qt-3.3/bin:/usr/kerber
os/bin:/opt/jre1.6.0_03/bin:/usr/lib/ccache:/usr/local/bin:/usr/bin:/bin:/home
/me/bin)
```

This is a fancy way of saying "command not found."

Getting a Command's Documentation

With this knowledge of what a command is, we can now search for the documentation available for each kind of command.

help—Get Help for Shell Builtins

bash has a built-in help facility for each of the shell builtins. To use it, type **help** followed by the name of the shell builtin. For example:

```
[me@linuxbox ~]$ help cd
cd: cd [-L|-P] [dir]
Change the current directory to DIR. The variable $HOME is the default DIR.
The variable CDPATH defines the search path for the directory containing DIR.
Alternative directory names in CDPATH are separated by a colon (:). A null
directory name is the same as the current directory, i.e. `.'. If DIR begins
with a slash (/), then CDPATH is not used. If the directory is not found, and
the shell option `cdable_vars' is set, then try the word as a variable name.
If that variable has a value, then cd to the value of that variable. The -P
option says to use the physical directory structure instead of following
symbolic links; the -L option forces symbolic links to be followed.
```

A note on notation: When square brackets appear in the description of a command's syntax, they indicate optional items. A vertical bar character indicates mutually exclusive items. An example is the cd command above: cd [-L|-P] [dir].

This notation says that the command cd may be followed optionally by either a -L or a -P and further, optionally followed by the argument dir.

While the output of help for the cd command is concise and accurate, it is by no means a tutorial, and as we can see, it also seems to mention a lot of things we haven't talked about yet! Don't worry. We'll get there.

--help—Display Usage Information

Many executable programs support a --help option that displays a description of the command's supported syntax and options. For example:

```
[me@linuxbox ~]$ mkdir --help
Usage: mkdir [OPTION] DIRECTORY...
Create the DIRECTORY(ies), if they do not already exist.

  -Z, --context=CONTEXT (SELinux) set security context to CONTEXT
Mandatory arguments to long options are mandatory for short options too.
  -m, --mode=MODE   set file mode (as in chmod), not a=rwx - umask
  -p, --parents     no error if existing, make parent directories as
                    needed
  -v, --verbose     print a message for each created directory
      --help        display this help and exit
      --version     output version information and exit
Report bugs to <bug-coreutils@gnu.org>.
```

Some programs don't support the --help option, but try it anyway. Often it results in an error message that will reveal the same usage information.

man—Display a Program's Manual Page

Most executable programs intended for command-line use provide a formal piece of documentation called a *manual* or *man page*. A special paging program called man is used to view them, like this:

    man *program*

where *program* is the name of the command to view.

Man pages vary somewhat in format but generally contain a title, a synopsis of the command's syntax, a description of the command's purpose, and a listing and description of each of the command's options. Man pages, however, do not usually include examples, and they are intended as a reference, not a tutorial. As an example, let's try viewing the man page for the ls command:

```
[me@linuxbox ~]$ man ls
```

On most Linux systems, man uses less to display the manual page, so all of the familiar less commands work while displaying the page.

The "manual" that man displays is broken into sections and covers not only user commands but also system administration commands, programming interfaces, file formats, and more. Table 5-1 describes the layout of the manual.

Table 5-1: Man Page Organization

Section	Contents
1	User commands
2	Programming interfaces for kernel system calls
3	Programming interfaces to the C library
4	Special files such as device nodes and drivers
5	File formats
6	Games and amusements such as screensavers
7	Miscellaneous
8	System administration commands

Sometimes we need to look in a specific section of the manual to find what we are looking for. This is particularly true if we are looking for a file format that is also the name of a command. If we don't specify a section number, we will always get the first instance of a match, probably in section 1. To specify a section number, we use man like this:

```
man section search_term
```

For example:

```
[me@linuxbox ~]$ man 5 passwd
```

will display the man page describing the file format of the */etc/passwd* file.

apropos—Display Appropriate Commands

It is also possible to search the list of man pages for possible matches based on a search term. Though crude, this approach is sometimes helpful. Here is an example of a search for man pages using the search term *floppy*:

```
[me@linuxbox ~]$ apropos floppy
create_floppy_devices (8)  - udev callout to create all possible
                               floppy device based on the CMOS type
fdformat             (8)  - Low-level formats a floppy disk
floppy               (8)  - format floppy disks
gfloppy              (1)  - a simple floppy formatter for the GNOME
mbadblocks           (1)  - tests a floppy disk, and marks the bad
                               blocks in the FAT
mformat              (1)  - add an MSDOS filesystem to a low-level
                               formatted floppy disk
```

The first field in each line of output is the name of the man page, and the second field shows the section. Note that the man command with the -k option performs exactly the same function as apropos.

whatis—Display a Very Brief Description of a Command

The whatis program displays the name and a one-line description of a man page matching a specified keyword:

```
[me@linuxbox ~]$ whatis ls
ls                      (1)  - list directory contents
```

THE MOST BRUTAL MAN PAGE OF THEM ALL

As we have seen, the manual pages supplied with Linux and other Unix-like systems are intended as reference documentation and not as tutorials. Many man pages are hard to read, but I think that the grand prize for difficulty has to go to the man page for bash. As I was doing my research for this book, I gave it a careful review to ensure that I was covering most of its topics. When printed, it's over 80 pages long and extremely dense, and its structure makes absolutely no sense to a new user.

On the other hand, it is very accurate and concise, as well as being extremely complete. So check it out if you dare, and look forward to the day when you can read it and it all makes sense.

info—Display a Program's Info Entry

The GNU Project provides an alternative to man pages called *info pages*. Info pages are displayed with a reader program named, appropriately enough, info. Info pages are *hyperlinked* much like web pages. Here is a sample:

```
File: coreutils.info,  Node: ls invocation,  Next: dir invocation, Up:
Directory listing


10.1 `ls': List directory contents
==================================

The `ls' program lists information about files (of any type, including
directories). Options and file arguments can be intermixed arbitrarily, as
usual.


   For non-option command-line arguments that are directories, by default `ls'
lists the contents of directories, not recursively, and omitting files with
names beginning with `.'. For other non-option arguments, by default `ls'
lists just the filename. If no non-option argument is specified, `ls' operates
on the current directory, acting as if it had been invoked with a single
argument of `.'.


   By default, the output is sorted alphabetically, according to the
--zz-Info: (coreutils.info.gz)ls invocation, 63 lines --Top----------
```

The `info` program reads *info files*, which are tree-structured into individual *nodes*, each containing a single topic. Info files contain hyperlinks that can move you from node to node. A hyperlink can be identified by its leading asterisk and is activated by placing the cursor upon it and pressing the ENTER key.

To invoke `info`, enter **info** followed optionally by the name of a program. Table 5-2 lists commands used to control the reader while displaying an info page.

Table 5-2: info Commands

Command	Action
?	Display command help.
PAGE UP or BACKSPACE	Display previous page.
PAGE DOWN or Spacebar	Display next page.
n	Next—Display the next node.
p	Previous—Display the previous node.
u	Up—Display the parent node of the currently displayed node, usually a menu.
ENTER	Follow the hyperlink at the cursor location.
q	Quit.

Most of the command-line programs we have discussed so far are part of the GNU Project's coreutils package, so you can find more information about them by typing

```
[me@linuxbox ~]$ info coreutils
```

which will display a menu page containing hyperlinks to documentation for each program provided by the coreutils package.

README and Other Program Documentation Files

Many software packages installed on your system have documentation files residing in the */usr/share/doc* directory. Most of these are stored in plaintext format and can be viewed with less. Some of the files are in HTML format and can be viewed with a web browser. We may encounter some files ending with a *.gz* extension. This indicates that they have been compressed with the gzip compression program. The gzip package includes a special version of less called zless, which will display the contents of gzip-compressed text files.

Creating Your Own Commands with alias

Now for our very first experience with programming! We will create a command of our own using the alias command. But before we start, we need to reveal a small command-line trick. It's possible to put more than one command on a line by separating each command with a semicolon character. It works like this:

    command1; *command2*; *command3*...

Here's the example we will use:

```
[me@linuxbox ~]$ cd /usr; ls; cd -
bin  games    kerberos  lib64    local  share  tmp
etc  include  lib       libexec  sbin   src
/home/me
[me@linuxbox ~]$
```

As we can see, we have combined three commands on one line. First we change directory to */usr*, then we list the directory, and finally we return to the original directory (by using cd -) so we end up where we started. Now let's turn this sequence into a new command using alias. The first thing we have to do is dream up a name for our new command. Let's try test. Before we do that, it would be a good idea to find out if the name test is already being used. To find out, we can use the type command again:

```
[me@linuxbox ~]$ type test
test is a shell builtin
```

Oops! The name test is already taken. Let's try foo:

```
[me@linuxbox ~]$ type foo
bash: type: foo: not found
```

Great! foo is not taken. So let's create our alias:

```
[me@linuxbox ~]$ alias foo='cd /usr; ls; cd -'
```

Notice the structure of this command:

    alias *name*='*string*'

After the command alias we give the alias a name followed immediately (no whitespace allowed) by an equal sign, which is followed immediately by a quoted string containing the meaning to be assigned to the name. After we define our alias, it can be used anywhere the shell would expect a command.

Let's try it:

```
[me@linuxbox ~]$ foo
bin   games     kerberos  lib64    local  share  tmp
etc   include   lib       libexec  sbin   src
/home/me
[me@linuxbox ~]$
```

We can also use the type command again to see our alias:

```
[me@linuxbox ~]$ type foo
foo is aliased to `cd /usr; ls; cd -'
```

To remove an alias, the unalias command is used, like so:

```
[me@linuxbox ~]$ unalias foo
[me@linuxbox ~]$ type foo
bash: type: foo: not found
```

While we purposely avoided naming our alias with an existing command name, it is sometimes desirable to do so. This is often done to apply a commonly desired option to each invocation of a common command. For instance, we saw earlier how the ls command is often aliased to add color support:

```
[me@linuxbox ~]$ type ls
ls is aliased to `ls --color=tty'
```

To see all the aliases defined in the environment, use the alias command without arguments. Here are some of the aliases defined by default on a Fedora system. Try to figure out what they all do:

```
[me@linuxbox ~]$ alias
alias l.='ls -d .* --color=tty'
alias ll='ls -l --color=tty'
alias ls='ls --color=tty'
```

There is one tiny problem with defining aliases on the command line. They vanish when your shell session ends. In a later chapter we will see how to add our own aliases to the files that establish the environment each time we log on, but for now, enjoy the fact that we have taken our first, albeit tiny, step into the world of shell programming!

Revisiting Old Friends

Now that we have learned how to find the documentation for commands, go and look up the documentation for all the commands we have encountered so far. Study what additional options are available and try them out!

6

REDIRECTION

In this lesson we are going to unleash what may be
the coolest feature of the command line: *I/O redirection.* The *I/O* stands for *input/output,* and with this facility you can redirect the input and output of
commands to and from files, as well as connect multiple commands to
make powerful command *pipelines.* To show off this facility, we will introduce the following commands:

- cat—Concatenate files.
- sort—Sort lines of text.
- uniq—Report or omit repeated lines.
- wc—Print newline, word, and byte counts for each file.
- grep—Print lines matching a pattern.
- head—Output the first part of a file.
- tail—Output the last part of a file.
- tee—Read from standard input and write to standard output and files.

Standard Input, Output, and Error

Many of the programs that we have used so far produce output of some kind. This output often consists of two types. First, we have the program's results; that is, the data the program is designed to produce. Second, we have status and error messages that tell us how the program is getting along. If we look at a command like ls, we can see that it displays its results and its error messages on the screen.

Keeping with the Unix theme of "everything is a file," programs such as ls actually send their results to a special file called *standard output* (often expressed as *stdout*) and their status messages to another file called *standard error* (*stderr*). By default, both standard output and standard error are linked to the screen and not saved into a disk file.

In addition, many programs take input from a facility called *standard input* (*stdin*), which is, by default, attached to the keyboard.

I/O redirection allows us to change where output goes and where input comes from. Normally, output goes to the screen and input comes from the keyboard, but with I/O redirection we can change that.

Redirecting Standard Output

I/O redirection allows us to redefine where standard output goes. To redirect standard output to another file instead of the screen, we use the > redirection operator followed by the name of the file. Why would we want to do this? It's often useful to store the output of a command in a file. For example, we could tell the shell to send the output of the ls command to the file *ls-output.txt* instead of the screen:

```
[me@linuxbox ~]$ ls -l /usr/bin > ls-output.txt
```

Here, we created a long listing of the */usr/bin* directory and sent the results to the file *ls-output.txt*. Let's examine the redirected output of the command:

```
[me@linuxbox ~]$ ls -l ls-output.txt
-rw-rw-r-- 1 me    me    167878 2012-02-01 15:07 ls-output.txt
```

Good—a nice, large, text file. If we look at the file with less, we will see that the file *ls-output.txt* does indeed contain the results from our ls command:

```
[me@linuxbox ~]$ less ls-output.txt
```

Now, let's repeat our redirection test but this time with a twist. We'll change the name of the directory to one that does not exist:

```
[me@linuxbox ~]$ ls -l /bin/usr > ls-output.txt
ls: cannot access /bin/usr: No such file or directory
```

We received an error message. This makes sense because we specified the nonexistent directory */bin/usr*, but why was the error message displayed on the screen rather than being redirected to the file *ls-output.txt*? The answer is that the ls program does not send its error messages to standard output. Instead, like most well-written Unix programs, it sends its error messages to standard error. Since we redirected only standard output and not standard error, the error message was still sent to the screen. We'll see how to redirect standard error in just a minute, but first, let's look at what happened to our output file:

```
[me@linuxbox ~]$ ls -l ls-output.txt
-rw-rw-r-- 1 me    me    0 2012-02-01 15:08 ls-output.txt
```

The file now has zero length! This is because, when we redirect output with the > redirection operator, the destination file is always rewritten from the beginning. Since our ls command generated no results and only an error message, the redirection operation started to rewrite the file and then stopped because of the error, resulting in its truncation. In fact, if we ever need to actually truncate a file (or create a new, empty file) we can use a trick like this:

```
[me@linuxbox ~]$ > ls-output.txt
```

Simply using the redirection operator with no command preceding it will truncate an existing file or create a new, empty file.

So, how can we append redirected output to a file instead of overwriting the file from the beginning? For that, we use the >> redirection operator, like so:

```
[me@linuxbox ~]$ ls -l /usr/bin >> ls-output.txt
```

Using the >> operator will result in the output being appended to the file. If the file does not already exist, it is created just as though the > operator had been used. Let's put it to the test:

```
[me@linuxbox ~]$ ls -l /usr/bin >> ls-output.txt
[me@linuxbox ~]$ ls -l /usr/bin >> ls-output.txt
[me@linuxbox ~]$ ls -l /usr/bin >> ls-output.txt
[me@linuxbox ~]$ ls -l ls-output.txt
-rw-rw-r-- 1 me    me    503634 2012-02-01 15:45 ls-output.txt
```

We repeated the command three times, resulting in an output file three times as large.

Redirecting Standard Error

Redirecting standard error lacks the ease of using a dedicated redirection operator. To redirect standard error we must refer to its *file descriptor*. A program can produce output on any of several numbered file streams. While we have referred to the first three of these file streams as standard input, output, and error, the shell references them internally as file descriptors 0, 1, and 2, respectively. The shell provides a notation for redirecting files using the file descriptor number. Since standard error is the same as file descriptor 2, we can redirect standard error with this notation:

```
[me@linuxbox ~]$ ls -l /bin/usr 2> ls-error.txt
```

The file descriptor 2 is placed immediately before the redirection operator to perform the redirection of standard error to the file *ls-error.txt*.

Redirecting Standard Output and Standard Error to One File

There are cases in which we may wish to capture all of the output of a command to a single file. To do this, we must redirect both standard output and standard error at the same time. There are two ways to do this. First, here is the traditional way, which works with old versions of the shell:

```
[me@linuxbox ~]$ ls -l /bin/usr > ls-output.txt 2>&1
```

Using this method, we perform two redirections. First we redirect standard output to the file *ls-output.txt*, and then we redirect file descriptor 2 (standard error) to file descriptor 1 (standard output) using the notation 2>&1.

Note: *Notice that the order of the redirections is significant. The redirection of standard error must always occur after redirecting standard output or it doesn't work. In the example above, >* ls-output.txt 2>&1 *redirects standard error to the file* ls-output.txt, *but if the order is changed to 2>&1 >* ls-output.txt, *standard error is directed to the screen.*

Recent versions of bash provide a second, more streamlined method for performing this combined redirection:

```
[me@linuxbox ~]$ ls -l /bin/usr &> ls-output.txt
```

In this example, we use the single notation &> to redirect both standard output and standard error to the file *ls-output.txt*.

Disposing of Unwanted Output

Sometimes silence really is golden, and we don't want output from a command—we just want to throw it away. This applies particularly to error and status messages. The system provides a way to do this by redirecting output to a special file called */dev/null*. This file is a system device called a *bit bucket*, which accepts input and does nothing with it. To suppress error messages from a command, we do this:

```
[me@linuxbox ~]$ ls -l /bin/usr 2> /dev/null
```

Redirecting Standard Input

Up to now, we haven't encountered any commands that make use of standard input (actually we have, but we'll reveal that surprise a little bit later), so we need to introduce one.

cat—Concatenate Files

The cat command reads one or more files and copies them to standard output like so:

```
cat [file...]
```

In most cases, you can think of cat as being analogous to the TYPE command in DOS. You can use it to display files without paging. For example,

```
[me@linuxbox ~]$ cat ls-output.txt
```

will display the contents of the file *ls-output.txt.* cat is often used to display short text files. Since cat can accept more than one file as an argument, it can also be used to join files together. Say we have downloaded a large file that has been split into multiple parts (multimedia files are often split this way on Usenet), and we want to join them back together. If the files were named

```
movie.mpeg.001  movie.mpeg.002 ... movie.mpeg.099
```

we could rejoin them with this command:

```
[me@linuxbox ~]$ cat movie.mpeg.0* > movie.mpeg
```

Since wildcards always expand in sorted order, the arguments will be arranged in the correct order.

This is all well and good, but what does this have to do with standard input? Nothing yet, but let's try something else. What happens if we enter cat with no arguments?

```
[me@linuxbox ~]$ cat
```

Nothing happens—it just sits there like it's hung. It may seem that way, but it's really doing exactly what it's supposed to.

If cat is not given any arguments, it reads from standard input, and since standard input is, by default, attached to the keyboard, it's waiting for us to type something!

Try this:

```
[me@linuxbox ~]$ cat
The quick brown fox jumped over the lazy dog.
```

Next, type CTRL-D (i.e., hold down the CTRL key and press D) to tell cat that it has reached *end-of-file (EOF)* on standard input:

```
[me@linuxbox ~]$ cat
The quick brown fox jumped over the lazy dog.
The quick brown fox jumped over the lazy dog.
```

In the absence of filename arguments, cat copies standard input to standard output, so we see our line of text repeated. We can use this behavior to create short text files. Let's say that we wanted to create a file called *lazy_dog.txt* containing the text in our example. We would do this:

```
[me@linuxbox ~]$ cat > lazy_dog.txt
The quick brown fox jumped over the lazy dog.
```

Enter the command followed by the text we want to place in the file. Remember to type CTRL-D at the end. Using the command line, we have implemented the world's dumbest word processor! To see our results, we can use cat to copy the file to standard output again:

```
[me@linuxbox ~]$ cat lazy_dog.txt
The quick brown fox jumped over the lazy dog.
```

Now that we know how cat accepts standard input in addition to filename arguments, let's try redirecting standard input:

```
[me@linuxbox ~]$ cat < lazy_dog.txt
The quick brown fox jumped over the lazy dog.
```

Using the < redirection operator, we change the source of standard input from the keyboard to the file *lazy_dog.txt*. We see that the result is the same as passing a single filename argument. This is not particularly useful compared to passing a filename argument, but it serves to demonstrate using a file as a source of standard input. Other commands make better use of standard input, as we shall soon see.

Before we move on, check out the man page for cat, as it has several interesting options.

Pipelines

The ability of commands to read data from standard input and send to standard output is utilized by a shell feature called *pipelines*. Using the pipe operator | (vertical bar), the standard output of one command can be *piped* into the standard input of another.

> command1 | command2

To fully demonstrate this, we are going to need some commands. Remember how we said there was one we already knew that accepts standard input? It's less. We can use less to display, page by page, the output of any command that sends its results to standard output:

```
[me@linuxbox ~]$ ls -l /usr/bin | less
```

This is extremely handy! Using this technique, we can conveniently examine the output of any command that produces standard output.

Filters

Pipelines are often used to perform complex operations on data. It is possible to put several commands together into a pipeline. Frequently, the commands used this way are referred to as *filters*. Filters take input, change it somehow, and then output it. The first one we will try is sort. Imagine we want to make a combined list of all of the executable programs in */bin* and */usr/bin*, put them in sorted order, and then view the list:

```
[me@linuxbox ~]$ ls /bin /usr/bin | sort | less
```

Since we specified two directories (*/bin* and */usr/bin*), the output of ls would have consisted of two sorted lists, one for each directory. By including sort in our pipeline, we changed the data to produce a single, sorted list.

uniq—Report or Omit Repeated Lines

The uniq command is often used in conjunction with sort. uniq accepts a sorted list of data from either standard input or a single filename argument (see the uniq man page for details) and, by default, removes any duplicates from the list. So, to make sure our list has no duplicates (that is, any programs of the same name that appear in both the */bin* and */usr/bin* directories) we will add uniq to our pipeline:

```
[me@linuxbox ~]$ ls /bin /usr/bin | sort | uniq | less
```

In this example, we use uniq to remove any duplicates from the output of the sort command. If we want to see the list of duplicates instead, we add the -d option to uniq like so:

```
[me@linuxbox ~]$ ls /bin /usr/bin | sort | uniq -d | less
```

wc—Print Line, Word, and Byte Counts

The wc (word count) command is used to display the number of lines, words, and bytes contained in files. For example:

```
[me@linuxbox ~]$ wc ls-output.txt
 7902  64566 503634 ls-output.txt
```

In this case it prints out three numbers: lines, words, and bytes contained in *ls-output.txt*. Like our previous commands, if executed without command-line arguments, wc accepts standard input. The -l option limits its output to only report lines. Adding it to a pipeline is a handy way to count things. To see the number of items we have in our sorted list, we can do this:

```
[me@linuxbox ~]$ ls /bin /usr/bin | sort | uniq | wc -l
2728
```

grep—Print Lines Matching a Pattern

grep is a powerful program used to find text patterns within files, like this:

grep *pattern* [*file...*]

When grep encounters a "pattern" in the file, it prints out the lines containing it. The patterns that grep can match can be very complex, but for now we will concentrate on simple text matches. We'll cover the advanced patterns, called *regular expressions*, in Chapter 19.

Let's say we want to find all the files in our list of programs that have the word *zip* in the name. Such a search might give us an idea of which programs on our system have something to do with file compression. We would do this:

```
[me@linuxbox ~]$ ls /bin /usr/bin | sort | uniq | grep zip
bunzip2
bzip2
gunzip
gzip
unzip
zip
zipcloak
zipgrep
zipinfo
zipnote
zipsplit
```

There are a couple of handy options for grep: -i, which causes grep to ignore case when performing the search (normally searches are case sensitive) and -v, which tells grep to print only lines that do not match the pattern.

head/tail—Print First/Last Part of Files

Sometimes you don't want all the output from a command. You may want only the first few lines or the last few lines. The head command prints the first 10 lines of a file, and the tail command prints the last 10 lines. By default, both commands print 10 lines of text, but this can be adjusted with the -n option:

```
[me@linuxbox ~]$ head -n 5 ls-output.txt
total 343496
-rwxr-xr-x 1 root root      31316 2011-12-05 08:58 [
```

```
-rwxr-xr-x 1 root root        8240 2011-12-09 13:39 411toppm
-rwxr-xr-x 1 root root      111276 2011-11-26 14:27 a2p
-rwxr-xr-x 1 root root       25368 2010-10-06 20:16 a52dec
[me@linuxbox ~]$ tail -n 5 ls-output.txt
-rwxr-xr-x 1 root root        5234 2011-06-27 10:56 znew
-rwxr-xr-x 1 root root         691 2009-09-10 04:21 zonetab2pot.py
-rw-r--r-- 1 root root         930 2011-11-01 12:23 zonetab2pot.pyc
-rw-r--r-- 1 root root         930 2011-11-01 12:23 zonetab2pot.pyo
lrwxrwxrwx 1 root root           6 2012-01-31 05:22 zsoelim -> soelim
```

These can be used in pipelines as well:

```
[me@linuxbox ~]$ ls /usr/bin | tail -n 5
znew
zonetab2pot.py
zonetab2pot.pyc
zonetab2pot.pyo
zsoelim
```

tail has an option that allows you to view files in real time. This is useful for watching the progress of log files as they are being written. In the following example, we will look at the *messages* file in */var/log*. Superuser privileges are required to do this on some Linux distributions, because the */var/log/messages* file may contain security information.

```
[me@linuxbox ~]$ tail -f /var/log/messages
Feb  8 13:40:05 twin4 dhclient: DHCPACK from 192.168.1.1
Feb  8 13:40:05 twin4 dhclient: bound to 192.168.1.4 -- renewal in 1652
seconds.
Feb  8 13:55:32 twin4 mountd[3953]: /var/NFSv4/musicbox exported to both
192.168.1.0/24 and twin7.localdomain in 192.168.1.0/24,twin7.localdomain
Feb  8 14:07:37 twin4 dhclient: DHCPREQUEST on eth0 to 192.168.1.1 port 67
Feb  8 14:07:37 twin4 dhclient: DHCPACK from 192.168.1.1
Feb  8 14:07:37 twin4 dhclient: bound to 192.168.1.4 -- renewal in 1771
seconds.
Feb  8 14:09:56 twin4 smartd[3468]: Device: /dev/hda, SMART Prefailure
Attribute: 8 Seek_Time_Performance changed from 237 to 236
Feb  8 14:10:37 twin4 mountd[3953]: /var/NFSv4/musicbox exported to both
192.168.1.0/24 and twin7.localdomain in 192.168.1.0/24,twin7.localdomain
Feb  8 14:25:07 twin4 sshd(pam_unix)[29234]: session opened for user me by
(uid=0)
Feb  8 14:25:36 twin4 su(pam_unix)[29279]: session opened for user root by
me(uid=500)
```

Using the -f option, tail continues to monitor the file and when new lines are appended, they immediately appear on the display. This continues until you type CTRL-C.

tee—Read from Stdin and Output to Stdout and Files

In keeping with our plumbing analogy, Linux provides a command called tee which creates a "T" fitting on our pipe. The tee program reads standard input and copies it to both standard output (allowing the data to continue down the pipeline) and to one or more files. This is useful for capturing a pipeline's contents at an intermediate stage of processing. Here we repeat one of our earlier examples, this time including tee to capture the entire directory listing to the file *ls.txt* before grep filters the pipeline's contents:

```
[me@linuxbox ~]$ ls /usr/bin | tee ls.txt | grep zip
bunzip2
bzip2
gunzip
gzip
unzip
zip
zipcloak
zipgrep
zipinfo
zipnote
zipsplit
```

Final Note

As always, check out the documentation of each of the commands we have covered in this chapter. We have seen only their most basic usage, and they all have a number of interesting options. As we gain Linux experience, we will see that the redirection feature of the command line is extremely useful for solving specialized problems. Many commands make use of standard input and output, and almost all command-line programs use standard error to display their informative messages.

LINUX IS ABOUT IMAGINATION

When I am asked to explain the difference between Windows and Linux, I often use a toy analogy.

Windows is like a Game Boy. You go to the store and buy one all shiny new in the box. You take it home, turn it on, and play with it. Pretty graphics, cute sounds. After a while, though, you get tired of the game that came with it, so you go back to the store and buy another one. This cycle repeats over and over. Finally, you go back to the store and say to the person behind the counter, "I want a game that does this!" only to be told that no such game exists because there is no "market demand" for it. Then you say, "But I only need to change this one thing!" The person behind the counter says you can't change it. The games are all sealed up in their cartridges. You discover that your toy is limited to the games that others have decided that you need and no more.

Linux, on the other hand, is like the world's largest Erector Set. You open it up, and it's just a huge collection of parts—a lot of steel struts, screws, nuts, gears, pulleys, and motors and a few suggestions on what to build. So you start to play with it. You build one of the suggestions and then another. After a while you discover that you have your own ideas of what to make. You don't ever have to go back to the store, because you already have everything you need. The Erector Set takes on the shape of your imagination. It does what you want.

Your choice of toys is, of course, a personal thing, so which toy would you find more satisfying?

7

SEEING THE WORLD AS
THE SHELL SEES IT

In this chapter we are going to look at some of the "magic" that occurs on the command line when you press the ENTER key. While we will examine several interesting and complex features of the shell, we will do it with just one new command:

- echo—Display a line of text.

Expansion

Each time you type a command line and press the ENTER key, bash performs several processes upon the text before it carries out your command. We've seen a couple of cases of how a simple character sequence, for example *, can have a lot of meaning to the shell. The process that makes this happen is called *expansion*. With expansion, you enter something, and it is expanded into something else before the shell acts upon it. To demonstrate what we mean by this, let's take a look at the echo command. echo is a shell builtin that performs a very simple task: It prints out its text arguments on standard output.

```
[me@linuxbox ~]$ echo this is a test
this is a test
```

That's pretty straightforward. Any argument passed to echo gets displayed. Let's try another example:

```
[me@linuxbox ~]$ echo *
Desktop Documents ls-output.txt Music Pictures Public Templates Videos
```

So what just happened? Why didn't echo print *? As you recall from our work with wildcards, the * character means "match any characters in a filename," but what we didn't see in our original discussion was how the shell does that. The simple answer is that the shell expands the * into something else (in this instance, the names of the files in the current working directory) before the echo command is executed. When the ENTER key is pressed, the shell automatically expands any qualifying characters on the command line before the command is carried out, so the echo command never saw the *, only its expanded result. Knowing this, we can see that echo behaved as expected.

Pathname Expansion

The mechanism by which wildcards work is called *pathname expansion*. If we try some of the techniques that we employed in our earlier chapters, we will see that they are really expansions. Given a home directory that looks like this:

```
[me@linuxbox ~]$ ls
Desktop     ls-output.txt  Pictures  Templates
Documents   Music          Public    Videos
```

we could carry out the following expansions:

```
[me@linuxbox ~]$ echo D*
Desktop Documents
```

and

```
[me@linuxbox ~]$ echo *s
Documents Pictures Templates Videos
```

or even

```
[me@linuxbox ~]$ echo [[:upper:]]*
Desktop Documents Music Pictures Public Templates Videos
```

And looking beyond our home directory:

```
[me@linuxbox ~]$ echo /usr/*/share
/usr/kerberos/share /usr/local/share
```

PATHNAME EXPANSION OF HIDDEN FILES

As we know, filenames that begin with a period character are hidden. Pathname expansion also respects this behavior. An expansion such as

```
echo *
```

does not reveal hidden files.

It might appear at first glance that we could include hidden files in an expansion by starting the pattern with a leading period, like this:

```
echo .*
```

It almost works. However, if we examine the results closely, we will see that the names . and .. will also appear in the results. Since these names refer to the current working directory and its parent directory, using this pattern will likely produce an incorrect result. We can see this if we try the command

```
ls -d .* | less
```

To correctly perform pathname expansion in this situation, we have to employ a more specific pattern. This will work correctly:

```
ls -d .[!.]?*
```

This pattern expands into every filename that begins with a period, does not include a second period, contains at least one additional character, and may be followed by any other characters.

Tilde Expansion

As you may recall from our introduction to the cd command, the tilde character (~) has a special meaning. When used at the beginning of a word, it expands into the name of the home directory of the named user or, if no user is named, the home directory of the current user:

```
[me@linuxbox ~]$ echo ~
/home/me
```

If user *foo* has an account, then

```
[me@linuxbox ~]$ echo ~foo
/home/foo
```

Arithmetic Expansion

The shell allows arithmetic to be performed by expansion. This allows us to use the shell prompt as a calculator:

```
[me@linuxbox ~]$ echo $((2 + 2))
4
```

Arithmetic expansion uses the following form:

$((expression))

where *expression* is an arithmetic expression consisting of values and arithmetic operators.

Arithmetic expansion supports only integers (whole numbers, no decimals) but can perform quite a number of different operations. Table 7-1 lists a few of the supported operators.

Table 7-1: Arithmetic Operators

Operator	Description
+	Addition
-	Subtraction
*	Multiplication
/	Division (But remember, because expansion supports only integer arithmetic, results are integers.)
%	Modulo, which simply means *remainder*
**	Exponentiation

Spaces are not significant in arithmetic expressions, and expressions may be nested. For example, multiply 5^2 by 3:

```
[me@linuxbox ~]$ echo $(($((5**2)) * 3))
75
```

Single parentheses may be used to group multiple subexpressions. With this technique, we can rewrite the example above and get the same result using a single expansion instead of two:

```
[me@linuxbox ~]$ echo $(((5**2) * 3))
75
```

Here is an example using the division and remainder operators. Notice the effect of integer division:

```
[me@linuxbox ~]$ echo Five divided by two equals $((5/2))
Five divided by two equals 2
```

```
[me@linuxbox ~]$ echo with $((5%2)) left over.
with 1 left over.
```

Arithmetic expansion is covered in greater detail in Chapter 34.

Brace Expansion

Perhaps the strangest expansion is called *brace expansion*. With it, you can create multiple text strings from a pattern containing braces. Here's an example:

```
[me@linuxbox ~]$ echo Front-{A,B,C}-Back
Front-A-Back Front-B-Back Front-C-Back
```

Patterns to be brace expanded may contain a leading portion called a *preamble* and a trailing portion called a *postscript*. The brace expression itself may contain either a comma-separated list of strings or a range of integers or single characters. The pattern may not contain embedded whitespace. Here is an example using a range of integers:

```
[me@linuxbox ~]$ echo Number_{1..5}
Number_1 Number_2 Number_3 Number_4 Number_5
```

Here we get a range of letters in reverse order:

```
[me@linuxbox ~]$ echo {Z..A}
Z Y X W V U T S R Q P O N M L K J I H G F E D C B A
```

Brace expansions may be nested:

```
[me@linuxbox ~]$ echo a{A{1,2},B{3,4}}b
aA1b aA2b aB3b aB4b
```

So what is this good for? The most common application is to make lists of files or directories to be created. For example, if we were photographers and had a large collection of images that we wanted to organize by years and months, the first thing we might do is create a series of directories named in numeric year-month format. This way, the directory names will sort in chronological order. We could type out a complete list of directories, but that's a lot of work and it's error prone too. Instead, we could do this:

```
[me@linuxbox ~]$ mkdir Pics
[me@linuxbox ~]$ cd Pics
[me@linuxbox Pics]$ mkdir {2009..2011}-0{1..9} {2009..2011}-{10..12}
[me@linuxbox Pics]$ ls
2009-01  2009-07  2010-01  2010-07  2011-01  2011-07
2009-02  2009-08  2010-02  2010-08  2011-02  2011-08
2009-03  2009-09  2010-03  2010-09  2011-03  2011-09
2009-04  2009-10  2010-04  2010-10  2011-04  2011-10
2009-05  2009-11  2010-05  2010-11  2011-05  2011-11
2009-06  2009-12  2010-06  2010-12  2011-06  2011-12
```

Pretty slick!

Parameter Expansion

We're only going to touch briefly on parameter expansion in this chapter, but we'll be covering it extensively later. It's a feature that is more useful in shell scripts than directly on the command line. Many of its capabilities have to do with the system's ability to store small chunks of data and to give each chunk a name. Many such chunks, more properly called *variables*, are available for your examination. For example, the variable named USER contains your username. To invoke parameter expansion and reveal the contents of USER, you would do this:

```
[me@linuxbox ~]$ echo $USER
me
```

To see a list of available variables, try this:

```
[me@linuxbox ~]$ printenv | less
```

You may have noticed that with other types of expansion, if you mistype a pattern, the expansion will not take place and the echo command will simply display the mistyped pattern. With parameter expansion, if you misspell the name of a variable, the expansion will still take place but will result in an empty string:

```
[me@linuxbox ~]$ echo $SUER

[me@linuxbox ~]$
```

Command Substitution

Command substitution allows us to use the output of a command as an expansion:

```
[me@linuxbox ~]$ echo $(ls)
Desktop Documents ls-output.txt Music Pictures Public Templates Videos
```

One of my favorites goes something like this:

```
[me@linuxbox ~]$ ls -l $(which cp)
-rwxr-xr-x 1 root root 71516 2012-12-05 08:58 /bin/cp
```

Here we passed the results of which cp as an argument to the ls command, thereby getting the listing of the cp program without having to know its full pathname. We are not limited to just simple commands. Entire pipelines can be used (only partial output shown):

```
[me@linuxbox ~]$ file $(ls /usr/bin/* | grep zip)
/usr/bin/bunzip2:      symbolic link to `bzip2'
/usr/bin/bzip2:        ELF 32-bit LSB executable, Intel 80386, version 1 (SYSV
), dynamically linked (uses shared libs), for GNU/Linux 2.6.9, stripped
/usr/bin/bzip2recover: ELF 32-bit LSB executable, Intel 80386, version 1
(SYSV), dynamically linked (uses shared libs), for GNU/Linux 2.6.9, stripped
/usr/bin/funzip:       ELF 32-bit LSB executable, Intel 80386, version 1 (SYSV
```

```
), dynamically linked (uses shared libs), for GNU/Linux 2.6.9, stripped
/usr/bin/gpg-zip:       Bourne shell script text executable
/usr/bin/gunzip:        symbolic link to `../../bin/gunzip'
/usr/bin/gzip:          symbolic link to `../../bin/gzip'
/usr/bin/mzip:          symbolic link to `mtools'
```

In this example, the results of the pipeline became the argument list of the file command.

There is an alternative syntax for command substitution in older shell programs that is also supported in bash. It uses *back quotes* instead of the dollar sign and parentheses:

```
[me@linuxbox ~]$ ls -l `which cp`
-rwxr-xr-x 1 root root 71516 2012-12-05 08:58 /bin/cp
```

Quoting

Now that we've seen how many ways the shell can perform expansions, it's time to learn how we can control it. For example, take this:

```
[me@linuxbox ~]$ echo this is a       test
this is a test
```

Or this:

```
[me@linuxbox ~]$ echo The total is $100.00
The total is 00.00
```

In the first example, *word splitting* by the shell removed extra whitespace from the echo command's list of arguments. In the second example, parameter expansion substituted an empty string for the value of $1 because it was an undefined variable. The shell provides a mechanism called *quoting* to selectively suppress unwanted expansions.

Double Quotes

The first type of quoting we will look at is *double quotes*. If you place text inside double quotes, all the special characters used by the shell lose their special meaning and are treated as ordinary characters. The exceptions are $ (dollar sign), \ (backslash), and ` (back tick). This means that word splitting, pathname expansion, tilde expansion, and brace expansion are suppressed, but parameter expansion, arithmetic expansion, and command substitution are still carried out. Using double quotes, we can cope with filenames containing embedded spaces. Say we were the unfortunate victim of a file called *two words.txt*. If we tried to use this on the command line, word splitting would cause this to be treated as two separate arguments rather than the desired single argument:

```
[me@linuxbox ~]$ ls -l two words.txt
ls: cannot access two: No such file or directory
ls: cannot access words.txt: No such file or directory
```

By using double quotes, we stop the word splitting and get the desired result; further, we can even repair the damage:

```
[me@linuxbox ~]$ ls -l "two words.txt"
-rw-rw-r-- 1 me    me    18 2012-02-20 13:03 two words.txt
[me@linuxbox ~]$ mv "two words.txt" two_words.txt
```

There! Now we don't have to keep typing those pesky double quotes.

Remember: Parameter expansion, arithmetic expansion, and command substitution still take place within double quotes:

```
[me@linuxbox ~]$ echo "$USER $((2+2)) $(cal)"
me 4    February 2012
Su Mo Tu We Th Fr Sa
          1  2  3  4
 5  6  7  8  9 10 11
12 13 14 15 16 17 18
19 20 21 22 23 24 25
26 27 28 29
```

We should take a moment to look at the effect of double quotes on command substitution. First let's look a little deeper at how word splitting works. In our earlier example, we saw how word splitting appears to remove extra spaces in our text:

```
[me@linuxbox ~]$ echo this is a      test
this is a test
```

By default, word splitting looks for the presence of spaces, tabs, and newlines (linefeed characters) and treats them as *delimiters* between words. This means that unquoted spaces, tabs, and newlines are not considered to be part of the text. They serve only as separators. Since they separate the words into different arguments, our example command line contains a command followed by four distinct arguments. If we add double quotes, however, word splitting is suppressed and the embedded spaces are not treated as delimiters; rather, they become part of the argument:

```
[me@linuxbox ~]$ echo "this is a      test"
this is a      test
```

Once the double quotes are added, our command line contains a command followed by a single argument.

The fact that newlines are considered delimiters by the word splitting mechanism causes an interesting, albeit subtle, effect on command substitution. Consider the following:

```
[me@linuxbox ~]$ echo $(cal)
February 2012 Su Mo Tu We Th Fr Sa 1 2 3 4 5 6 7 8 9 10 11 12 13 14 15 16 17
18 19 20 21 22 23 24 25 26 27 28 29
[me@linuxbox ~]$ echo "$(cal)"
```

```
        February 2012
Su Mo Tu We Th Fr Sa
            1  2  3  4
 5  6  7  8  9 10 11
12 13 14 15 16 17 18
19 20 21 22 23 24 25
26 27 28 29
```

In the first instance, the unquoted command substitution resulted in a command line containing 38 arguments; in the second, the result was a command line with 1 argument that includes the embedded spaces and newlines.

Single Quotes

If we need to suppress *all* expansions, we use *single quotes*. Here is a comparison of unquoted, double quotes, and single quotes:

```
[me@linuxbox ~]$ echo text ~/*.txt {a,b} $(echo foo) $((2+2)) $USER
text /home/me/ls-output.txt a b foo 4 me
[me@linuxbox ~]$ echo "text ~/*.txt {a,b} $(echo foo) $((2+2)) $USER"
text ~/*.txt {a,b} foo 4 me
[me@linuxbox ~]$ echo 'text ~/*.txt {a,b} $(echo foo) $((2+2)) $USER'
text ~/*.txt {a,b} $(echo foo) $((2+2)) $USER
```

As we can see, with each succeeding level of quoting, more and more expansions are suppressed.

Escaping Characters

Sometimes we want to quote only a single character. To do this, we can precede a character with a backslash, which in this context is called the *escape character*. Often this is done inside double quotes to selectively prevent an expansion.

```
[me@linuxbox ~]$ echo "The balance for user $USER is: \$5.00"
The balance for user me is: $5.00
```

It is also common to use escaping to eliminate the special meaning of a character in a filename. For example, it is possible to use characters in filenames that normally have special meaning to the shell. These would include $, !, &, (a space), and others. To include a special character in a filename, you can do this:

```
[me@linuxbox ~]$ mv bad\&filename good_filename
```

To allow a backslash character to appear, escape it by typing \\. Note that within single quotes, the backslash loses its special meaning and is treated as an ordinary character.

BACKSLASH ESCAPE SEQUENCES

In addition to its role as the escape character, the backslash is also used as part of a notation to represent certain special characters called *control codes*. The first 32 characters in the ASCII coding scheme are used to transmit commands to teletype-like devices. Some of these codes are familiar (tab, backspace, line-feed, and carriage return), while others are not (null, end-of-transmission, and acknowledge), as shown in Table 7-2.

Table 7-2: Backslash Escape Sequences

Escape Sequence	Meaning
\a	Bell ("alert"—causes the computer to beep)
\b	Backspace
\n	Newline (on Unix-like systems, this produces a linefeed)
\r	Carriage return
\t	Tab

This table lists some of the common backslash escape sequences. The idea behind using the backslash originated in the C programming language and has been adopted by many others, including the shell.

Adding the -e option to echo will enable interpretation of escape sequences. You may also place them inside $' '. Here, using the sleep command, a simple program that just waits for the specified number of seconds and then exits, we can create a primitive countdown timer.

```
sleep 10; echo -e  "Time's up\a"
```

We could also do this:

```
sleep 10; echo "Time's up" $'\a'
```

Final Note

As we move forward with using the shell, we will find that expansions and quoting will be used with increasing frequency, so it makes sense to get a good understanding of the way they work. In fact, it could be argued that they are the most important subjects to learn about the shell. Without a proper understanding of expansion, the shell will always be a source of mystery and confusion, and much of its potential power will be wasted.

8

ADVANCED KEYBOARD TRICKS

I often kiddingly describe Unix as "the operating system for people who like to type." Of course, the fact that it even has a command line is a testament to that. But command line users don't like to type *that* much. Why else would so many commands have such short names, like cp, ls, mv, and rm?

In fact, one of the most cherished goals of the command line is laziness—doing the most work with the fewest keystrokes. Another goal is never having to lift your fingers from the keyboard—never reaching for the mouse. In this chapter, we will look at bash features that make keyboard use faster and more efficient.

The following commands will make an appearance:

- clear—Clear the screen.
- history—Display the contents of the history list.

Command Line Editing

bash uses a library (a shared collection of routines that different programs can use) called *Readline* to implement command line editing. We have already seen some of this. We know, for example, that the arrow keys move the cursor, but there are many more features. Think of these as additional tools that we can employ in our work. It's not important to learn all of them, but many of them are very useful. Pick and choose as desired.

Note: *Some of the key sequences below (particularly those that use the ALT key) may be intercepted by the GUI for other functions. All of the key sequences should work properly when using a virtual console.*

Cursor Movement

Table 8-1 lists the keys used to move the cursor.

Table 8-1: Cursor Movement Commands

Key	Action
CTRL-A	Move cursor to the beginning of the line.
CTRL-E	Move cursor to the end of the line.
CTRL-F	Move cursor forward one character; same as the right arrow key.
CTRL-B	Move cursor backward one character; same as the left arrow key.
ALT-F	Move cursor forward one word.
ALT-B	Move cursor backward one word.
CTRL-L	Clear the screen and move the cursor to the top left corner. The clear command does the same thing.

Modifying Text

Table 8-2 lists keyboard commands that are used to edit characters on the command line.

Cutting and Pasting (Killing and Yanking) Text

The Readline documentation uses the terms *killing* and *yanking* to refer to what we would commonly call cutting and pasting. Table 8-3 lists the commands for cutting and pasting. Items that are cut are stored in a buffer called the *kill-ring*.

Table 8-2: Text Editing Commands

Key	Action
CTRL-D	Delete the character at the cursor location.
CTRL-T	Transpose (exchange) the character at the cursor location with the one preceding it.
ALT-T	Transpose the word at the cursor location with the one preceding it.
ALT-L	Convert the characters from the cursor location to the end of the word to lowercase.
ALT-U	Convert the characters from the cursor location to the end of the word to uppercase.

Table 8-3: Cut and Paste Commands

Key	Action
CTRL-K	Kill text from the cursor location to the end of line.
CTRL-U	Kill text from the cursor location to the beginning of the line.
ALT-D	Kill text from the cursor location to the end of the current word.
ALT-BACKSPACE	Kill text from the cursor location to the beginning of the current word. If the cursor is at the beginning of a word, kill the previous word.
CTRL-Y	Yank text from the kill-ring and insert it at the cursor location.

THE META KEY

If you venture into the Readline documentation, which can be found in the "READLINE" section of the bash man page, you will encounter the term *meta key*. On modern keyboards this maps to the ALT key, but it wasn't always so.

Back in the dim times (before PCs but after Unix) not everybody had their own computer. What they might have had was a device called a *terminal*. A terminal was a communication device that featured a text-display screen and a keyboard and had just enough electronics inside to display text characters and move the cursor around. It was attached (usually by serial cable) to a larger computer or the communication network of a larger computer. There were many different brands of terminals, and they all had different keyboards and display feature sets. Since they all tended to at least understand ASCII, software developers wanting portable applications wrote to the lowest common denominator. Unix systems have a very elaborate way of dealing with terminals and their different display features. Since the developers of Readline could not be sure of the presence of a dedicated extra control key, they invented one and called it *meta*. While the ALT key serves as the meta key on modern keyboards, you can also press and release the ESC key to get the same effect as holding down the ALT key if you're still using a terminal (which you can still do in Linux!).

Completion

Another way that the shell can help you is through a mechanism called *completion*. Completion occurs when you press the TAB key while typing a command. Let's see how this works. Say your home directory looks like this:

```
[me@linuxbox ~]$ ls
Desktop     ls-output.txt  Pictures  Templates     Videos
Documents   Music          Public
```

Try typing the following but *don't press the ENTER key*:

```
[me@linuxbox ~]$ ls l
```

Now press the TAB key:

```
[me@linuxbox ~]$ ls ls-output.txt
```

See how the shell completed the line for you? Let's try another one. Again, don't press ENTER:

```
[me@linuxbox ~]$ ls D
```

Press TAB:

```
[me@linuxbox ~]$ ls D
```

No completion—just a beep. This happened because D matches more than one entry in the directory. For completion to be successful, the "clue" you give it has to be unambiguous. We can go further:

```
[me@linuxbox ~]$ ls Do
```

Then press TAB:

```
[me@linuxbox ~]$ ls Documents
```

The completion is successful.

While this example shows completion of pathnames, which is completion's most common use, completion will also work on variables (if the beginning of the word is a $), usernames (if the word begins with ~), commands (if the word is the first word on the line), and hostnames (if the beginning of the word is @). Hostname completion works only for hostnames listed in *\/etc\/hosts.*

A number of control and meta key sequences are associated with completion (see Table 8-4).

Table 8-4: Completion Commands

Key	Action
ALT-?	Display list of possible completions. On most systems you can also do this by pressing the TAB key a second time, which is much easier.
ALT-*	Insert all possible completions. This is useful when you want to use more than one possible match.

There are quite a few more that I find rather obscure. You can see a list in the bash man page under the "READLINE" section.

PROGRAMMABLE COMPLETION

Recent versions of bash have a facility called *programmable completion.* Programmable completion allows you (or, more likely, your distribution provider) to add additional completion rules. Usually this is done to add support for specific applications. For example, it is possible to add completions for the option list of a command or match particular file types that an application supports. Ubuntu has a fairly large set defined by default. Programmable completion is implemented by shell functions, a kind of mini shell script that we will cover in later chapters. If you are curious, try

```
set | less
```

and see if you can find them. Not all distributions include them by default.

Using History

As we discovered in Chapter 1, bash maintains a history of commands that have been entered. This list of commands is kept in your home directory in a file called *.bash_history.* The history facility is a useful resource for reducing the amount of typing you have to do, especially when combined with command-line editing.

Searching History

At any time, we can view the contents of the history list:

```
[me@linuxbox ~]$ history | less
```

By default, bash stores the last 500 commands you have entered. We will see how to adjust this value in Chapter 11. Let's say we want to find the commands we used to list */usr/bin*. Here is one way we could do this:

```
[me@linuxbox ~]$ history | grep /usr/bin
```

And let's say that among our results we got a line containing an interesting command like this:

```
  88  ls -l /usr/bin > ls-output.txt
```

The number 88 is the line number of the command in the history list. We could use this immediately with another type of expansion called *history expansion*. To use our discovered line, we could do this:

```
[me@linuxbox ~]$ !88
```

bash will expand !88 into the contents of the 88th line in the history list. We will cover other forms of history expansion a little later.

bash also provides the ability to search the history list incrementally. This means that we can tell bash to search the history list as we enter characters, with each additional character further refining our search. To start an incremental search, enter CTRL-R followed by the text you are looking for. When you find it, you can either press ENTER to execute the command or press CTRL-J to copy the line from the history list to the current command line. To find the next occurrence of the text (moving "up" the history list), press CTRL-R again. To quit searching, press either CTRL-G or CTRL-C. Here we see it in action:

```
[me@linuxbox ~]$
```

First press CTRL-R:

```
(reverse-i-search)`':
```

The prompt changes to indicate that we are performing a reverse incremental search. It is "reverse" because we are searching from "now" to some time in the past. Next, we start typing our search text, which in this example is /usr/bin:

```
(reverse-i-search)`/usr/bin': ls -l /usr/bin > ls-output.txt
```

Immediately, the search returns its result. Now we can execute the command by pressing ENTER, or we can copy the command to our current command line for further editing by pressing CTRL-J. Let's copy it. Press CTRL-J:

```
[me@linuxbox ~]$ ls -l /usr/bin > ls-output.txt
```

Our shell prompt returns, and our command line is loaded and ready for action!

Table 8-5 lists some of the keystrokes used to manipulate the history list.

Table 8-5: History Commands

Key	Action
CTRL-P	Move to the previous history entry. Same action as the up arrow.
CTRL-N	Move to the next history entry. Same action as the down arrow.
ALT-<	Move to the beginning (top) of the history list.
ALT->	Move to the end (bottom) of the history list; i.e., the current command line.
CTRL-R	Reverse incremental search. Searches incrementally from the current command line up the history list.
ALT-P	Reverse search, non-incremental. With this key, type the search string and press ENTER before the search is performed.
ALT-N	Forward search, non-incremental.
CTRL-O	Execute the current item in the history list and advance to the next one. This is handy if you are trying to re-execute a sequence of commands in the history list.

History Expansion

The shell offers a specialized type of expansion for items in the history list by using the ! character. We have already seen how the exclamation point can be followed by a number to insert an entry from the history list. There are a number of other expansion features (see Table 8-6).

I would caution against using the !string and !?string forms unless you are absolutely sure of the contents of the history list items.

Many more elements are available in the history expansion mechanism, but this subject is already too arcane and our heads may explode if we continue. The "HISTORY EXPANSION" section of the bash man page goes into all the gory details. Feel free to explore!

Table 8-6: History Expansion Commands

Sequence	Action
!!	Repeat the last command. It is probably easier to press the up arrow and ENTER.
!number	Repeat history list item number.
!string	Repeat last history list item starting with string.
!?string	Repeat last history list item containing string.

SCRIPT

In addition to the command history feature in bash, most Linux distributions include a program called script, which can be used to record an entire shell session and store it in a file. The basic syntax of the command is

    script [file]

where file is the name of the file used for storing the recording. If no file is specified, the file typescript is used. See the script man page for a complete list of the program's options and features.

Final Note

In this chapter we have covered *some* of the keyboard tricks that the shell provides to help hardcore typists reduce their workloads. I suspect that as time goes by and you become more involved with the command line, you will refer to this chapter to pick up more of these tricks. For now, consider them optional and potentially helpful.

9

PERMISSIONS

Operating systems in the Unix tradition differ from those in the MS-DOS tradition in that they are not only *multitasking* systems but also *multiuser* systems.

What exactly does this mean? It means that more than one person can use the computer at the same time. While a typical computer will likely have only one keyboard and monitor, it can still be used by more than one user. For example, if a computer is attached to a network or the Internet, remote users can log in via ssh (secure shell) and operate the computer. In fact, remote users can execute graphical applications and have the graphical output appear on a remote display. The X Window System supports this as part of its basic design.

The multiuser capability of Linux is not a recent "innovation" but rather a feature that is deeply embedded into the design of the operating system. Considering the environment in which Unix was created, this makes perfect sense. Years ago, before computers were "personal," they were large, expensive, and centralized. A typical university computer system, for example, consisted of a large central computer located in one building and terminals located throughout the campus, each connected to the large central computer. The computer would support many users at the same time.

In order to make this practical, a method had to be devised to protect the users from each other. After all, the actions of one user could not be allowed to crash the computer, nor could one user interfere with the files belonging to another user.

In this chapter we are going to look at this essential part of system security and introduce the following commands:

- `id`—Display user identity.
- `chmod`—Change a file's mode.
- `umask`—Set the default file permissions.
- `su`—Run a shell as another user.
- `sudo`—Execute a command as another user.
- `chown`—Change a file's owner.
- `chgrp`—Change a file's group ownership.
- `passwd`—Change a user's password.

Owners, Group Members, and Everybody Else

When we were exploring the system back in Chapter 3, we may have encountered the following problem when trying to examine a file such as */etc/shadow*.

```
[me@linuxbox ~]$ file /etc/shadow
/etc/shadow: regular file, no read permission
[me@linuxbox ~]$ less /etc/shadow
/etc/shadow: Permission denied
```

The reason for this error message is that, as regular users, we do not have permission to read this file.

In the Unix security model, a user may *own* files and directories. When a user owns a file or directory, the user has control over its access. Users can, in turn, belong to a *group* consisting of one or more users who are given access to files and directories by their owners. In addition to granting access to a group, an owner may also grant some set of access rights to everybody, which in Unix terms is referred to as the *world*. To find out information about your identity, use the `id` command:

```
[me@linuxbox ~]$ id
uid=500(me) gid=500(me) groups=500(me)
```

Let's look at the output. When user accounts are created, users are assigned a number called a *user ID*, or *uid*. This is then, for the sake of the humans, mapped to a username. The user is assigned a *primary group ID,* or *gid*, and may belong to additional groups. The previous example is from a Fedora system. On other systems, such as Ubuntu, the output may look a little different.

```
[me@linuxbox ~]$ id
uid=1000(me) gid=1000(me)
groups=4(adm),20(dialout),24(cdrom),25(floppy),29(audio),30(dip),44(video),46(
plugdev),108(lpadmin),114(admin),1000(me)
```

As we can see, the uid and gid numbers are different. This is simply because Fedora starts its numbering of regular user accounts at 500, while Ubuntu starts at 1000. We can also see that the Ubuntu user belongs to a lot more groups. This has to do with the way Ubuntu manages privileges for system devices and services.

So where does this information come from? Like so many things in Linux, it comes from a couple of text files. User accounts are defined in the */etc/passwd* file, and groups are defined in the */etc/group* file. When user accounts and groups are created, these files are modified along with */etc/shadow*, which holds information about the user's password. For each user account, the */etc/passwd* file defines the user (login) name, the uid, the gid, the account's real name, the home directory, and the login shell. If you examine the contents of */etc/passwd* and */etc/group*, you will notice that besides the regular user accounts there are accounts for the superuser (uid 0) and various other system users.

In Chapter 10, when we cover processes, you will see that some of these other "users" are, in fact, quite busy.

While many Unix-like systems assign regular users to a common group such as *users*, modern Linux practice is to create a unique, single-member group with the same name as the user. This makes certain types of permission assignment easier.

Reading, Writing, and Executing

Access rights to files and directories are defined in terms of read access, write access, and execution access. If we look at the output of the ls command, we can get some clue as to how this is implemented:

```
[me@linuxbox ~]$ > foo.txt
[me@linuxbox ~]$ ls -l foo.txt
-rw-rw-r-- 1 me     me    0 2012-03-06 14:52 foo.txt
```

The first 10 characters of the listing are the *file attributes* (see Figure 9-1). The first of these characters is the *file type*. Table 9-1 lists the file types you are most likely to see (there are other, less common types too).

The remaining nine characters of the file attributes, called the *file mode*, represent the read, write, and execute permissions for the file's owner, the file's group owner, and everybody else.

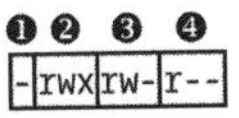

❶ ❷ ❸ ❹
`-|rwx|rw-|r--`

❶ File type (see Table 9-1)
❷ Owner permissions (see Table 9-2)
❸ Group permissions (see Table 9-2)
❹ World permissions (see Table 9-2)

Figure 9-1: Breakdown of file attributes

When set, the r, w, and x mode attributes have certain effects on files and directories, as shown in Table 9-2.

Table 9-1: File Types

Attribute	File Type
-	A regular file.
d	A directory.
l	A symbolic link. Notice that with symbolic links, the remaining file attributes are always rwxrwxrwx and are dummy values. The real file attributes are those of the file the symbolic link points to.
c	A *character special file*. This file type refers to a device that handles data as a stream of bytes, such as a terminal or modem.
b	A *block special file*. This file type refers to a device that handles data in blocks, such as a hard drive or CD-ROM drive.

Table 9-2: Permission Attributes

Attribute	Files	Directories
r	Allows a file to be opened and read.	Allows a directory's contents to be listed if the execute attribute is also set.
w	Allows a file to be written to or truncated; however, this attribute does not allow files to be renamed or deleted. The ability to delete or rename files is determined by directory attributes.	Allows files within a directory to be created, deleted, and renamed if the execute attribute is also set.
x	Allows a file to be treated as a program and executed. Program files written in scripting languages must also be set as readable to be executed.	Allows a directory to be entered; e.g., cd *directory*.

Table 9-3 shows some examples of file attribute settings.

Table 9-3: Permission Attribute Examples

File Attributes	Meaning
-rwx------	A regular file that is readable, writable, and executable by the file's owner. No one else has any access.
-rw-------	A regular file that is readable and writable by the file's owner. No one else has any access.

Table 9-3 (*continued*)

File Attributes	Meaning
-rw-r--r--	A regular file that is readable and writable by the file's owner. Members of the file's owner group may read the file. The file is world readable.
-rwxr-xr-x	A regular file that is readable, writable, and executable by the file's owner. The file may be read and executed by everybody else.
-rw-rw----	A regular file that is readable and writable by the file's owner and members of the file's owner group only.
lrwxrwxrwx	A symbolic link. All symbolic links have "dummy" permissions. The real permissions are kept with the actual file pointed to by the symbolic link.
drwxrwx---	A directory. The owner and the members of the owner group may enter the directory and create, rename, and remove files within the directory.
drwxr-x---	A directory. The owner may enter the directory and create, rename, and delete files within the directory. Members of the owner group may enter the directory but cannot create, delete, or rename files.

chmod—Change File Mode

To change the mode (permissions) of a file or directory, the chmod command is used. Be aware that only the file's owner or the superuser can change the mode of a file or directory. chmod supports two distinct ways of specifying mode changes: octal number representation and symbolic representation. We will cover octal number representation first.

Octal Representation

With octal notation we use octal numbers to set the pattern of desired permissions. Since each digit in an octal number represents three binary digits, this maps nicely to the scheme used to store the file mode. Table 9-4 shows what we mean.

Table 9-4: File Modes in Binary and Octal

Octal	Binary	File Mode	
0	000	---	
1	001	--x	
2	010	-w-	(continued)

Table 9-4 (*continued*)

Octal	Binary	File Mode
3	011	-wx
4	100	r--
5	101	r-x
6	110	rw-
7	111	rwx

WHAT THE HECK IS OCTAL?

Octal (base 8) and its cousin *hexadecimal* (base 16) are number systems often used to express numbers on computers. We humans, owing to the fact that we (or at least most of us) were born with 10 fingers, count using a base 10 number system. Computers, on the other hand, were born with only one finger and thus do all all their counting in *binary* (base 2). Their number system has only two numerals, zero and one. So in binary, counting looks like this: 0, 1, 10, 11, 100, 101, 110, 111, 1000, 1001, 1010, 1011 . . .

In octal, counting is done with the numerals zero through seven, like so: 0, 1, 2, 3, 4, 5, 6, 7, 10, 11, 12, 13, 14, 15, 16, 17, 20, 21 . . .

Hexadecimal counting uses the numerals zero through nine plus the letters *A* through *F*: 0, 1, 2, 3, 4, 5, 6, 7, 8, 9, A, B, C, D, E, F, 10, 11, 12, 13 . . .

While we can see the sense in binary (since computers have only one finger), what are octal and hexadecimal good for? The answer has to do with human convenience. Many times, small portions of data are represented on computers as *bit patterns.* Take for example an RGB color. On most computer displays, each pixel is composed of three color components: 8 bits of red, 8 bits of green, and 8 bits of blue. A lovely medium blue would be a 24-digit number: 010000110110111111001101.

How would you like to read and write those kinds of numbers all day? I didn't think so. Here's where another number system would help. Each digit in a hexadecimal number represents four digits in binary. In octal, each digit represents three binary digits. So our 24-digit medium blue could be condensed to a 6-digit hexadecimal number: 436FCD. Since the digits in the hexadecimal number "line up" with the bits in the binary number, we can see that the red component of our color is 43, the green 6F, and the blue CD.

These days, hexadecimal notation (often called *hex*) is more common than octal, but as we shall soon see, octal's ability to express three bits of binary is very useful.

By using three octal digits, we can set the file mode for the owner, group owner, and world.

```
[me@linuxbox ~]$ > foo.txt
[me@linuxbox ~]$ ls -l foo.txt
-rw-rw-r-- 1 me    me   0 2012-03-06 14:52 foo.txt
[me@linuxbox ~]$ chmod 600 foo.txt
[me@linuxbox ~]$ ls -l foo.txt
-rw------- 1 me    me   0 2012-03-06 14:52 foo.txt
```

By passing the argument 600, we were able to set the permissions of the owner to read and write while removing all permissions from the group owner and world. Though remembering the octal-to-binary mapping may seem inconvenient, you will usually have to use only a few common ones: 7 (rwx), 6 (rw-), 5 (r-x), 4 (r--), and 0 (---).

Symbolic Representation

chmod also supports a symbolic notation for specifying file modes. Symbolic notation is divided into three parts: whom the change will affect, which operation will be performed, and which permission will be set. To specify who is affected, a combination of the characters *u*, *g*, *o*, and *a* is used, as shown in Table 9-5.

Table 9-5: chmod Symbolic Notation

Symbol	Meaning
u	Short for *user* but means the file or directory owner.
g	Group owner.
o	Short for *others* but means world.
a	Short for *all*; the combination of *u*, *g*, and *o*.

If no character is specified, *all* will be assumed. The operation may be a + indicating that a permission is to be added, a - indicating that a permission is to be taken away, or a = indicating that only the specified permissions are to be applied and that all others are to be removed.

Permissions are specified with the r, w, and x characters. Table 9-6 lists some examples of symbolic notation.

Table 9-6: chmod Symbolic Notation Examples

Notation	Meaning
u+x	Add execute permission for the owner.
u-x	Remove execute permission from the owner.
+x	Add execute permission for the owner, group, and world. Equivalent to a+x.

(continued)

Table 9-6 (continued)

Notation	Meaning
o-rw	Remove the read and write permissions from anyone besides the owner and group owner.
go=rw	Set the group owner and anyone besides the owner to have read and write permission. If either the group owner or world previously had execute permissions, remove them.
u+x,go=rx	Add execute permission for the owner and set the permissions for the group and others to read and execute. Multiple specifications may be separated by commas.

Some people prefer to use octal notation; some folks really like the symbolic. Symbolic notation does offer the advantage of allowing you to set a single attribute without disturbing any of the others.

Take a look at the chmod man page for more details and a list of options. A word of caution regarding the --recursive option: It acts on both files and directories, so it's not as useful as one would hope because we rarely want files and directories to have the same permissions.

Setting File Mode with the GUI

Now that we have seen how the permissions on files and directories are set, we can better understand the permission dialogs in the GUI. In both Nautilus (GNOME) and Konqueror (KDE), right-clicking a file or directory icon will expose a properties dialog. Figure 9-2 is an example from KDE 3.5.

Here we can see the settings for the owner, group, and world. In KDE, clicking the Advanced Permissions button brings up another dialog that allows you to set each of the mode attributes individually. Another victory for understanding brought to us by the command line!

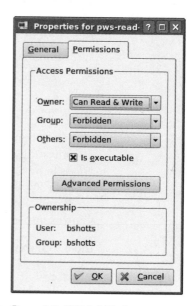

Figure 9-2: KDE 3.5 File Properties dialog

umask—Set Default Permissions

The umask command controls the default permissions given to a file when it is created. It uses octal notation to express a *mask* of bits to be removed from a file's mode attributes.

Let's take a look:

```
[me@linuxbox ~]$ rm -f foo.txt
[me@linuxbox ~]$ umask
0002
[me@linuxbox ~]$ > foo.txt
[me@linuxbox ~]$ ls -l foo.txt
-rw-rw-r-- 1 me     me    0 2012-03-06 14:53 foo.txt
```

We first removed any existing copy of *foo.txt* to make sure we were starting fresh. Next, we ran the umask command without an argument to see the current value. It responded with the value 0002 (the value 0022 is another common default value), which is the octal representation of our mask. We then created a new instance of the file *foo.txt* and observed its permissions.

We can see that both the owner and group get read and write permissions, while everyone else gets only read permission. World does not have write permission because of the value of the mask. Let's repeat our example, this time setting the mask ourselves:

```
[me@linuxbox ~]$ rm foo.txt
[me@linuxbox ~]$ umask 0000
[me@linuxbox ~]$ > foo.txt
[me@linuxbox ~]$ ls -l foo.txt
-rw-rw-rw- 1 me     me    0 2012-03-06 14:58 foo.txt
```

When we set the mask to 0000 (effectively turning it off), we see that the file is now world writable. To understand how this works, we have to look at octal numbers again. If we expand the mask into binary and then compare it to the attributes, we can see what happens:

Original file mode	--- rw- rw- rw-
Mask	000 000 000 010
Result	--- rw- rw- r--

Ignore for the moment the leading 0s (we'll get to those in a minute) and observe that where the 1 appears in our mask, an attribute was removed—in this case, the world write permission. That's what the mask does. Everywhere a 1 appears in the binary value of the mask, an attribute is unset. If we look at a mask value of 0022, we can see what it does:

Original file mode	--- rw- rw- rw-
Mask	000 000 010 010
Result	--- rw- r-- r--

Again, where a 1 appears in the binary value, the corresponding attribute is unset. Play with some values (try some 7s) to get used to how this works. When you're done, remember to clean up:

```
[me@linuxbox ~]$ rm foo.txt; umask 0002
```

Most of the time you won't have to change the mask; the default provided by your distribution will be fine. In some high-security situations, however, you will want to control it.

SOME SPECIAL PERMISSIONS

Though we usually see an octal permission mask expressed as a three-digit number, it is more technically correct to express it in four digits. Why? Because, in addition to read, write, and execute permissions, there are some other, less-used permission settings.

The first of these is the *setuid bit* (octal 4000). When applied to an executable file, it sets the *effective user ID* from that of the real user (the user actually running the program) to that of the program's owner. Most often this is given to a few programs owned by the superuser. When an ordinary user runs a program that is *setuid root,* the program runs with the effective privileges of the superuser. This allows the program to access files and directories that an ordinary user would normally be prohibited from accessing. Clearly, because this raises security concerns, the number of setuid programs must be held to an absolute minimum.

The second less-used setting is the *setgid bit* (octal 2000). This, like the setuid bit, changes the *effective group ID* from that of the *real group ID* of the user to that of the file owner. If the setgid bit is set on a directory, newly created files in the directory will be given the group ownership of the directory rather the group ownership of the file's creator. This is useful in a shared directory when members of a common group need access to all the files in the directory, regardless of the file owner's primary group.

The third is called the *sticky bit* (octal 1000). This is a holdover from ancient Unix, where it was possible to mark an executable file as "not swappable." On files, Linux ignores the sticky bit, but if applied to a directory, it prevents users from deleting or renaming files unless the user is either the owner of the directory, the owner of the file, or the superuser. This is often used to control access to a shared directory, such as */tmp*.

Here are some examples of using chmod with symbolic notation to set these special permissions. First, assign setuid to a program:

    chmod u+s *program*

Next, assign setgid to a directory:

    chmod g+s *dir*

Finally, assign the sticky bit to a directory:

```
chmod +t dir
```

By viewing the output from ls, you can determine the special permissions. Here are some examples. First, a program that is setuid:

```
-rwsr-xr-x
```

Now, a directory that has the setgid attribute:

```
drwxrwsr-x
```

Finally, a directory with the sticky bit set:

```
drwxrwxrwt
```

Changing Identities

At various times, we may find it necessary to take on the identity of another user. Often we want to gain superuser privileges to carry out some administrative task, but it is also possible to "become" another regular user to perform such tasks as testing an account. There are three ways to take on an alternate identity:

- Log out and log back in as the alternate user.
- Use the su command.
- Use the sudo command.

We will skip the first technique because we know how to do it and it lacks the convenience of the other two. From within your own shell session, the su command allows you to assume the identity of another user and either start a new shell session with that user's ID or issue a single command as that user. The sudo command allows an administrator to set up a configuration file called */etc/sudoers* and define specific commands that particular users are permitted to execute under an assumed identity. The choice of which command to use is largely determined by which Linux distribution you use. Your distribution probably includes both commands, but its configuration will favor either one or the other. We'll start with su.

su—Run a Shell with Substitute User and Group IDs

The su command is used to start a shell as another user. The command syntax looks like this:

```
su [-[l]] [user]
```

If the -1 option is included, the resulting shell session is a *login shell* for the specified user. This means that the user's environment is loaded and the working directory is changed to the user's home directory. This is usually what we want. If the user is not specified, the superuser is assumed. Notice that (strangely) the -1 may be abbreviated as -, which is how it is most often used. To start a shell for the superuser, we would do this:

```
[me@linuxbox ~]$ su -
Password:
[root@linuxbox ~]#
```

After entering the command, we are prompted for the superuser's password. If it is successfully entered, a new shell prompt appears indicating that this shell has superuser privileges (the trailing # rather than a $) and that the current working directory is now the home directory for the superuser (normally */root*). Once in the new shell, we can carry out commands as the superuser. When finished, enter exit to return to the previous shell:

```
[root@linuxbox ~]# exit
[me@linuxbox ~]$
```

It is also possible to execute a single command rather than starting a new interactive command by using su this way:

```
su -c 'command'
```

Using this form, a single command line is passed to the new shell for execution. It is important to enclose the command in quotes, as we do not want expansion to occur in our shell but rather in the new shell:

```
[me@linuxbox ~]$ su -c 'ls -l /root/*'
Password:
-rw------- 1 root root      754 2011-08-11 03:19 /root/anaconda-ks.cfg

/root/Mail:
total 0
[me@linuxbox ~]$
```

sudo—Execute a Command as Another User

The sudo command is like su in many ways but has some important additional capabilities. The administrator can configure sudo to allow an ordinary user to execute commands as a different user (usually the superuser) in a very controlled way. In particular, a user may be restricted to one or more specific commands and no others. Another important difference is that the use of sudo does not require access to the superuser's password. To authenticate using sudo, the user enters his own password. Let's say, for example, that sudo has been configured to allow us to run a fictitious backup program called backup_script, which requires superuser privileges.

With sudo it would be done like this:

```
[me@linuxbox ~]$ sudo backup_script
Password:
System Backup Starting...
```

After entering the command, we are prompted for our password (not the superuser's), and once the authentication is complete, the specified command is carried out. One important difference between su and sudo is that sudo does not start a new shell, nor does it load another user's environment. This means that commands do not need to be quoted any differently than they would be without using sudo. Note that this behavior can be overridden by specifying various options. See the sudo man page for details.

To see what privileges are granted by sudo, use the -l option to list them:

```
[me@linuxbox ~]$ sudo -l
User me may run the following commands on this host:
    (ALL) ALL
```

UBUNTU AND SUDO

One of the recurrent problems for regular users is how to perform certain tasks that require superuser privileges. These tasks include installing and updating software, editing system configuration files, and accessing devices. In the Windows world, this is often done by giving users administrative privileges. This allows users to perform these tasks. However, it also enables programs executed by the user to have the same abilities. This is desirable in most cases, but it also permits *malware* (malicious software) such as viruses to have free run of the computer.

In the Unix world, there has always been a larger division between regular users and administrators, owing to the multiuser heritage of Unix. The approach taken in Unix is to grant superuser privileges only when needed. To do this, the su and sudo commands are commonly used.

Up until a few of years ago, most Linux distributions relied on su for this purpose. su didn't require the configuration that sudo required, and having a root account is traditional in Unix. This introduced a problem. Users were tempted to operate as root unnecessarily. In fact, some users operated their systems as the root user exclusively, because it does away with all those annoying "permission denied" messages. This is how you reduce the security of a Linux system to that of a Windows system. Not a good idea.

When Ubuntu was introduced, its creators took a different tack. By default, Ubuntu disables logins to the root account (by failing to set a password for the account) and instead uses sudo to grant superuser privileges. The initial user account is granted full access to superuser privileges via sudo and may grant similar powers to subsequent user accounts.

chown—Change File Owner and Group

The chown command is used to change the owner and group owner of a file or directory. Superuser privileges are required to use this command. The syntax of chown looks like this:

```
chown [owner][:[group]] file...
```

chown can change the file owner and/or the file group owner depending on the first argument of the command. Table 9-7 lists some examples.

Table 9-7: chown Argument Examples

Argument	Results
bob	Changes the ownership of the file from its current owner to user *bob*.
bob:users	Changes the ownership of the file from its current owner to user *bob* and changes the file group owner to group *users*.
:admins	Changes the group owner to the group *admins*. The file owner is unchanged.
bob:	Change the file owner from the current owner to user *bob* and changes the group owner to the login group of user *bob*.

Let's say that we have two users: *janet*, who has access to superuser privileges, and *tony*, who does not. User *janet* wants to copy a file from her home directory to the home directory of user *tony*. Since user *janet* wants *tony* to be able to edit the file, *janet* changes the ownership of the copied file from *janet* to *tony*:

```
[janet@linuxbox ~]$ sudo cp myfile.txt ~tony
Password:
[janet@linuxbox ~]$ sudo ls -l ~tony/myfile.txt
-rw-r--r-- 1 root   root  8031 2012-03-20 14:30 /home/tony/myfile.txt
[janet@linuxbox ~]$ sudo chown tony: ~tony/myfile.txt
[janet@linuxbox ~]$ sudo ls -l ~tony/myfile.txt
-rw-r--r-- 1 tony   tony  8031 2012-03-20 14:30 /home/tony/myfile.txt
```

Here we see user *janet* copy the file from her directory to the home directory of user *tony*. Next, *janet* changes the ownership of the file from *root* (a result of using sudo) to *tony*. Using the trailing colon in the first argument, *janet* also changed the group ownership of the file to the login group of *tony*, which happens to be group *tony*.

Notice that after the first use of sudo, *janet* was not prompted for her password? This is because sudo, in most configurations, "trusts" you for several minutes (until its timer runs out).

chgrp—Change Group Ownership

In older versions of Unix, the chown command changed only file ownership, not group ownership. For that purpose a separate command, chgrp, was used. It works much the same way as chown, except for being more limited.

Exercising Your Privileges

Now that we have learned how this permissions thing works, it's time to show it off. We are going to demonstrate the solution to a common problem—setting up a shared directory. Let's imagine that we have two users named *bill* and *karen*. They both have music CD collections and wish to set up a shared directory, where they will each store their music files as Ogg Vorbis or MP3. User *bill* has access to superuser privileges via sudo.

The first thing that needs to happen is the creation of a group that will have both *bill* and *karen* as members. Using GNOME's graphical user management tool, *bill* creates a group called *music* and adds users *bill* and *karen* to it, as shown in Figure 9-3.

Figure 9-3: Creating a new group with GNOME

Next, *bill* creates the directory for the music files:

```
[bill@linuxbox ~]$ sudo mkdir /usr/local/share/Music
Password:
```

Since *bill* is manipulating files outside his home directory, superuser privileges are required. After the directory is created, it has the following ownerships and permissions:

```
[bill@linuxbox ~]$ ls -ld /usr/local/share/Music
drwxr-xr-x 2 root root 4096 2012-03-21 18:05 /usr/local/share/Music
```

As we can see, the directory is owned by *root* and has 755 permissions. To make this directory shareable, *bill* needs to change the group ownership and the group permissions to allow writing:

```
[bill@linuxbox ~]$ sudo chown :music /usr/local/share/Music
[bill@linuxbox ~]$ sudo chmod 775 /usr/local/share/Music
[bill@linuxbox ~]$ ls -ld /usr/local/share/Music
drwxrwxr-x 2 root music 4096 2012-03-21 18:05 /usr/local/share/Music
```

So what does this all mean? It means that we now have a directory */usr/local/share/Music* that is owned by *root* and allows read and write access to group *music*. Group *music* has members *bill* and *karen*; thus *bill* and *karen* can create files in directory */usr/local/share/Music*. Other users can list the contents of the directory but cannot create files there.

But we still have a problem. With the current permissions, files and directories created within the *Music* directory will have the normal permissions of the users *bill* and *karen*:

```
[bill@linuxbox ~]$ > /usr/local/share/Music/test_file
[bill@linuxbox ~]$ ls -l /usr/local/share/Music
-rw-r--r-- 1 bill   bill   0 2012-03-24 20:03 test_file
```

Actually there are two problems. First, the default umask on this system is 0022, which prevents group members from writing files belonging to other members of the group. This would not be a problem if the shared directory contained only files, but since this directory will store music and music is usually organized in a hierarchy of artists and albums, members of the group will need the ability to create files and directories inside directories created by other members. We need to change the umask used by *bill* and *karen* to 0002 instead.

Second, each file and directory created by one member will be set to the primary group of the user, rather than the group *music*. This can be fixed by setting the setgid bit on the directory:

```
[bill@linuxbox ~]$ sudo chmod g+s /usr/local/share/Music
[bill@linuxbox ~]$ ls -ld /usr/local/share/Music
drwxrwsr-x 2 root music 4096 2012-03-24 20:03 /usr/local/share/Music
```

Now we test to see if the new permissions fix the problem. *bill* sets his umask to 0002, removes the previous test file, and creates a new test file and directory:

```
[bill@linuxbox ~]$ umask 0002
[bill@linuxbox ~]$ rm /usr/local/share/Music/test_file
[bill@linuxbox ~]$ > /usr/local/share/Music/test_file
[bill@linuxbox ~]$ mkdir /usr/local/share/Music/test_dir
[bill@linuxbox ~]$ ls -l /usr/local/share/Music
drwxrwsr-x 2 bill   music 4096 2012-03-24 20:24 test_dir
-rw-rw-r-- 1 bill   music 0 2012-03-24 20:22 test_file
[bill@linuxbox ~]$
```

Both files and directories are now created with the correct permissions to allow all members of the group *music* to create files and directories inside the *Music* directory.

The one remaining issue is umask. The necessary setting lasts only until the end of the session and then must be reset. In Chapter 11, we'll look at making the change to umask permanent.

Changing Your Password

The last topic we'll cover in this chapter is setting passwords for yourself (and for other users if you have access to superuser privileges). To set or change a password, the passwd command is used. The command syntax looks like this:

passwd [*user*]

To change your password, just enter the passwd command. You will be prompted for your old password and your new password:

```
[me@linuxbox ~]$ passwd
(current) UNIX password:
New UNIX password:
```

The passwd command will try to enforce use of "strong" passwords. This means it will refuse to accept passwords that are too short, are too similar to previous passwords, are dictionary words, or are too easily guessed:

```
[me@linuxbox ~]$ passwd
(current) UNIX password:
New UNIX password:
BAD PASSWORD: is too similar to the old one
New UNIX password:
BAD PASSWORD: it is WAY too short
New UNIX password:
BAD PASSWORD: it is based on a dictionary word
```

If you have superuser privileges, you can specify a username as an argument to the passwd command to set the password for another user. Other options are available to the superuser to allow account locking, password expiration, and so on. See the passwd man page for details.

10

PROCESSES

Modern operating systems are usually *multitasking*, meaning that they create the illusion of doing more than one thing at once by rapidly switching from one executing program to another. The Linux kernel manages this through the use of *processes*. Processes are how Linux organizes the different programs waiting for their turn at the CPU.

Sometimes a computer will become sluggish, or an application will stop responding. In this chapter, we will look at some of the tools available at the command line that let us examine what programs are doing and how to terminate processes that are misbehaving.

This chapter will introduce the following commands:

- ps—Report a snapshot of current processes.
- top—Display tasks.
- jobs—List active jobs.

- bg—Place a job in the background.
- fg—Place a job in the foreground.
- kill—Send a signal to a process.
- killall—Kill processes by name.

How a Process Works

When a system starts up, the kernel initiates a few of its own activities as processes and launches a program called init. init, in turn, runs a series of shell scripts (located in */etc*) called *init scripts*, which start all the system services. Many of these services are implemented as *daemon programs*, programs that just sit in the background and do their thing without having any user interface. So even if we are not logged in, the system is at least a little busy performing routine stuff.

The fact that a program can launch other programs is expressed in the process scheme as a *parent process* producing a *child process*.

The kernel maintains information about each process to help keep things organized. For example, each process is assigned a number called a *process ID (PID)*. PIDs are assigned in ascending order, with init always getting PID 1. The kernel also keeps track of the memory assigned to each process, as well as the processes' readiness to resume execution. Like files, processes also have owners and user IDs, effective user IDs, and so on.

Viewing Processes with ps

The most commonly used command to view processes (there are several) is ps. The ps program has a lot of options, but in it simplest form it is used like this:

```
[me@linuxbox ~]$ ps
  PID TTY          TIME CMD
 5198 pts/1    00:00:00 bash
10129 pts/1    00:00:00 ps
```

The result in this example lists two processes: process 5198 and process 10129, which are bash and ps respectively. As we can see, by default ps doesn't show us very much, just the processes associated with the current terminal session. To see more, we need to add some options, but before we do that, let's look at the other fields produced by ps. TTY is short for *teletype* and refers to the *controlling terminal* for the process. Unix is showing its age here. The TIME field is the amount of CPU time consumed by the process. As we can see, neither process makes the computer work very hard.

If we add an option, we can get a bigger picture of what the system is doing:

```
[me@linuxbox ~]$ ps x
  PID TTY      STAT   TIME COMMAND
 2799 ?        Ssl    0:00 /usr/libexec/bonobo-activation-server -ac
 2820 ?        Sl     0:01 /usr/libexec/evolution-data-server-1.10 --
15647 ?        Ss     0:00 /bin/sh /usr/bin/startkde
15751 ?        Ss     0:00 /usr/bin/ssh-agent /usr/bin/dbus-launch --
15754 ?        S      0:00 /usr/bin/dbus-launch --exit-with-session
15755 ?        Ss     0:01 /bin/dbus-daemon --fork --print-pid 4 -pr
15774 ?        Ss     0:02 /usr/bin/gpg-agent -s -daemon
15793 ?        S      0:00 start_kdeinit --new-startup +kcminit_start
15794 ?        Ss     0:00 kdeinit Running...
15797 ?        S      0:00 dcopserver -nosid
```

and many more...

Adding the x option (note that there is no leading dash) tells ps to show all of our processes regardless of what terminal (if any) they are controlled by. The presence of a ? in the TTY column indicates no controlling terminal. Using this option, we see a list of every process that we own.

Since the system is running a lot of processes, ps produces a long list. It is often helpful to pipe the output from ps into less for easier viewing. Some option combinations also produce long lines of output, so maximizing the terminal emulator window may be a good idea, too.

A new column titled STAT has been added to the output. STAT is short for *state* and reveals the current status of the process, as shown in Table 10-1.

Table 10-1: Process States

State	Meaning
R	Running. The process is running or ready to run.
S	Sleeping. The process is not running; rather, it is waiting for an event, such as a keystroke or network packet.
D	Uninterruptible sleep. Process is waiting for I/O such as a disk drive.
T	Stopped. Process has been instructed to stop (more on this later).
Z	A defunct or "zombie" process. This is a child process that has terminated but has not been cleaned up by its parent.
<	A high-priority process. It's possible to grant more importance to a process, giving it more time on the CPU. This property of a process is called *niceness*. A process with high priority is said to be less nice because it's taking more of the CPU's time, which leaves less for everybody else.
N	A low-priority process. A process with low priority (a nice process) will get processor time only after other processes with higher priority have been serviced.

The process state may be followed by other characters. These indicate various exotic process characteristics. See the ps man page for more detail.

Another popular set of options is aux (without a leading dash). This gives us even more information:

```
[me@linuxbox ~]$ ps aux
USER      PID %CPU %MEM    VSZ   RSS TTY      STAT START   TIME COMMAND
root        1  0.0  0.0   2136   644 ?        Ss   Mar05   0:31 init
root        2  0.0  0.0      0     0 ?        S<   Mar05   0:00 [kt]
root        3  0.0  0.0      0     0 ?        S<   Mar05   0:00 [mi]
root        4  0.0  0.0      0     0 ?        S<   Mar05   0:00 [ks]
root        5  0.0  0.0      0     0 ?        S<   Mar05   0:06 [wa]
root        6  0.0  0.0      0     0 ?        S<   Mar05   0:36 [ev]
root        7  0.0  0.0      0     0 ?        S<   Mar05   0:00 [kh]

and many more...
```

This set of options displays the processes belonging to every user. Using the options without the leading dash invokes the command with "BSD-style" behavior. The Linux version of ps can emulate the behavior of the ps program found in several Unix implementations. With these options, we get the additional columns shown in Table 10-2.

Table 10-2: BSD-Style ps Column Headers

Header	Meaning
USER	User ID. This is the owner of the process.
%CPU	CPU usage as a percent.
%MEM	Memory usage as a percent.
VSZ	Virtual memory size.
RSS	Resident Set Size. The amount of physical memory (RAM) the process is using in kilobytes.
START	Time when the process started. For values over 24 hours, a date is used.

Viewing Processes Dynamically with top

While the ps command can reveal a lot about what the machine is doing, it provides only a snapshot of the machine's state at the moment the ps command is executed. To see a more dynamic view of the machine's activity, we use the top command:

```
[me@linuxbox ~]$ top
```

The top program displays a continuously updating (by default, every 3 seconds) display of the system processes listed in order of process activity.

Its name comes from the fact that the top program is used to see the "top" processes on the system. The top display consists of two parts: a system summary at the top of the display, followed by a table of processes sorted by CPU activity:

```
top - 14:59:20 up  6:30,   2 users,  load average: 0.07, 0.02, 0.00
Tasks: 109 total,   1 running, 106 sleeping,   0 stopped,   2 zombie
Cpu(s):  0.7%us,  1.0%sy,  0.0%ni, 98.3%id,  0.0%wa,  0.0%hi,  0.0%si
Mem:     319496k total,   314860k used,     4636k free,    19392k buff
Swap:    875500k total,   149128k used,   726372k free,   114676k cach

  PID USER      PR  NI  VIRT  RES  SHR S %CPU %MEM    TIME+  COMMAND
 6244 me        39  19 31752 3124 2188 S  6.3  1.0 16:24.42 trackerd
11071 me        20   0  2304 1092  840 R  1.3  0.3  0:00.14 top
 6180 me        20   0  2700 1100  772 S  0.7  0.3  0:03.66 dbus-dae
 6321 me        20   0 20944 7248 6560 S  0.7  2.3  2:51.38 multiloa
 4955 root      20   0  104m 9668 5776 S  0.3  3.0  2:19.39 Xorg
    1 root      20   0  2976  528  476 S  0.0  0.2  0:03.14 init
    2 root      15  -5     0    0    0 S  0.0  0.0  0:00.00 kthreadd
    3 root      RT  -5     0    0    0 S  0.0  0.0  0:00.00 migratio
    4 root      15  -5     0    0    0 S  0.0  0.0  0:00.72 ksoftirq
    5 root      RT  -5     0    0    0 S  0.0  0.0  0:00.04 watchdog
    6 root      15  -5     0    0    0 S  0.0  0.0  0:00.42 events/0
    7 root      15  -5     0    0    0 S  0.0  0.0  0:00.06 khelper
   41 root      15  -5     0    0    0 S  0.0  0.0  0:01.08 kblockd/
   67 root      15  -5     0    0    0 S  0.0  0.0  0:00.00 kseriod
  114 root      20   0     0    0    0 S  0.0  0.0  0:01.62 pdflush
  116 root      15  -5     0    0    0 S  0.0  0.0  0:02.44 kswapd0
```

The system summary contains a lot of good stuff; see Table 10-3 for a rundown.

Table 10-3: top Information Fields

Row	Field	Meaning
1	top	Name of the program.
	14:59:20	Current time of day.
	up 6:30	This is called *uptime*. It is the amount of time since the machine was last booted. In this example, the system has been up for 6½ hours.
	2 users	Two users are logged in.
	load average:	*Load average* refers to the number of processes that are waiting to run; that is, the number of processes that are in a runnable state and are sharing the CPU. Three values are shown, each for a different period of time. The first is the average for the last 60 seconds, the next the previous 5 minutes, and finally the previous 15 minutes. Values under 1.0 indicate that the machine is not busy.

(continued)

Table 10-3 (*continued*)

Row	Field	Meaning
2	Tasks:	This summarizes the number of processes and their various process states.
3	Cpu(s):	This row describes the character of the activities that the CPU is performing.
	0.7%us	0.7% of the CPU is being used for *user processes*. This means processes outside of the kernel itself.
	1.0%sy	1.0% of the CPU is being used for *system* (kernel) processes.
	0.0%ni	0.0% of the CPU is being used by nice (low-priority) processes.
	98.3%id	98.3% of the CPU is idle.
	0.0%wa	0.0% of the CPU is waiting for I/O.
4	Mem:	Shows how physical RAM is being used.
5	Swap:	Shows how swap space (virtual memory) is being used.

The top program accepts a number of keyboard commands. The two most interesting are h, which displays the program's help screen, and q, which quits top.

Both major desktop environments provide graphical applications that display information similar to top (in much the same way that Task Manager in Windows does), but I find that top is better than the graphical versions because it is faster and consumes far fewer system resources. After all, our system monitor program shouldn't add to the system slowdown that we are trying to track.

Controlling Processes

Now that we can see and monitor processes, let's gain some control over them. For our experiments, we're going to use a little program called xlogo as our guinea pig. The xlogo program is a sample program supplied with the X Window System (the underlying engine that makes the graphics on our display go), which simply displays a resizable window containing the X logo. First, we'll get to know our test subject:

```
[me@linuxbox ~]$ xlogo
```

After we enter the command, a small window containing the logo should appear somewhere on the screen. On some systems, xlogo may print a warning message, but it may be safely ignored.

Note: *If your system does not include the* xlogo *program, try using* gedit *or* kwrite *instead.*

We can verify that xlogo is running by resizing its window. If the logo is redrawn in the new size, the program is running.

Notice how our shell prompt has not returned? This is because the shell is waiting for the program to finish, just like all the other programs we have used so far. If we close the xlogo window, the prompt returns.

Interrupting a Process

Let's observe what happens when we run xlogo again. First, enter the xlogo command and verify that the program is running. Next, return to the terminal window and press CTRL-C.

```
[me@linuxbox ~]$ xlogo
[me@linuxbox ~]$
```

In a terminal, pressing CTRL-C *interrupts* a program. This means that we politely asked the program to terminate. After we pressed CTRL-C, the xlogo window closed and the shell prompt returned.

Many (but not all) command-line programs can be interrupted by using this technique.

Putting a Process in the Background

Let's say we wanted to get the shell prompt back without terminating the xlogo program. We'll do this by placing the program in the *background*. Think of the terminal as having a *foreground* (with stuff visible on the surface, like the shell prompt) and a background (with hidden stuff below the surface). To launch a program so that it is immediately placed in the background, we follow the command with an ampersand character (&):

```
[me@linuxbox ~]$ xlogo &
[1] 28236
[me@linuxbox ~]$
```

After the command was entered, the xlogo window appeared and the shell prompt returned, but some funny numbers were printed too. This message is part of a shell feature called *job control*. With this message, the shell is telling us that we have started job number 1 ([1]) and that it has PID 28236. If we run ps, we can see our process:

```
[me@linuxbox ~]$ ps
  PID TTY          TIME CMD
10603 pts/1    00:00:00 bash
```

```
28236 pts/1    00:00:00 xlogo
28239 pts/1    00:00:00 ps
```

The shell's job control facility also gives us a way to list the jobs that have been launched from our terminal. Using the jobs command, we can see the following list:

```
[me@linuxbox ~]$ jobs
[1]+  Running              xlogo &
```

The results show that we have one job, numbered 1, that it is running, and that the command was xlogo &.

Returning a Process to the Foreground

A process in the background is immune from keyboard input, including any attempt to interrupt it with a CTRL-C. To return a process to the foreground, use the fg command, as in this example:

```
[me@linuxbox ~]$ jobs
[1]+  Running              xlogo &
[me@linuxbox ~]$ fg %1
xlogo
```

The command fg followed by a percent sign and the job number (called a *jobspec*) does the trick. If we have only one background job, the jobspec is optional. To terminate xlogo, type CTRL-C.

Stopping (Pausing) a Process

Sometimes we'll want to stop a process without terminating it. This is often done to allow a foreground process to be moved to the background. To stop a foreground process, type CTRL-Z. Let's try it. At the command prompt, type xlogo, press the ENTER key, and then type CTRL-Z:

```
[me@linuxbox ~]$ xlogo
[1]+  Stopped              xlogo
[me@linuxbox ~]$
```

After stopping xlogo, we can verify that the program has stopped by attempting to resize the xlogo window. We will see that it appears quite dead. We can either restore the program to the foreground, using the fg command, or move the program to the background with the bg command:

```
[me@linuxbox ~]$ bg %1
[1]+ xlogo &
[me@linuxbox ~]$
```

As with the fg command, the jobspec is optional if there is only one job.

Moving a process from the foreground to the background is handy if we launch a graphical program from the command but forget to place it in the background by appending the trailing &.

Why would you want to launch a graphical program from the command line? There are two reasons. First, the program you wish to run might not be listed on the window manager's menus (such as xlogo).

Second, by launching a program from the command line, you might be able to see error messages that would be invisible if the program were launched graphically. Sometimes, a program will fail to start up when launched from the graphical menu. By launching it from the command line instead, we may see an error message that will reveal the problem. Also, some graphical programs have many interesting and useful command-line options.

Signals

The kill command is used to "kill" (terminate) processes. This allows us to end the execution of a program that is behaving badly or otherwise refuses to terminate on its own. Here's an example:

```
[me@linuxbox ~]$ xlogo &
[1] 28401
[me@linuxbox ~]$ kill 28401
[1]+  Terminated              xlogo
```

We first launch xlogo in the background. The shell prints the jobspec and the PID of the background process. Next, we use the kill command and specify the PID of the process we want to terminate. We could also have specified the process using a jobspec (for example, %1) instead of a PID.

While this is all very straightforward, there is more to it. The kill command doesn't exactly "kill" processes; rather it sends them *signals*. Signals are one of several ways that the operating system communicates with programs. We have already seen signals in action with the use of CTRL-C and CTRL-Z. When the terminal receives one of these keystrokes, it sends a signal to the program in the foreground. In the case of CTRL-C, a signal called INT (Interrupt) is sent; with CTRL-Z, a signal called TSTP (Terminal Stop) is sent. Programs, in turn, "listen" for signals and may act upon them as they are received. The fact that a program can listen and act upon signals allows it to do things like save work in progress when it is sent a termination signal.

Sending Signals to Processes with kill

The most common syntax for the kill command looks like this:

    kill [-signal] PID...

If no signal is specified on the command line, then the TERM (Terminate) signal is sent by default. The kill command is most often used to send the signals shown in Table 10-4.

Table 10-4: Common Signals

Number	Name	Meaning
1	HUP	Hang up. This is a vestige of the good old days when terminals were attached to remote computers with phone lines and modems. The signal is used to indicate to programs that the controlling terminal has "hung up." The effect of this signal can be demonstrated by closing a terminal session. The foreground program running on the terminal will be sent the signal and will terminate. This signal is also used by many daemon programs to cause a reinitialization. This means that when a daemon is sent this signal, it will restart and reread its configuration file. The Apache web server is an example of a daemon that uses the HUP signal in this way.
2	INT	Interrupt. Performs the same function as the CTRL-C key sent from the terminal. It will usually terminate a program.
9	KILL	Kill. This signal is special. Whereas programs may choose to handle signals sent to them in different ways, including by ignoring them altogether, the KILL signal is never actually sent to the target program. Rather, the kernel immediately terminates the process. When a process is terminated in this manner, it is given no opportunity to "clean up" after itself or save its work. For this reason, the KILL signal should be used only as a last resort when other termination signals fail.
15	TERM	Terminate. This is the default signal sent by the kill command. If a program is still "alive" enough to receive signals, it will terminate.
18	CONT	Continue. This will restore a process after a STOP signal.
19	STOP	Stop. This signal causes a process to pause without terminating. Like the KILL signal, it is not sent to the target process, and thus it cannot be ignored.

Let's try out the kill command:

```
[me@linuxbox ~]$ xlogo &
[1] 13546
[me@linuxbox ~]$ kill -1 13546
[1]+  Hangup                  xlogo
```

In this example, we start the xlogo program in the background and then send it a HUP signal with kill. The xlogo program terminates, and the shell indicates that the background process has received a hangup signal. You may need to press the ENTER key a couple of times before you see the message. Note that signals may be specified either by number or by name, including the name prefixed with the letters *SIG*:

```
[me@linuxbox ~]$ xlogo &
[1] 13601
[me@linuxbox ~]$ kill -INT 13601
[1]+  Interrupt               xlogo
[me@linuxbox ~]$ xlogo &
[1] 13608
[me@linuxbox ~]$ kill -SIGINT 13608
[1]+  Interrupt               xlogo
```

Repeat the example above and try out the other signals. Remember, you can also use jobspecs in place of PIDs.

Processes, like files, have owners, and you must be the owner of a process (or the superuser) in order to send it signals with kill.

In addition to the signals listed in Table 10-4, which are most often used with kill, other signals are frequently used by the system. Table 10-5 lists the other common signals.

Table 10-5: Other Common Signals

Number	Name	Meaning
3	QUIT	Quit.
11	SEGV	Segmentation violation. This signal is sent if a program makes illegal use of memory; that is, it tried to write somewhere it was not allowed to.
20	TSTP	Terminal stop. This is the signal sent by the terminal when CTRL-Z is pressed. Unlike the STOP signal, the TSTP signal is received by the program but the program may choose to ignore it.
28	WINCH	Window change. This is a signal sent by the system when a window changes size. Some programs, like top and less, will respond to this signal by redrawing themselves to fit the new window dimensions.

For the curious, a complete list of signals can be seen with the following command:

```
[me@linuxbox ~]$ kill -l
```

Sending Signals to Multiple Processes with killall

It's also possible to send signals to multiple processes matching a specified program or username by using the killall command. Here is the syntax:

```
killall [-u user] [-signal] name...
```

To demonstrate, we will start a couple of instances of the xlogo program and then terminate them:

```
[me@linuxbox ~]$ xlogo &
[1] 18801
[me@linuxbox ~]$ xlogo &
[2] 18802
[me@linuxbox ~]$ killall xlogo
[1]-  Terminated                  xlogo
[2]+  Terminated                  xlogo
```

Remember, as with kill, you must have superuser privileges to send signals to processes that do not belong to you.

More Process-Related Commands

Since monitoring processes is an important system administration task, there are a lot of commands for it. Table 10-6 lists some to play with.

Table 10-6: Other Process-Related Commands

Command	Description
pstree	Outputs a process list arranged in a tree-like pattern showing the parent/child relationships between processes.
vmstat	Outputs a snapshot of system resource usage including memory, swap, and disk I/O. To see a continuous display, follow the command with a time delay (in seconds) for updates (e.g., vmstat 5). Terminate the output with CTRL-C.
xload	A graphical program that draws a graph showing system load over time.
tload	Similar to the xload program, but draws the graph in the terminal. Terminate the output with CTRL-C.

PART 2

CONFIGURATION AND THE ENVIRONMENT

11

THE ENVIRONMENT

As we discussed earlier, the shell maintains a body of information during our shell session called the *environment*. Data stored in the environment is used by programs to determine facts about our configuration. While most programs use *configuration files* to store program settings, some programs will also look for values stored in the environment to adjust their behavior. Knowing this, we can use the environment to customize our shell experience.

In this chapter, we will work with the following commands:

- printenv—Print part or all of the environment.
- set—Set shell options.
- export—Export environment to subsequently executed programs.
- alias—Create an alias for a command.

What Is Stored in the Environment?

The shell stores two basic types of data in the environment, although, with bash, the types are largely indistinguishable. They are *environment variables* and *shell variables*. Shell variables are bits of data placed there by bash, and environment variables are basically everything else. In addition to variables, the shell also stores some programmatic data, namely *aliases* and *shell functions*. We covered aliases in Chapter 5, and shell functions (which are related to shell scripting) will be covered in Part 4.

Examining the Environment

To see what is stored in the environment, we can use either the set built in bash or the printenv program. The set command will show both the shell and environment variables, while printenv will display only the latter. Since the list of environment contents will be fairly long, it is best to pipe the output of either command into less:

```
[me@linuxbox ~]$ printenv | less
```

Doing so, we should get something that looks like this:

```
KDE_MULTIHEAD=false
SSH_AGENT_PID=6666
HOSTNAME=linuxbox
GPG_AGENT_INFO=/tmp/gpg-PdOt7g/S.gpg-agent:6689:1
SHELL=/bin/bash
TERM=xterm
XDG_MENU_PREFIX=kde-
HISTSIZE=1000
XDG_SESSION_COOKIE=6d7b05c65846c3eaf3101b0046bd2b00-1208521990.996705-1177056199
GTK2_RC_FILES=/etc/gtk-2.0/gtkrc:/home/me/.gtkrc-2.0:/home/me/.kde/share/config/gtkrc-2.0
GTK_RC_FILES=/etc/gtk/gtkrc:/home/me/.gtkrc:/home/me/.kde/share/config/gtkrc
GS_LIB=/home/me/.fonts
WINDOWID=29360136
QTDIR=/usr/lib/qt-3.3
QTINC=/usr/lib/qt-3.3/include
KDE_FULL_SESSION=true
USER=me
LS_COLORS=no=00:fi=00:di=00;34:ln=00;36:pi=40;33:so=00;35:bd=40;33;01:cd=40;33;01:or=01;05;37;41:mi=01;05;37;41:ex=00;32:*.cmd=00;32:*.exe:
```

What we see is a list of environment variables and their values. For example, we see a variable called USER, which contains the value me. The printenv command can also list the value of a specific variable:

```
[me@linuxbox ~]$ printenv USER
me
```

The set command, when used without options or arguments, will display both the shell and environment variables, as well as any defined shell functions.

```
[me@linuxbox ~]$ set | less
```

Unlike printenv, its output is courteously sorted in alphabetical order.

It is also possible to view the contents of a single variable using the echo command, like this:

```
[me@linuxbox ~]$ echo $HOME
/home/me
```

One element of the environment that neither set nor printenv displays is aliases. To see them, enter the alias command without arguments:

```
[me@linuxbox ~]$ alias
alias l.='ls -d .* --color=tty'
alias ll='ls -l --color=tty'
alias ls='ls --color=tty'
alias vi='vim'
alias which='alias | /usr/bin/which --tty-only --read-alias --show-dot --show-tilde'
```

Some Interesting Variables

The environment contains quite a few variables, and though your environment may differ from the one presented here, you will likely see the variables shown in Table 11-1 in your environment.

Table 11-1: Environment Variables

Variable	Contents
DISPLAY	The name of your display if you are running a graphical environment. Usually this is :0, meaning the first display generated by the X server.
EDITOR	The name of the program to be used for text editing.
SHELL	The name of your shell program.
HOME	The pathname of your home directory.
LANG	Defines the character set and collation order of your language.
OLD_PWD	The previous working directory.
PAGER	The name of the program to be used for paging output. This is often set to /usr/bin/less.
PATH	A colon-separated list of directories that are searched when you enter the name of an executable program.

(continued)

Table 11-1 (*continued*)

Variable	Contents
PS1	Prompt String 1. This defines the contents of your shell prompt. As we will later see, this can be extensively customized.
PWD	The current working directory.
TERM	The name of your terminal type. Unix-like systems support many terminal protocols; this variable sets the protocol to be used with your terminal emulator.
TZ	Specifies your time zone. Most Unix-like systems maintain the computer's internal clock in *Coordinated Universal Time (UTC)* and then display the local time by applying an offset specified by this variable.
USER	Your username.

Don't worry if some of these values are missing. They vary by distribution.

How Is the Environment Established?

When we log on to the system, the bash program starts and reads a series of configuration scripts called *startup files,* which define the default environment shared by all users. This is followed by more startup files in our home directory that define our personal environment. The exact sequence depends on the type of shell session being started.

Login and Non-login Shells

There are two kinds of shell sessions: a login shell session and a non-login shell session.

A *login shell session* is one in which we are prompted for our username and password; for example, when we start a virtual console session. A *non-login shell session* typically occurs when we launch a terminal session in the GUI.

Login shells read one or more startup files, as shown in Table 11-2.

Table 11-2: Startup Files for Login Shell Sessions

File	Contents
/etc/profile	A global configuration script that applies to all users.
~/.bash_profile	A user's personal startup file. Can be used to extend or override settings in the global configuration script.

Table 11-2 (*continued*)

File	Contents
~/.bash_login	If ~/.bash_profile is not found, bash attempts to read this script.
~/.profile	If neither ~/.bash_profile nor ~/.bash_login is found, bash attempts to read this file. This is the default in Debian-based distributions, such as Ubuntu.

Non-login shell sessions read the startup files as shown in Table 11-3.

Table 11-3: Startup Files for Non-Login Shell Sessions

File	Contents
/etc/bash.bashrc	A global configuration script that applies to all users.
~/.bashrc	A user's personal startup file. Can be used to extend or override settings in the global configuration script.

In addition to reading the startup files above, non-login shells inherit the environment from their parent process, usually a login shell.

Take a look at your system and see which of these startup files you have. Remember: Since most of the filenames listed above start with a period (meaning that they are hidden), you will need to use the -a option when using ls.

The ~/.bashrc file is probably the most important startup file from the ordinary user's point of view, since it is almost always read. Non-login shells read it by default, and most startup files for login shells are written in such a way as to read the ~/.bashrc file as well.

What's in a Startup File?

If we take a look inside a typical .bash_profile (taken from a CentOS-4 system), it looks something like this:

```
# .bash_profile

# Get the aliases and functions
if [ -f ~/.bashrc ]; then
        . ~/.bashrc
fi

# User specific environment and startup programs

PATH=$PATH:$HOME/bin
export PATH
```

Lines that begin with a # are *comments* and are not read by the shell. These are there for human readability. The first interesting thing occurs on the fourth line, with the following code:

```
if [ -f ~/.bashrc ]; then
        . ~/.bashrc
fi
```

This is called an *if compound command*, which we will cover fully when we get to shell scripting in Part 4, but for now we will translate:

```
If the file "~/.bashrc" exists, then
        read the "~/.bashrc" file.
```

We can see that this bit of code is how a login shell gets the contents of *.bashrc*. The next thing in our startup file has to do with the PATH variable.

Ever wonder how the shell knows where to find commands when we enter them on the command line? For example, when we enter ls, the shell does not search the entire computer to find */bin/ls* (the full pathname of the ls command); rather, it searches a list of directories that are contained in the PATH variable.

The PATH variable is often (but not always, depending on the distribution) set by the */etc/profile* startup file and with this code:

```
PATH=$PATH:$HOME/bin
```

PATH is modified to add the directory *$HOME/bin* to the end of the list. This is an example of parameter expansion, which we touched on in Chapter 7. To demonstrate how this works, try the following:

```
[me@linuxbox ~]$ foo="This is some"
[me@linuxbox ~]$ echo $foo
This is some
[me@linuxbox ~]$ foo=$foo" text."
[me@linuxbox ~]$ echo $foo
This is some text.
```

Using this technique, we can append text to the end of a variable's contents.

By adding the string $HOME/bin to the end of the PATH variable's contents, the directory *$HOME/bin* is added to the list of directories searched when a command is entered. This means that when we want to create a directory within our home directory for storing our own private programs, the shell is ready to accommodate us. All we have to do is call it *bin*, and we're ready to go.

Note: *Many distributions provide this PATH setting by default. Some Debian-based distributions, such as Ubuntu, test for the existence of the ~/bin directory at login and dynamically add it to the PATH variable if the directory is found.*

Lastly, we have this:

```
export PATH
```

The export command tells the shell to make the contents of PATH available to child processes of this shell.

Modifying the Environment

Since we know where the startup files are and what they contain, we can modify them to customize our environment.

Which Files Should We Modify?

As a general rule, to add directories to your PATH or define additional environment variables, place those changes in *.bash_profile* (or equivalent, according to your distribution—for example, Ubuntu uses *.profile*). For everything else, place the changes in *.bashrc*. Unless you are the system administrator and need to change the defaults for all users of the system, restrict your modifications to the files in your home directory. It is certainly possible to change the files in */etc* such as *profile*, and in many cases it would be sensible to do so, but for now let's play it safe.

Text Editors

To edit (i.e., modify) the shell's startup files, as well as most of the other configuration files on the system, we use a program called a *text editor*. A text editor is a program that is, in some ways, like a word processor in that it allows you to edit the words on the screen with a moving cursor. It differs from a word processor by supporting only pure text, and it often contains features designed for writing programs. Text editors are the central tool used by software developers to write code and by system administrators to manage the configuration files that control the system.

A lot of text editors are available for Linux; your system probably has several installed. Why so many different ones? Probably because programmers like writing them, and since programmers use editors extensively, they like to express their own desires as to how editors should work.

Text editors fall into two basic categories: graphical and text based. GNOME and KDE both include some popular graphical editors. GNOME ships with an editor called gedit, which is usually called Text Editor in the GNOME menu. KDE usually ships with three, which are (in order of increasing complexity) kedit, kwrite, and kate.

There are many text-based editors. The popular ones you will encounter are nano, vi, and emacs. The nano editor is a simple, easy-to-use editor designed as a replacement for the pico editor supplied with the PINE email suite. The vi editor (on most Linux systems replaced by a program named vim, which is short for *Vi IMproved*) is the traditional editor for Unix-like systems. It is the subject of Chapter 12. The emacs editor was originally written by Richard Stallman. It is a gigantic, all-purpose, does-everything programming environment. Though readily available, it is seldom installed on most Linux systems by default.

Using a Text Editor

All text editors can be invoked from the command line by typing the name of the editor followed by the name of the file you want to edit. If the file does not already exist, the editor will assume that you want to create a new file. Here is an example using gedit:

```
[me@linuxbox ~]$ gedit some_file
```

This command will start the gedit text editor and load the file named *some_file*, if it exists.

All graphical text editors are pretty self-explanatory, so we won't cover them here. Instead, we will concentrate on our first text-based text editor, nano. Let's fire up nano and edit the *.bashrc* file. But before we do that, let's practice some safe computing. Whenever we edit an important configuration file, it is always a good idea to create a backup copy of the file first. This protects us in case we mess the file up while editing. To create a backup of the *.bashrc* file, do this:

```
[me@linuxbox ~]$ cp .bashrc .bashrc.bak
```

It doesn't matter what you call the backup file; just pick an understandable name. The extensions *.bak*, *.sav*, *.old*, and *.orig* are all popular ways of indicating a backup file. Oh, and remember that cp will *overwrite existing files silently*.

Now that we have a backup file, we'll start the editor:

```
[me@linuxbox ~]$ nano .bashrc
```

Once nano starts, we'll get a screen like this:

```
  GNU nano 2.0.3          File: .bashrc

# .bashrc

# Source global definitions
if [ -f /etc/bashrc ]; then
        . /etc/bashrc
fi

# User specific aliases and functions



                         [ Read 8 lines ]
^G Get Help^O WriteOut^R Read Fil^Y Prev Pag^K Cut Text^C Cur Pos
^X Exit    ^J Justify ^W Where Is^V Next Pag^U UnCut Te^T To Spell
```

Note: *If your system does not have nano installed, you may use a graphical editor instead.*

The screen consists of a header at the top, the text of the file being edited in the middle, and a menu of commands at the bottom. Since nano was designed to replace the text editor supplied with an email client, it is rather short on editing features.

The first command you should learn in any text editor is how to exit the program. In the case of nano, you press CTRL-X to exit. This is indicated in the menu at the bottom of the screen. The notation ^X means CTRL-X. This is a common notation for the control characters used by many programs.

The second command we need to know is how to save our work. With nano it's CTRL-O. With this knowledge under our belts, we're ready to do some editing. Using the down-arrow key and/or the page-down key, move the cursor to the end of the file, and then add the following lines to the *.bashrc* file:

```
umask 0002
export HISTCONTROL=ignoredups
export HISTSIZE=1000
alias l.='ls -d .* --color=auto'
alias ll='ls -l --color=auto'
```

Note: *Your distribution may already include some of these, but duplicates won't hurt anything.*

Table 11-4 lists the meanings of our additions.

Table 11-4: Additions to Our *.bashrc* File

Line	Meaning
Umask 0002	Sets the umask to solve the problem with shared directories we discussed in Chapter 9.
export HISTCONTROL=ignoredups	Causes the shell's history recording feature to ignore a command if the same command was just recorded.
export HISTSIZE=1000	Increases the size of the command history from the default of 500 lines to 1000 lines.
alias l.='ls -d .* --color=auto'	Creates a new command called l., which displays all directory entries that begin with a dot.
alias ll='ls -l –color=auto'	Creates a new command called ll, which displays a long-format directory listing.

As we can see, many of our additions are not intuitively obvious, so it would be a good idea to add some comments to our *.bashrc* file to help explain things to the humans. Using the editor, change our additions to look like this:

```
# Change umask to make directory sharing easier
umask 0002

# Ignore duplicates in command history and increase
# history size to 1000 lines
export HISTCONTROL=ignoredups
export HISTSIZE=1000

# Add some helpful aliases
alias l.='ls -d .* --color=auto'
alias ll='ls -l --color=auto'
```

Ah, much better! With our changes complete, press CTRL-O to save our modified *.bashrc* file and CTRL-X to exit nano.

Activating Our Changes

The changes we have made to our *.bashrc* will not take effect until we close our terminal session and start a new one, because the *.bashrc* file is only read at the beginning of a session. However, we can force bash to reread the modified *.bashrc* file with the following command:

```
[me@linuxbox ~]$ source .bashrc
```

After doing this, we should be able to see the effect of our changes. Try out one of the new aliases:

```
[me@linuxbox ~]$ ll
```

WHY COMMENTS ARE IMPORTANT

Whenever you modify configuration files, it's a good idea to add some comments to document your changes. Sure, you will remember what you changed tomorrow, but what about six months from now? Do yourself a favor and add some comments. While you're at it, it's not a bad idea to keep a log of what changes you make.

Shell scripts and bash startup files use a # symbol to begin a comment. Other configuration files may use other symbols. Most configuration files will have comments. Use them as a guide.

You will often see lines in configuration files that are *commented out* to prevent them from being used by the affected program. This is done to give the reader suggestions for possible configuration choices or examples of correct configuration syntax. For example, the *.bashrc* file of Ubuntu 8.04 contains these lines:

```
# some more ls aliases
#alias ll='ls -l'
#alias la='ls -A'
#alias l='ls -CF'
```

The last three lines are valid alias definitions that have been commented out. If you remove the leading # symbols from these three lines, a technique called *uncommenting*, you will activate the aliases. Conversely, if you add a # symbol to the beginning of a line, you can deactivate a configuration line while preserving the information it contains.

Final Note

In this chapter we learned an essential skill—editing configuration files with a text editor. Moving forward, as we read man pages for commands, take note of the environment variables that commands support. There may be a gem or two. In later chapters we will learn about shell functions, a powerful feature that you can also include in the bash startup files to add to your arsenal of custom commands.

12

A GENTLE INTRODUCTION TO VI

There is an old joke about a visitor to New York City asking a passerby for directions to the city's famous classical music venue:

> Visitor: Excuse me, how do I get to Carnegie Hall?
> Passerby: Practice, practice, practice!

Learning the Linux command line, like becoming an accomplished pianist, is not something that we pick up in an afternoon. It takes years of practice. In this chapter, we will introduce the vi (pronounced "vee eye") text editor, one of the core programs in the Unix tradition. vi is somewhat notorious for its difficult user interface, but when we see a master sit down at the keyboard and begin to "play," we will indeed be witness to some great art. We won't become masters in this chapter, but when we are done, we will know how to play "Chopsticks" in vi.

Why We Should Learn vi

In this modern age of graphical editors and easy-to-use text-based editors such as nano, why should we learn vi? There are three good reasons:

- vi is always available. This can be a lifesaver if we have a system with no graphical interface, such as a remote server or a local system with a broken X configuration. nano, while increasingly popular, is still not universal. POSIX, a standard for program compatibility on Unix systems, requires that vi be present.

- vi is lightweight and fast. For many tasks, it's easier to bring up vi than it is to find the graphical text editor in the menus and wait for its multiple megabytes to load. In addition, vi is designed for typing speed. As we shall see, a skilled vi user never has to lift his or her fingers from the keyboard while editing.

- We don't want other Linux and Unix users to think we are sissies.

  Okay, maybe two good reasons.

A Little Background

The first version of vi was written in 1976 by Bill Joy, a University of California, Berkeley student who later went on to co-found Sun Microsystems. vi derives its name from the word *visual*, because it was intended to allow editing on a video terminal with a moving cursor. Before *visual editors* there were *line editors,* which operated on a single line of text at a time. To specify a change, we tell a line editor to go to a particular line and describe what change to make, such as adding or deleting text. With the advent of video terminals (rather than printer-based terminals like teletypes), visual editing became possible. vi actually incorporates a powerful line editor called ex, and we can use line-editing commands while using vi.

Most Linux distributions don't include real vi; rather, they ship with an enhanced replacement called vim (which is short for *Vi IMproved*) written by Bram Moolenaar. vim is a substantial improvement over traditional Unix vi and is usually symbolically linked (or aliased) to the name vi on Linux systems. In the discussions that follow, we will assume that we have a program called vi that is really vim.

Starting and Stopping vi

To start vi, we simply enter the following:

```
[me@linuxbox ~]$ vi
```

A screen like this should appear:

```
~
~
~                        VIM - Vi Improved
~
~                         version 7.1.138
~                       by Bram Moolenaar et al.
~              Vim is open source and freely distributable
~
~                       Sponsor Vim development!
~         type  :help sponsor<Enter>    for information
~
~         type  :q<Enter>               to exit
~         type  :help<Enter>  or  <F1>  for on-line help
~         type  :help version7<Enter>   for version info
~
~                  Running in Vi compatible mode
~         type  :set nocp<Enter>        for Vim defaults
~         type  :help cp-default<Enter> for info on this
~
~
~
```

Just as we did with nano earlier, the first thing to learn is how to exit. To exit, we enter the following command (note that the colon character is part of the command):

```
:q
```

The shell prompt should return. If, for some reason, vi will not quit (usually because we made a change to a file that has not yet been saved), we can tell vi that we really mean it by adding an exclamation point to the command:

```
:q!
```

Note: *If you get "lost" in vi, try pressing the ESC key twice to find your way again.*

Editing Modes

Let's start up vi again, this time passing to it the name of a nonexistent file. This is how we can create a new file with vi:

```
[me@linuxbox ~]$ rm -f foo.txt
[me@linuxbox ~]$ vi foo.txt
```

If all goes well, we should get a screen like this:

```
~
~
~
~
~
~
~
~
~
~
~
~
~
~
~
~
~
~
~
~
~
~
~
"foo.txt" [New File]
```

The leading tilde characters (~) indicate that no text exists on that line. This shows that we have an empty file. *Do not type anything yet!*

The second most important thing to learn about vi (after learning how to exit) is that vi is a *modal editor*. When vi starts up, it begins in *command mode*. In this mode, almost every key is a command, so if we were to start typing, vi would basically go crazy and make a big mess.

Entering Insert Mode

In order to add some text to our file, we must first enter *insert mode*. To do this, we press the I key (i). Afterward, we should see the following at the bottom of the screen if vim is running in its usual enhanced mode (this will not appear in vi-compatible mode):

```
-- INSERT --
```

Now we can enter some text. Try this:

```
The quick brown fox jumped over the lazy dog.
```

To exit insert mode and return to command mode, press the ESC key.

Saving Our Work

To save the change we just made to our file, we must enter an *ex command* while in command mode. This is easily done by pressing the : key. After doing this, a colon character should appear at the bottom of the screen:

```
:
```

To write our modified file, we follow the colon with a w, then ENTER:

```
:w
```

The file will be written to the hard drive, and we should get a confirmation message at the bottom of the screen, like this:

```
"foo.txt" [New] 1L, 46C written
```

Note: *If you read the vim documentation, you will notice that (confusingly) command mode is called normal mode and ex commands are called command mode. Beware.*

COMPATIBILITY MODE

In the example startup screen shown at the beginning of this section (taken from Ubuntu 8.04), we see the text Running in Vi compatible mode. This means that vim will run in a mode that is closer to the normal behavior of vi rather than the enhanced behavior of vim. For purposes of this chapter, we will want to run vim with its enhanced behavior. To do this, you have a couple of options:

- Try running vim instead of vi (if that works, consider adding alias vi='vim' to your *.bashrc* file).

- Use this command to add a line to your vim configuration file:

  ```
  echo "set nocp" >> ~/.vimrc
  ```

Different Linux distributions package vim in different ways. Some distributions install a minimal version of vim by default that supports only a limited set of vim features. While performing the lessons that follow, you may encounter missing features. If this is the case, install the full version of vim.

Moving the Cursor Around

While it is in command mode, vi offers a large number of movement commands, some of which it shares with less. Table 12-1 lists a subset.

Table 12-1: Cursor Movement Keys

Key	Moves the cursor
L or right arrow	Right one character
H or left arrow	Left one character
J or down arrow	Down one line
K or up arrow	Up one line

(continued)

Table 12-1 (*continued*)

Key	Moves the cursor
0 (zero)	To the beginning of the current line
SHIFT-6 (^)	To the first non-whitespace character on the current line
SHIFT-4 ($)	To the end of the current line
W	To the beginning of the next word or punctuation character
SHIFT-W (W)	To the beginning of the next word, ignoring punctuation characters
B	To the beginning of the previous word or punctuation character
SHIFT-B (B)	To the beginning of the previous word, ignoring punctuation characters
CTRL-F or PAGE DOWN	Down one page
CTRL-B or PAGE UP	Up one page
number-SHIFT-G	To line *number* (for example, 1G moves to the first line of the file)
SHIFT-G (G)	To the last line of the file

Why are the H, J, K, and L keys used for cursor movement? Because when vi was originally written, not all video terminals had arrow keys, and skilled typists could use regular keyboard keys to move the cursor without ever having to lift their fingers from the keyboard.

Many commands in vi can be prefixed with a number, as with the G command listed in Table 12-1. By prefixing a command with a number, we may specify the number of times a command is to be carried out. For example, the command 5j causes vi to move the cursor down five lines.

Basic Editing

Most editing consists of a few basic operations such as inserting text, deleting text, and moving text around by cutting and pasting. vi, of course, supports all of these operations in its own unique way. vi also provides a limited form of undo. If we press the U key while in command mode, vi will undo the last change that you made. This will come in handy as we try out some of the basic editing commands.

Appending Text

vi has several ways of entering insert mode. We have already used the i command to insert text.

Let's go back to our *foo.txt* file for a moment:

```
The quick brown fox jumped over the lazy dog.
```

If we wanted to add some text to the end of this sentence, we would discover that the i command will not do it, because we can't move the cursor beyond the end of the line. vi provides a command to append text, the sensibly named a command. If we move the cursor to the end of the line and type a, the cursor will move past the end of the line, and vi will enter insert mode. This will allow us to add some more text:

```
The quick brown fox jumped over the lazy dog. It was cool.
```

Remember to press the ESC key to exit insert mode.

Since we will almost always want to append text to the end of a line, vi offers a shortcut to move to the end of the current line and start appending. It's the A command. Let's try it and add some more lines to our file.

First, we'll move the cursor to the beginning of the line using the 0 (zero) command. Now we type A and add the following lines of text:

```
The quick brown fox jumped over the lazy dog. It was cool.
Line 2
Line 3
Line 4
Line 5
```

Again, press the ESC key to exit insert mode.

As we can see, the A command is more useful because it moves the cursor to the end of the line before starting insert mode.

Opening a Line

Another way we can insert text is by "opening" a line. This inserts a blank line between two existing lines and enters insert mode. This has two variants, as shown in Table 12-2.

Table 12-2: Line Opening Keys

Command	Opens
o	The line below the current line
O	The line above the current line

We can demonstrate this as follows: Place the cursor on Line 3 and then
o.

```
quick brown fox jumped over the lazy dog. It was cool.
e 2
e 3

ne 4
ne 5
```

A new line was opened below the third line, and we entered insert mode. Exit insert mode by pressing the ESC key. Type **u** to undo our change. Type **O** to open the line above the cursor:

```
The quick brown fox jumped over the lazy dog. It was cool.
Line 2

Line 3
Line 4
Line 5
```

Exit insert mode by pressing the ESC key and undo our change by typing **u**.

Deleting Text

As we might expect, vi offers a variety of ways to delete text, all of which contain one of two keystrokes. First, the X key will delete a character at the cursor location. x may be preceded by a number specifying how many characters are to be deleted. The D key is more general purpose. Like x, it may be preceded by a number specifying the number of times the deletion is to be performed. In addition, d is always followed by a movement command that controls the size of the deletion. Table 12-3 lists some examples.

Place the cursor on the word It on the first line of our text. Type **x** repeatedly until the rest of the sentence is deleted. Next, type **u** repeatedly until the deletion is undone.

Note: *Real vi supports only a single level of undo. vim supports multiple levels.*

Table 12-3: Text Deletion Commands

Command	Deletes
x	The current character
3x	The current character and the next two characters
dd	The current line
5dd	The current line and the next four lines

Table 12-3 (*continued*)

Command	Deletes
dW	From the current cursor location to the beginning of the next word
d$	From the current cursor location to the end of the current line
d0	From the current cursor location to the beginning of the line
d^	From the current cursor location to the first non-whitespace character in the line
dG	From the current line to the end of the file
d20G	From the current line to the 20th line of the file

Let's try the deletion again, this time using the d command. Again, move the cursor to the word It and type **dW** to delete the word:

```
The quick brown fox jumped over the lazy dog. was cool.
Line 2
Line 3
Line 4
Line 5
```

Type **d$** to delete from the cursor position to the end of the line:

```
The quick brown fox jumped over the lazy dog.
Line 2
Line 3
Line 4
Line 5
```

Type **dG** to delete from the current line to the end of the file:

```
~
~
~
~
~
```

Type **u** three times to undo the deletions.

Cutting, Copying, and Pasting Text

The d command not only deletes text, it also "cuts" text. Each time we use the d command, the deletion is copied into a paste buffer (think clipboard) that we can later recall with the p command to paste the contents of the buffer after the cursor or with the P command to paste the contents before the cursor.

The y command is used to "yank" (copy) text in much the same way the d command is used to cut text. Table 12-4 lists some examples combining the y command with various movement commands.

Table 12-4: Yanking Commands

Command	Copies
yy	The current line
5yy	The current line and the next four lines
yW	From the current cursor location to the beginning of the next word
y$	From the current cursor location to the end of the current line
y0	From the current cursor location to the beginning of the line
y^	From the current cursor location to the first non-whitespace character in the line
yG	From the current line to the end of the file
y20G	From the current line to the 20th line of the file

Let's try some copy and paste. Place the cursor on the first line of the text and type **yy** to copy the current line. Next, move the cursor to the last line (G) and type **p** to paste the copied line below the current line:

```
The quick brown fox jumped over the lazy dog. It was cool.
Line 2
Line 3
Line 4
Line 5
The quick brown fox jumped over the lazy dog. It was cool.
```

Just as before, the u command will undo our change. With the cursor still positioned on the last line of the file, type **P** to paste the text above the current line:

```
The quick brown fox jumped over the lazy dog. It was cool.
Line 2
Line 3
Line 4
The quick brown fox jumped over the lazy dog. It was cool.
Line 5
```

Try out some of the other y commands in Table 12-4 and get to know the behavior of both the p and P commands. When you are done, return the file to its original state.

Joining Lines

vi is rather strict about its idea of a line. Normally, it is not possible to move the cursor to the end of a line and delete the end-of-line character to join one line with the one below it. Because of this, vi provides a specific command, J (not to be confused with j, which is for cursor movement), to join lines together.

If we place the cursor on line 3 and type the J command, here's what happens:

```
The quick brown fox jumped over the lazy dog. It was cool.
Line 2
Line 3 Line 4
Line 5
```

Search and Replace

vi has the ability to move the cursor to locations based on searches. It can do this on either a single line or over an entire file. It can also perform text replacements with or without confirmation from the user.

Searching Within a Line

The f command searches a line and moves the cursor to the next instance of a specified character. For example, the command fa would move the cursor to the next occurrence of the character *a* within the current line. After performing a character search within a line, the search may be repeated by typing a semicolon.

Searching the Entire File

To move the cursor to the next occurrence of a word or phrase, the / command is used. This works the same way as in the less program we covered in Chapter 3. When you type the / command, a forward slash will appear at the bottom of the screen. Next, type the word or phrase to be searched for, followed by the ENTER key. The cursor will move to the next location containing the search string. A search may be repeated using the previous search string with the n command. Here's an example:

```
The quick brown fox jumped over the lazy dog. It was cool.
Line 2
Line 3
Line 4
Line 5
```

Place the cursor on the first line of the file. Type

```
/Line
```

followed by the ENTER key. The cursor will move to line 2. Next, type n, and the cursor will move to line 3. Repeating the n command will move the cursor down the file until it runs out of matches. While we have so far used only words and phrases for our search patterns, vi allows the use of *regular expressions*, a powerful method of expressing complex text patterns. We will cover regular expressions in some detail in Chapter 19.

Global Search and Replace

vi uses an ex command to perform search-and-replace operations (called *substitution* in vi) over a range of lines or the entire file. To change the word *Line* to *line* for the entire file, we would enter the following command:

```
:%s/Line/line/g
```

Let's break this command down into separate items and see what each one does (see Table 12-5).

Table 12-5: An Example of Global Search-and-Replace Syntax

Item	Meaning
:	The colon character starts an ex command.
%	Specifies the range of lines for the operation. % is a shortcut meaning from the first line to the last line. Alternatively, the range could have been specified 1,5 (because our file is five lines long), or 1,$, which means "from line 1 to the last line in the file." If the range of lines is omitted, the operation is performed only on the current line.
s	Specifies the operation—in this case, substitution (search and replace).
/Line/line/	The search pattern and the replacement text.
g	This means *global*, in the sense that the substitution is performed on every instance of the search string in each line. If g is omitted, only the first instance of the search string on each line is replaced.

After executing our search-and-replace command, our file looks like this:

```
The quick brown fox jumped over the lazy dog. It was cool.
line 2
line 3
line 4
line 5
```

We can also specify a substitution command with user confirmation. This is done by adding a c to the end of the command. For example:

```
:%s/line/Line/gc
```

This command will change our file back to its previous form; however, before each substitution, vi stops and asks us to confirm the substitution with this message:

```
replace with Line (y/n/a/q/l/^E/^Y)?
```

Each of the characters within the parentheses is a possible response, as shown in Table 12-6.

Table 12-6: Replace Confirmation Keys

Key	Action
y	Perform the substitution.
n	Skip this instance of the pattern.
a	Perform the substitution on this and all subsequent instances of the pattern.
q or ESC	Quit substituting.
l	Perform this substitution and then quit. Short for *last*.
CTRL-E, CTRL-Y	Scroll down and scroll up, respectively. Useful for viewing the context of the proposed substitution.

Editing Multiple Files

It's often useful to edit more than one file at a time. You might need to make changes to multiple files, or you may need to copy content from one file into another. With vi we can open multiple files for editing by specifying them on the command line:

```
vi file1 file2 file3...
```

Let's exit our existing vi session and create a new file for editing. Type :wq to exit vi, saving our modified text. Next, we'll create an additional file in our home directory that we can play with. We'll create the file by capturing some output from the ls command:

```
[me@linuxbox ~]$ ls -l /usr/bin > ls-output.txt
```

Let's edit our old file and our new one with vi:

```
[me@linuxbox ~]$ vi foo.txt ls-output.txt
```

vi will start up, and we will see the first file on the screen:

```
The quick brown fox jumped over the lazy dog. It was cool.
Line 2
Line 3
Line 4
Line 5
```

Switching Between Files

To switch from one file to the next, use this ex command:

```
:n
```

To move back to the previous file, use:

```
:N
```

While we can move from one file to another, vi enforces a policy that prevents us from switching files if the current file has unsaved changes. To force vi to switch files and abandon your changes, add an exclamation point (!) to the command.

In addition to the switching method described above, vim (and some versions of vi) provides some ex commands that make multiple files easier to manage. We can view a list of files being edited with the :buffers command. Doing so will display a list of the files at the bottom of the display:

```
:buffers
  1 %a   "foo.txt"                  line 1
  2      "ls-output.txt"            line 0
Press ENTER or type command to continue
```

To switch to another buffer (file), type **:buffer** followed by the number of the buffer you wish to edit. For example, to switch from buffer 1, which contains the file *foo.txt*, to buffer 2, which contains the file *ls-output.txt*, we would type this:

```
:buffer 2
```

and our screen now displays the second file.

Opening Additional Files for Editing

It's also possible to add files to our current editing session. The ex command :e (short for *edit*) followed by a filename will open an additional file. Let's end our current editing session and return to the command line.

Start vi again with just one file:

```
[me@linuxbox ~]$ vi foo.txt
```

To add our second file, enter:

```
:e ls-output.txt
```

and it should appear on the screen. The first file is still present, as we can verify:

```
:buffers
  1 #    "foo.txt"                      line 1
  2 %a   "ls-output.txt"                line 0
Press ENTER or type command to continue
```

Note: *You cannot switch to files loaded with the :e command using either the :n or :N command. To switch files, use the :buffer command followed by the buffer number.*

Copying Content from One File into Another

Often while editing multiple files, we will want to copy a portion of one file into another file that we are editing. This is easily done using the usual yank and paste commands we used earlier. We can demonstrate as follows. First, using our two files, switch to buffer 1 (*foo.txt*) by entering

```
:buffer 1
```

This should give us the following:

```
The quick brown fox jumped over the lazy dog. It was cool.
Line 2
Line 3
Line 4
Line 5
```

Next, move the cursor to the first line and type **yy** to yank (copy) the line.

Switch to the second buffer by entering

```
:buffer 2
```

The screen will now contain some file listings like this (only a portion is shown here):

```
total 343700
-rwxr-xr-x 1 root root          31316 2011-12-05 08:58 [
-rwxr-xr-x 1 root root           8240 2011-12-09 13:39 411toppm
-rwxr-xr-x 1 root root         111276 2012-01-31 13:36 a2p
-rwxr-xr-x 1 root root          25368 2010-10-06 20:16 a52dec
-rwxr-xr-x 1 root root          11532 2011-05-04 17:43 aafire
-rwxr-xr-x 1 root root           7292 2011-05-04 17:43 aainfo
```

Move the cursor to the first line and paste the line we copied from the preceding file by typing the **p** command:

```
total 343700
The quick brown fox jumped over the lazy dog. It was cool.
-rwxr-xr-x 1 root root          31316 2011-12-05 08:58 [
-rwxr-xr-x 1 root root           8240 2011-12-09 13:39 411toppm
-rwxr-xr-x 1 root root         111276 2012-01-31 13:36 a2p
-rwxr-xr-x 1 root root          25368 2010-10-06 20:16 a52dec
-rwxr-xr-x 1 root root          11532 2011-05-04 17:43 aafire
-rwxr-xr-x 1 root root           7292 2011-05-04 17:43 aainfo
```

Inserting an Entire File into Another

It's also possible to insert an entire file into one that we are editing. To see this in action, let's end our vi session and start a new one with just a single file:

```
[me@linuxbox ~]$ vi ls-output.txt
```

We will see our file listing again:

```
total 343700
-rwxr-xr-x 1 root root          31316 2011-12-05 08:58 [
-rwxr-xr-x 1 root root           8240 2011-12-09 13:39 411toppm
-rwxr-xr-x 1 root root         111276 2012-01-31 13:36 a2p
-rwxr-xr-x 1 root root          25368 2010-10-06 20:16 a52dec
-rwxr-xr-x 1 root root          11532 2011-05-04 17:43 aafire
-rwxr-xr-x 1 root root           7292 2011-05-04 17:43 aainfo
```

Move the cursor to the third line and then enter the following ex command:

```
:r foo.txt
```

The :r command (short for *read*) inserts the specified file before the cursor position. Our screen should now look like this:

```
total 343700
-rwxr-xr-x 1 root root          31316 2011-12-05 08:58 [
-rwxr-xr-x 1 root root           8240 2011-12-09 13:39 411toppm
The quick brown fox jumped over the lazy dog. It was cool.
Line 2
Line 3
Line 4
Line 5
-rwxr-xr-x 1 root root         111276 2012-01-31 13:36 a2p
-rwxr-xr-x 1 root root          25368 2010-10-06 20:16 a52dec
-rwxr-xr-x 1 root root          11532 2011-05-04 17:43 aafire
-rwxr-xr-x 1 root root           7292 2011-05-04 17:43 aainfo
```

Saving Our Work

Like everything else in vi, there are several ways to save our edited files. We have already covered the ex command :w, but there are some others we may also find helpful.

In command mode, typing ZZ will save the current file and exit vi. Likewise, the ex command :wq will combine the :w and :q commands into one that will both save the file and exit.

The :w command may also specify an optional filename. This acts like a Save As command. For example, if we were editing *foo.txt* and wanted to save an alternative version called *foo1.txt*, we would enter the following:

```
:w foo1.txt
```

Note: *While this saves the file under a new name, it does not change the name of the file you are editing. As you continue to edit, you will still be editing* foo.txt, *not* foo1.txt.

13

CUSTOMIZING THE PROMPT

In this chapter we will look at a seemingly trivial detail: our shell prompt. This examination will reveal some of the inner workings of the shell and the terminal emulator program itself.

Like so many things in Linux, the shell prompt is highly configurable, and while we have pretty much taken it for granted, the prompt is a really useful device once we learn how to control it.

Anatomy of a Prompt

Our default prompt looks something like this:

```
[me@linuxbox ~]$
```

Notice that it contains our username, our hostname, and our current working directory, but how did it get that way? Very simply, it turns out. The prompt is defined by an environment variable named PS1 (short for *prompt string 1*). We can view the contents of PS1 with the echo command:

```
[me@linuxbox ~]$ echo $PS1
[\u@\h \W]\$
```

Note: *Don't worry if your results are not exactly the same as the example above. Every Linux distribution defines the prompt string a little differently, some quite exotically.*

From the results, we can see that PS1 contains a few of the characters we see in our prompt, such as the square brackets, the @ sign, and the dollar sign, but the rest are a mystery. The astute among us will recognize these as *backslash-escaped special characters* like those we saw in Table 7-2. Table 13-1 is a partial list of the characters that the shell treats specially in the prompt string.

Table 13-1: Escape Codes Used in Shell Prompts

Sequence	Value Displayed
\a	ASCII bell. This makes the computer beep when it is encountered.
\d	Current date in day, month, date format; for example, "Mon May 26"
\h	Hostname of the local machine minus the trailing domain name
\H	Full hostname
\j	Number of jobs running in the current shell session
\l	Name of the current terminal device
\n	A newline character
\r	A carriage return
\s	Name of the shell program
\t	Current time in 24-hour, hours:minutes:seconds format
\T	Current time in 12-hour format
\@	Current time in 12-hour, AM/PM format
\A	Current time in 24-hour, hours:minutes format
\u	Username of the current user
\v	Version number of the shell
\V	Version and release numbers of the shell
\w	Name of the current working directory

Table 13-1 (*continued*)

Sequence	Value Displayed
\W	Last part of the current working directory name
\!	History number of the current command
\#	Number of commands entered during this shell session
\$	This displays a "$" character unless you have superuser privileges. In that case, it displays a "#" instead.
\[	This signals the start of a series of one or more non-printing characters. It is used to embed non-printing control characters that manipulate the terminal emulator in some way, such as moving the cursor or changing text colors.
\]	This signals the end of a non-printing character sequence.

Trying Some Alternative Prompt Designs

With this list of special characters, we can change the prompt to see the effect. First, we'll back up the existing string so we can restore it later. To do this, we will copy the existing string into another shell variable that we create ourselves:

```
[me@linuxbox ~]$ ps1_old="$PS1"
```

We create a new variable called ps1_old and assign the value of PS1 to it. We can verify that the string has been copied by using the echo command:

```
[me@linuxbox ~]$ echo $ps1_old
[\u@\h \W]\$
```

We can restore the original prompt at any time during our terminal session by simply reversing the process:

```
[me@linuxbox ~]$ PS1="$ps1_old"
```

Now that we are ready to proceed, let's see what happens if we have an empty prompt string:

```
[me@linuxbox ~]$ PS1=
```

If we assign nothing to the prompt string, we get nothing. No prompt string at all! The prompt is still there but displays nothing, just as we asked it to. Since this is kind of disconcerting to look at, we'll replace it with a minimal prompt:

```
PS1="\$ "
```

That's better. At least now we can see what we are doing. Notice the trailing space within the double quotes. This provides the space between the dollar sign and the cursor when the prompt is displayed.

Let's add a bell to our prompt:

```
$ PS1="\a\$ "
```

Now we should hear a beep each time the prompt is displayed. This could get annoying, but it might be useful if we needed notification when an especially long-running command has been executed.

Next, let's try to make an informative prompt with some hostname and time-of-day information:

```
$ PS1="\A \h \$ "
17:33 linuxbox $
```

Adding time-of-day to our prompt will be useful if we need to keep track of when we perform certain tasks. Finally, we'll make a new prompt that is similar to our original:

```
17:37 linuxbox $ PS1="<\u@\h \W>\$ "
<me@linuxbox ~>$
```

Try out the other sequences listed in Table 13-1 and see if you can come up with a brilliant new prompt.

Adding Color

Most terminal emulator programs respond to certain non-printing character sequences to control such things as character attributes (like color, bold text, and the dreaded blinking text) and cursor position. We'll cover cursor position in a little bit, but first we'll look at color.

TERMINAL CONFUSION

Back in ancient times, when terminals were hooked to remote computers, there were many competing brands of terminals and they all worked differently. They had different keyboards, and they all had different ways of interpreting control information. Unix and Unix-like systems have two rather complex subsystems (called termcap and terminfo) to deal with the babel of terminal control. If you look into the deepest recesses of your terminal emulator settings, you may find a setting for the type of terminal emulation.

In an effort to make terminals speak some sort of common language, the American National Standards Institute (ANSI) developed a standard set of character sequences to control video terminals. Old-time DOS users will remember the *ANSI.SYS* file that was used to enable interpretation of these codes.

Character color is controlled by sending the terminal emulator an *ANSI escape code* embedded in the stream of characters to be displayed. The control code does not "print out" on the display; rather it is interpreted by the terminal as an instruction. As we saw in Table 13-1, the \[and \] sequences are used to encapsulate non-printing characters. An ANSI escape code begins with an octal 033 (the code generated by the ESC key), followed by an optional character attribute, followed by an instruction. For example, the code to set the text color to normal (attribute = 0) black text is \033[0;30m.

Table 13-2 lists available text colors. Notice that the colors are divided into two groups, differentiated by the application of the bold character attribute (1), which creates the appearance of "light" colors.

Table13-2: Escape Sequences Used to Set Text Colors

Sequence	Text Color
\033[0;30m	Black
\033[0;31m	Red
\033[0;32m	Green
\033[0;33m	Brown
\033[0;34m	Blue
\033[0;35m	Purple
\033[0;36m	Cyan
\033[0;37m	Light Gray
\033[1;30m	Dark Gray
\033[1;31m	Light Red
\033[1;32m	Light Green
\033[1;33m	Yellow
\033[1;34m	Light Blue
\033[1;35m	Light Purple
\033[1;36m	Light Cyan
\033[1;37m	White

Let's try to make a red prompt (seen here as gray). We'll insert the escape code at the beginning:

```
<me@linuxbox ~>$ PS1="\[\033[0;31m\]<\u@\h \W>\$ "
<me@linuxbox ~>$
```

That works, but notice that all the text that we type after the prompt is also red. To fix this, we will add another escape code to the end of the prompt that tells the terminal emulator to return to the previous color:

```
<me@linuxbox ~>$ PS1="\[\033[0;31m\]<\u@\h \W>\$\[\033[0m\] "
<me@linuxbox ~>$
```

That's better!

It's also possible to set the text background color using the codes listed in Table 13-3. The background colors do not support the bold attribute.

Table 13-3: Escape Sequences Used to Set Background Color

Sequence	Background Color
\033[0;40m	Black
\033[0;41m	Red
\033[0;42m	Green
\033[0;43m	Brown
\033[0;44m	Blue
\033[0;45m	Purple
\033[0;46m	Cyan
\033[0;47m	Light Gray

We can create a prompt with a red background by applying a simple change to the first escape code:

```
<me@linuxbox ~>$ PS1="\[\033[0;41m\]<\u@\h \W>\$\[\033[0m\] "
<me@linuxbox ~>$
```

Try out the color codes and see what you can create!

Note: *Besides the normal (0) and bold (1) character attributes, text may also be given underscore (4), blinking (5), and inverse (7) attributes. In the interests of good taste, many terminal emulators refuse to honor the blinking attribute.*

Moving the Cursor

Escape codes can be used to position the cursor. This is commonly used to provide a clock or some other kind of information at a different location on the screen, such as an upper corner, each time the prompt is drawn. Table 13-4 lists the escape codes that position the cursor.

Table 13-4: Cursor Movement Escape Sequences

Escape Code	Action
\033[*l*;*c*H	Move the cursor to line *l* and column *c*.
\033[*n*A	Move the cursor up *n* lines.
\033[*n*B	Move the cursor down *n* lines.
\033[*n*C	Move the cursor forward *n* characters.
\033[*n*D	Move the cursor backward *n* characters.
\033[2J	Clear the screen and move the cursor to the upper-left corner (line 0, column 0).
\033[K	Clear from the cursor position to the end of the current line.
\033[s	Store the current cursor position.
\033[u	Recall the stored cursor position.

Using these codes, we'll construct a prompt that draws a red bar at the top of the screen containing a clock (rendered in yellow text) each time the prompt is displayed. The code for the prompt is this formidable looking string:

```
PS1="\[\033[s\033[0;0H\033[0;41m\033[K\033[1;33m\t\033[0m\033[u\]<\u@\h \W>\$ "
```

Table 13-5 takes a look at each part of the string to see what it does.

Table 13-5: Breakdown of Complex Prompt String

Sequence	Action
\[	Begins a non-printing character sequence. The real purpose of this is to allow bash to correctly calculate the size of the visible prompt. Without this, command line editing features will improperly position the cursor.
\033[s	Store the cursor position. This is needed to return to the prompt location after the bar and clock have been drawn at the top of the screen. *Be aware that some terminal emulators do not honor this code.*
\033[0;0H	Move the cursor to the upper-left corner, which is line 0, column 0.
\033[0;41m	Set the background color to red.

(continued)

Table 13-5 (continued)

Sequence	Action
\033[K	Clear from the current cursor location (the top-left corner) to the end of the line. Since the background color is now red, the line is cleared to that color, creating our bar. Note that clearing to the end of the line does not change the cursor position, which remains at the upper-left corner.
\033[1;33m	Set the text color to yellow.
\t	Display the current time. While this is a "printing" element, we still include it in the non-printing portion of the prompt, because we don't want bash to include the clock when calculating the true size of the displayed prompt.
\033[0m	Turn off color. This affects both the text and the background.
\033[u	Restore the cursor position saved earlier.
\]	End the non-printing characters sequence.
<\u@\h \W>\$	Prompt string.

Saving the Prompt

Obviously, we don't want to be typing that monster all the time, so we'll want to store our prompt someplace. We can make the prompt permanent by adding it to our *.bashrc* file. To do so, add these two lines to the file:

```
PS1="\[\033[s\033[0;0H\033[0;41m\033[K\033[1;33m\t\033[0m\033[u\]<\u@\h \W>\$ "

export PS1
```

Final Note

Believe it or not, much more can be done with prompts involving shell functions and scripts that we haven't covered here, but this is a good start. Not everyone will care enough to change the prompt, since the default prompt is usually satisfactory. But for those of us who like to tinker, the shell provides an opportunity for many hours of trivial fun.

PART 3

COMMON TASKS AND ESSENTIAL TOOLS

14

PACKAGE MANAGEMENT

If we spend any time in the Linux community, we hear many opinions as to which of the many Linux distributions is "best." Often, these discussions get really silly, focusing on such things as the prettiness of the desktop background (some people won't use Ubuntu because of its default color scheme!) and other trivial matters.

The most important determinant of distribution quality is the *packaging system* and the vitality of the distribution's support community. As we spend more time with Linux, we see that its software landscape is extremely dynamic. Things are constantly changing. Most of the top-tier Linux distributions release new versions every six months and many individual program updates every day. To keep up with this blizzard of software, we need good tools for package management.

Package management is a method of installing and maintaining software on the system. Today, most people can satisfy all of their software needs by installing *packages* from their Linux distributor. This contrasts with the early days of Linux, when one had to download and compile *source code* in order to install software. Not that there is anything wrong with compiling source code; in fact, having access to source code is the great wonder of Linux. It gives us (and everybody else) the ability to examine and improve the system. It's just that working with a precompiled package is faster and easier.

In this chapter, we will look at some of the command-line tools used for package management. While all of the major distributions provide powerful and sophisticated graphical programs for maintaining the system, it is important to learn about the command-line programs, too. They can perform many tasks that are difficult (or impossible) to do using their graphical counterparts.

Packaging Systems

Different distributions use different packaging systems, and as a general rule a package intended for one distribution is not compatible with another distribution. Most distributions fall into one of two camps of packaging technologies: the Debian *.deb* camp and the Red Hat *.rpm* camp. There are some important exceptions, such as Gentoo, Slackware, and Foresight, but most others use one of the two basic systems shown in Table 14-1.

Table 14-1: Major Packaging System Families

Packaging System	Distributions (partial listing)
Debian style (*.deb*)	Debian, Ubuntu, Xandros, Linspire
Red Hat style (*.rpm*)	Fedora, CentOS, Red Hat Enterprise Linux, openSUSE, Mandriva, PCLinuxOS

How a Package System Works

The method of software distribution found in the proprietary software industry usually entails buying a piece of installation media such as an "install disk" and then running an "installation wizard" to install a new application on the system.

Linux doesn't work that way. Virtually all software for a Linux system is found on the Internet. Most of it is provided by the distribution vendor in the form of package files, and the rest is available in source code form, which can be installed manually. We'll talk a little about how to install software by compiling source code in Chapter 23.

Package Files

The basic unit of software in a packaging system is the package file. A *package file* is a compressed collection of files that comprise the software package. A package may consist of numerous programs and data files that support the programs. In addition to the files to be installed, the package file also includes metadata about the package, such as a text description of the package and its contents. Additionally, many packages contain pre- and post-installation scripts that perform configuration tasks before and after the package installation.

Package files are created by a person known as a *package maintainer*, often (but not always) an employee of the distribution vendor. The package maintainer gets the software in source code form from the *upstream provider* (the author of the program), compiles it, and creates the package metadata and any necessary installation scripts. Often, the package maintainer will apply modifications to the original source code to improve the program's integration with the other parts of the Linux distribution.

Repositories

While some software projects choose to perform their own packaging and distribution, most packages today are created by the distribution vendors and interested third parties. Packages are made available to the users of a distribution in central repositories, which may contain many thousands of packages, each specially built and maintained for the distribution.

A distribution may maintain several different repositories for different stages of the software development life cycle. For example, there will usually be a *testing repository*, which contains packages that have just been built and are intended for use by brave souls who are looking for bugs before the packages are released for general distribution. A distribution will often have a *development repository* where work-in-progress packages destined for inclusion in the distribution's next major release are kept.

A distribution may also have related third-party repositories. These are often needed to supply software that, for legal reasons such as patents or Digital Rights Management (DRM) anticircumvention issues, cannot be included with the distribution. Perhaps the best-known case is that of encrypted DVD support, which is not legal in the United States. The third-party repositories operate in countries where software patents and anti-circumvention laws do not apply. These repositories are usually wholly independent of the distribution they support, and to use them one must know about them and manually include them in the configuration files for the package management system.

Dependencies

Programs seldom stand alone; rather, they rely on the presence of other software components to get their work done. Common activities, such as input/output for example, are handled by routines shared by many programs. These routines are stored in what are called *shared libraries*, which provide essential services to more than one program. If a package requires a shared resource such as a shared library, it is said to have a *dependency*. Modern package management systems all provide some method of *dependency resolution* to ensure that when a package is installed, all of its dependencies are installed, too.

High- and Low-Level Package Tools

Package management systems usually consist of two types of tools: low-level tools that handle tasks such as installing and removing package files, and high-level tools that perform metadata searching and dependency resolution. In this chapter, we will look at the tools supplied with Debian-style systems (such as Ubuntu and many others) and those used by recent Red Hat products. While all Red Hat–style distributions rely on the same low-level program (rpm), they use different high-level tools. For our discussion, we will cover the high-level program yum, used by Fedora, Red Hat Enterprise Linux, and CentOS. Other Red Hat–style distributions provide high-level tools with comparable features (see Table 14-2).

Table14-2: Packaging System Tools

Distributions	Low-Level Tools	High-Level Tools
Debian style	dpkg	apt-get, aptitude
Fedora, Red Hat Enterprise Linux, CentOS	rpm	yum

Common Package Management Tasks

Many operations can be performed with the command-line package management tools. We will look at the most common. Be aware that the low-level tools also support creation of package files, an activity outside the scope of this book.

In the following discussion, the term *package_name* refers to the actual name of a package, as opposed to *package_file*, which is the name of the file that contains the package.

Finding a Package in a Repository

By using the high-level tools to search repository metadata, one can locate a package based on its name or description (see Table 14-3).

Table 14-3: Package Search Commands

Style	Command(s)
Debian	apt-get update apt-cache search *search_string*
Red Hat	yum search *search_string*

Example: Search a yum repository for the emacs text editor on a Red Hat system:

```
yum search emacs
```

Installing a Package from a Repository

High-level tools permit a package to be downloaded from a repository and installed with full dependency resolution (see Table 14-4).

Table 14-4: Package Installation Commands

Style	Command(s)
Debian	apt-get update apt-get install *package_name*
Red Hat	yum install *package_name*

Example: Install the emacs text editor from an apt repository on a Debian-style system:

```
apt-get update; apt-get install emacs
```

Installing a Package from a Package File

If a package file has been downloaded from a source other than a repository, it can be installed directly (though without dependency resolution) using a low-level tool (see Table 14-5).

Table 14-5: Low-Level Package Installation Commands

Style	Command
Debian	dpkg --install *package_file*
Red Hat	rpm -i *package_file*

Example: If the *emacs-22.1-7.fc7-i386.rpm* package file has been downloaded from a non-repository site, install it on a Red Hat system this way:

```
rpm -i emacs-22.1-7.fc7-i386.rpm
```

Note: *Since this technique uses the low-level* rpm *program to perform the installation, no dependency resolution is performed. If* rpm *discovers a missing dependency,* rpm *will exit with an error.*

Removing a Package

Packages can be uninstalled using either the high-level or low-level tools. The high-level tools are shown in Table 14-6.

Table 14-6: Package Removal Commands

Style	Command
Debian	apt-get remove *package_name*
Red Hat	yum erase *package_name*

Example: Uninstall the emacs package from a Debian-style system:

```
apt-get remove emacs
```

Updating Packages from a Repository

The most common package management task is keeping the system up-to-date with the latest packages. The high-level tools can perform this vital task in one single step (see Table 14-7).

Table 14-7: Package Update Commands

Style	Command(s)
Debian	apt-get update; apt-get upgrade
Red Hat	yum update

Example: Apply any available updates to the installed packages on a Debian-style system:

```
apt-get update; apt-get upgrade
```

Upgrading a Package from a Package File

If an updated version of a package has been downloaded from a non-repository source, it can be installed, replacing the previous version (see Table 14-8).

Table 14-8: Low-Level Package Upgrade Commands

Style	Command
Debian	dpkg --install *package_file*
Red Hat	rpm -U *package_file*

Example: Update an existing installation of emacs to the version contained in the package file *emacs-22.1-7.fc7-i386.rpm* on a Red Hat system:

```
rpm -U emacs-22.1-7.fc7-i386.rpm
```

Note: *dpkg does not have a specific option for upgrading a package versus installing one, as rpm does.*

Listing Installed Packages

The commands shown in Table 14-9 can be used to display a list of all the packages installed on the system.

Table 14-9: Package Listing Commands

Style	Command
Debian	dpkg --list
Red Hat	rpm -qa

Determining Whether a Package Is Installed

The low-level tools shown in Table 14-10 can be used to display whether a specified package is installed.

Table 14-10: Package Status Commands

Style	Command
Debian	dpkg --status *package_name*
Red Hat	rpm -q *package_name*

Example: Determine whether the emacs package is installed on a Debian-style system:

```
dpkg --status emacs
```

Displaying Information About an Installed Package

If the name of an installed package is known, the commands shown in Table 14-11 can be used to display a description of the package.

Table 14-11: Package Information Commands

Style	Command
Debian	apt-cache show *package_name*
Red Hat	yum info *package_name*

Example: See a description of the emacs package on a Debian-style system:

```
apt-cache show emacs
```

Finding Which Package Installed a File

To determine which package is responsible for the installation of a particular file, the commands shown in Table 14-12 can be used.

Table 14-12: Package File Identification Commands

Style	Command
Debian	dpkg --search *file_name*
Red Hat	rpm -qf *file_name*

Example: See which package installed the */usr/bin/vim* file on a Red Hat system:

```
rpm -qf /usr/bin/vim
```

Final Note

In the chapters that follow, we will explore many programs covering a wide range of application areas. While most of these programs are commonly installed by default, sometimes we may need to install additional packages. With our newfound knowledge (and appreciation) of package management, we should have no problem installing and managing the programs we need.

THE LINUX SOFTWARE INSTALLATION MYTH

People migrating from other platforms sometimes fall victim to the myth that software is somehow difficult to install under Linux and that the variety of packaging schemes used by different distributions is a hindrance. Well, it is a hindrance, but only to proprietary software vendors who wish to distribute binary-only versions of their secret software.

The Linux software ecosystem is based on the idea of open source code. If a program developer releases source code for a product, it is likely that a person associated with a distribution will package the product and include it in the repository. This method ensures that the product is well integrated into the distribution and the user is given the convenience of one-stop shopping for software, rather than having to search for each product's website.

Device drivers are handled in much the same way, except that instead of being separate items in a distribution's repository, they become part of the Linux kernel itself. Generally speaking, there is no such thing as a "driver disk" in Linux. Either the kernel supports a device or it doesn't, and the Linux kernel supports a lot of devices. Many more, in fact, than Windows does. Of course, this is no consolation if the particular device you need is not supported. When that happens, you need to look at the cause. A lack of driver support is usually caused by one of three things:

- **The device is too new.** Since many hardware vendors don't actively support Linux development, it falls upon a member of the Linux community to write the kernel driver code. This takes time.

- **The device is too exotic.** Not all distributions include every possible device driver. Each distribution builds its own kernels, and since kernels are very configurable (which is what makes it possible to run Linux on everything from wristwatches to mainframes), the distribution may have overlooked a particular device. By locating and downloading the source code for the driver, it is possible for you (yes, you) to compile and install the driver yourself. This process is not overly difficult, but it is rather involved. We'll talk about compiling software in Chapter 23.

- **The hardware vendor is hiding something.** It has neither released source code for a Linux driver, nor has it released the technical documentation for somebody else to create one. This means that the hardware vendor is trying to keep the programming interfaces to the device a secret. Since we don't want secret devices in our computers, I suggest that you remove the offending hardware and pitch it into the trash with your other useless items.

15

STORAGE MEDIA

In previous chapters we've looked at manipulating data at the file level. In this chapter, we will consider data at the device level. Linux has amazing capabilities for handling storage devices, whether physical storage such as hard disks, network storage, or virtual storage devices like RAID (redundant array of independent disks) and LVM (logical volume manager).

However, since this is not a book about system administration, we will not try to cover this entire topic in depth. What we will do is introduce some of the concepts and key commands that are used to manage storage devices.

To carry out the exercises in this chapter, we will use a USB flash drive, a CD-RW disc (for systems equipped with a CD-ROM burner), and a floppy disk (again, if the system is so equipped).

We will look at the following commands:

- mount—Mount a filesystem.
- umount—Unmount a filesystem.

- `fdisk`—Partition table manipulator.

- `fsck`—Check and repair a filesystem.

- `fdformat`—Format a floppy disk.

- `mkfs`—Create a filesystem.

- `dd`—Write block-oriented data directly to a device.

- `genisoimage (mkisofs)`—Create an ISO 9660 image file.

- `wodim (cdrecord)`—Write data to optical storage media.

- `md5sum`—Calculate an MD5 checksum.

Mounting and Unmounting Storage Devices

Recent advances in the Linux desktop have made storage device management extremely easy for desktop users. For the most part, we attach a device to our system and it just works. Back in the old days (say, 2004), this stuff had to be done manually. On non-desktop systems (i.e., servers) this is still a largely manual procedure, because servers often have extreme storage needs and complex configuration requirements.

The first step in managing a storage device is attaching the device to the filesystem tree. This process, called *mounting*, allows the device to participate with the operating system. As we recall from Chapter 2, Unix-like operating systems, like Linux, maintain a single filesystem tree with devices attached at various points. This contrasts with other operating systems such as MS-DOS and Windows that maintain separate trees for each device (for example *C:*, *D:*, etc.).

A file named */etc/fstab* lists the devices (typically hard disk partitions) that are to be mounted at boot time. Here is an example */etc/fstab* file from a Fedora 7 system:

```
LABEL=/12           /              ext3    defaults         1 1
LABEL=/home         /home          ext3    defaults         1 2
LABEL=/boot         /boot          ext3    defaults         1 2
tmpfs               /dev/shm       tmpfs   defaults         0 0
devpts              /dev/pts       devpts  gid=5,mode=620   0 0
sysfs               /sys           sysfs   defaults         0 0
proc                /proc          proc    defaults         0 0
LABEL=SWAP-sda3     swap           swap    defaults         0 0
```

Most of the filesystems listed in this example file are virtual and are not applicable to our discussion. For our purposes, the interesting ones are the first three:

```
LABEL=/12           /              ext3    defaults         1 1
LABEL=/home         /home          ext3    defaults         1 2
LABEL=/boot         /boot          ext3    defaults         1 2
```

These are the hard disk partitions. Each line of the file consists of six fields, as shown in Table 15-1.

Table 15-1: */etc/fstab* **Fields**

Field	Contents	Description
1	Device	Traditionally, this field contains the actual name of a device file associated with the physical device, such as */dev/hda1* (the first partition of the master device on the first IDE channel). But with today's computers, which have many devices that are hot pluggable (like USB drives), many modern Linux distributions associate a device with a text label instead. This label (which is added to the storage medium when it is formatted) is read by the operating system when the device is attached to the system. That way, no matter which device file is assigned to the actual physical device, it can still be correctly identified.
2	Mount point	The directory where the device is attached to the filesystem tree
3	Filesystem type	Linux allows many filesystem types to be mounted. Most native Linux filesystems are ext3, but many others are supported, such as FAT16 (msdos), FAT32 (vfat), NTFS (ntfs), CD-ROM (iso9660), etc.
4	Options	Filesystems can be mounted with various options. It is possible, for example, to mount filesystems as read only or to prevent any programs from being executed from them (a useful security feature for removable media).
5	Frequency	A single number that specifies if and when a filesystem is to be backed up with the dump command
6	Order	A single number that specifies in what order filesystems should be checked with the fsck command

Viewing a List of Mounted Filesystems

The mount command is used to mount filesystems. Entering the command without arguments will display a list of the filesystems currently mounted:

```
[me@linuxbox ~]$ mount
/dev/sda2 on / type ext3 (rw)
proc on /proc type proc (rw)
sysfs on /sys type sysfs (rw)
```

```
devpts on /dev/pts type devpts (rw,gid=5,mode=620)
/dev/sda5 on /home type ext3 (rw)
/dev/sda1 on /boot type ext3 (rw)
tmpfs on /dev/shm type tmpfs (rw)
none on /proc/sys/fs/binfmt_misc type binfmt_misc (rw)
sunrpc on /var/lib/nfs/rpc_pipefs type rpc_pipefs (rw)
fusectl on /sys/fs/fuse/connections type fusectl (rw)
/dev/sdd1 on /media/disk type vfat (rw,nosuid,nodev,noatime,
uhelper=hal,uid=500,utf8,shortname=lower)
twin4:/musicbox on /misc/musicbox type nfs4 (rw,addr=192.168.1.4)
```

The format of the listing is *device* on *mount_point* type *filesystem_type*
(*options*). For example, the first line shows that device */dev/sda2* is mounted
as the root filesystem, is of type ext3, and is both readable and writable
(the option rw). This listing also has two interesting entries at the bottom.
The next-to-last entry shows a 2-gigabyte SD memory card in a card reader
mounted at */media/disk*, and the last entry is a network drive mounted at
/misc/musicbox.

For our first experiment, we will work with a CD-ROM. First, let's look at
a system before a CD-ROM is inserted:

```
[me@linuxbox ~]$ mount
/dev/mapper/VolGroup00-LogVol00 on / type ext3 (rw)
proc on /proc type proc (rw)
sysfs on /sys type sysfs (rw)
devpts on /dev/pts type devpts (rw,gid=5,mode=620)
/dev/hda1 on /boot type ext3 (rw)
tmpfs on /dev/shm type tmpfs (rw)
none on /proc/sys/fs/binfmt_misc type binfmt_misc (rw)
sunrpc on /var/lib/nfs/rpc_pipefs type rpc_pipefs (rw)
```

This listing is from a CentOS 5 system that is using LVM to create its
root filesystem. Like many modern Linux distributions, this system will
attempt to automatically mount the CD-ROM after insertion. After we
insert the disc, we see the following:

```
[me@linuxbox ~]$ mount
/dev/mapper/VolGroup00-LogVol00 on / type ext3 (rw)
proc on /proc type proc (rw)
sysfs on /sys type sysfs (rw)
devpts on /dev/pts type devpts (rw,gid=5,mode=620)
/dev/hda1 on /boot type ext3 (rw)
tmpfs on /dev/shm type tmpfs (rw)
none on /proc/sys/fs/binfmt_misc type binfmt_misc (rw)
sunrpc on /var/lib/nfs/rpc_pipefs type rpc_pipefs (rw)
/dev/hdc on /media/live-1.0.10-8 type iso9660 (ro,noexec,nosuid,nodev,uid=500)
```

We see the same listing as before, with one additional entry. At the end
of the listing, we see that the CD-ROM (which is device */dev/hdc* on this system) has been mounted on */media/live-1.0.10-8* and is type iso9660 (a CD-
ROM). For the purposes of our experiment, we're interested in the name
of the device. When you conduct this experiment yourself, the device name
will most likely be different.

Warning: *In the examples that follow, it is vitally important that you pay close attention to the actual device names in use on your system and **do not use the names used in this text!***

Also, note that audio CDs are not the same as CD-ROMs. Audio CDs do not contain filesystems and thus cannot be mounted in the usual sense.

Now that we have the device name of the CD-ROM drive, let's unmount the disc and remount it at another location in the filesystem tree. To do this, we become the superuser (using the command appropriate for our system) and unmount the disc with the umount (notice the spelling) command:

```
[me@linuxbox ~]$ su -
Password:
[root@linuxbox ~]# umount /dev/hdc
```

The next step is to create a new mount point for the disc. A *mount point* is simply a directory somewhere on the filesystem tree. Nothing special about it. It doesn't even have to be an empty directory, though if you mount a device on a non-empty directory, you will not be able to see the directory's previous contents until you unmount the device. For our purposes, we will create a new directory:

```
[root@linuxbox ~]# mkdir /mnt/cdrom
```

Finally, we mount the CD-ROM at the new mount point. The -t option is used to specify the filesystem type:

```
[root@linuxbox ~]# mount -t iso9660 /dev/hdc /mnt/cdrom
```

Afterward, we can examine the contents of the CD-ROM via the new mount point:

```
[root@linuxbox ~]# cd /mnt/cdrom
[root@linuxbox cdrom]# ls
```

Notice what happens when we try to unmount the CD-ROM:

```
[root@linuxbox cdrom]# umount /dev/hdc
umount: /mnt/cdrom: device is busy
```

Why is this? We cannot unmount a device if the device is being used by someone or some process. In this case, we changed our working directory to the mount point for the CD-ROM, which causes the device to be busy. We can easily remedy the issue by changing the working directory to something other than the mount point:

```
[root@linuxbox cdrom]# cd
[root@linuxbox ~]# umount /dev/hdc
```

Now the device unmounts successfully.

WHY UNMOUNTING IS IMPORTANT

If you look at the output of the free command, which displays statistics about memory usage, you will see a statistic called *buffers*. Computer systems are designed to go as fast as possible. One of the impediments to system speed is slow devices. Printers are a good example. Even the fastest printer is extremely slow by computer standards. A computer would be very slow indeed if it had to stop and wait for a printer to finish printing a page. In the early days of PCs (before multitasking), this was a real problem. If you were working on a spreadsheet or text document, the computer would stop and become unavailable every time you printed. The computer would send the data to the printer as fast as the printer could accept it, but it was very slow because printers don't print very fast. This problem was solved by the advent of the *printer buffer*, a device containing some RAM memory, that would sit between the computer and the printer. With the printer buffer in place, the computer would send the printer output to the buffer, and it would quickly be stored in the fast RAM so the computer could go back to work without waiting. Meanwhile, the printer buffer would slowly *spool* the data to the printer from the buffer's memory at the speed at which the printer could accept it.

This idea of buffering is used extensively in computers to make them faster. Don't let the need to occasionally read or write data to or from slow devices impede the speed of the system. Operating systems store data that has been read from, and is to be written to, storage devices in memory for as long as possible before actually having to interact with the slower device. On a Linux system, for example, you will notice that the system seems to fill up memory the longer it is used. This does not mean Linux is "using" all the memory, it means that Linux is taking advantage of all the available memory to do as much buffering as it can.

This buffering allows writing to storage devices to be done very quickly, because the writing to the physical device is being deferred to a future time. In the meantime, the data destined for the device is piling up in memory. From time to time, the operating system will write this data to the physical device.

Unmounting a device entails writing all the remaining data to the device so that it can be safely removed. If the device is removed without first being unmounted, the possibility exists that not all the data destined for the device has been transferred. In some cases, this data may include vital directory updates, which will lead to *filesystem corruption*, one of the worst things that can happen on a computer.

Determining Device Names

It's sometimes difficult to determine the ameof a device. Back in the old days, it wasn't very hard. A device was always in the same place and didn't change. Unix-like systems like it that way. Back when Unix was developed, "changing a disk drive" involved using a forklift to remove a washing machine–sized device from the computer room. In recent years, the typical desktop hardware configuration has become quite dynamic, and Linux has evolved to become more flexible than its ancestors.

In the examples above, we took advantage of the modern Linux desktop's ability to "automagically" mount the device and then determine the name after the fact. But what if we are managing a server or some other environment where this does not occur? How can we figure it out?

First, let's look at how the system names devices. If we list the contents of the */dev* directory (where all devices live), we can see that there are lots and lots of devices:

```
[me@linuxbox ~]$ ls /dev
```

The contents of this listing reveal some patterns of device naming. Table 15-2 lists a few.

Table 15-2: Linux Storage Device Names

Pattern	Device
/dev/fd*	Floppy disk drives
/dev/hd*	IDE (PATA) disks on older systems. Typical motherboards contain two IDE connectors, or *channels*, each with a cable with two attachment points for drives. The first drive on the cable is called the *master* device and the second is called the *slave* device. The device names are ordered such that */dev/hda* refers to the master device on the first channel, */dev/hdb* is the slave device on the first channel; */dev/hdc*, the master device on the second channel, and so on. A trailing digit indicates the partition number on the device. For example, */dev/hda1* refers to the first partition on the first hard drive on the system while */dev/hda* refers to the entire drive.
/dev/lp*	Printers
/dev/sd*	SCSI disks. On recent Linux systems, the kernel treats all disk-like devices (including PATA/SATA hard disks, flash drives, and USB mass storage devices such as portable music players and digital cameras) as SCSI disks. The rest of the naming system is similar to the older */dev/hd** naming scheme described above.
/dev/sr*	Optical drives (CD/DVD readers and burners)

In addition, we often see symbolic links such as */dev/cdrom*, */dev/dvd*, and */dev/floppy*, which point to the actual device files, provided as a convenience.

If you are working on a system that does not automatically mount removable devices, you can use the following technique to determine how the removable device is named when it is attached. First, start a real-time view of the */var/log/messages* file (you may require superuser privileges for this):

```
[me@linuxbox ~]$ sudo tail -f /var/log/messages
```

The last few lines of the file will be displayed and then pause. Next, plug in the removable device. In this example, we will use a 16MB flash drive. Almost immediately, the kernel will notice the device and probe it:

```
Jul 23 10:07:53 linuxbox kernel: usb 3-2: new full speed USB device using uhci_h
cd and address 2
Jul 23 10:07:53 linuxbox kernel: usb 3-2: configuration #1 chosen from 1 choice
Jul 23 10:07:53 linuxbox kernel: scsi3 : SCSI emulation for USB Mass Storage dev
ices
Jul 23 10:07:58 linuxbox kernel: scsi scan: INQUIRY result too short (5), using
36
Jul 23 10:07:58 linuxbox kernel: scsi 3:0:0:0: Direct-Access Easy Disk 1.00 PQ:
0 ANSI: 2
Jul 23 10:07:59 linuxbox kernel: sd 3:0:0:0: [sdb] 31263 512-byte hardware secto
rs (16 MB)
Jul 23 10:07:59 linuxbox kernel: sd 3:0:0:0: [sdb] Write Protect is off
Jul 23 10:07:59 linuxbox kernel: sd 3:0:0:0: [sdb] Assuming drive cache: write t
hrough
Jul 23 10:07:59 linuxbox kernel: sd 3:0:0:0: [sdb] 31263 512-byte hardware secto
rs (16 MB)
Jul 23 10:07:59 linuxbox kernel: sd 3:0:0:0: [sdb] Write Protect is off
Jul 23 10:07:59 linuxbox kernel: sd 3:0:0:0: [sdb] Assuming drive cache: write t
hrough
Jul 23 10:07:59 linuxbox kernel:  sdb: sdb1
Jul 23 10:07:59 linuxbox kernel: sd 3:0:0:0: [sdb] Attached SCSI removable disk
Jul 23 10:07:59 linuxbox kernel: sd 3:0:0:0: Attached scsi generic sg3 type 0
```

After the display pauses again, press CTRL-C to get the prompt back. The interesting parts of the output are the repeated references to [sdb], which matches our expectation of a SCSI disk device name. Knowing this, two lines become particularly illuminating:

```
Jul 23 10:07:59 linuxbox kernel:  sdb: sdb1
Jul 23 10:07:59 linuxbox kernel: sd 3:0:0:0: [sdb] Attached SCSI removable disk
```

This tells us the device name is */dev/sdb* for the entire device and */dev/sdb1* for the first partition on the device. As we have seen, working with Linux means lots of interesting detective work!

Note: *Using the* tail -f /var/log/messages *technique is a great way to watch what the system is doing in near realtime.*

With our device name in hand, we can now mount the flash drive:

```
[me@linuxbox ~]$ sudo mkdir /mnt/flash
[me@linuxbox ~]$ sudo mount /dev/sdb1 /mnt/flash
[me@linuxbox ~]$ df
```

```
Filesystem           1K-blocks      Used Available Use% Mounted on
/dev/sda2            15115452    5186944   9775164  35% /
/dev/sda5            59631908   31777376  24776480  57% /home
/dev/sda1              147764      17277    122858  13% /boot
tmpfs                  776808          0    776808   0% /dev/shm
/dev/sdb1               15560          0     15560   0% /mnt/flash
```

The device name will remain the same as long as it remains physically attached to the computer and the computer is not rebooted.

Creating New Filesystems

Let's say that we want to reformat the flash drive with a Linux native filesystem, rather than the FAT32 system it has now. This involves two steps: first, (optionally) creating a new partition layout if the existing one is not to our liking, and second, creating a new, empty filesystem on the drive.

Warning: *In the following exercise, we are going to format a flash drive. Use a drive that contains nothing you care about because it will be erased! Again, **make absolutely sure you are specifying the correct device name for your system, not the one shown in the text. Failure to heed this warning could result in formatting (i.e., erasing) the wrong drive!***

Manipulating Partitions with fdisk

The fdisk program allows us to interact directly with disk-like devices (such as hard disk drives and flash drives) at a very low level. With this tool we can edit, delete, and create partitions on the device. To work with our flash drive, we must first unmount it (if needed) and then invoke the fdisk program as follows:

```
[me@linuxbox ~]$ sudo umount /dev/sdb1
[me@linuxbox ~]$ sudo fdisk /dev/sdb
```

Notice that we must specify the device in terms of the entire device, not by partition number. After the program starts up, we will see the following prompt:

```
Command (m for help):
```

Entering an m will display the program menu:

```
Command action
   a   toggle a bootable flag
   b   edit bsd disklabel
   c   toggle the dos compatibility flag
   d   delete a partition
   l   list known partition types
   m   print this menu
   n   add a new partition
```

```
o   create a new empty DOS partition table
p   print the partition table
q   quit without saving changes
s   create a new empty Sun disklabel
t   change a partition's system id
u   change display/entry units
v   verify the partition table
w   write table to disk and exit
x   extra functionality (experts only)
```

Command (m for help):

The first thing we want to do is examine the existing partition layout. We do this by entering p to print the partition table for the device:

```
Command (m for help): p

Disk /dev/sdb: 16 MB, 16006656 bytes
1 heads, 31 sectors/track, 1008 cylinders
Units = cylinders of 31 * 512 = 15872 bytes

   Device Boot      Start         End      Blocks   Id  System
/dev/sdb1                2        1008       15608+   b   W95 FAT32
```

In this example, we see a 16MB device with a single partition (1) that uses 1006 of the available 1008 cylinders on the device. The partition is identified as a Windows 95 FAT32 partition. Some programs will use this identifier to limit the kinds of operation that can be done to the disk, but most of the time changing the identifier is not critical. However, in the interest of demonstration, we will change it to indicate a Linux partition. To do this, we must first find out what ID is used to identify a Linux partition. In the listing above, we see that the ID b is used to specify the existing partition. To see a list of the available partition types, we refer back to the program menu. There we can see the following choice:

```
l   list known partition types
```

If we enter l at the prompt, a large list of possible types is displayed. Among them we see b for our existing partition type and 83 for Linux.

Going back to the menu, we see this choice to change a partition ID:

```
t   change a partition's system id
```

We enter t at the prompt and enter the new ID:

```
Command (m for help): t
Selected partition 1
Hex code (type L to list codes): 83
Changed system type of partition 1 to 83 (Linux)
```

This completes all the changes that we need to make. Up to this point, the device has been untouched (all the changes have been stored in memory, not on the physical device), so we will write the modified partition table to the device and exit.

To do this, we enter w at the prompt:

```
Command (m for help): w
The partition table has been altered!

Calling ioctl() to re-read partition table.

WARNING: If you have created or modified any DOS 6.x
partitions, please see the fdisk manual page for additional
information.
Syncing disks.
[me@linuxbox ~]$
```

If we had decided to leave the device unaltered, we could have entered q at the prompt, which would have exited the program without writing the changes. We can safely ignore the ominous-sounding warning message.

Creating a New Filesystem with mkfs

With our partition editing done (lightweight though it might have been), it's time to create a new filesystem on our flash drive. To do this, we will use mkfs (short for *make filesystem*), which can create filesystems in a variety of formats. To create an ext3 filesystem on the device, we use the -t option to specify the ext3 system type, followed by the name of the device containing the partition we wish to format:

```
[me@linuxbox ~]$ sudo mkfs -t ext3 /dev/sdb1
mke2fs 1.40.2 (12-Jul-2012)
Filesystem label=
OS type: Linux
Block size=1024 (log=0)
Fragment size=1024 (log=0)
3904 inodes, 15608 blocks
780 blocks (5.00%) reserved for the super user
First data block=1
Maximum filesystem blocks=15990784
2 block groups
8192 blocks per group, 8192 fragments per group
1952 inodes per group
Superblock backups stored on blocks:
        8193

Writing inode tables: done
Creating journal (1024 blocks): done
Writing superblocks and filesystem accounting information: done

This filesystem will be automatically checked every 34 mounts or
180 days, whichever comes first. Use tune2fs -c or -i to override.
[me@linuxbox ~]$
```

The program will display a lot of information when ext3 is the chosen filesystem type. To reformat the device to its original FAT32 filesystem, specify vfat as the filesystem type:

```
[me@linuxbox ~]$ sudo mkfs -t vfat /dev/sdb1
```

This process of partitioning and formatting can be used anytime additional storage devices are added to the system. While we worked with a tiny flash drive, the same process can be applied to internal hard disks and other removable storage devices like USB hard drives.

Testing and Repairing Filesystems

In our earlier discussion of the */etc/fstab* file, we saw some mysterious digits at the end of each line. Each time the system boots, it routinely checks the integrity of the filesystems before mounting them. This is done by the fsck program (short for *filesystem check*). The last number in each *fstab* entry specifies the order in which the devices are to be checked. In our example above, we see that the root filesystem is checked first, followed by the *home* and *boot* filesystems. Devices with a zero as the last digit are not routinely checked.

In addition to checking the integrity of filesystems, fsck can also repair corrupt filesystems with varying degrees of success, depending on the amount of damage. On Unix-like filesystems, recovered portions of files are placed in the *lost+found* directory, located in the root of each filesystem.

To check our flash drive (which should be unmounted first), we could do the following:

```
[me@linuxbox ~]$ sudo fsck /dev/sdb1
fsck 1.40.8 (13-Mar-2012)
e2fsck 1.40.8 (13-Mar-2012)
/dev/sdb1: clean, 11/3904 files, 1661/15608 blocks
```

In my experience, filesystem corruption is quite rare unless there is a hardware problem, such as a failing disk drive. On most systems, filesystem corruption detected at boot time will cause the system to stop and direct you to run fsck before continuing.

WHAT THE FSCK?

In Unix culture, fsck is often used in place of a popular word with which it shares three letters. This is especially appropriate, given that you will probably be uttering the aforementioned word if you find yourself in a situation where you are forced to run fsck.

Formatting Floppy Disks

For those of us still using computers old enough to be equipped with floppy-disk drives, we can manage those devices, too. Preparing a blank floppy for use is a two-step process. First, we perform a low-level format on the disk, and then we create a filesystem. To accomplish the formatting, we use the dformat program specifying the name of the floppy device (usually */dev/fd0*):

```
[me@linuxbox ~]$ sudo fdformat /dev/fd0
Double-sided, 80 tracks, 18 sec/track. Total capacity 1440 kB.
Formatting ... done
Verifying ... done
```

Next, we apply a FAT filesystem to the disk with mkfs:

```
[me@linuxbox ~]$ sudo mkfs -t msdos /dev/fd0
```

Notice that we use the msdos filesystem type to get the older (and smaller) style file allocation tables. After a disk is prepared, it may be mounted like other devices.

Moving Data Directly to and from Devices

While we usually think of data on our computers as being organized into files, it is also possible to think of the data in "raw" form. If we look at a disk drive, for example, we see that it consists of a large number of "blocks" of data that the operating system sees as directories and files. If we could treat a disk drive as simply a large collection of data blocks, we could perform useful tasks, such as cloning devices.

The dd program performs this task. It copies blocks of data from one place to another. It uses a unique syntax (for historical reasons) and is usually used this way:

```
dd if=input_file of=output_file [bs=block_size [count=blocks]]
```

Let's say we had two USB flash drives of the same size and we wanted to exactly copy the first drive to the second. If we attached both drives to the computer and they were assigned to devices */dev/sdb* and */dev/sdc* respectively, we could copy everything on the first drive to the second drive with the following:

```
dd if=/dev/sdb of=/dev/sdc
```

Alternatively, if only the first device were attached to the computer, we could copy its contents to an ordinary file for later restoration or copying:

```
dd if=/dev/sdb of=flash_drive.img
```

Warning: *The dd command is very powerful. Though its name derives from data definition, it is sometimes called* destroy disk *because users often mistype either the* if *or* of *specifications.* **Always double-check your input and output specifications before pressing ENTER!**

Creating CD-ROM Images

Writing a recordable CD-ROM (either a CD-R or CD-RW) consists of two steps: first, constructing an *ISO image file* that is the exact filesystem image of the CD-ROM, and second, writing the image file onto the CD-ROM medium.

Creating an Image Copy of a CD-ROM

If we want to make an ISO image of an existing CD-ROM, we can use dd to read all the data blocks off the CD-ROM and copy them to a local file. Say we had an Ubuntu CD and we wanted to make an ISO file that we could later use to make more copies. After inserting the CD and determining its device name (we'll assume */dev/cdrom*), we can make the ISO file like so:

```
dd if=/dev/cdrom of=ubuntu.iso
```

This technique works for data DVDs as well, but it will not work for audio CDs as they do not use a filesystem for storage. For audio CDs, look at the cdrdao command.

A PROGRAM BY ANY OTHER NAME...

If you look at online tutorials for creating and burning optical media like CD-ROMs and DVDs, you will frequently encounter two programs called mkisofs and cdrecord. These programs were part of a popular package called cdrtools authored by Jörg Schilling. In the summer of 2006, Mr. Schilling made a license change to a portion of the cdrtools package that, in the opinion of many in the Linux community, created a license incompatibility with the GNU GPL. As a result, a *fork* of the cdrtools project was started, which now includes replacement programs for cdrecord and mkisofs named wodim and genisoimage, respectively.

Creating an Image from a Collection of Files

To create an ISO image file containing the contents of a directory, we use the enisoimage program. To do this, we first create a directory containing all the files we wish to include in the image and then execute the genisoimage command to create the image file. For example, if we had created a directory called *~/cd-rom-files* and filled it with files for our CD-ROM, we could create an image file named *cd-rom.iso* with the following command:

```
genisoimage -o cd-rom.iso -R -J ~/cd-rom-files
```

The -R option adds metadata for the *Rock Ridge extensions*, which allow the use of long filenames and POSIX-style file permissions. Likewise, the -J option enables the *Joliet extensions*, which permit long filenames in Windows.

Writing CD-ROM Images

After we have an image file, we can burn it onto our optical media. Most of the commands we discuss below can be applied to both recordable CD-ROM and DVD media.

Mounting an ISO Image Directly

There is a trick that we can use to mount an ISO image while it is still on our hard disk and treat it as though it were already on optical media. By adding the -o loop option to mount (along with the required -t iso9660 filesystem type), we can mount the image file as though it were a device and attach it to the filesystem tree:

```
mkdir /mnt/iso_image
mount -t iso9660 -o loop image.iso /mnt/iso_image
```

In the example above, we created a mount point named */mnt/iso_image* and then mounted the image file *image.iso* at that mount point. After the image is mounted, it can be treated just as though it were a real CD-ROM or DVD. *Remember to unmount the image when it is no longer needed.*

Blanking a Rewritable CD-ROM

Rewritable CD-RW media need to be erased or *blanked* before being reused. To do this, we can use wodim, specifying the device name for the CD writer and the type of blanking to be performed. The wodim program offers several types. The most minimal (and fastest) is the fast type:

```
wodim dev=/dev/cdrw blank=fast
```

Writing an Image

To write an image, we again use wodim, specifying the name of the optical media writer device and the name of the image file:

```
wodim dev=/dev/cdrw image.iso
```

In addition to the device name and image file, wodim supports a very large set of options. Two common ones are -v for verbose output and -dao, which writes the disc in *disc-at-once* mode. This mode should be used if you are preparing a disc for commercial reproduction. The default mode for wodim is *track-at-once*, which is useful for recording music tracks.

Extra Credit

It's often useful to verify the integrity of an ISO image that we have downloaded. In most cases, a distributor of an ISO image will also supply a *checksum file*. A checksum is the result of an exotic mathematical calculation resulting in a number that represents the content of the target file. If the contents of the file change by even one bit, the resulting checksum will be much different. The most common method of checksum generation uses the md5sum program. When you use md5sum, it produces a unique hexadecimal number:

```
md5sum image.iso
34e354760f9bb7fbf85c96f6a3f94ece  image.iso
```

After you download an image, you should run md5sum against it and compare the results with the md5sum value supplied by the publisher.

In addition to checking the integrity of a downloaded file, we can use md5sum to verify newly written optical media. To do this, we first calculate the checksum of the image file and then calculate a checksum for the medium. The trick to verifying the medium is to limit the calculation to only the portion of the optical medium that contains the image. We do this by determining the number of 2048-byte blocks the image contains (optical media is always written in 2048-byte blocks) and reading that many blocks from the medium. On some types of media, this is not required. A CD-R written in disc-at-once mode can be checked this way:

```
md5sum /dev/cdrom
34e354760f9bb7fbf85c96f6a3f94ece  /dev/cdrom
```

Many types of media, such as DVDs, require a precise calculation of the number of blocks. In the example below, we check the integrity of the image file *dvd-image.iso* and the disc in the DVD reader */dev/dvd*. Can you figure out how this works?

```
md5sum dvd-image.iso; dd if=/dev/dvd bs=2048 count=$(( $(stat -c "%s" dvd-image
.iso) / 2048 )) | md5sum
```

16

NETWORKING

When it comes to networking, there is probably nothing that cannot be done with Linux. Linux is used to build all sorts of networking systems and appliances, including firewalls, routers, name servers, NAS (network-attached storage) boxes, and on and on.

Just as the subject of networking is vast, so is the number of commands that can be used to configure and control it. We will focus our attention on just a few of the most frequently used ones. The commands chosen for examination include those used to monitor networks and those used to transfer files. In addition, we are going to explore the ssh program, which is used to perform remote logins. This chapter will cover the following:

- ping—Send an ICMP ECHO_REQUEST to network hosts.
- traceroute—Print the route packets take to a network host.
- netstat—Print network connections, routing tables, interface statistics, masquerade connections, and multicast memberships.
- ftp—Internet file transfer program.

- `lftp`—An improved Internet file transfer program.
- `wget`—Non-interactive network downloader.
- `ssh`—OpenSSH SSH client (remote login program).
- `scp`—Secure copy (remote file copy program).
- `sftp`—Secure file transfer program.

We're going to assume a little background in networking. In this, the Internet age, everyone using a computer needs a basic understanding of networking concepts. To make full use of this chapter, you should be familiar with the following terms:

- IP (Internet protocol) address
- Host and domain name
- URI (uniform resource identifier)

Note: *Some of the commands we will cover may (depending on your distribution) require the installation of additional packages from your distribution's repositories, and some may require superuser privileges to execute.*

Examining and Monitoring a Network

Even if you're not the system administrator, it's often helpful to examine the performance and operation of a network.

ping—Send a Special Packet to a Network Host

The most basic network command is `ping`. The `ping` command sends a special network packet called an ICMP ECHO_REQUEST to a specified host. Most network devices receiving this packet will reply to it, allowing the network connection to be verified.

Note: *It is possible to configure most network devices (including Linux hosts) to ignore these packets. This is usually done for security reasons, to partially obscure a host from a potential attacker. It is also common for firewalls to be configured to block ICMP traffic.*

For example, to see if we can reach *http://www.linuxcommand.org/* (one of my favorite sites ;-)), we can use `ping` like this:

```
[me@linuxbox ~]$ ping linuxcommand.org
```

Once started, `ping` continues to send packets at a specified interval (default is 1 second) until it is interrupted:

```
[me@linuxbox ~]$ ping linuxcommand.org
PING linuxcommand.org (66.35.250.210) 56(84) bytes of data.
```

```
64 bytes from vhost.sourceforge.net (66.35.250.210): icmp_seq=1 ttl=43 time=10
7 ms
64 bytes from vhost.sourceforge.net (66.35.250.210): icmp_seq=2 ttl=43 time=10
8 ms
64 bytes from vhost.sourceforge.net (66.35.250.210): icmp_seq=3 ttl=43 time=10
6 ms
64 bytes from vhost.sourceforge.net (66.35.250.210): icmp_seq=4 ttl=43 time=10
6 ms
64 bytes from vhost.sourceforge.net (66.35.250.210): icmp_seq=5 ttl=43 time=10
5 ms
64 bytes from vhost.sourceforge.net (66.35.250.210): icmp_seq=6 ttl=43 time=10
7 ms

--- linuxcommand.org ping statistics ---
6 packets transmitted, 6 received, 0% packet loss, time 6010ms
rtt min/avg/max/mdev = 105.647/107.052/108.118/0.824 ms
```

After it is interrupted (in this case after the sixth packet) by the pressing of CTRL-C, ping prints performance statistics. A properly performing network will exhibit zero percent packet loss. A successful ping will indicate that the elements of the network (its interface cards, cabling, routing, and gateways) are in generally good working order.

traceroute—Trace the Path of a Network Packet

The traceroute program (some systems use the similar tracepath program instead) displays a listing of all the "hops" network traffic takes to get from the local system to a specified host. For example, to see the route taken to reach *http://www.slashdot.org/*, we would do this:

```
[me@linuxbox ~]$ traceroute slashdot.org
```

The output looks like this:

```
traceroute to slashdot.org (216.34.181.45), 30 hops max, 40 byte packets
 1  ipcop.localdomain (192.168.1.1)  1.066 ms  1.366 ms  1.720 ms
 2  * * *
 3  ge-4-13-ur01.rockville.md.bad.comcast.net (68.87.130.9)  14.622 ms  14.885
ms  15.169 ms
 4  po-30-ur02.rockville.md.bad.comcast.net (68.87.129.154)  17.634 ms  17.626
ms  17.899 ms
 5  po-60-ur03.rockville.md.bad.comcast.net (68.87.129.158)  15.992 ms  15.983
ms  16.256 ms
 6  po-30-ar01.howardcounty.md.bad.comcast.net (68.87.136.5)  22.835 ms  14.23
3 ms  14.405 ms
 7  po-10-ar02.whitemarsh.md.bad.comcast.net (68.87.129.34)  16.154 ms  13.600
ms  18.867 ms
 8  te-0-3-0-1-cr01.philadelphia.pa.ibone.comcast.net (68.86.90.77)  21.951 ms
21.073 ms  21.557 ms
 9  pos-0-8-0-0-cr01.newyork.ny.ibone.comcast.net (68.86.85.10)  22.917 ms  21
.884 ms  22.126 ms
10  204.70.144.1 (204.70.144.1)  43.110 ms  21.248 ms  21.264 ms
11  cr1-pos-0-7-3-1.newyork.savvis.net (204.70.195.93)  21.857 ms cr2-pos-0-0-
3-1.newyork.savvis.net (204.70.204.238)  19.556 ms cr1-pos-0-7-3-1.newyork.sav
vis.net (204.70.195.93)  19.634 ms
```

```
12  cr2-pos-0-7-3-0.chicago.savvis.net (204.70.192.109)  41.586 ms  42.843 ms
cr2-tengig-0-0-2-0.chicago.savvis.net (204.70.196.242)  43.115 ms
13  hr2-tengigabitethernet-12-1.elkgrovech3.savvis.net (204.70.195.122)  44.21
5 ms  41.833 ms  45.658 ms
14  csr1-ve241.elkgrovech3.savvis.net (216.64.194.42)  46.840 ms  43.372 ms  4
7.041 ms
15  64.27.160.194 (64.27.160.194)  56.137 ms  55.887 ms  52.810 ms
16  slashdot.org (216.34.181.45)  42.727 ms  42.016 ms  41.437 ms
```

In the output, we can see that connecting from our test system to *http://www.slashdot.org/* requires traversing 16 routers. For routers that provide identifying information, we see their hostnames, IP addresses, and performance data, which include three samples of round-trip time from the local system to the router. For routers that do not provide identifying information (because of router configuration, network congestion, firewalls, etc.), we see asterisks as in the line for hop number two.

netstat—Examine Network Settings and Statistics

The netstat program is used to examine various network settings and statistics. Through the use of its many options, we can look at a variety of features in our network setup. Using the -ie option, we can examine the network interfaces in our system:

```
[me@linuxbox ~]$ netstat -ie
eth0    Link encap:Ethernet  HWaddr 00:1d:09:9b:99:67
        inet addr:192.168.1.2 Bcast:192.168.1.255 Mask:255.255.255.0
        inet6 addr: fe80::21d:9ff:fe9b:9967/64 Scope:Link
        UP BROADCAST RUNNING MULTICAST  MTU:1500  Metric:1
        RX packets:238488 errors:0 dropped:0 overruns:0 frame:0
        TX packets:403217 errors:0 dropped:0 overruns:0 carrier:0
        collisions:0 txqueuelen:100
        RX bytes:153098921 (146.0 MB)  TX bytes:261035246 (248.9 MB)
        Memory:fdfc0000-fdfe0000

lo      Link encap:Local Loopback
        inet addr:127.0.0.1  Mask:255.0.0.0
        inet6 addr: ::1/128 Scope:Host
        UP LOOPBACK RUNNING  MTU:16436  Metric:1
        RX packets:2208 errors:0 dropped:0 overruns:0 frame:0
        TX packets:2208 errors:0 dropped:0 overruns:0 carrier:0
        collisions:0 txqueuelen:0
        RX bytes:111490 (108.8 KB)  TX bytes:111490 (108.8 KB)
```

In the example above, we see that our test system has two network interfaces. The first, called eth0, is the Ethernet interface; the second, called lo, is the *loopback interface*, a virtual interface that the system uses to "talk to itself."

When performing causal network diagnostics, the important things to look for are the presence of the word UP at the beginning of the fourth line for each interface, indicating that the network interface is enabled, and the presence of a valid IP address in the inet addr field on the second line. For systems using Dynamic Host Configuration Protocol (DHCP), a valid IP address in this field will verify that the DHCP is working.

Using the -r option will display the kernel's network routing table. This shows how the network is configured to send packets from network to network:

```
[me@linuxbox ~]$ netstat -r
Kernel IP routing table
Destination  Gateway   Genmask        Flags  MSS Window  irtt Iface
192.168.1.0  *         255.255.255.0  U        0 0          0 eth0  default
192.168.1.1  0.0.0.0   UG        0 0           0 eth0
```

In this simple example, we see a typical routing table for a client machine on a local area network (LAN) behind a firewall/router. The first line of the listing shows the destination 192.168.1.0. IP addresses that end in zero refer to networks rather than individual hosts, so this destination means any host on the LAN. The next field, Gateway, is the name or IP address of the gateway (router) used to go from the current host to the destination network. An asterisk in this field indicates that no gateway is needed.

The last line contains the destination default. This means any traffic destined for a network that is not otherwise listed in the table. In our example, we see that the gateway is defined as a router with the address of 192.168.1.1, which presumably knows what to do with the destination traffic.

The netstat program has many options, and we have looked at only a couple. Check out the netstat man page for a complete list.

Transporting Files over a Network

What good is a network unless we know how to move files across it? There are many programs that move data over networks. We will cover two of them now and several more in later sections.

ftp—Transfer Files with the File Transfer Protocol

One of the true "classic" programs, ftp gets its name from the protocol it uses, the *File Transfer Protocol*. FTP is used widely on the Internet for file downloads. Most, if not all, web browsers support it, and you often see URIs starting with the protocol *ftp://*.

Before there were web browsers, there was the ftp program. ftp is used to communicate with *FTP servers*, machines that contain files that can be uploaded and downloaded over a network.

FTP (in its original form) is not secure, because it sends account names and passwords in *cleartext*. This means that they are not encrypted and anyone sniffing the network can see them. Because of this, almost all FTP done over the Internet is done by *anonymous FTP servers*. An anonymous server allows anyone to log in using the login name *anonymous* and a meaningless password.

In the following example, we show a typical session with the ftp program downloading an Ubuntu ISO image located in the */pub/cd_images/ Ubuntu-8.04* directory of the anonymous FTP server *fileserver*.

```
[me@linuxbox ~]$ ftp fileserver
Connected to fileserver.localdomain.
220 (vsFTPd 2.0.1)
Name (fileserver:me): anonymous
331 Please specify the password.
Password:
230 Login successful.
Remote system type is UNIX.
Using binary mode to transfer files.
ftp> cd pub/cd_images/Ubuntu-8.04
250 Directory successfully changed.
ftp> ls
200 PORT command successful. Consider using PASV.
150 Here comes the directory listing.
-rw-rw-r--    1 500      500        733079552 Apr 25 03:53 ubuntu-8.04-desktop-
i386.iso
226 Directory send OK.
ftp> lcd Desktop
Local directory now /home/me/Desktop
ftp> get ubuntu-8.04-desktop-i386.iso
local: ubuntu-8.04-desktop-i386.iso remote: ubuntu-8.04-desktop-i386.iso
200 PORT command successful. Consider using PASV.
150 Opening BINARY mode data connection for ubuntu-8.04-desktop-i386.iso
(733079552 bytes).
226 File send OK.
733079552 bytes received in 68.56 secs (10441.5 kB/s)
ftp> bye
```

Table 16-1 gives an explanation of the commands entered during this session.

Table 16-1: Examples of Interactive ftp Commands

Command	Meaning
ftp fileserver	Invoke the ftp program and have it connect to the FTP server *fileserver*.
anonymous	Login name. After the login prompt, a password prompt will appear. Some servers will accept a blank password. Others will require a password in the form of an email address. In that case, try something like *user@example.com*.
cd pub/cd_images/Ubuntu-8.04	Change to the directory on the remote system containing the desired file. Note that on most anonymous FTP servers, the files for public downloading are found somewhere under the *pub* directory.
ls	List the directory on the remote system.

Table 16-1 (*continued*)

Command	Meaning
`lcd Desktop`	Change the directory on the local system to *~/Desktop*. In the example, the `ftp` program was invoked when the working directory was *~*. This command changes the working directory to *~/Desktop*.
`get ubuntu-8.04-desktop-i386.iso`	Tell the remote system to transfer the file *ubuntu-8.04-desktop-i386.iso* to the local system. Since the working directory on the local system was changed to *~/Desktop*, the file will be downloaded there.
`bye`	Log off the remote server and end the `ftp` program session. The commands `quit` and `exit` may also be used.

Typing `help` at the `ftp>` prompt will display a list of the supported commands. Using `ftp` on a server where sufficient permissions have been granted, it is possible to perform many ordinary file management tasks. It's clumsy, but it does work.

lftp—A Better ftp

`ftp` is not the only command-line FTP client. In fact, there are many. One of the better (and more popular) ones is `lftp` by Alexander Lukyanov. It works much like the traditional `ftp` program but has many additional convenience features, including multiple-protocol support (including HTTP), automatic retry on failed downloads, background processes, tab completion of pathnames, and many more.

wget—Non-interactive Network Downloader

Another popular command-line program for file downloading is `wget`. It is useful for downloading content from both web and FTP sites. Single files, multiple files, and even entire sites can be downloaded. To download the first page of *http://www.linuxcommand.org/*, we could do this:

```
[me@linuxbox ~]$ wget http://linuxcommand.org/index.php
--11:02:51--  http://linuxcommand.org/index.php
           => `index.php'
Resolving linuxcommand.org... 66.35.250.210
Connecting to linuxcommand.org|66.35.250.210|:80... connected.
```

```
HTTP request sent, awaiting response... 200 OK
Length: unspecified [text/html]

    [ <=>                                      ] 3,120           --.--K/s

11:02:51 (161.75 MB/s) - `index.php' saved [3120]
```

The program's many options allow wget to recursively download, download files in the background (allowing you to log off but continue downloading), and complete the download of a partially downloaded file. These features are well documented in its better-than-average man page.

Secure Communication with Remote Hosts

For many years, Unix-like operating systems have had the ability to be administered remotely via a network. In the early days, before the general adoption of the Internet, there were a couple of popular programs used to log in to remote hosts: the rlogin and telnet programs. These programs, however, suffer from the same fatal flaw that the ftp program does; they transmit all their communications (including login names and passwords) in cleartext. This makes them wholly inappropriate for use in the Internet age.

ssh—Securely Log in to Remote Computers

To address this problem, a new protocol called SSH (Secure Shell) was developed. SSH solves the two basic problems of secure communication with a remote host. First, it authenticates that the remote host is who it says it is (thus preventing man-in-the-middle attacks), and second, it encrypts all of the communications between the local and remote hosts.

SSH consists of two parts. An SSH server runs on the remote host, listening for incoming connections on port 22, while an SSH client is used on the local system to communicate with the remote server.

Most Linux distributions ship an implementation of SSH called OpenSSH from the BSD project. Some distributions include both the client and the server packages by default (for example, Red Hat), while others (such as Ubuntu) supply only the client. To enable a system to receive remote connections, it must have the OpenSSH-server package installed, configured, and running, and (if the system is either running or behind a firewall) it must allow incoming network connections on TCP port 22.

Note: *If you don't have a remote system to connect to but want to try these examples, make sure the OpenSSH-server package is installed on your system and use localhost as the name of the remote host. That way, your machine will create network connections with itself.*

The SSH client program used to connect to remote SSH servers is called, appropriately enough, ssh. To connect to a remote host named remote-sys, we would use the ssh client program like so:

```
[me@linuxbox ~]$ ssh remote-sys
The authenticity of host 'remote-sys (192.168.1.4)' can't be established.
RSA key fingerprint is 41:ed:7a:df:23:19:bf:3c:a5:17:bc:61:b3:7f:d9:bb.
Are you sure you want to continue connecting (yes/no)?
```

The first time the connection is attempted, a message is displayed indicating that the authenticity of the remote host cannot be established. This is because the client program has never seen this remote host before. To accept the credentials of the remote host, enter yes when prompted. Once the connection is established, the user is prompted for a password:

```
Warning: Permanently added 'remote-sys,192.168.1.4' (RSA) to the list of known
hosts.
me@remote-sys's password:
```

After the password is successfully entered, we receive the shell prompt from the remote system:

```
Last login: Tue Aug 30 13:00:48 2011
[me@remote-sys ~]$
```

The remote shell session continues until the user enters the exit command at the remote shell prompt, thereby closing the remote connection. At this point, the local shell session resumes, and the local shell prompt reappears.

It is also possible to connect to remote systems using a different username. For example, if the local user *me* had an account named *bob* on a remote system, user *me* could log in to the account *bob* on the remote system as follows:

```
[me@linuxbox ~]$ ssh bob@remote-sys
bob@remote-sys's password:
Last login: Tue Aug 30 13:03:21 2011
[bob@remote-sys ~]$
```

As stated before, ssh verifies the authenticity of the remote host. If the remote host does not successfully authenticate, the following message appears:

```
[me@linuxbox ~]$ ssh remote-sys
@@@@@@@@@@@@@@@@@@@@@@@@@@@@@@@@@@@@@@@@@@@@@@@@@@@@@@@@@@@
@    WARNING: REMOTE HOST IDENTIFICATION HAS CHANGED!     @
@@@@@@@@@@@@@@@@@@@@@@@@@@@@@@@@@@@@@@@@@@@@@@@@@@@@@@@@@@@
IT IS POSSIBLE THAT SOMEONE IS DOING SOMETHING NASTY!
Someone could be eavesdropping on you right now (man-in-the-middle attack)!
It is also possible that the RSA host key has just been changed.
```

```
The fingerprint for the RSA key sent by the remote host is
41:ed:7a:df:23:19:bf:3c:a5:17:bc:61:b3:7f:d9:bb.
Please contact your system administrator.
Add correct host key in /home/me/.ssh/known_hosts to get rid of this message.
Offending key in /home/me/.ssh/known_hosts:1
RSA host key for remote-sys has changed and you have requested strict
checking.
Host key verification failed.
```

This message is caused by one of two possible situations. First, an attacker may be attempting a man-in-the-middle attack. This is rare, because everybody knows that ssh alerts the user to this. The more likely culprit is that the remote system has been changed somehow; for example, its operating system or SSH server has been reinstalled. In the interests of security and safety, however, the first possibility should not be dismissed out of hand. Always check with the administrator of the remote system when this message occurs.

After determining that the message is due to a benign cause, it is safe to correct the problem on the client side. This is done by using a text editor (vim perhaps) to remove the obsolete key from the *~/.ssh/known_hosts* file. In the example message above, we see this:

```
Offending key in /home/me/.ssh/known_hosts:1
```

This means that line 1 of the *known_hosts* file contains the offending key. Delete this line from the file, and the ssh program will be able to accept new authentication credentials from the remote system.

Besides opening a shell session on a remote system, ssh also allows us to execute a single command on a remote system. For example, we can execute the free command on a remote host named *remote-sys* and have the results displayed on the local system:

```
[me@linuxbox ~]$ ssh remote-sys free
me@twin4's password:
             total     used     free   shared    buffers     cached
Mem:        775536   507184   268352        0     110068     154596
-/+ buffers/cache:   242520   533016
Swap:      1572856        0  1572856
[me@linuxbox ~]$
```

It's possible to use this technique in more interesting ways, such as this example in which we perform an ls on the remote system and redirect the output to a file on the local system:

```
[me@linuxbox ~]$ ssh remote-sys 'ls *' > dirlist.txt
me@twin4's password:
[me@linuxbox ~]$
```

Notice the use of the single quotes. This is done because we do not want the pathname expansion performed on the local machine; rather, we want it to be performed on the remote system. Likewise, if we had wanted the output redirected to a file on the remote machine, we could have placed the redirection operator and the filename within the single quotes:

```
[me@linuxbox ~]$ ssh remote-sys 'ls * > dirlist.txt'
```

TUNNELING WITH SSH

Part of what happens when you establish a connection with a remote host via SSH is that an *encrypted tunnel* is created between the local and remote systems. Normally, this tunnel is used to allow commands typed at the local system to be transmitted safely to the remote system and the results to be transmitted safely back. In addition to this basic function, the SSH protocol allows most types of network traffic to be sent through the encrypted tunnel, creating a sort of *VPN* (virtual private network) between the local and remote systems.

Perhaps the most common use of this feature is to allow X Window system traffic to be transmitted. On a system running an X server (that is, a machine displaying a GUI), it is possible to launch and run an X client program (a graphical application) on a remote system and have its display appear on the local system. It's easy to do—here's an example. Let's say we are sitting at a Linux system called *linuxbox* that is running an X server, and we want to run the xload program on a remote system named *remote-sys* and see the program's graphical output on our local system. We could do this:

```
[me@linuxbox ~]$ ssh -X remote-sys
me@remote-sys's password:
Last login: Mon Sep 05 13:23:11 2011
[me@remote-sys ~]$ xload
```

After the xload command is executed on the remote system, its window appears on the local system. On some systems, you may need to use the -Y option rather than the -X option to do this.

scp and sftp—Securely Transfer Files

The OpenSSH package also includes two programs that can make use of an SSH-encrypted tunnel to copy files across the network. The first, scp (secure copy) is used much like the familiar cp program to copy files. The most notable difference is that the source or destination pathname may be preceded with the name of a remote host followed by a colon character. For example, if we wanted to copy a document named *document.txt* from our home directory on the remote system, *remote-sys*, to the current working directory on our local system, we could do this:

```
[me@linuxbox ~]$ scp remote-sys:document.txt .
me@remote-sys's password:
document.txt                     100% 5581      5.5KB/s   00:00
[me@linuxbox ~]$
```

As with ssh, you may apply a username to the beginning of the remote host's name if the desired remote host account name does not match that of the local system:

```
[me@linuxbox ~]$ scp bob@remote-sys:document.txt .
```

The second SSH file-copying program is sftp, which, as its name implies, is a secure replacement for the ftp program. sftp works much like the original ftp program that we used earlier; however, instead of transmitting everything in cleartext, it uses an SSH-encrypted tunnel. sftp has an important advantage over conventional ftp in that it does not require an FTP server to be running on the remote host. It requires only the SSH server. This means that any remote machine that can connect with the SSH client can also be used as a FTP-like server. Here is a sample session:

```
[me@linuxbox ~]$ sftp remote-sys
Connecting to remote-sys...
me@remote-sys's password:
sftp> ls
ubuntu-8.04-desktop-i386.iso
sftp> lcd Desktop
sftp> get ubuntu-8.04-desktop-i386.iso
Fetching /home/me/ubuntu-8.04-desktop-i386.iso to ubuntu-8.04-desktop-i386.iso

/home/me/ubuntu-8.04-desktop-i386.iso 100%  699MB   7.4MB/s   01:35
sftp> bye
```

Note: *The SFTP protocol is supported by many of the graphical file managers found in Linux distributions. Using either Nautilus (GNOME) or Konqueror (KDE), we can enter a URI beginning with* sftp:// *into the location bar and operate on files stored on a remote system running an SSH server.*

AN SSH CLIENT FOR WINDOWS?

Let's say you are sitting at a Windows machine but you need to log in to your Linux server and get some real work done. What do you do? Get an SSH client program for your Windows box, of course! There are a number of these. The most popular one is probably PuTTY by Simon Tatham and his team. The PuTTY program displays a terminal window and allows a Windows user to open an SSH (or telnet) session on a remote host. The program also provides analogs for the scp and sftp programs.

PuTTY is available at *http://www.chiark.greenend.org.uk/~sgtatham/putty/.*

17

SEARCHING FOR FILES

As we have wandered around our Linux system, one thing has become abundantly clear: A typical Linux system has a lot of files! This raises the question "How do we find things?" We already know that the Linux filesystem is well organized according to conventions that have been passed down from one generation of Unix-like systems to the next, but the sheer number of files can present a daunting problem.

In this chapter, we will look at two tools that are used to find files on a system:

- locate—Find files by name.
- find—Search for files in a directory hierarchy.

We will also look at a command that is often used with file-search commands to process the resulting list of files:

- xargs—Build and execute command lines from standard input.

In addition, we will introduce a couple of commands to assist us in our explorations:

- touch—Change file times.

- stat—Display file or filesystem status.

locate—Find Files the Easy Way

The locate program performs a rapid database search of pathnames and then outputs every name that matches a given substring. Say, for example, we want to find all the programs with names that begin with *zip*. Since we are looking for programs, we can assume that the name of the directory containing the programs would end with *bin/*. Therefore, we could try to use locate this way to find our files:

```
[me@linuxbox ~]$ locate bin/zip
```

locate will search its database of pathnames and output any that contain the string bin/zip:

```
/usr/bin/zip
/usr/bin/zipcloak
/usr/bin/zipgrep
/usr/bin/zipinfo
/usr/bin/zipnote
/usr/bin/zipsplit
```

If the search requirement is not so simple, locate can be combined with other tools, such as grep, to design more interesting searches:

```
[me@linuxbox ~]$ locate zip | grep bin
/bin/bunzip2
/bin/bzip2
/bin/bzip2recover
/bin/gunzip
/bin/gzip
/usr/bin/funzip
/usr/bin/gpg-zip
/usr/bin/preunzip
/usr/bin/prezip
/usr/bin/prezip-bin
/usr/bin/unzip
/usr/bin/unzipsfx
/usr/bin/zip
/usr/bin/zipcloak
/usr/bin/zipgrep
/usr/bin/zipinfo
/usr/bin/zipnote
/usr/bin/zipsplit
```

The locate program has been around for a number of years, and several different variants are in common use. The two most common ones found in modern Linux distributions are slocate and mlocate, though they are usually accessed by a symbolic link named locate. The different versions of locate have overlapping options sets. Some versions include regular-expression matching (which we'll cover in Chapter 19) and wildcard support. Check the man page for locate to determine which version of locate is installed.

WHERE DOES THE LOCATE DATABASE COME FROM?

You may notice that, on some distributions, locate fails to work just after the system is installed, but if you try again the next day, it works fine. What gives? The locate database is created by another program named updatedb. Usually, it is run periodically as a *cron job*; that is, a task performed at regular intervals by the cron daemon. Most systems equipped with locate run updatedb once a day. Since the database is not updated continuously, you will notice that very recent files do not show up when using locate. To overcome this, it's possible to run the updatedb program manually by becoming the superuser and running updatedb at the prompt.

find—Find Files the Hard Way

While the locate program can find a file based solely on its name, the find program searches a given directory (and its subdirectories) for files based on a variety of attributes. We're going to spend a lot of time with find because it has a bunch of interesting features that we will see again and again when we start to cover programming concepts in later chapters.

In its simplest use, find is given one or more names of directories to search. For example, it can produce a list of our home directory:

```
[me@linuxbox ~]$ find ~
```

On most active user accounts, this will produce a large list. Since the list is sent to standard output, we can pipe the list into other programs. Let's use wc to count the number of files:

```
[me@linuxbox ~]$ find ~ | wc -l
47068
```

Wow, we've been busy! The beauty of find is that it can be used to identify files that meet specific criteria. It does this through the (slightly strange) application of *tests*, *actions*, and *options*. We'll look at the tests first.

Tests

Let's say that we want a list of directories from our search. To do this, we could add the following test:

```
[me@linuxbox ~]$ find ~ -type d | wc -l
1695
```

Adding the test -type d limited the search to directories. Conversely, we could have limited the search to regular files with this test:

```
[me@linuxbox ~]$ find ~ -type f | wc -l
38737
```

Table 17-1 lists the common file-type tests supported by find.

Table 17-1: find File Types

File Type	Description
b	Block special device file
c	Character special device file
d	Directory
f	Regular file
l	Symbolic link

We can also search by file size and filename by adding some additional tests. Let's look for all the regular files that match the wildcard pattern *.JPG and are larger than 1 megabyte:

```
[me@linuxbox ~]$ find ~ -type f -name "*.JPG" -size +1M | wc -l
840
```

In this example, we add the -name test followed by the wildcard pattern. Notice that we enclose it in quotes to prevent pathname expansion by the shell. Next, we add the -size test followed by the string +1M. The leading plus sign indicates that we are looking for files larger than the specified number. A leading minus sign would change the string to mean "smaller than the specified number." Using no sign means "match the value exactly." The trailing letter M indicates that the unit of measurement is megabytes. The characters shown in Table 17-2 may be used to specify units.

Table 17-2: find Size Units

Character	Unit
b	512-byte blocks (the default if no unit is specified)
c	Bytes
w	2-byte words
k	Kilobytes (units of 1024 bytes)
M	Megabytes (units of 1,048,576 bytes)
G	Gigabytes (units of 1,073,741,824 bytes)

find supports a large number of different tests. Table 17-3 provides a rundown of the common ones. Note that in cases where a numeric argument is required, the same + and - notation discussed above can be applied.

Table 17-3: find Tests

Test	Description
-cmin *n*	Match files or directories whose content or attributes were last modified exactly *n* minutes ago. To specify fewer than *n* minutes ago, use -*n*; to specify more than *n* minutes ago, use +*n*.
-cnewer *file*	Match files or directories whose contents or attributes were last modified more recently than those of *file*.
-ctime *n*	Match files or directories whose contents or attributes (i.e., permissions) were last modified *n**24 hours ago.
-empty	Match empty files and directories.
-group *name*	Match file or directories belonging to group *name*. *name* may be expressed as either a group name or as a numeric group ID.
-iname *pattern*	Like the -name test but case insensitive.
-inum *n*	Match files with inode number *n*. This is helpful for finding all the hard links to a particular inode.
-mmin *n*	Match files or directories whose contents were modified *n* minutes ago.
-mtime *n*	Match files or directories whose contents only were last modified *n**24 hours ago.
-name *pattern*	Match files and directories with the specified wildcard *pattern*.
-newer *file*	Match files and directories whose contents were modified more recently than the specified *file*. This is very useful when writing shell scripts that perform file backups. Each time you make a backup, update a file (such as a log) and then use find to determine which files have changed since the last update.
-nouser	Match file and directories that do not belong to a valid user. This can be used to find files belonging to deleted accounts or to detect activity by attackers.
-nogroup	Match files and directories that do not belong to a valid group.

(continued)

Table 17-3 (*continued*)

Test	Description
-perm *mode*	Match files or directories that have permissions set to the specified *mode*. *mode* may be expressed by either octal or symbolic notation.
-samefile *name*	Similar to the -inum test. Matches files that share the same inode number as file *name*.
-size *n*	Match files of size *n*.
-type *c*	Match files of type *c*.
-user *name*	Match files or directories belonging to *name*. *name* may be expressed by a username or by a numeric user ID.

This is not a complete list. The find man page has all the details.

Operators

Even with all the tests that find provides, we may still need a better way to describe the *logical relationships* between the tests. For example, what if we needed to determine if all the files and subdirectories in a directory had secure permissions? We would look for all the files with permissions that are not 0600 and the directories with permissions that are not 0700. Fortunately, find provides a way to combine tests using *logical operators* to create more complex logical relationships. To express the aforementioned test, we could do this:

```
[me@linuxbox ~]$ find ~ \( -type f -not -perm 0600 \) -or \( -type d -not -perm
0700 \)
```

Yikes! That sure looks weird. What is all this stuff? Actually, the operators are not that complicated once you get to know them (see Table 17-4).

Table 17-4: find Logical Operators

Operator	Description
-and	Match if the tests on both sides of the operator are true. May be shortened to -a. Note that when no operator is present, -and is implied by default.
-or	Match if a test on either side of the operator is true. May be shortened to -o.
-not	Match if the test following the operator is false. May be shortened to -!.

Table 17-4 (*continued*)

Operator	Description
( )	Groups tests and operators together to form larger expressions. This is used to control the precedence of the logical evaluations. By default, find evaluates from left to right. It is often necessary to override the default evaluation order to obtain the desired result. Even if not needed, it is helpful sometimes to include the grouping characters to improve readability of the command. Note that since the parentheses characters have special meaning to the shell, they must be quoted when using them on the command line to allow them to be passed as arguments to find. Usually the backslash character is used to escape them.

With this list of operators in hand, let's deconstruct our find command. When viewed from the uppermost level, we see that our tests are arranged as two groupings separated by an -or operator:

```
(expression 1) -or (expression 2)
```

This makes sense, since we are searching for files with a certain set of permissions and for directories with a different set. If we are looking for both files and directories, why do we use -or instead of -and? Because as find scans through the files and directories, each one is evaluated to see if it matches the specified tests. We want to know if it is *either* a file with bad permissions *or* a directory with bad permissions. It can't be both at the same time. So if we expand the grouped expressions, we can see it this way:

```
(file with bad perms) -or (directory with bad perms)
```

Our next challenge is how to test for "bad permissions." How do we do that? Actually we don't. What we will test for is "not good permissions," since we know what "good permissions" are. In the case of files, we define *good* as 0600; for directories, 0700. The expression that will test files for "not good" permissions is:

```
-type f -and -not -perm 0600
```

and the expression for directories is:

```
-type d -and -not -perm 0700
```

As noted in Table 17-4, the -and operator can be safely removed, since it is implied by default. So if we put this all back together, we get our final command:

```
find ~ (-type f -not -perm 0600) -or (-type d -not -perm 0700)
```

However, since the parentheses have special meaning to the shell, we must escape them to prevent the shell from trying to interpret them. Preceding each one with a backslash character does the trick.

There is another feature of logical operators that is important to understand. Let's say that we have two expressions separated by a logical operator:

```
expr1 -operator expr2
```

In all cases, *expr1* will always be performed; however, the operator will determine if *expr2* is performed. Table 17-5 shows how it works.

Table 17-5: find AND/OR Logic

Results of *expr1*	Operator	*expr2* is...
True	-and	Always performed
False	-and	Never performed
True	-or	Never performed
False	-or	Always performed

Why does this happen? It's done to improve performance. Take -and, for example. We know that the expression *expr1* -and *expr2* cannot be true if the result of *expr1* is false, so there is no point in performing *expr2*. Likewise, if we have the expression *expr1* -or *expr2* and the result of *expr1* is true, there is no point in performing *expr2*, as we already know that the expression *expr1* -or *expr2* is true.

Okay, so this helps things go faster. Why is this important? Because we can rely on this behavior to control how actions are performed, as we shall soon see.

Actions

Let's get some work done! Having a list of results from our find command is useful, but what we really want to do is act on the items on the list. Fortunately, find allows actions to be performed based on the search results.

Predefined Actions

There are a set of predefined actions and several ways to apply user-defined actions. First let's look at a few of the predefined actions in Table 17-6.

Table 17-6: Predefined find Actions

Action	Description
-delete	Delete the currently matching file.
-ls	Perform the equivalent of ls -dils on the matching file. Output is sent to standard output.
-print	Output the full pathname of the matching file to standard output. This is the default action if no other action is specified.

Table 17-6 (*continued*)

Action	Description
-quit	Quit once a match has been made.

As with the tests, there are many more actions. See the find man page for full details.

In our very first example, we did this:

```
find ~
```

This command produced a list of every file and subdirectory contained within our home directory. It produced a list because the -print action is implied if no other action is specified. Thus, our command could also be expressed as

```
find ~ -print
```

We can use find to delete files that meet certain criteria. For example, to delete files that have the file extension *.BAK* (which is often used to designate backup files), we could use this command:

```
find ~ -type f -name '*.BAK' -delete
```

In this example, every file in the user's home directory (and its subdirectories) is searched for filenames ending in *.BAK*. When they are found, they are deleted.

Warning: *It should go without saying that you should **use extreme caution** when using the -delete action. Always test the command first by substituting the -print action for -delete to confirm the search results.*

Before we go on, let's take another look at how the logical operators affect actions. Consider the following command:

```
find ~ -type f -name '*.BAK' -print
```

As we have seen, this command will look for every regular file (-type f) whose name ends with *.BAK* (-name '*.BAK') and will output the relative pathname of each matching file to standard output (-print). However, the reason the command performs the way it does is determined by the logical relationships between each of the tests and actions. Remember, there is, by default, an implied -and relationship between each test and action. We could also express the command this way to make the logical relationships easier to see:

```
find ~ -type f -and -name '*.BAK' -and -print
```

With our command fully expressed, let's look at Table 17-7 to see how the logical operators affect its execution.

Table 17-7: Effect of Logical Operators

Test/Action	Is performed when...
-print	-type f and -name '*.BAK' are true.
-name '*.BAK'	-type f is true.
-type f	Is always performed, since it is the first test/action in an -and relationship.

Since the logical relationship between the tests and actions determines which of them are performed, we can see that the order of the tests and actions is important. For instance, if we were to reorder the tests and actions so that the -print action was the first one, the command would behave much differently:

```
find ~ -print -and -type f -and -name '*.BAK'
```

This version of the command will print each file (the -print action always evaluates to true) and then test for file type and the specified file extension.

User-Defined Actions

In addition to the predefined actions, we can also invoke arbitrary commands. The traditional way of doing this is with the -exec action, like this:

```
-exec command {} ;
```

where *command* is the name of a command, {} is a symbolic representation of the current pathname, and the semicolon is a required delimiter indicating the end of the command. Here's an example of using -exec to act like the -delete action discussed earlier:

```
-exec rm '{}' ';'
```

Again, since the brace and semicolon characters have special meaning to the shell, they must be quoted or escaped.

It's also possible to execute a user-defined action interactively. By using the -ok action in place of -exec, the user is prompted before execution of each specified command:

```
find ~ -type f -name 'foo*' -ok ls -l '{}' ';'
< ls ... /home/me/bin/foo > ? y
-rwxr-xr-x 1 me    me 224 2011-10-29 18:44 /home/me/bin/foo
< ls ... /home/me/foo.txt > ? y
-rw-r--r-- 1 me    me   0 2012-09-19 12:53 /home/me/foo.txt
```

In this example, we search for files with names starting with the string foo and execute the command ls -l each time one is found. Using the -ok action prompts the user before the ls command is executed.

Improving Efficiency

When the -exec action is used, it launches a new instance of the specified command each time a matching file is found. There are times when we might prefer to combine all of the search results and launch a single instance of the command. For example, rather than executing the commands like this,

```
ls -l file1
ls -l file2
```

we may prefer to execute them this way:

```
ls -l file1 file2
```

Here we cause the command to be executed only one time rather than multiple times. There are two ways we can do this: the traditional way, using the external command xargs, and the alternative way, using a new feature in find itself. We'll talk about the alternative way first.

By changing the trailing semicolon character to a plus sign, we activate the ability of find to combine the results of the search into an argument list for a single execution of the desired command. Going back to our example,

```
find ~ -type f -name 'foo*' -exec ls -l '{}' ';'
-rwxr-xr-x 1 me    me  224 2011-10-29 18:44 /home/me/bin/foo
-rw-r--r-- 1 me    me    0 2012-09-19 12:53 /home/me/foo.txt
```

will execute ls each time a matching file is found. By changing the command to

```
find ~ -type f -name 'foo*' -exec ls -l '{}' +
-rwxr-xr-x 1 me    me  224 2011-10-29 18:44 /home/me/bin/foo
-rw-r--r-- 1 me    me    0 2012-09-19 12:53 /home/me/foo.txt
```

we get the same results, but the system has to execute the ls command only once.

We can also use the xargs command to get the same result. xargs accepts input from standard input and converts it into an argument list for a specified command. With our example, we would use it like this:

```
find ~ -type f -name 'foo*' -print | xargs ls -l
-rwxr-xr-x 1 me    me  224 2011-10-29 18:44 /home/me/bin/foo
-rw-r--r-- 1 me    me    0 2012-09-19 12:53 /home/me/foo.txt
```

Here we see the output of the find command piped into xargs, which, in turn, constructs an argument list for the ls command and then executes it.

Note: *While the number of arguments that can be placed into a command line is quite large, it's not unlimited. It is possible to create commands that are too long for the shell to accept. When a command line exceeds the maximum length supported by the system, xargs executes the specified command with the maximum number of arguments possible and then repeats this process until standard input is exhausted. To see the maximum size of the command line, execute xargs with the --show-limits option.*

A Return to the Playground

It's time to put find to some (almost) practical use. First, let's create a playground with lots of subdirectories and files:

```
[me@linuxbox ~]$ mkdir -p playground/dir-{00{1..9},0{10..99},100}
[me@linuxbox ~]$ touch playground/dir-{00{1..9},0{10..99},100}/file-{A..Z}
```

Marvel in the power of the command line! With these two lines, we created a playground directory containing 100 subdirectories, each containing 26 empty files. Try that with the GUI!

The method we employed to accomplish this magic involved a familiar command (mkdir); an exotic shell expansion (braces); and a new command, touch. By combining mkdir with the -p option (which causes mkdir to create the parent directories of the specified paths) with brace expansion, we were able to create 100 directories.

The touch command is usually used to set or update the modification times of files. However, if a filename argument is that of a non-existent file, an empty file is created.

In our playground, we created 100 instances of a file named *file-A*. Let's find them:

```
[me@linuxbox ~]$ find playground -type f -name 'file-A'
```

Note that unlike ls, find does not produce results in sorted order. Its order is determined by the layout of the storage device. We can confirm that we actually have 100 instances of the file this way:

```
[me@linuxbox ~]$ find playground -type f -name 'file-A' | wc -l
100
```

Next, let's look at finding files based on their modification times. This will be helpful when creating backups or organizing files in chronological order. To do this, we will first create a reference file against which we will compare modification time:

```
[me@linuxbox ~]$ touch playground/timestamp
```

This creates an empty file named timestamp and sets its modification time to the current time. We can verify this by using another handy command, stat, which is a kind of souped-up version of ls. The stat command reveals all that the system understands about a file and its attributes:

```
[me@linuxbox ~]$ stat playground/timestamp
  File: `playground/timestamp'
  Size: 0          Blocks: 0          IO Block: 4096 regular empty file
Device: 803h/2051d Inode: 14265061 Links: 1
Access: (0644/-rw-r--r--) Uid: ( 1001/ me)   Gid: ( 1001/ me)
Access: 2012-10-08 15:15:39.000000000 -0400
Modify: 2012-10-08 15:15:39.000000000 -0400
Change: 2012-10-08 15:15:39.000000000 -0400
```

If we touch the file again and then examine it with stat, we will see that the file's times have been updated:

```
[me@linuxbox ~]$ touch playground/timestamp
[me@linuxbox ~]$ stat playground/timestamp
  File: `playground/timestamp'
  Size: 0          Blocks: 0          IO Block: 4096 regular empty file
Device: 803h/2051d Inode: 14265061 Links: 1
Access: (0644/-rw-r--r--) Uid: ( 1001/ me)   Gid: ( 1001/ me)
Access: 2012-10-08 15:23:33.000000000 -0400
Modify: 2012-10-08 15:23:33.000000000 -0400
Change: 2012-10-08 15:23:33.000000000 -0400
```

Next, let's use find to update some of our playground files:

```
[me@linuxbox ~]$ find playground -type f -name 'file-B' -exec touch '{}' ';'
```

This updates all files in the playground that are named *file-B*. Next we'll use find to identify the updated files by comparing all the files to the reference file *timestamp*:

```
[me@linuxbox ~]$ find playground -type f -newer playground/timestamp
```

The results contain all 100 instances of *file-B*. Since we performed a touch on all the files in the playground that are named *file-B* after we updated *timestamp*, they are now "newer" than *timestamp* and thus can be identified with the -newer test.

Finally, let's go back to the bad permissions test we performed earlier and apply it to *playground*:

```
[me@linuxbox ~]$ find playground \( -type f -not -perm 0600 \) -or \( -type d
-not -perm 0700 \)
```

This command lists all 100 directories and 2,600 files in *playground* (as well as *timestamp* and *playground* itself, for a total of 2,702) because none of them meets our definition of "good permissions." With our knowledge of operators and actions, we can add actions to this command to apply new permissions to the files and directories in our playground:

```
[me@linuxbox ~]$ find playground \( -type f -not -perm 0600 -exec chmod 0600
'{}' ';' \) -or \( -type d -not -perm 0700 -exec chmod 0700 '{}' ';' \)
```

On a day-to-day basis, we might find it easier to issue two commands, one for the directories and one for the files, rather than this one large compound command, but it's nice to know that we can do it this way. The important point here is to understand how operators and actions can be used together to perform useful tasks.

Options

Finally, we have the options. The options are used to control the scope of a find search. They may be included with other tests and actions when constructing find expressions. Table 17-8 lists the most commonly used options.

Table 17-8: find Options

Option	Description
-depth	Direct find to process a directory's files before the directory itself. This option is automatically applied when the -delete action is specified.
-maxdepth *levels*	Set the maximum number of levels that find will descend into a directory tree when performing tests and actions.
-mindepth *levels*	Set the minimum number of levels that find will descend into a directory tree before applying tests and actions.
-mount	Direct find not to traverse directories that are mounted on other filesystems.
-noleaf	Direct find not to optimize its search based on the assumption that it is searching a Unix-like filesystem. This is needed when scanning DOS/Windows filesystems and CD-ROMs.

18

ARCHIVING AND BACKUP

One of the primary tasks of a computer system's administrator is to keep the system's data secure. One way this is done is by performing timely backups of the system's files. Even if you're not a system administrator, it is often useful to make copies of things and to move large collections of files from place to place and from device to device.

In this chapter, we will look at several common programs that are used to manage collections of files. There are the file compression programs:

- gzip—Compress or expand files.
- bzip2—A block sorting file compressor.

the archiving programs:

- tar—Tape-archiving utility.
- zip—Package and compress files.

and the file synchronization program:

- rsync—Remote file and directory synchronization.

Compressing Files

Throughout the history of computing, there has been a struggle to get the most data into the smallest available space, whether that space be memory, storage devices, or network bandwidth. Many of the data services that we take for granted today, such as portable music players, high-definition television, or broadband Internet, owe their existence to effective *data compression* techniques.

Data compression is the process of removing *redundancy* from data. Let's consider an imaginary example. Say we had an entirely black picture file with the dimensions of 100 pixels by 100 pixels. In terms of data storage (assuming 24 bits, or 3 bytes per pixel), the image will occupy 30,000 bytes of storage: $100 \times 100 \times 3 = 30,000$.

An image that is all one color contains entirely redundant data. If we were clever, we could encode the data in such a way as to simply describe the fact that we have a block of 10,000 black pixels. So, instead of storing a block of data containing 30,000 zeros (black is usually represented in image files as zero), we could compress the data into the number 30,000, followed by a zero to represent our data. Such a data compression scheme, called *run-length encoding*, is one of the most rudimentary compression techniques. Today's techniques are much more advanced and complex, but the basic goal remains the same—get rid of redundant data.

Compression algorithms (the mathematical techniques used to carry out the compression) fall into two general categories, *lossless* and *lossy*. Lossless compression preserves all the data contained in the original. This means that when a file is restored from a compressed version, the restored file is exactly the same as the original, uncompressed version. Lossy compression, on the other hand, removes data as the compression is performed, to allow more compression to be applied. When a lossy file is restored, it does not match the original version; rather, it is a close approximation. Examples of lossy compression are JPEG (for images) and MP3 (for music). In our discussion, we will look exclusively at lossless compression, since most data on computers cannot tolerate any data loss.

gzip—Compress or Expand Files

The gzip program is used to compress one or more files. When executed, it replaces the original file with a compressed version of the original. The corresponding gunzip program is used to restore compressed files to their original, uncompressed form. Here is an example:

```
[me@linuxbox ~]$ ls -l /etc > foo.txt
[me@linuxbox ~]$ ls -l foo.*
```

```
-rw-r--r-- 1 me      me      15738 2012-10-14 07:15 foo.txt
[me@linuxbox ~]$ gzip foo.txt
[me@linuxbox ~]$ ls -l foo.*
-rw-r--r-- 1 me      me       3230 2012-10-14 07:15 foo.txt.gz
[me@linuxbox ~]$ gunzip foo.txt
[me@linuxbox ~]$ ls -l foo.*
-rw-r--r-- 1 me      me      15738 2012-10-14 07:15 foo.txt
```

In this example, we create a text file named *foo.txt* from a directory listing. Next, we run gzip, which replaces the original file with a compressed version named *foo.txt.gz*. In the directory listing of *foo.**, we see that the original file has been replaced with the compressed version and that the compressed version is about one-fifth the size of the original. We can also see that the compressed file has the same permissions and time stamp as the original.

Next, we run the gunzip program to uncompress the file. Afterward, we can see that the compressed version of the file has been replaced with the original, again with the permissions and timestamp preserved.

gzip has many options. Table 18-1 lists a few.

Table 18-1: gzip Options

Option	Description
-c	Write output to standard output and keep original files. May also be specified with --stdout and --to-stdout.
-d	Decompress. This causes gzip to act like gunzip. May also be specified with --decompress or --uncompress.
-f	Force compression even if a compressed version of the original file already exists. May also be specified with --force.
-h	Display usage information. May also be specified with --help.
-l	List compression statistics for each file compressed. May also be specified with --list.
-r	If one or more arguments on the command line are directories, recursively compress files contained within them. May also be specified with --recursive.
-t	Test the integrity of a compressed file. May also be specified with --test.
-v	Display verbose messages while compressing. May also be specified with --verbose.
-*number*	Set amount of compression. *number* is an integer in the range of 1 (fastest, least compression) to 9 (slowest, most compression). The values 1 and 9 may also be expressed as --fast and --best, respectively. The default value is 6.

Let's look again at our earlier example:

```
[me@linuxbox ~]$ gzip foo.txt
[me@linuxbox ~]$ gzip -tv foo.txt.gz
foo.txt.gz:         OK
[me@linuxbox ~]$ gzip -d foo.txt.gz
```

Here, we replaced the file *foo.txt* with a compressed version named *foo.txt.gz*. Next, we tested the integrity of the compressed version, using the -t and -v options. Finally, we decompressed the file back to its original form.

gzip can also be used in interesting ways via standard input and output:

```
[me@linuxbox ~]$ ls -l /etc | gzip > foo.txt.gz
```

This command creates a compressed version of a directory listing.

The gunzip program, which uncompresses gzip files, assumes that file-names end in the extension *.gz*, so it's not necessary to specify it, as long as the specified name is not in conflict with an existing uncompressed file:

```
[me@linuxbox ~]$ gunzip foo.txt
```

If our goal were only to view the contents of a compressed text file, we could do this:

```
[me@linuxbox ~]$ gunzip -c foo.txt | less
```

Alternatively, a program supplied with gzip, called zcat, is equivalent to gunzip with the -c option. It can be used like the cat command on gzip-compressed files:

```
[me@linuxbox ~]$ zcat foo.txt.gz | less
```

Note: *There is a zless program, too. It performs the same function as the pipeline above.*

bzip2—Higher Compression at the Cost of Speed

The bzip2 program, by Julian Seward, is similar to gzip but uses a different compression algorithm, which achieves higher levels of compression at the cost of compression speed. In most regards, it works in the same fashion as gzip. A file compressed with bzip2 is denoted with the extension *.bz2*:

```
[me@linuxbox ~]$ ls -l /etc > foo.txt
[me@linuxbox ~]$ ls -l foo.txt
-rw-r--r-- 1 me    me    15738 2012-10-17 13:51 foo.txt
[me@linuxbox ~]$ bzip2 foo.txt
[me@linuxbox ~]$ ls -l foo.txt.bz2
-rw-r--r-- 1 me    me     2792 2012-10-17 13:51 foo.txt.bz2
[me@linuxbox ~]$ bunzip2 foo.txt.bz2
```

As we can see, bzip2 can be used the same way as gzip. All the options (except for -r) that we discussed for gzip are also supported in bzip2. Note, however, that the compression level option (-*number*) has a somewhat different meaning to bzip2. bzip2 comes with bunzip2 and bzcat for decompressing files.

bzip2 also comes with the bzip2recover program, which will try to recover damaged *.bz2* files.

DON'T BE COMPRESSIVE COMPULSIVE

I occasionally see people attempting to compress a file that has already been compressed with an effective compression algorithm, by doing something like this:

```
$ gzip picture.jpg
```

Don't do it. You're probably just wasting time and space! If you apply compression to a file that is already compressed, you will actually end up with a larger file. This is because all compression techniques involve some overhead that is added to the file to describe the compression. If you try to compress a file that already contains no redundant information, the compression will not result in any savings to offset the additional overhead.

Archiving Files

A common file-management task used in conjunction with compression is *archiving*. Archiving is the process of gathering up many files and bundling them into a single large file. Archiving is often done as a part of system backups. It is also used when old data is moved from a system to some type of long-term storage.

tar—Tape Archiving Utility

In the Unix-like world of software, the tar program is the classic tool for archiving files. Its name, short for *tape archive*, reveals its roots as a tool for making backup tapes. While it is still used for that traditional task, it is equally adept on other storage devices. We often see filenames that end with the extension *.tar* or *.tgz*, which indicate a "plain" tar archive and a gzipped archive, respectively. A tar archive can consist of a group of separate files, one or more directory hierarchies, or a mixture of both. The command syntax works like this:

```
tar mode[options] pathname...
```

where *mode* is one of the operating modes shown in Table 18-2 (only a partial list is shown here; see the tar man page for a complete list).

Table 18-2: tar Modes

Mode	Description
c	Create an archive from a list of files and/or directories.
x	Extract an archive.
r	Append specified pathnames to the end of an archive.
t	List the contents of an archive.

tar uses a slightly odd way of expressing options, so we'll need some examples to show how it works. First, let's re-create our playground from the previous chapter:

```
[me@linuxbox ~]$ mkdir -p playground/dir-{00{1..9},0{10..99},100}
[me@linuxbox ~]$ touch playground/dir-{00{1..9},0{10..99},100}/file-{A..Z}
```

Next, let's create a tar archive of the entire playground:

```
[me@linuxbox ~]$ tar cf playground.tar playground
```

This command creates a tar archive named *playground.tar*, which contains the entire playground directory hierarchy. We can see that the mode and the f option, which is used to specify the name of the tar archive, may be joined together and do not require a leading dash. Note, however, that the mode must always be specified first, before any other option.

To list the contents of the archive, we can do this:

```
[me@linuxbox ~]$ tar tf playground.tar
```

For a more detailed listing, we can add the v (verbose) option:

```
[me@linuxbox ~]$ tar tvf playground.tar
```

Now, let's extract the playground in a new location. We will do this by creating a new directory named *foo*, changing the directory, and extracting the tar archive:

```
[me@linuxbox ~]$ mkdir foo
[me@linuxbox ~]$ cd foo
[me@linuxbox foo]$ tar xf ../playground.tar
[me@linuxbox foo]$ ls
playground
```

If we examine the contents of *~/foo/playground*, we see that the archive was successfully installed, creating a precise reproduction of the original files. There is one caveat, however: Unless you are operating as the superuser, files and directories extracted from archives take on the ownership of the user performing the restoration, rather than the original owner.

Another interesting behavior of tar is the way it handles pathnames in archives. The default for pathnames is relative, rather than absolute. tar does this by simply removing any leading slash from the pathname when creating the archive. To demonstrate, we will re-create our archive, this time specifying an absolute pathname:

```
[me@linuxbox foo]$ cd
[me@linuxbox ~]$ tar cf playground2.tar ~/playground
```

Remember, *~/playground* will expand into */home/me/playground* when we press the ENTER key, so we will get an absolute pathname for our demonstration. Next, we will extract the archive as before and watch what happens:

```
[me@linuxbox ~]$ cd foo
[me@linuxbox foo]$ tar xf ../playground2.tar
[me@linuxbox foo]$ ls
home     playground
[me@linuxbox foo]$ ls home
me
[me@linuxbox foo]$ ls home/me
playground
```

Here we can see that when we extracted our second archive, it re-created the directory *home/me/playground* relative to our current working directory, *~/foo*, not relative to the root directory, as would have been the case with an absolute pathname. This may seem like an odd way for it to work, but it's actually more useful this way, as it allows us to extract archives to any location rather than being forced to extract them to their original locations. Repeating the exercise with the inclusion of the verbose option (v) will give a clearer picture of what's going on.

Let's consider a hypothetical, yet practical, example of tar in action. Imagine we want to copy the home directory and its contents from one system to another and we have a large USB hard drive that we can use for the transfer. On our modern Linux system, the drive is "automagically" mounted in the */media* directory. Let's also imagine that the disk has a volume name of *BigDisk* when we attach it. To make the tar archive, we can do the following:

```
[me@linuxbox ~]$ sudo tar cf /media/BigDisk/home.tar /home
```

After the tar file is written, we unmount the drive and attach it to the second computer. Again, it is mounted at */media/BigDisk*. To extract the archive, we do this:

```
[me@linuxbox2 ~]$ cd /
[me@linuxbox2 /]$ sudo tar xf /media/BigDisk/home.tar
```

What's important to see here is that we must first change directory to / so that the extraction is relative to the root directory, since all pathnames within the archive are relative.

When extracting an archive, it's possible to limit what is extracted. For example, if we wanted to extract a single file from an archive, it could be done like this:

```
tar xf archive.tar pathname
```

By adding the trailing *pathname* to the command, we ensure that tar will restore only the specified file. Multiple pathnames may be specified. Note that the pathname must be the full, exact relative pathname as stored in the archive. When specifying pathnames, wildcards are not normally supported; however, the GNU version of tar (which is the version most often found in Linux distributions) supports them with the --wildcards option. Here is an example using our previous *playground.tar* file:

```
[me@linuxbox ~]$ cd foo
[me@linuxbox foo]$ tar xf ../playground2.tar --wildcards 'home/me/playground/
dir-*/file-A'
```

This command will extract only files matching the specified pathname including the wildcard *dir-**.

tar is often used in conjunction with find to produce archives. In this example, we will use find to produce a set of files to include in an archive:

```
[me@linuxbox ~]$ find playground -name 'file-A' -exec tar rf playground.tar '{
}' '+'
```

Here we use find to match all the files in *playground* named *file-A* and then, using the -exec action, we invoke tar in the append mode (r) to add the matching files to the archive *playground.tar*.

Using tar with find is a good way to create *incremental backups* of a directory tree or an entire system. By using find to match files newer than a timestamp file, we could create an archive that contains only files newer than the last archive, assuming that the timestamp file is updated right after each archive is created.

tar can also make use of both standard input and output. Here is a comprehensive example:

```
[me@linuxbox foo]$ cd
[me@linuxbox ~]$ find playground -name 'file-A' | tar cf - --files-from=- | gzip
> playground.tgz
```

In this example, we used the find program to produce a list of matching files and piped them into tar. If the filename - is specified, it is taken to mean standard input or output, as needed. (By the way, this convention of using - to represent standard input/output is used by a number of other programs, too.) The --files-from option (which may also be specified as -T) causes tar to read its list of pathnames from a file rather than the command line. Lastly, the archive produced by tar is piped into gzip to create the compressed archive *playground.tgz*. The *.tgz* extension is the conventional extension given to gzip-compressed tar files. The extension *.tar.gz* is also used sometimes.

While we used the gzip program externally to produce our compressed archive, modern versions of GNU tar support both gzip and bzip2 compression directly with the use of the z and j options, respectively. Using our previous example as a base, we can simplify it this way:

```
[me@linuxbox ~]$ find playground -name 'file-A' | tar czf playground.tgz -T -
```

If we had wanted to create a bzip2-compressed archive instead, we could have done this:

```
[me@linuxbox ~]$ find playground -name 'file-A' | tar cjf playground.tbz -T -
```

By simply changing the compression option from z to j (and changing the output file's extension to .tbz to indicate a bzip2-compressed file), we enabled bzip2 compression.

Another interesting use of standard input and output with the tar command involves transferring files between systems over a network. Imagine that we had two machines running a Unix-like system equipped with tar and ssh. In such a scenario, we could transfer a directory from a remote system (named remote-sys for this example) to our local system:

```
[me@linuxbox ~]$ mkdir remote-stuff
[me@linuxbox ~]$ cd remote-stuff
[me@linuxbox remote-stuff]$ ssh remote-sys 'tar cf - Documents' | tar xf -
me@remote-sys's password:
[me@linuxbox remote-stuff]$ ls
Documents
```

Here we were able to copy a directory named *Documents* from the remote system *remote-sys* to a directory within the directory named *remote-stuff* on the local system. How did we do this? First, we launched the tar program on the remote system using ssh. You will recall that ssh allows us to execute a program remotely on a networked computer and "see" the results on the local system—the standard output produced on the remote system is sent to the local system for viewing. We can take advantage of this by having tar create an archive (the c mode) and send it to standard output, rather than a file (the f option with the dash argument), thereby transporting the archive over the encrypted tunnel provided by ssh to the local system. On the local system, we execute tar and have it expand an archive (the x mode) supplied from standard input (again, the f option with the dash argument).

zip—Package and Compress Files

The zip program is both a compression tool and an archiver. The file format used by the program is familiar to Windows users, as it reads and writes *.zip* files. In Linux, however, gzip is the predominant compression program with bzip2 being a close second. Linux users mainly use zip for exchanging files with Windows systems, rather than performing compression and archiving.

In its most basic usage, zip is invoked like this:

```
zip options zipfile file...
```

For example, to make a zip archive of our playground, we would do this:

```
[me@linuxbox ~]$ zip -r playground.zip playground
```

Unless we include the -r option for recursion, only the *playground* directory (but none of its contents) is stored. Although the addition of the extension *.zip* is automatic, we will include the file extension for clarity.

During the creation of the zip archive, zip will normally display a series of messages like this:

```
  adding: playground/dir-020/file-Z (stored 0%)
  adding: playground/dir-020/file-Y (stored 0%)
  adding: playground/dir-020/file-X (stored 0%)
  adding: playground/dir-087/ (stored 0%)
  adding: playground/dir-087/file-S (stored 0%)
```

These messages show the status of each file added to the archive. zip will add files to the archive using one of two storage methods: Either it will "store" a file without compression, as shown here, or it will "deflate" the file, which performs compression. The numeric value displayed after the storage method indicates the amount of compression achieved. Since our playground contains only empty files, no compression is performed on its contents.

Extracting the contents of a zip file is straightforward when using the unzip program:

```
[me@linuxbox ~]$ cd foo
[me@linuxbox foo]$ unzip ../playground.zip
```

One thing to note about zip (as opposed to tar) is that if an existing archive is specified, it is updated rather than replaced. This means that the existing archive is preserved, but new files are added and matching files are replaced.

Files may be listed and extracted selectively from a zip archive by specifying them to unzip:

```
[me@linuxbox ~]$ unzip -l playground.zip playground/dir-087/file-Z
Archive:  ./playground.zip
  Length     Date   Time    Name
 --------    ----   ----    ----
        0  10-05-12 09:25   playground/dir-087/file-Z
 --------                   -------
        0                   1 file
[me@linuxbox ~]$ cd foo
[me@linuxbox foo]$ unzip ../playground.zip playground/dir-087/file-Z
Archive:  ../playground.zip
replace playground/dir-087/file-Z? [y]es, [n]o, [A]ll, [N]one, [r]ename: y
 extracting: playground/dir-087/file-Z
```

Using the -l option causes unzip to merely list the contents of the archive without extracting the file. If no file(s) are specified, unzip will list all files in the archive. The -v option can be added to increase the verbosity of the listing. Note that when the archive extraction conflicts with an existing file, the user is prompted before the file is replaced.

Like tar, zip can make use of standard input and output, though its implementation is somewhat less useful. It is possible to pipe a list of filenames to zip via the -@ option:

```
[me@linuxbox foo]$ cd
[me@linuxbox ~]$ find playground -name "file-A" | zip -@ file-A.zip
```

Here we use find to generate a list of files matching the test -name "file-A" and then pipe the list into zip, which creates the archive *file-A.zip* containing the selected files.

zip also supports writing its output to standard output, but its use is limited because very few programs can make use of the output. Unfortunately, the unzip program does not accept standard input. This prevents zip and unzip from being used together to perform network file copying like tar.

zip can, however, accept standard input, so it can be used to compress the output of other programs:

```
[me@linuxbox ~]$ ls -l /etc/ | zip ls-etc.zip -
  adding: - (deflated 80%)
```

In this example, we pipe the output of ls into zip. Like tar, zip interprets the trailing dash as "use standard input for the input file."

The unzip program allows its output to be sent to standard output when the -p (for pipe) option is specified:

```
[me@linuxbox ~]$ unzip -p ls-etc.zip | less
```

We touched on some of the basic things that zip and unzip can do. They both have a lot of options that add to their flexibility, though some are platform specific to other systems. The man pages for both zip and unzip are pretty good and contain useful examples.

Synchronizing Files and Directories

A common strategy for maintaining a backup copy of a system involves keeping one or more directories synchronized with another directory (or directories) located on either the local system (usually a removable storage device of some kind) or a remote system. We might, for example, have a local copy of a website under development and synchronize it from time to time with the "live" copy on a remote web server.

rsync—Remote File and Directory Synchronization

In the Unix-like world, the preferred tool for this task is rsync. This program can synchronize both local and remote directories by using the *rsync remote-update protocol*, which allows rsync to quickly detect the differences between two directories and perform the minimum amount of copying required to bring them into sync. This makes rsync very fast and economical to use, compared to other kinds of copy programs.

rsync is invoked like this:

```
rsync options source destination
```

where *source* and *destination* are each one of the following:

- A local file or directory
- A remote file or directory in the form of *[user@]host:path*
- A remote rsync server specified with a URI of *rsync://[user@]host[:port]/path*

Note that either the source or the destination must be a local file. Remote-to-remote copying is not supported.

Let's try rsync out on some local files. First, let's clean out our *foo* directory:

```
[me@linuxbox ~]$ rm -rf foo/*
```

Next, we'll synchronize the *playground* directory with a corresponding copy in *foo*:

```
[me@linuxbox ~]$ rsync -av playground foo
```

We've included both the -a option (for archiving—causes recursion and preservation of file attributes) and the -v option (verbose output) to make a *mirror* of the *playground* directory within *foo*. While the command runs, we will see a list of the files and directories being copied. At the end, we will see a summary message like this, indicating the amount of copying performed:

```
sent 135759 bytes  received 57870 bytes  387258.00 bytes/sec
total size is 3230  speedup is 0.02
```

If we run the command again, we will see a different result:

```
[me@linuxbox ~]$ rsync -av playgound foo
building file list ... done

 sent 22635 bytes  received 20 bytes  45310.00 bytes/sec
total size is 3230  speedup is 0.14
```

Notice that there was no listing of files. This is because rsync detected that there were no differences between *~/playground* and *~/foo/playground*, and therefore it didn't need to copy anything. If we modify a file in *playground* and run rsync again, we see that rsync detected the change and copied only the updated file.

```
[me@linuxbox ~]$ touch playground/dir-099/file-Z
[me@linuxbox ~]$ rsync -av playground foo
building file list ... done
playground/dir-099/file-Z
sent 22685 bytes  received 42 bytes  45454.00 bytes/sec
total size is 3230  speedup is 0.14
```

As a practical example, let's consider the imaginary external hard drive that we used earlier with tar. If we attach the drive to our system and, once again, it is mounted at */media/BigDisk*, we can perform a useful system backup by first creating a directory named */backup* on the external drive and then using rsync to copy the most important stuff from our system to the external drive:

```
[me@linuxbox ~]$ mkdir /media/BigDisk/backup
[me@linuxbox ~]$ sudo rsync -av --delete /etc /home /usr/local /media/BigDisk/
backup
```

In this example, we copied the */etc, /home,* and */usr/local* directories from our system to our imaginary storage device. We included the --delete option to remove files that may have existed on the backup device that no longer existed on the source device (this is irrelevant the first time we make a backup but will be useful on subsequent copies). Repeating the procedure of attaching the external drive and running this rsync command would be a useful (though not ideal) way of keeping a small system backed up. Of course, an alias would be helpful here, too. We could create an alias and add it to our *.bashrc* file to provide this feature:

```
alias backup='sudo rsync -av --delete /etc /home /usr/local /media/BigDisk/bac
kup'
```

Now all we have to do is attach our external drive and run the backup command to do the job.

Using rsync over a Network

One of the real beauties of rsync is that it can be used to copy files over a network. After all, the *r* in rsync stands for *remote*. Remote copying can be done in one of two ways.

The first way is with another system that has rsync installed, along with a remote shell program such as ssh. Let's say we had another system on our local network with a lot of available hard drive space and we wanted to perform our backup operation using the remote system instead of an external drive. Assuming that it already had a directory named */backup* where we could deliver our files, we could do this:

```
[me@linuxbox ~]$ sudo rsync -av --delete --rsh=ssh /etc /home /usr/local remote-
sys:/backup
```

We made two changes to our command to facilitate the network copy. First, we added the --rsh=ssh option, which instructs rsync to use the ssh program as its remote shell. In this way, we were able to use an SSH-encrypted tunnel to securely transfer the data from the local system to the remote host. Second, we specified the remote host by prefixing its name (in this case the remote host is named *remote-sys*) to the destination pathname.

The second way that rsync can be used to synchronize files over a network is by using an *rysnc server*. rsync can be configured to run as a daemon and listen to incoming requests for synchronization. This is often done to allow mirroring of a remote system. For example, Red Hat Software maintains a large repository of software packages under development for its Fedora distribution. It is useful for software testers to mirror this collection during the testing phase of the distribution release cycle. Since files in the repository change frequently (often more than once a day), it is desirable to maintain a local mirror by periodic synchronization, rather than by bulk copying of the repository. One of these repositories is kept at Georgia Tech; we could mirror it using our local copy of rsync and Georgia Tech's rsync server like this:

```
[me@linuxbox ~]$ mkdir fedora-devel
[me@linuxbox ~]$ rsync -av --delete rsync://rsync.gtlib.gatech.edu/fedora-
linux-core/development/i386/os fedora-devel
```

In this example, we use the URI of the remote rsync server, which consists of a protocol (*rsync://*), followed by the remote hostname (*rsync.gtlib .gatech.edu*), followed by the pathname of the repository.

19

REGULAR EXPRESSIONS

In the next few chapters, we are going to look at tools used to manipulate text. As we have seen, text data plays an important role on all Unix-like systems, such as Linux. But before we can fully appreciate all of the features offered by these tools, we have to examine a technology that is frequently associated with the most sophisticated uses of these tools—regular expressions.

As we have navigated the many features and facilities offered by the command line, we have encountered some truly arcane shell features and commands, such as shell expansion and quoting, keyboard shortcuts, and command history, not to mention the vi editor. Regular expressions continue this "tradition" and may be (arguably) the most arcane feature of them all. This is not to suggest that the time it takes to learn about them is not worth the effort. Quite the contrary. A good understanding will enable us to perform amazing feats, though their full value may not be immediately apparent.

Are Regular Expressions?

Simply put, *regular expressions* are symbolic notations used to identify patterns in text. In some ways, they resemble the shell's wildcard method of matching file- and pathnames but on a much grander scale. Regular expressions are supported by many command-line tools and by most programming languages to facilitate the solution of text manipulation problems. However, to further confuse things, not all regular expressions are the same; they vary slightly from tool to tool and from programming language to language. For our discussion, we will limit ourselves to regular expressions as described in the POSIX standard (which will cover most of the command-line tools), as opposed to many programming languages (most notably Perl), which use slightly larger and richer sets of notations.

grep—Search Through Text

The main program we will use to work with regular expressions is our old pal, grep. The name *grep* is actually derived from the phrase *global regular expression print*, so we can see that grep has something to do with regular expressions. In essence, grep searches text files for the occurrence of a specified regular expression and outputs any line containing a match to standard output.

So far, we have used grep with fixed strings, like so:

```
[me@linuxbox ~]$ ls /usr/bin | grep zip
```

This will list all the files in the */usr/bin* directory whose names contain the substring zip.

The grep program accepts options and arguments this way:

grep [*options*] *regex* [*file*...]

where *regex* is a regular expression.

Table 19-1 lists the commonly used grep options.

Table19-1: grep Options

Option	Description
-i	Ignore case. Do not distinguish between upper- and lowercase characters. May also be specified --ignore-case.
-v	Invert match. Normally, grep prints lines that contain a match. This option causes grep to print every line that does not contain a match. May also be specified --invert-match.
-c	Print the number of matches (or non-matches if the -v option is also specified) instead of the lines themselves. May also be specified --count.

Table 19-1 (*continued*)

Option	Description
-l	Print the name of each file that contains a match instead of the lines themselves. May also be specified --files-with-matches.
-L	Like the -l option, but print only the names of files that do not contain matches. May also be specified --files-without-match.
-n	Prefix each matching line with the number of the line within the file. May also be specified --line-number.
-h	For multifile searches, suppress the output of filenames. May also be specified --no-filename.

In order to more fully explore grep, let's create some text files to search:

```
[me@linuxbox ~]$ ls /bin > dirlist-bin.txt
[me@linuxbox ~]$ ls /usr/bin > dirlist-usr-bin.txt
[me@linuxbox ~]$ ls /sbin > dirlist-sbin.txt
[me@linuxbox ~]$ ls /usr/sbin > dirlist-usr-sbin.txt
[me@linuxbox ~]$ ls dirlist*.txt
dirlist-bin.txt    dirlist-sbin.txt      dirlist-usr-sbin.txt
dirlist-usr-bin.txt
```

We can perform a simple search of our list of files like this:

```
[me@linuxbox ~]$ grep bzip dirlist*.txt
dirlist-bin.txt:bzip2
dirlist-bin.txt:bzip2recover
```

In this example, grep searches all of the listed files for the string bzip and finds two matches, both in the file *dirlist-bin.txt*. If we were interested in only the files that contained matches rather than the matches themselves, we could specify the -l option:

```
[me@linuxbox ~]$ grep -l bzip dirlist*.txt
dirlist-bin.txt
```

Conversely, if we wanted to see a list of only the files that did not contain a match, we could do this:

```
[me@linuxbox ~]$ grep -L bzip dirlist*.txt
dirlist-sbin.txt
dirlist-usr-bin.txt
dirlist-usr-sbin.txt
```

Metacharacters and Literals

While it may not seem apparent, our grep searches have been using regular expressions all along, albeit very simple ones. The regular expression bzip is taken to mean that a match will occur only if the line in the file contains at least four characters and that somewhere in the line the characters *b, z, i,* and *p* are found in that order, with no other characters in between. The characters in the string bzip are all *literal characters*, in that they match themselves. In addition to literals, regular expressions may also include *metacharacters,* which are used to specify more complex matches. Regular expression metacharacters consist of the following:

Metacharacters :

```
^ $ . [ ] { } - ? * + ( ) | \
```

All other characters are considered literals, though the backslash character is used in a few cases to create *metasequences,* as well as allowing the metacharacters to be escaped and treated as literals instead of being interpreted as metacharacters.

Note: *As we can see, many of the regular-expression metacharacters are also characters that have meaning to the shell when expansion is performed. When we pass regular expressions containing metacharacters on the command line, it is vital that they be enclosed in quotes to prevent the shell from attempting to expand them.*

The Any Character

The first metacharacter we will look at is the dot or period character, which is used to match any character. If we include it in a regular expression, it will match any character in that character position. Here's an example:

```
[me@linuxbox ~]$ grep -h '.zip' dirlist*.txt
bunzip2
bzip2
bzip2recover
gunzip
gzip
funzip
gpg-zip
preunzip
prezip
prezip-bin
unzip
unzipsfx
```

to demonstrate . is metacharacter rather than normal character

We searched for any line in our files that matches the regular expression .zip. There are a couple of interesting things to note about the results. Notice that the zip program was not found. This is because the inclusion of the dot metacharacter in our regular expression increased the length of the required match to four characters; because the name *zip* contains only three, it does not match. Also, if any files in our lists had contained the file extension *.zip,* they would have been matched, because the period character in the file extension is treated as "any character," too.

pre-fix *postfix*

Anchors

The caret (^) and dollar sign ($) characters are treated as *anchors* in regular expressions. This means that they cause the match to occur only if the regular expression is found at the beginning of the line (^) or at the end of the line ($).

```
[me@linuxbox ~]$ grep -h '^zip' dirlist*.txt
zip
zipcloak
zipgrep
zipinfo
zipnote
zipsplit
[me@linuxbox ~]$ grep -h 'zip$' dirlist*.txt
gunzip
gzip
funzip
gpg-zip
preunzip
prezip
unzip
zip
[me@linuxbox ~]$ grep -h '^zip$' dirlist*.txt
zip
```

Here we searched the list of files for the string zip located at the beginning of the line, the end of the line, and on a line where it is at both the beginning and the end of the line (i.e., by itself on the line.) Note that the regular expression ^$ (a beginning and an end with nothing in between) will match blank lines.

A CROSSWORD PUZZLE HELPER

My wife loves crossword puzzles, and she will sometimes ask me for help with a particular question. Something like, "What's a five-letter word whose third letter is *j* and last letter is *r* that means . . . ?" This kind of question got me thinking.

Did you know that your Linux system contains a dictionary? It does. Take a look in the */usr/share/dict* directory and you might find one, or several. The dictionary files located there are just long lists of words, one per line, arranged in alphabetical order. On my system, the *words* file contains just over 98,500 words. To find possible answers to the crossword puzzle question above, we could do this:

```
[me@linuxbox ~]$ grep -i '^..j.r$' /usr/share/dict/words
Major
major
```

Using this regular expression, we can find all the words in our dictionary file that are five letters long and have a *j* in the third position and an *r* in the last position.

Bracket Expressions and Character Classes

In addition to matching any character at a given position in our regular expression, we can also match a single character from a specified set of characters by using *bracket expressions*. With bracket expressions, we can specify a set of characters (including characters that would otherwise be interpreted as metacharacters) to be matched. In this example, using a two-character set, we match any line that contains the string bzip or gzip:

```
[me@linuxbox ~]$ grep -h '[bg]zip' dirlist*.txt
bzip2
bzip2recover
gzip
```

A set may contain any number of characters, and metacharacters lose their special meaning when placed within brackets. However, there are two cases in which metacharacters are used within bracket expressions and have different meanings. The first is the caret (^), which is used to indicate negation; the second is the dash (-), which is used to indicate a character range.

Negation

If the first character in a bracket expression is a caret (^), the remaining characters are taken to be a set of characters that must not be present at the given character position. We do this by modifying our previous example:

```
[me@linuxbox ~]$ grep -h '[^bg]zip' dirlist*.txt
bunzip2
gunzip
funzip
gpg-zip
preunzip
prezip
prezip-bin
unzip
unzipsfx
```

With negation activated, we get a list of files that contain the string zip preceded by any character except *b* or *g*. Notice that the file *zip* was not found. A negated character set still requires a character at the given position, but the character must not be a member of the negated set.

The caret character invokes negation only if it is the first character within a bracket expression; otherwise, it loses its special meaning and becomes an ordinary character in the set.

Traditional Character Ranges

If we wanted to construct a regular expression that would find every file in our lists whose name begins with an uppercase letter, we could do this:

```
[me@linuxbox ~]$ grep -h '^[ABCDEFGHIJKLMNOPQRSTUVWXZY]' dirlist*.txt
```

It's just a matter of putting all 26 uppercase letters in a bracket expression. But the idea of all that typing is deeply troubling, so there is another way:

```
[me@linuxbox ~]$ grep -h '^[A-Z]' dirlist*.txt
MAKEDEV
ControlPanel
GET
HEAD
POST
X
X11
Xorg
MAKEFLOPPIES
NetworkManager
NetworkManagerDispatcher
```

By using a 3-character range, we can abbreviate the 26 letters. Any range of characters can be expressed this way, including multiple ranges such as this expression, which matches all filenames starting with letters and numbers:

```
[me@linuxbox ~]$ grep -h '^[A-Za-z0-9]' dirlist*.txt
```
normal expression

In character ranges, we see that the dash character is treated specially, so how do we actually include a dash character in a bracket expression? By making it the first character in the expression. Consider

```
[me@linuxbox ~]$ grep -h '[A-Z]' dirlist*.txt
```

This will match every filename containing an uppercase letter. This, on the other hand,

```
[me@linuxbox ~]$ grep -h '[-AZ]' dirlist*.txt
```

will match every filename containing a dash, an uppercase *A*, or an uppercase *Z*.

POSIX Character Classes

The traditional character ranges are an easily understood and effective way to handle the problem of quickly specifying sets of characters. Unfortunately, they don't always work. While we have not encountered any problems with our use of grep so far, we might run into problems using other programs.

Back in Chapter 4, we looked at how wildcards are used to perform pathname expansion. In that discussion, we said that character ranges could be used in a manner almost identical to the way they are used in regular expressions, but here's the problem:

```
[me@linuxbox ~]$ ls /usr/sbin/[ABCDEFGHIJKLMNOPQRSTUVWXYZ]*
/usr/sbin/MAKEFLOPPIES
/usr/sbin/NetworkManagerDispatcher
/usr/sbin/NetworkManager
```

(Depending on the Linux distribution, we will get a different list of files, possibly an empty list. This example is from Ubuntu.) This command produces the expected result—a list of only the files whose names begin with an uppercase letter. But with this command we get an entirely different result (only a partial listing of the results is shown):

```
[me@linuxbox ~]$ ls /usr/sbin/[A-Z]*
/usr/sbin/biosdecode
/usr/sbin/chat
/usr/sbin/chgpasswd
/usr/sbin/chpasswd
/usr/sbin/chroot
/usr/sbin/cleanup-info
/usr/sbin/complain
/usr/sbin/console-kit-daemon
```

Why is that? It's a long story, but here's the short version.

Back when Unix was first developed, it only knew about ASCII characters, and this feature reflects that fact. In ASCII, the first 32 characters (numbers 0–31) are control codes (things like tabs, backspaces, and carriage returns). The next 32 (32–63) contain printable characters, including most punctuation characters and the numerals zero through nine. The next 32 (numbers 64–95) contain the uppercase letters and a few more punctuation symbols. The final 31 (numbers 96–127) contain the lowercase letters and yet more punctuation symbols. Based on this arrangement, systems using ASCII used a *collation order* that looked like this:

ABCDEFGHIJKLMNOPQRSTUVWXYZabcdefghijklmnopqrstuvwxyz

This differs from proper dictionary order, which is like this:

aAbBcCdDeEfFgGhHiIjJkKlLmMnNoOpPqQrRsStTuUvVwWxXyYzZ

As the popularity of Unix spread beyond the United States, there grew a need to support characters not found in US English. The ASCII table was expanded to use a full 8 bits, adding character numbers 128–255, which accommodated many more languages. To support this ability, the POSIX standards introduced a concept called a *locale*, which could be adjusted to select the character set needed for a particular location. We can see the language setting of our system using this command:

```
[me@linuxbox ~]$ echo $LANG
en_US.UTF-8
```

With this setting, POSIX-compliant applications will use a dictionary collation order rather than ASCII order. This explains the behavior of the commands above. A character range of [A-Z], when interpreted in dictionary order, includes all of the alphabetic characters except the lowercase *a*—hence our results.

To partially work around this problem, the POSIX standard includes a number of character classes, which provide useful ranges of characters. They are described in Table 19-2.

Table 19-2: POSIX Character Classes

Character Class	Description
[:alnum:]	The alphanumeric characters; in ASCII, equivalent to [A-Za-z0-9]
[:word:]	The same as [:alnum:], with the addition of the underscore character (_)
[:alpha:]	The alphabetic characters; in ASCII, equivalent to [A-Za-z]
[:blank:]	Includes the space and tab characters
[:cntrl:]	The ASCII control codes; includes the ASCII characters 0 through 31 and 127
[:digit:]	The numerals 0 through 9
[:graph:]	The visible characters; in ASCII, includes characters 33 through 126
[:lower:]	The lowercase letters
[:punct:]	The punctuation characters; in ASCII, equivalent to [-!"#$%&'()*+,./:;<=>?@[\\\]_`{|}~]
[:print:]	The printable characters; all the characters in [:graph:] plus the space character
[:space:]	The whitespace characters including space, tab, carriage return, newline, vertical tab, and form feed; in ASCII, equivalent to [\t\r\n\v\f]
[:upper:]	The uppercase characters
[:xdigit:]	Characters used to express hexadecimal numbers; in ASCII, equivalent to [0-9A-Fa-f]

Even with the character classes, there is still no convenient way to express partial ranges, such as [A-M].

Using character classes, we can repeat our directory listing and see an improved result.

```
[me@linuxbox ~]$ ls /usr/sbin/[[:upper:]]*
/usr/sbin/MAKEFLOPPIES
/usr/sbin/NetworkManagerDispatcher
/usr/sbin/NetworkManager
```

Remember, however, that this is not an example of a regular expression; rather it is the shell performing pathname expansion. We show it here because POSIX character classes can be used for both.

REVERTING TO TRADITIONAL COLLATION ORDER

You can opt to have your system use the traditional (ASCII) collation order by changing the value of the LANG environment variable. As we saw in the previous section, the LANG variable contains the name of the language and character set used in your locale. This value was originally determined when you selected an installation language as your Linux was installed.

To see the locale settings, use the locale command:

```
[me@linuxbox ~]$ locale
LANG=en_US.UTF-8
LC_CTYPE="en_US.UTF-8"
LC_NUMERIC="en_US.UTF-8"
LC_TIME="en_US.UTF-8"
LC_COLLATE="en_US.UTF-8"
LC_MONETARY="en_US.UTF-8"
LC_MESSAGES="en_US.UTF-8"
LC_PAPER="en_US.UTF-8"
LC_NAME="en_US.UTF-8"
LC_ADDRESS="en_US.UTF-8"
LC_TELEPHONE="en_US.UTF-8"
LC_MEASUREMENT="en_US.UTF-8"
LC_IDENTIFICATION="en_US.UTF-8"
LC_ALL=
```

To change the locale to use the traditional Unix behaviors, set the LANG variable to POSIX:

```
[me@linuxbox ~]$ export LANG=POSIX
```

Note that this change converts the system to use US English (more specifically, ASCII) for its character set, so be sure this is really what you want.

You can make this change permanent by adding this line to your *.bashrc* file:

```
export LANG=POSIX
```

POSIX Basic vs. Extended Regular Expressions

Just when we thought this couldn't get any more confusing, we discover that POSIX also splits regular expression implementations into two kinds: *basic regular expressions (BRE)* and *extended regular expressions (ERE)*. The features we have covered so far are supported by any application that is POSIX compliant and implements BRE. Our grep program is one such program.

What's the difference between BRE and ERE? It's a matter of metacharacters. With BRE, the following metacharacters are recognized: ^ $. [ ] *
All other characters are considered literals. With ERE, the following metacharacters (and their associated functions) are added: ( ) { } ? + |

However (and this is the fun part), the characters () {} are treated as metacharacters in BRE *if* they are escaped with a backslash, whereas with ERE, preceding any metacharacter with a backslash causes it to be treated as a literal.

Since the features we are going to discuss next are part of ERE, we are going to need to use a different grep. Traditionally, this has been performed by the egrep program, but the GNU version of grep also supports extended regular expressions when the -E option is used.

POSIX

During the 1980s, Unix became a very popular commercial operating system, but by 1988, the Unix world was in turmoil. Many computer manufacturers had licensed the Unix source code from its creators AT&T, and were supplying various versions of the operating system with their systems. However, in their efforts to create product differentiation, each manufacturer added proprietary changes and extensions. This started to limit the compatibility of the software. As always with proprietary vendors, each was trying to play a winning game of "lock-in" with their customers. This dark time in the history of Unix is known today as *the Balkanization*.

Enter the IEEE (Institute of Electrical and Electronics Engineers). In the mid-1980s, the IEEE began developing a set of standards that would define how Unix (and Unix-like) systems would perform. These standards, formally known as IEEE 1003, define the *application programming interfaces (APIs)*, the shell and utilities that are to be found on a standard Unix-like system. The name *POSIX*, which stands for *Portable Operating System Interface* (with the *X* added to the end for extra snappiness), was suggested by Richard Stallman (yes, *that* Richard Stallman) and was adopted by the IEEE.

Alternation

The first of the extended regular expression features we will discuss is called *alternation*, which is the facility that allows a match to occur from among a set of expressions. Just as a bracket expression allows a single character to match from a set of specified characters, alternation allows matches from a set of strings or other regular expressions.

To demonstrate, we'll use grep in conjunction with echo. First, let's try a plain old string match:

```
[me@linuxbox ~]$ echo "AAA" | grep AAA
AAA
[me@linuxbox ~]$ echo "BBB" | grep AAA
[me@linuxbox ~]$
```

A pretty straightforward example, in which we pipe the output of echo into grep and see the results. When a match occurs, we see it printed out; when no match occurs, we see no results.

Now we'll add alternation, signified by the vertical pipe metacharacter:

```
[me@linuxbox ~]$ echo "AAA" | grep -E 'AAA|BBB'
AAA
[me@linuxbox ~]$ echo "BBB" | grep -E 'AAA|BBB'
BBB
[me@linuxbox ~]$ echo "CCC" | grep -E 'AAA|BBB'
[me@linuxbox ~]$
```

Here we see the regular expression 'AAA|BBB', which means "match either the string AAA or the string BBB." Notice that since this is an extended feature, we added the -E option to grep (though we could have used the egrep program instead), and we enclosed the regular expression in quotes to prevent the shell from interpreting the vertical pipe metacharacter as a pipe operator. Alternation is not limited to two choices:

```
[me@linuxbox ~]$ echo "AAA" | grep -E 'AAA|BBB|CCC'
AAA
```

To combine alternation with other regular-expression elements, we can use () to separate the alternation:

```
[me@linuxbox ~]$ grep -Eh '^(bz|gz|zip)' dirlist*.txt
```

This expression will match the filenames in our lists that start with either bz, gz, or zip. If we leave off the parentheses, the meaning of this regular expression changes to match any filename that begins with bz *or contains* gz *or contains* zip:

```
[me@linuxbox ~]$ grep -Eh '^bz|gz|zip' dirlist*.txt
```

Quantifiers

Extended regular expressions support several ways to specify the number of times an element is matched.

?—Match an Element Zero Times or One Time

This quantifier means, in effect, "Make the preceding element optional." Let's say we wanted to check a phone number for validity and we considered a phone number to be valid if it matched either of these two forms, *(nnn) nnn-nnnn* or *nnn nnn-nnnn*, where *n* is a numeral. We could construct a regular expression like this:

$$^\(?[0-9][0-9][0-9]\)?\ [0-9][0-9][0-9]-[0-9][0-9][0-9][0-9]\$$$

In this expression, we follow the parentheses characters with question marks to indicate that they are to be matched zero or one time. Again, since the parentheses are normally metacharacters (in ERE), we precede them with backslashes to cause them to be treated as literals instead.

Let's try it:

```
[me@linuxbox ~]$ echo "(555) 123-4567" | grep -E '^\(?[0-9][0-9][0-9]\)? [0-9]
[0-9][0-9]$'
(555) 123-4567
[me@linuxbox ~]$ echo "555 123-4567" | grep -E '^\(?[0-9][0-9][0-9]\)? [0-9]
[0-9][0-9]-[0-9][0-9][0-9][0-9]$'
555 123-4567
[me@linuxbox ~]$ echo "AAA 123-4567" | grep -E '^\(?[0-9][0-9][0-9]\)? [0-9]
[0-9][0-9]-[0-9][0-9][0-9][0-9]$'
[me@linuxbox ~]$
```

Here we see that the expression matches both forms of the phone number but does not match one containing non-numeric characters.

*—Match an Element Zero or More Times

Like the ? metacharacter, the * is used to denote an optional item; however, unlike the ?, the item may occur any number of times, not just once. Let's say we want to see if a string is a sentence; that is, it starts with an uppercase letter, then contains any number of upper- and lowercase letters and spaces, and ends with a period. To match this (very crude) definition of a sentence, we could use a regular expression like this:

[[:upper:]][[:upper:][:lower:]]*\.

The expression consists of three items: a bracket expression containing the [:upper:] character class, a bracket expression containing both the [:upper:] and [:lower:] character classes and a space, and a period escaped with a backslash. The second element is trailed with an * metacharacter so that after the leading uppercase letter in our sentence, any number of upper- and lowercase letters and spaces may follow it and still match:

```
[me@linuxbox ~]$ echo "This works." | grep -E '[[:upper:]][[:upper:][:lower:]
 ]*\.'
This works.
[me@linuxbox ~]$ echo "This Works." | grep -E '[[:upper:]][[:upper:][:lower:]
 ]*\.'
This Works.
[me@linuxbox ~]$ echo "this does not" | grep -E '[[:upper:]][[:upper:][:lower:
] ]*\.'
[me@linuxbox ~]$
```

The expression matches the first two tests, but not the third, since it lacks the required leading uppercase character and trailing period.

+—Match an Element One or More Times

The + metacharacter works much like the *, except it requires at least one instance of the preceding element to cause a match. Here is a regular expression that will match only lines consisting of groups of one or more alphabetic characters separated by single spaces:

^([[:alpha:]]+ ?)+$

Let's try it:

```
[me@linuxbox ~]$ echo "This that" | grep -E '^([[:alpha:]]+ ?)+$'
This that
[me@linuxbox ~]$ echo "a b c" | grep -E '^([[:alpha:]]+ ?)+$'
a b c
[me@linuxbox ~]$ echo "a b 9" | grep -E '^([[:alpha:]]+ ?)+$'
[me@linuxbox ~]$ echo "abc  d" | grep -E '^([[:alpha:]]+ ?)+$'
[me@linuxbox ~]$
```

We see that this expression does not match the line "a b 9", because it contains a non-alphabetic character; nor does it match "abc d", because more than one space character separates the characters *c* and *d*.

{ }—Match an Element a Specific Number of Times

The { and } metacharacters are used to express minimum and maximum numbers of required matches. They may be specified in four possible ways, as shown in Table 19-3.

Table 19-3: Specifying the Number of Matches

Specifier	Meaning
{*n*}	Match the preceding element if it occurs exactly *n* times.
{*n,m*}	Match the preceding element if it occurs at least *n* times, but no more than *m* times.
{*n,*}	Match the preceding element if it occurs *n* or more times.
{*,m*}	Match the preceding element if it occurs no more than *m* times.

Going back to our earlier example with the phone numbers, we can use this method of specifying repetitions to simplify our original regular expression from

$$^\backslash(?[0-9][0-9][0-9]\backslash)? \ \ [0-9][0-9][0-9]-[0-9][0-9][0-9][0-9]\$$$

to

$$^\backslash(?[0-9]\{3\}\backslash)? \ \ [0-9]\{3\}-[0-9]\{4\}\$$$

Let's try it:

```
[me@linuxbox ~]$ echo "(555) 123-4567" | grep -E '^\(?[0-9]{3}\)? [0-
9]{4}$'
(555) 123-4567
[me@linuxbox ~]$ echo "555 123-4567" | grep -E '^\(?[0-9]{3}\)? [0-9]{3}-[0-9]
{4}$'
555 123-4567
[me@linuxbox ~]$ echo "5555 123-4567" | grep -E '^\(?[0-9]{3}\)? [0-9]{3}-[0-9
]{4}$'
[me@linuxbox ~]$
```

As we can see, our revised expression can successfully validate numbers both with and without the parentheses, while rejecting those numbers that are not properly formatted.

Putting Regular Expressions to Work

Let's look at some of the commands we already know and see how they can be used with regular expressions.

Validating a Phone List with grep

In our earlier example, we looked at single phone numbers and checked them for proper formatting. A more realistic scenario would be checking a list of numbers instead, so let's make a list. We'll do this by reciting a magical incantation to the command line. It will be magic because we have not covered most of the commands involved, but worry not—we will get there in future chapters. Here is the incantation:

```
[me@linuxbox ~]$ for i in {1..10}; do echo "(${RANDOM:0:3}) ${RANDOM:0:3}-$
{RANDOM:0:4}" >> phonelist.txt; done
```

This command will produce a file named *phonelist.txt* containing 10 phone numbers. Each time the command is repeated, another 10 numbers are added to the list. We can also change the value 10 near the beginning of the command to produce more or fewer phone numbers. If we examine the contents of the file, however, we see we have a problem:

```
[me@linuxbox ~]$ cat phonelist.txt
(232) 298-2265
(624) 381-1078
(540) 126-1980
(874) 163-2885
(286) 254-2860
(292) 108-518
(129) 44-1379
(458) 273-1642
(686) 299-8268
(198) 307-2440
```

Some of the numbers are malformed, which is perfect for our purposes because we will use grep to validate them.

One useful method of validation would be to scan the file for invalid numbers and display the resulting list.

```
[me@linuxbox ~]$ grep -Ev '^\([0-9]{3}\) [0-9]{3}-[0-9]{4}$' phonelist.txt
(292) 108-518
(129) 44-1379
[me@linuxbox ~]$
```

Here we use the -v option to produce an inverse match so that we will output only the lines in the list that do not match the specified expression.

The expression itself includes the anchor metacharacters at each end to ensure that the number has no extra characters at either end. This expression also requires that the parentheses be present in a valid number, unlike our earlier phone number example.

Finding Ugly Filenames with find

The find command supports a test based on a regular expression. There is an important consideration to keep in mind when using regular expressions in find versus grep. Whereas grep will print a line when the line *contains* a string that matches an expression, find requires that the pathname *exactly match* the regular expression. In the following example, we will use find with a regular expression to find every pathname that contains any character that is not a member of the following set:

    [-_./0-9a-zA-Z]

Such a scan would reveal pathnames that contain embedded spaces and other potentially offensive characters:

```
[me@linuxbox ~]$ find . -regex '.*[^-_./0-9a-zA-Z].*'
```

Due to the requirement for an exact match of the entire pathname, we use .* at both ends of the expression to match zero or more instances of any character. In the middle of the expression, we use a negated bracket expression containing our set of acceptable pathname characters.

Searching for Files with locate

The locate program supports both basic (the --regexp option) and extended (the --regex option) regular expressions. With it, we can perform many of the same operations that we performed earlier with our *dirlist* files:

```
[me@linuxbox ~]$ locate --regex 'bin/(bz|gz|zip)'
/bin/bzcat
/bin/bzcmp
/bin/bzdiff
/bin/bzegrep
/bin/bzexe
/bin/bzfgrep
/bin/bzgrep
/bin/bzip2
/bin/bzip2recover
/bin/bzless
/bin/bzmore
/bin/gzexe
/bin/gzip
/usr/bin/zip
/usr/bin/zipcloak
/usr/bin/zipgrep
/usr/bin/zipinfo
/usr/bin/zipnote
/usr/bin/zipsplit
```

Using alternation, we perform a search for pathnames that contain either *bin/bz*, *bin/gz*, or */bin/zip*.

Searching for Text with less and vim

less and vim share the same method of searching for text. Pressing the / key followed by a regular expression will perform a search. We use less to view our *phonelist.txt* file:

```
[me@linuxbox ~]$ less phonelist.txt
```

Then we search for our validation expression:

```
(232) 298-2265
(624) 381-1078
(540) 126-1980
(874) 163-2885
(286) 254-2860
(292) 108-518
(129) 44-1379
(458) 273-1642
(686) 299-8268
(198) 307-2440
~
~
~
/^\([0-9]{3}\) [0-9]{3}-[0-9]{4}$
```

less will highlight the strings that match, leaving the invalid ones easy to spot:

```
(232) 298-2265
(624) 381-1078
(540) 126-1980
(874) 163-2885
(286) 254-2860
(292) 108-518
(129) 44-1379
(458) 273-1642
(686) 299-8268
(198) 307-2440
~
~
~
(END)
```

vim, on the other hand, supports basic regular expressions, so our search expression would look like this:

```
/([0-9]\{3\}) [0-9]\{3\}-[0-9]\{4\}
```

We can see that the expression is mostly the same; however, many of the characters that are considered metacharacters in extended expressions are considered literals in basic expressions. They are treated as metacharacters only when escaped with a backslash. Depending on the particular configuration of vim on our system, the matching will be highlighted. If not, try the command-mode command :hlsearch to activate search highlighting.

Note: *Depending on your distribution, vim may or may not support text-search highlighting. Ubuntu, in particular, supplies a very stripped-down version of vim by default. On such systems, you may want to use your package manager to install a more complete version of vim.*

Final Note

In this chapter, we've seen a few of the many uses of regular expressions. We can find even more if we use regular expressions to search for additional applications that use them. We can do that by searching the man pages:

```
[me@linuxbox ~]$ cd /usr/share/man/man1
[me@linuxbox man1]$ zgrep -El 'regex|regular expression' *.gz
```

The zgrep program provides a frontend for grep, allowing it to read compressed files. In our example, we search the compressed Section 1 man page files in their usual location. The result of this command is a list of files containing the string regex or regular expression. As we can see, regular expressions show up in a lot of programs.

There is one feature found in basic regular expressions that we did not cover. Called *back references*, this feature will be discussed in the next chapter.

20

TEXT PROCESSING

All Unix-like operating systems rely heavily on text
files for several types of data storage. So it makes sense
that there are many tools for manipulating text. In
this chapter, we will look at programs that are used
to "slice and dice" text. In the next chapter, we will look at more text processing, focusing on programs that are used to format text for printing and
other kinds of human consumption.

This chapter will revisit some old friends and introduce us to some
new ones:

- cat—Concatenate files and print on the standard output.

- sort—Sort lines of text files.

- uniq—Report or omit repeated lines.

- cut—Remove sections from each line of files.

- paste—Merge lines of files.

- join—Join lines of two files on a common field.

- comm—Compare two sorted files line by line.

- `diff`—Compare files line by line.
- `patch`—Apply a diff file to an original.
- `tr`—Translate or delete characters.
- `sed`—Stream editor for filtering and transforming text.
- `aspell`—Interactive spell checker.

Applications of Text

So far, we have learned about a couple of text editors (`nano` and `vim`), looked at a bunch of configuration files, and witnessed the output of dozens of commands, all in text. But what else is text used for? Many things, it turns out.

Documents

Many people write documents using plaintext formats. While it is easy to see how a small text file could be useful for keeping simple notes, it is also possible to write large documents in text format. One popular approach is to write a large document in a text format and then use a *markup language* to describe the formatting of the finished document. Many scientific papers are written using this method, as Unix-based text-processing systems were among the first systems that supported the advanced typographical layout needed by writers in technical disciplines.

Web Pages

The world's most popular type of electronic document is probably the web page. Web pages are text documents that use either *HTML (Hypertext Markup Language)* or *XML (Extensible Markup Language)* as a markup language to describe the document's visual format.

Email

Email is an intrinsically text-based medium. Even non-text attachments are converted into a text representation for transmission. We can see this for ourselves by downloading an email message and then viewing it in `less`. We will see that the message begins with a *header* that describes the source of the message and the processing it received during its journey, followed by the *body* of the message with its content.

Printer Output

On Unix-like systems, output destined for a printer is sent as plaintext or, if the page contains graphics, is converted into a text format page-description language known as *PostScript*, which is then sent to a program that generates the graphic dots to be printed.

Program Source Code

Many of the command-line programs found on Unix-like systems were created to support system administration and software development, and text-processing programs are no exception. Many of them are designed to solve software development problems. The reason text processing is important to software developers is that all software starts out as text. *Source code*, the part of the program the programmer actually writes, is always in text format.

Revisiting Some Old Friends

Back in Chapter 6, we learned about some commands that are able to accept standard input in addition to command-line arguments. We touched on them only briefly then, but now we will take a closer look at how they can be used to perform text processing.

cat—Concatenate Files and Print on Standard Output

The cat program has a number of interesting options. Many of them are used to better visualize text content. One example is the -A option, which is used to display non-printing characters in the text. There are times when we want to know if control characters are embedded in our otherwise visible text. The most common of these are tab characters (as opposed to spaces) and carriage returns, often present as end-of-line characters in MS-DOS-style text files. Another common situation is a file containing lines of text with trailing spaces.

Let's create a test file using cat as a primitive word processor. To do this, we'll just enter the command cat (along with specifying a file for redirected output) and type our text, followed by ENTER to properly end the line, then CTRL-D to indicate to cat that we have reached end-of-file. In this example, we enter a leading tab character and follow the line with some trailing spaces:

```
[me@linuxbox ~]$ cat > foo.txt
        The quick brown fox jumped over the lazy dog.
[me@linuxbox ~]$
```

Next, we will use cat with the -A option to display the text:

```
[me@linuxbox ~]$ cat -A foo.txt
^IThe quick brown fox jumped over the lazy dog. $
[me@linuxbox ~]$
```

As we can see in the results, the tab character in our text is represented by ^I. This common notation means "CTRL-I," which, as it turns out, is the same as a tab character. We also see that a $ appears at the true end of the line, indicating that our text contains trailing spaces.

cat also has options that are used to modify text. The two most prominent are -n, which numbers lines, and -s, which suppresses the output of multiple blank lines. We can demonstrate thusly:

```
[me@linuxbox ~]$ cat > foo.txt
The quick brown fox


jumped over the lazy dog.
[me@linuxbox ~]$ cat -ns foo.txt
     1  The quick brown fox
     2
     3  jumped over the lazy dog.
[me@linuxbox ~]$
```

In this example, we create a new version of our *foo.txt* test file, which contains two lines of text separated by two blank lines. After processing by cat with the -ns options, the extra blank line is removed and the remaining lines are numbered. While this is not much of a process to perform on text, it is a process.

sort—Sort Lines of Text Files

The sort program sorts the contents of standard input, or one or more files specified on the command line, and sends the results to standard output. Using the same technique that we used with cat, we can demonstrate processing of standard input directly from the keyboard.

```
[me@linuxbox ~]$ sort > foo.txt
c
b
a
[me@linuxbox ~]$ cat foo.txt
a
b
c
```

After entering the command, we type the letters c, b, and a, followed once again by CTRL-D to indicate end-of-file. We then view the resulting file and see that the lines now appear in sorted order.

Since sort can accept multiple files on the command line as arguments, it is possible to *merge* multiple files into a single sorted whole. For example, if we had three text files and wanted to combine them into a single sorted file, we could do something like this:

```
sort file1.txt file2.txt file3.txt > final_sorted_list.txt
```

sort has several interesting options. Table 20-1 shows a partial list.

Table 20-1: Common sort Options

Option	Long Option	Description
-b	--ignore-leading-blanks	By default, sorting is performed on the entire line, starting with the first character in the line. This option causes sort to ignore leading spaces in lines and calculates sorting based on the first non-whitespace character on the line.
-f	--ignore-case	Makes sorting case insensitive.
-n	--numeric-sort	Performs sorting based on the numeric evaluation of a string. Using this option allows sorting to be performed on numeric values rather than alphabetic values.
-r	--reverse	Sort in reverse order. Results are in descending rather than ascending order.
-k	--key=*field1*[,*field2*]	Sort based on a key field located from *field1* to *field2* rather than the entire line.
-m	--merge	Treat each argument as the name of a presorted file. Merge multiple files into a single sorted result without performing any additional sorting.
-o	--output=*file*	Send sorted output to *file* rather than to standard output.
-t	--field-separator=*char*	Define the field-separator character. By default, fields are separated by spaces or tabs.

Although most of the options above are pretty self-explanatory, some are not. First, let's look at the -n option, used for numeric sorting. With this option, it is possible to sort values based on numeric values. We can demonstrate this by sorting the results of the du command to determine the largest users of disk space. Normally, the du command lists the results of a summary in pathname order:

```
[me@linuxbox ~]$ du -s /usr/share/* | head
252            /usr/share/aclocal
96             /usr/share/acpi-support
8              /usr/share/adduser
196            /usr/share/alacarte
344            /usr/share/alsa
8              /usr/share/alsa-base
12488          /usr/share/anthy
8              /usr/share/apmd
21440          /usr/share/app-install
48             /usr/share/application-registry
```

In this example, we pipe the results into *head* to limit the results to the first 10 lines. We can produce a numerically sorted list to show the 10 largest consumers of space this way:

```
[me@linuxbox ~]$ du -s /usr/share/* | sort -nr | head
509940         /usr/share/locale-langpack
242660         /usr/share/doc
197560         /usr/share/fonts
179144         /usr/share/gnome
146764         /usr/share/myspell
144304         /usr/share/gimp
135880         /usr/share/dict
76508          /usr/share/icons
68072          /usr/share/apps
62844          /usr/share/foomatic
```

By using the -nr options, we produce a reverse numerical sort, with the largest values appearing first in the results. This sort works because the numerical values occur at the beginning of each line. But what if we want to sort a list based on some value found within the line? For example, the result of ls -l looks like this:

```
[me@linuxbox ~]$ ls -l /usr/bin | head
total 152948
-rwxr-xr-x 1 root     root        34824 2012-04-04 02:42 [
-rwxr-xr-x 1 root     root       101556 2011-11-27 06:08 a2p
-rwxr-xr-x 1 root     root        13036 2012-02-27 08:22 aconnect
-rwxr-xr-x 1 root     root        10552 2011-08-15 10:34 acpi
-rwxr-xr-x 1 root     root         3800 2012-04-14 03:51 acpi_fakekey
-rwxr-xr-x 1 root     root         7536 2012-04-19 00:19 acpi_listen
-rwxr-xr-x 1 root     root         3576 2012-04-29 07:57 addpart
-rwxr-xr-x 1 root     root        20808 2012-01-03 18:02 addr2line
-rwxr-xr-x 1 root     root       489704 2012-10-09 17:02 adept_batch
```

Ignoring, for the moment, that ls can sort its results by size, we could use sort to sort this list by file size, as well.

```
[me@linuxbox ~]$ ls -l /usr/bin | sort -nr -k 5 | head
-rwxr-xr-x 1 root     root      8234216 2012-04-07 17:42 inkscape
-rwxr-xr-x 1 root     root      8222692 2012-04-07 17:42 inkview
-rwxr-xr-x 1 root     root      3746508 2012-03-07 23:45 gimp-2.4
-rwxr-xr-x 1 root     root      3654020 2012-08-26 16:16 quanta
-rwxr-xr-x 1 root     root      2928760 2012-09-10 14:31 gdbtui
-rwxr-xr-x 1 root     root      2928756 2012-09-10 14:31 gdb
-rwxr-xr-x 1 root     root      2602236 2012-10-10 12:56 net
-rwxr-xr-x 1 root     root      2304684 2012-10-10 12:56 rpcclient
-rwxr-xr-x 1 root     root      2241832 2012-04-04 05:56 aptitude
-rwxr-xr-x 1 root     root      2202476 2012-10-10 12:56 smbcacls
```

Many uses of sort involve the processing of *tabular data,* such as the results of the ls command above. If we apply database terminology to the table above, we would say that each row is a *record* and that each record consists of multiple *fields,* such as the file attributes, link count, filename, file size and so on. sort is able to process individual fields. In database terms, we are able to specify one or more *key fields* to use as *sort keys.* In the example above, we specify the n and r options to perform a reverse numerical sort and specify -k 5 to make sort use the fifth field as the key for sorting.

The k option is very interesting and has many features, but first we need to talk about how sort defines fields. Let's consider a very simple text file consisting of a single line containing the author's name:

```
William     Shotts
```

By default, sort sees this line as having two fields. The first field contains the characters William and the second field contains the characters   Shotts, meaning that whitespace characters (spaces and tabs) are used as delimiters between fields and that the delimiters are included in the field when sorting is performed.

Looking again at a line from our ls output, we can see that a line contains eight fields and that the fifth field is the file size:

```
-rwxr-xr-x 1 root     root      8234216 2012-04-07 17:42 inkscape
```

For our next series of experiments, let's consider the following file containing the history of three popular Linux distributions released from 2006 to 2008. Each line in the file has three fields: the distribution name, the version number, and the date of release in MM/DD/YYYY format:

```
SUSE        10.2    12/07/2006
Fedora      10      11/25/2008
SUSE        11.0    06/19/2008
Ubuntu      8.04    04/24/2008
Fedora      8       11/08/2007
SUSE        10.3    10/04/2007
Ubuntu      6.10    10/26/2006
Fedora      7       05/31/2007
Ubuntu      7.10    10/18/2007
Ubuntu      7.04    04/19/2007
SUSE        10.1    05/11/2006
Fedora      6       10/24/2006
```

```
Fedora    9       05/13/2008
Ubuntu    6.06    06/01/2006
Ubuntu    8.10    10/30/2008
Fedora    5       03/20/2006
```

Using a text editor (perhaps vim), we'll enter this data and name the resulting file *distros.txt*.

Next, we'll try sorting the file and observe the results:

```
[me@linuxbox ~]$ sort distros.txt
Fedora    10      11/25/2008
Fedora    5       03/20/2006
Fedora    6       10/24/2006
Fedora    7       05/31/2007
Fedora    8       11/08/2007
Fedora    9       05/13/2008
SUSE      10.1    05/11/2006
SUSE      10.2    12/07/2006
SUSE      10.3    10/04/2007
SUSE      11.0    06/19/2008
Ubuntu    6.06    06/01/2006
Ubuntu    6.10    10/26/2006
Ubuntu    7.04    04/19/2007
Ubuntu    7.10    10/18/2007
Ubuntu    8.04    04/24/2008
Ubuntu    8.10    10/30/2008
```

Well, it mostly worked. The problem occurs in the sorting of the Fedora version numbers. Since a 1 comes before a 5 in the character set, version 10 ends up at the top while version 9 falls to the bottom.

To fix this problem, we have to sort on multiple keys. We want to perform an alphabetic sort on the first field and then a numeric sort on the third field. sort allows multiple instances of the -k option so that multiple sort keys can be specified. In fact, a key may include a range of fields. If no range is specified (as has been the case with our previous examples), sort uses a key that begins with the specified field and extends to the end of the line.

Here is the syntax for our multikey sort:

```
[me@linuxbox ~]$ sort --key=1,1 --key=2n distros.txt
Fedora    5       03/20/2006
Fedora    6       10/24/2006
Fedora    7       05/31/2007
Fedora    8       11/08/2007
Fedora    9       05/13/2008
Fedora    10      11/25/2008
SUSE      10.1    05/11/2006
SUSE      10.2    12/07/2006
SUSE      10.3    10/04/2007
SUSE      11.0    06/19/2008
Ubuntu    6.06    06/01/2006
Ubuntu    6.10    10/26/2006
Ubuntu    7.04    04/19/2007
Ubuntu    7.10    10/18/2007
Ubuntu    8.04    04/24/2008
Ubuntu    8.10    10/30/2008
```

Though we used the long form of the option for clarity, -k 1,1 -k 2n would be exactly equivalent. In the first instance of the key option, we specified a range of fields to include in the first key. Since we wanted to limit the sort to just the first field, we specified 1,1, which means "start at field 1 and end at field 1." In the second instance, we specified 2n, which means that field 2 is the sort key and that the sort should be numeric. An option letter may be included at the end of a key specifier to indicate the type of sort to be performed. These option letters are the same as the global options for the sort program: b (ignore leading blanks), n (numeric sort), r (reverse sort), and so on.

The third field in our list contains a date in an inconvenient format for sorting. On computers, dates are usually formatted in YYYY-MM-DD order to make chronological sorting easy, but ours are in the American format of MM/DD/YYYY. How can we sort this list in chronological order?

Fortunately, sort provides a way. The key option allows specification of *offsets* within fields, so we can define keys within fields:

```
[me@linuxbox ~]$ sort -k 3.7nbr -k 3.1nbr -k 3.4nbr distros.txt
Fedora      10      11/25/2008
Ubuntu      8.10    10/30/2008
SUSE        11.0    06/19/2008
Fedora      9       05/13/2008
Ubuntu      8.04    04/24/2008
Fedora      8       11/08/2007
Ubuntu      7.10    10/18/2007
SUSE        10.3    10/04/2007
Fedora      7       05/31/2007
Ubuntu      7.04    04/19/2007
SUSE        10.2    12/07/2006
Ubuntu      6.10    10/26/2006
Fedora      6       10/24/2006
Ubuntu      6.06    06/01/2006
SUSE        10.1    05/11/2006
Fedora      5       03/20/2006
```

By specifying -k 3.7, we instruct sort to use a sort key that begins at the seventh character within the third field, which corresponds to the start of the year. Likewise, we specify -k 3.1 and -k 3.4 to isolate the month and day portions of the date. We also add the n and r options to achieve a reverse numeric sort. The b option is included to suppress the leading spaces (whose numbers vary from line to line, thereby affecting the outcome of the sort) in the date field.

Some files don't use tabs and spaces as field delimiters; take, for example, the */etc/passwd* file:

```
[me@linuxbox ~]$ head /etc/passwd
root:x:0:0:root:/root:/bin/bash
daemon:x:1:1:daemon:/usr/sbin:/bin/sh
bin:x:2:2:bin:/bin:/bin/sh
sys:x:3:3:sys:/dev:/bin/sh
sync:x:4:65534:sync:/bin:/bin/sync
games:x:5:60:games:/usr/games:/bin/sh
man:x:6:12:man:/var/cache/man:/bin/sh
```

```
lp:x:7:7:lp:/var/spool/lpd:/bin/sh
mail:x:8:8:mail:/var/mail:/bin/sh
news:x:9:9:news:/var/spool/news:/bin/sh
```

The fields in this file are delimited with colons (:), so how would we sort this file using a key field? sort provides the -t option to define the field separator character. To sort the passwd file on the seventh field (the account's default shell), we could do this:

```
[me@linuxbox ~]$ sort -t ':' -k 7 /etc/passwd | head
me:x:1001:1001:Myself,,,:/home/me:/bin/bash
root:x:0:0:root:/root:/bin/bash
dhcp:x:101:102::/nonexistent:/bin/false
gdm:x:106:114:Gnome Display Manager:/var/lib/gdm:/bin/false
hplip:x:104:7:HPLIP system user,,,:/var/run/hplip:/bin/false
klog:x:103:104::/home/klog:/bin/false
messagebus:x:108:119::/var/run/dbus:/bin/false
polkituser:x:110:122:PolicyKit,,,:/var/run/PolicyKit:/bin/false
pulse:x:107:116:PulseAudio daemon,,,:/var/run/pulse:/bin/false
```

By specifying the colon character as the field separator, we can sort on the seventh field.

uniq—Report or Omit Repeated Lines

Compared to sort, the uniq program is a lightweight. uniq performs a seemingly trivial task. When given a sorted file (including standard input), it removes any duplicate lines and sends the results to standard output. It is often used in conjunction with sort to clean the output of duplicates.

Note: *While uniq is a traditional Unix tool often used with sort, the GNU version of sort supports a -u option, which removes duplicates from the sorted output.*

Let's make a text file to try this out:

```
[me@linuxbox ~]$ cat > foo.txt
a
b
c
a
b
c
```

Remember to type CTRL-D to terminate standard input. Now, if we run uniq on our text file, the results are no different from our original file; the duplicates were not removed:

```
[me@linuxbox ~]$ uniq foo.txt
a
b
c
a
b
c
```

For uniq to actually do its job, the input must be sorted first:

```
[me@linuxbox ~]$ sort foo.txt | uniq
a
b
c
```

This is because uniq only removes duplicate lines that are adjacent to each other.

uniq has several options. Table 20-2 lists the common ones.

Table 20-2: Common uniq Options

Option	Description
-c	Output a list of duplicate lines preceded by the number of times the line occurs.
-d	Output only repeated lines, rather than unique lines.
-f *n*	Ignore *n* leading fields in each line. Fields are separated by whitespace as they are in sort; however, unlike sort, uniq has no option for setting an alternative field separator.
-i	Ignore case during the line comparisons.
-s *n*	Skip (ignore) the leading *n* characters of each line.
-u	Do not output any line that has a duplicate.

Here we see uniq used to report the number of duplicates found in our text file, using the -c option:

```
[me@linuxbox ~]$ sort foo.txt | uniq -c
      2 a
      2 b
      2 c
```

Slicing and Dicing

The next three programs we will discuss are used to peel columns of text out of files and recombine them in useful ways.

cut—Remove Sections from Each Line of Files

The cut program is used to extract a section of text from a line and output the extracted section to standard output. It can accept multiple file arguments or input from standard input.

Specifying the section of the line to be extracted is somewhat awkward and is specified using the options shown in Table 20-3.

Table 20-3: cut Selection Options

Option	Description
-c *char_list*	Extract the portion of the line defined by *char_list*. The list may consist of one or more comma-separated numerical ranges.
-f *field_list*	Extract one or more fields from the line as defined by *field_list*. The list may contain one or more fields or field ranges separated by commas.
-d *delim_char*	When -f is specified, use *delim_char* as the field delimiting character. By default, fields must be separated by a single tab character.
--complement	Extract the entire line of text, except for those portions specified by -c and/or -f.

As we can see, the way cut extracts text is rather inflexible. cut is best used to extract text from files that are produced by other programs, rather than text directly typed by humans. We'll take a look at our *distros.txt* file to see if it is "clean" enough to be a good specimen for our cut examples. If we use cat with the -A option, we can see if the file meets our requirements of tab-separated fields.

```
[me@linuxbox ~]$ cat -A distros.txt
SUSE^I10.2^I12/07/2006$
Fedora^I10^I11/25/2008$
SUSE^I11.0^I06/19/2008$
Ubuntu^I8.04^I04/24/2008$
Fedora^I8^I11/08/2007$
SUSE^I10.3^I10/04/2007$
Ubuntu^I6.10^I10/26/2006$
Fedora^I7^I05/31/2007$
Ubuntu^I7.10^I10/18/2007$
Ubuntu^I7.04^I04/19/2007$
SUSE^I10.1^I05/11/2006$
Fedora^I6^I10/24/2006$
Fedora^I9^I05/13/2008$
Ubuntu^I6.06^I06/01/2006$
Ubuntu^I8.10^I10/30/2008$
Fedora^I5^I03/20/2006$
```

It looks good—no embedded spaces, just single tab characters between the fields. Since the file uses tabs rather than spaces, we'll use the -f option to extract a field:

```
[me@linuxbox ~]$ cut -f 3 distros.txt
12/07/2006
11/25/2008
06/19/2008
04/24/2008
11/08/2007
```

```
10/04/2007
10/26/2006
05/31/2007
10/18/2007
04/19/2007
05/11/2006
10/24/2006
05/13/2008
06/01/2006
10/30/2008
03/20/2006
```

Because our *distros* file is tab delimited, it is best to use cut to extract fields rather than characters. This is because when a file is tab delimited, it is unlikely that each line will contain the same number of characters, which makes calculating character positions within the line difficult or impossible. In our example above, however, we now have extracted a field that luckily contains data of identical length, so we can show how character extraction works by extracting the year from each line:

```
[me@linuxbox ~]$ cut -f 3 distros.txt | cut -c 7-10
2006
2008
2008
2008
2007
2007
2006
2007
2007
2007
2006
2006
2008
2006
2008
2006
```

By running cut a second time on our list, we are able to extract character positions 7 through 10, which corresponds to the year in our date field. The 7-10 notation is an example of a range. The cut man page contains a complete description of how ranges can be specified.

When working with fields, it is possible to specify a different field delimiter rather than the tab character. Here we will extract the first field from the */etc/passwd* file:

```
[me@linuxbox ~]$ cut -d ':' -f 1 /etc/passwd | head
root
daemon
bin
sys
sync
games
man
```

```
lp
mail
news
```

Using the -d option, we are able to specify the colon character as the field delimiter.

EXPANDING TABS

Our *distros.txt* file is ideally formatted for extracting fields using cut. But what if we wanted a file that could be fully manipulated with cut by characters, rather than fields? This would require us to replace the tab characters within the file with the corresponding number of spaces. Fortunately, the GNU coreutils package includes a tool for that. Named expand, this program accepts either one or more file arguments or standard input, and it outputs the modified text to standard output.

If we process our *distros.txt* file with expand, we can use the cut -c to extract any range of characters from the file. For example, we could use the following command to extract the year of release from our list by expanding the file and using cut to extract every character from the 23rd position to the end of the line:

```
[me@linuxbox ~]$ expand distros.txt | cut -c 23-
```

coreutils also provides the unexpand program to substitute tabs for spaces.

---

paste—Merge Lines of Files

The paste command does the opposite of cut. Rather than extracting a column of text from a file, it adds one or more columns of text to a file. It does this by reading multiple files and combining the fields found in each file into a single stream of standard output. Like cut, paste accepts multiple file arguments and/or standard input. To demonstrate how paste operates, we will perform some surgery on our *distros.txt* file to produce a chronological list of releases.

From our earlier work with sort, we will first produce a list of distros sorted by date and store the result in a file called *distros-by-date.txt*:

```
[me@linuxbox ~]$ sort -k 3.7nbr -k 3.1nbr -k 3.4nbr distros.txt > distros-by-
date.txt
```

Next, we will use cut to extract the first two fields from the file (the distro name and version) and store that result in a file named *distro-versions.txt*:

```
[me@linuxbox ~]$ cut -f 1,2 distros-by-date.txt > distro-versions.txt
[me@linuxbox ~]$ head distro-versions.txt
```

Fedora	10
Ubuntu	8.10
SUSE	11.0
Fedora	9
Ubuntu	8.04
Fedora	8
Ubuntu	7.10
SUSE	10.3
Fedora	7
Ubuntu	7.04

The final piece of preparation is to extract the release dates and store them a file named *distro-dates.txt*:

```
[me@linuxbox ~]$ cut -f 3 distros-by-date.txt > distros-dates.txt
[me@linuxbox ~]$ head distros-dates.txt
11/25/2008
10/30/2008
06/19/2008
05/13/2008
04/24/2008
11/08/2007
10/18/2007
10/04/2007
05/31/2007
04/19/2007
```

We now have the parts we need. To complete the process, use paste to put the column of dates ahead of the distro names and versions, thus creating a chronological list. This is done simply by using paste and ordering its arguments in the desired arrangement.

```
[me@linuxbox ~]$ paste distros-dates.txt distros-versions.txt
11/25/2008    Fedora    10
10/30/2008    Ubuntu    8.10
06/19/2008    SUSE      11.0
05/13/2008    Fedora    9
04/24/2008    Ubuntu    8.04
11/08/2007    Fedora    8
10/18/2007    Ubuntu    7.10
10/04/2007    SUSE      10.3
05/31/2007    Fedora    7
04/19/2007    Ubuntu    7.04
12/07/2006    SUSE      10.2
10/26/2006    Ubuntu    6.10
10/24/2006    Fedora    6
06/01/2006    Ubuntu    6.06
05/11/2006    SUSE      10.1
03/20/2006    Fedora    5
```

join—Join Lines of Two Files on a Common Field

In some ways, join is like paste in that it adds columns to a file, but it does so in a unique way. A *join* is an operation usually associated with *relational databases* where data from multiple *tables* with a shared key field is combined to form a desired result. The `join` program performs the same operation. It joins data from multiple files based on a shared key field.

To see how a join operation is used in a relational database, let's imagine a very small database consisting of two tables, each containing a single record. The first table, called CUSTOMERS, has three fields: a customer number (CUSTNUM), the customer's first name (FNAME), and the customer's last name (LNAME):

```
CUSTNUM       FNAME    LNAME
=========     ======   ======
4681934       John     Smith
```

The second table is called ORDERS and contains four fields: an order number (ORDERNUM), the customer number (CUSTNUM), the quantity (QUAN), and the item ordered (ITEM):

```
ORDERNUM       CUSTNUM      QUAN    ITEM
==========     =========    =====   ====
3014953305     4681934      1       Blue Widget
```

Note that both tables share the field CUSTNUM. This is important, as it allows a relationship between the tables.

Performing a join operation would allow us to combine the fields in the two tables to achieve a useful result, such as preparing an invoice. Using the matching values in the CUSTNUM fields of both tables, a join operation could produce the following:

```
FNAME    LNAME    QUAN    ITEM
======   ======   =====   ====
John     Smith    1       Blue Widget
```

To demonstrate the `join` program, we'll need to make a couple of files with a shared key. To do this, we will use our *distros-by-date.txt* file. From this file, we will construct two additional files. One contains the release dates (which will be our shared key field for this demonstration) and the release names:

```
[me@linuxbox ~]$ cut -f 1,1 distros-by-date.txt > distros-names.txt
[me@linuxbox ~]$ paste distros-dates.txt distros-names.txt > distros-key-names
.txt
[me@linuxbox ~]$ head distros-key-names.txt
11/25/2008      Fedora
10/30/2008      Ubuntu
06/19/2008      SUSE
05/13/2008      Fedora
04/24/2008      Ubuntu
11/08/2007      Fedora
10/18/2007      Ubuntu
10/04/2007      SUSE
05/31/2007      Fedora
04/19/2007      Ubuntu
```

The second file contains the release dates and the version numbers:

```
[me@linuxbox ~]$ cut -f 2,2 distros-by-date.txt > distros-vernums.txt
[me@linuxbox ~]$ paste distros-dates.txt distros-vernums.txt > distros-key-
vernums.txt
[me@linuxbox ~]$ head distros-key-vernums.txt
11/25/2008      10
10/30/2008      8.10
06/19/2008      11.0
05/13/2008      9
04/24/2008      8.04
11/08/2007      8
10/18/2007      7.10
10/04/2007      10.3
05/31/2007      7
04/19/2007      7.04
```

We now have two files with a shared key (the "release date" field). It is important to point out that the files must be sorted on the key field for join to work properly.

```
[me@linuxbox ~]$ join distros-key-names.txt  distros-key-vernums.txt | head
11/25/2008 Fedora 10
10/30/2008 Ubuntu 8.10
06/19/2008 SUSE 11.0
05/13/2008 Fedora 9
04/24/2008 Ubuntu 8.04
11/08/2007 Fedora 8
10/18/2007 Ubuntu 7.10
10/04/2007 SUSE 10.3
05/31/2007 Fedora 7
04/19/2007 Ubuntu 7.04
```

Note also that, by default, join uses whitespace as the input field delimiter and a single space as the output field delimiter. This behavior can be modified by specifying options. See the join man page for details.

Comparing Text

It is often useful to compare versions of text files. For system administrators and software developers, this is particularly important. A system administrator may, for example, need to compare an existing configuration file to a previous version to diagnose a system problem. Likewise, a programmer frequently needs to see what changes have been made to programs over time.

comm—Compare Two Sorted Files Line by Line

The comm program compares two text files, displaying the lines that are unique to each one and the lines they have in common. To demonstrate, we will create two nearly identical text files using cat:

```
[me@linuxbox ~]$ cat > file1.txt
a
b
```

```
c
d
[me@linuxbox ~]$ cat > file2.txt
b
c
d
e
```

Next, we will compare the two files using comm:

```
[me@linuxbox ~]$ comm file1.txt file2.txt
a
                b
                c
                d
        e
```

As we can see, comm produces three columns of output. The first column
contains lines unique to the first file argument; the second column, the lines
unique to the second file argument; and the third column, the lines shared
by both files. comm supports options in the form -n where n is either 1, 2, or 3.
When used, these options specify which column(s) to suppress. For example,
if we wanted to output only the lines shared by both files, we would suppress
the output of columns 1 and 2:

```
[me@linuxbox ~]$ comm -12 file1.txt file2.txt
b
c
d
```

diff—Compare Files Line by Line

Like the comm program, diff is used to detect the differences between files.
However, diff is a much more complex tool, supporting many output formats and the ability to process large collections of text files at once. diff is
often used by software developers to examine changes between different
versions of program source code because it has the ability to recursively
examine directories of source code, often referred to as *source trees*. One
common use for diff is the creation of *diff files* or *patches* that are used by
programs such as patch (which we'll discuss shortly) to convert one version
of a file (or files) to another version.

If we use diff to look at our previous example files, we see its default
style of output: a terse description of the differences between the two files.

```
[me@linuxbox ~]$ diff file1.txt file2.txt
1d0
< a
4a4
> e
```

In the default format, each group of changes is preceded by a *change command* (see Table 20-4) in the form of *range operation range* to describe the positions and types of changes required to convert the first file to the second file.

Table 20-4: diff Change Commands

Change	Description
r1ar2	Append the lines at the position r2 in the second file to the position r1 in the first file.
r1cr2	Change (replace) the lines at position r1 with the lines at the position r2 in the second file.
r1dr2	Delete the lines in the first file at position r1, which would have appeared at range r2 in the second file

In this format, a range is a comma-separated list of the starting line and the ending line. While this format is the default (mostly for POSIX compliance and backward compatibility with traditional Unix versions of diff), it is not as widely used as other, optional formats. Two of the more popular formats are the *context format* and the *unified format.*

When viewed using the context format (the -c option), the output looks like this:

```
[me@linuxbox ~]$ diff -c file1.txt file2.txt
*** file1.txt    2012-12-23 06:40:13.000000000 -0500
--- file2.txt    2012-12-23 06:40:34.000000000 -0500
***************
*** 1,4 ****
- a
  b
  c
  d
--- 1,4 ----
  b

  c
  d
+ e
```

The output begins with the names of the two files and their timestamps. The first file is marked with asterisks, and the second file is marked with dashes. Throughout the remainder of the listing, these markers will signify their respective files. Next, we see groups of changes, including the default number of surrounding context lines. In the first group, we see *** 1,4 ****, which indicates lines 1 through 4 in the first file. Later we see --- 1,4 ----, which indicates lines 1 through 4 in the second file. Within a change group, lines begin with one of four indicators, as shown in Table 20-5.

Table 20-5: diff Context-Format Change Indicators

Indicator	Meaning
(none)	A line shown for context. It does not indicate a difference between the two files.
-	A line deleted. This line will appear in the first file but not in the second file.
+	A line added. This line will appear in the second file but not in the first file.
!	A line changed. The two versions of the line will be displayed, each in its respective section of the change group.

The unified format is similar to the context format but is more concise. It is specified with the -u option:

```
[me@linuxbox ~]$ diff -u file1.txt file2.txt
--- file1.txt    2012-12-23 06:40:13.000000000 -0500
+++ file2.txt    2012-12-23 06:40:34.000000000 -0500
@@ -1,4 +1,4 @@
-a
 b
 c
 d
+e
```

The most notable difference between the context and unified formats is the elimination of the duplicated lines of context, making the results of the unified format shorter than those of the context format. In our example above, we see file timestamps like those of the context format, followed by the string @@ -1,4 +1,4 @@. This indicates the lines in the first file and the lines in the second file described in the change group. Following this are the lines themselves, with the default three lines of context. As shown in Table 20-6, each line starts with one of three possible characters.

Table 20-6: diff Unified-Format Change Indicators

Character	Meaning
(none)	This line is shared by both files.
-	This line was removed from the first file.
+	This line was added to the first file.

patch—Apply a diff to an Original

The patch program is used to apply changes to text files. It accepts output from diff and is generally used to convert older version of files into newer versions. Let's consider a famous example. The Linux kernel is developed by a large, loosely organized team of contributors who submit a constant stream of small changes to the source code. The Linux kernel consists of several million lines of code, while the changes that are made by one contributor at one time are quite small. It makes no sense for a contributor to send each developer an entire kernel source tree each time a small change is made. Instead, a diff file is submitted. The diff file contains the change from the previous version of the kernel to the new version with the contributor's changes. The receiver then uses the patch program to apply the change to his own source tree. Using diff/patch offers two significant advantages:

- The diff file is very small, compared to the full size of the source tree.

- The diff file concisely shows the change being made, allowing reviewers of the patch to quickly evaluate it.

Of course, diff/patch will work on any text file, not just source code. It would be equally applicable to configuration files or any other text.

To prepare a diff file for use with patch, the GNU documentation suggests using diff as follows:

diff -Naur *old_file new_file* > *diff_file*

where *old_file* and *new_file* are either single files or directories containing files. The r option supports recursion of a directory tree.

Once the diff file has been created, we can apply it to patch the old file into the new file:

patch < *diff_file*

We'll demonstrate with our test file:

```
[me@linuxbox ~]$ diff -Naur file1.txt file2.txt > patchfile.txt
[me@linuxbox ~]$ patch < patchfile.txt
patching file file1.txt
[me@linuxbox ~]$ cat file1.txt
b
c
d
e
```

In this example, we created a diff file named *patchfile.txt* and then used the patch program to apply the patch. Note that we did not have to specify a target file to patch, as the diff file (in unified format) already contains the filenames in the header. Once the patch is applied, we can see that *file1.txt* now matches *file2.txt.*

patch has a large number of options, and additional utility programs can be used to analyze and edit patches.

Editing on the Fly

Our experience with text editors has been largely *interactive*, meaning that we manually move a cursor around and then type our changes. However, there are *non-interactive* ways to edit text as well. It's possible, for example, to apply a set of changes to multiple files with a single command.

tr—Transliterate or Delete Characters

The tr program is used to *transliterate* characters. We can think of this as a sort of character-based search-and-replace operation. Transliteration is the process of changing characters from one alphabet to another. For example, converting characters from lowercase to uppercase is transliteration. We can perform such a conversion with tr as follows:

```
[me@linuxbox ~]$ echo "lowercase letters" | tr a-z A-Z
LOWERCASE LETTERS
```

As we can see, tr operates on standard input and outputs its results on standard output. tr accepts two arguments: a set of characters to convert from and a corresponding set of characters to convert to. Character sets may be expressed in one of three ways:

- An enumerated list; for example, ABCDEFGHIJKLMNOPQRSTUVWXYZ.
- A character range; for example, A-Z. Note that this method is sometimes subject to the same issues as other commands (due to the locale collation order) and thus should be used with caution.
- POSIX character classes; for example, [:upper:].

In most cases, the character sets should be of equal length; however, it is possible for the first set to be larger than the second, particularly if we wish to convert multiple characters to a single character:

```
[me@linuxbox ~]$ echo "lowercase letters" | tr [:lower:] A
AAAAAAAAA AAAAAAA
```

In addition to transliteration, tr allows characters to simply be deleted from the input stream. Earlier in this chapter, we discussed the problem of converting MS-DOS text files to Unix-style text. To perform this conversion, carriage return characters need to be removed from the end of each line. This can be performed with tr as follows:

```
tr -d '\r' < dos_file > unix_file
```

where *dos_file* is the file to be converted and *unix_file* is the result. This form of the command uses the escape sequence \r to represent the carriage return character. To see a complete list of the sequences and character classes tr supports, try

```
[me@linuxbox ~]$ tr -help
```

ROT13: THE NOT-SO-SECRET DECODER RING

One amusing use of tr is to perform *ROT13 encoding* of text. ROT13 is a trivial type of encryption based on a simple substitution cipher. Calling ROT13 *encryption* is being generous; *text obfuscation* is more accurate. It is used sometimes on text to obscure potentially offensive content. The method simply moves each character 13 places up the alphabet. Since this is halfway up the possible 26 characters, performing the algorithm a second time on the text restores it to its original form. To perform this encoding with tr:

```
echo "secret text" | tr a-zA-Z n-za-mN-ZA-M
frperg grkg
```

Performing the same procedure a second time results in the translation:

```
echo "frperg grkg" | tr a-zA-Z n-za-mN-ZA-M
secret text
```

A number of email programs and Usenet news readers support ROT13 encoding. Wikipedia contains a good article on the subject: *http://en.wikipedia .org/wiki/ROT13.*

tr can perform another trick, too. Using the -s option, tr can "squeeze" (delete) repeated instances of a character:

```
[me@linuxbox ~]$ echo "aaabbbccc" | tr -s ab
abccc
```

Here we have a string containing repeated characters. By specifying the set ab to tr, we eliminate the repeated instances of the letters in the set, while leaving the character that is missing from the set (c) unchanged. Note that the repeating characters must be adjoining. If they are not, the squeezing will have no effect:

```
[me@linuxbox ~]$ echo "abcabcabc" | tr -s ab
abcabcabc
```

sed—Stream Editor for Filtering and Transforming Text

The name sed is short for *stream editor*. It performs text editing on a stream of text, either a set of specified files or standard input. sed is a powerful and somewhat complex program (there are entire books about it), so we will not cover it completely here.

In general, the way sed works is that it is given either a single editing command (on the command line) or the name of a script file containing multiple commands, and it then performs these commands upon each line in the stream of text. Here is a very simple example of sed in action:

```
[me@linuxbox ~]$ echo "front" | sed 's/front/back/'
back
```

In this example, we produce a one-word stream of text using echo and pipe it into sed. sed, in turn, carries out the instruction s/front/back/ upon the text in the stream and produces the output back as a result. We can also recognize this command as resembling the substitution (search and replace) command in vi.

Commands in sed begin with a single letter. In the example above, the substitution command is represented by the letter s and is followed by the search and replace strings, separated by the slash character as a delimiter. The choice of the delimiter character is arbitrary. By convention, the slash character is often used, but sed will accept any character that immediately follows the command as the delimiter. We could perform the same command this way:

```
[me@linuxbox ~]$ echo "front" | sed 's_front_back_'
back
```

When the underscore character is used immediately after the command, it becomes the delimiter. The ability to set the delimiter can be used to make commands more readable, as we shall see.

Most commands in sed may be preceded by an *address*, which specifies which line(s) of the input stream will be edited. If the address is omitted, then the editing command is carried out on every line in the input stream. The simplest form of address is a line number. We can add one to our example:

```
[me@linuxbox ~]$ echo "front" | sed '1s/front/back/'
back
```

Adding the address 1 to our command causes our substitution to be performed on the first line of our one-line input stream. We can specify another number:

```
[me@linuxbox ~]$ echo "front" | sed '2s/front/back/'
front
```

Now we see that the editing is not carried out, because our input stream does not have a line 2.

Addresses may be expressed in many ways. Table 20-7 lists the most common ones.

Table 20-7: sed Address Notation

Address	Description
n	A line number where *n* is a positive integer
$	The last line
/regexp/	Lines matching a POSIX basic regular expression. Note that the regular expression is delimited by slash characters. Optionally, the regular expression may be delimited by an alternate character, by specifying the expression with \c*regexp*c, where *c* is the alternate character.
addr1,addr2	A range of lines from *addr1* to *addr2*, inclusive. Addresses may be any of the single address forms above.
first~step	Match the line represented by the number *first* and then each subsequent line at *step* intervals. For example, 1~2 refers to each odd-numbered line, and 5~5 refers to the fifth line and every fifth line thereafter.
addr1,+n	Match *addr1* and the following *n* lines.
addr!	Match all lines except *addr*, which may be any of the forms above.

We'll demonstrate different kinds of addresses using the *distros.txt* file from earlier in this chapter. First, a range of line numbers:

```
[me@linuxbox ~]$ sed -n '1,5p' distros.txt
SUSE        10.2    12/07/2006
Fedora      10      11/25/2008
SUSE        11.0    06/19/2008
Ubuntu      8.04    04/24/2008
Fedora      8       11/08/2007
```

In this example, we print a range of lines, starting with line 1 and continuing to line 5. To do this, we use the p command, which simply causes a matched line to be printed. For this to be effective, however, we must include the option -n (the no autoprint option) to cause sed not to print every line by default.

Next, we'll try a regular expression:

```
[me@linuxbox ~]$ sed -n '/SUSE/p' distros.txt
SUSE        10.2    12/07/2006
SUSE        11.0    06/19/2008
SUSE        10.3    10/04/2007
SUSE        10.1    05/11/2006
```

By including the slash-delimited regular expression /SUSE/, we are able to isolate the lines containing it in much the same manner as grep.

Finally, we'll try negation by adding an exclamation point (!) to the address:

```
[me@linuxbox ~]$ sed -n '/SUSE/!p' distros.txt
Fedora      10      11/25/2008
Ubuntu      8.04    04/24/2008
Fedora      8       11/08/2007
Ubuntu      6.10    10/26/2006
Fedora      7       05/31/2007
Ubuntu      7.10    10/18/2007
Ubuntu      7.04    04/19/2007
Fedora      6       10/24/2006
Fedora      9       05/13/2008
Ubuntu      6.06    06/01/2006
Ubuntu      8.10    10/30/2008
Fedora      5       03/20/2006
```

Here we see the expected result: all of the lines in the file except the ones matched by the regular expression.

So far, we've looked at two of the sed editing commands, s and p. Table 20-8 is a more complete list of the basic editing commands.

Table 20-8: sed Basic Editing Commands

Command	Description
=	Output current line number.
a	Append text after the current line.
d	Delete the current line.
i	Insert text in front of the current line.
p	Print the current line. By default, sed prints every line and edits only lines that match a specified address within the file. The default behavior can be overridden by specifying the -n option.
q	Exit sed without processing any more lines. If the -n option is not specified, output the current line.

Table 20-8 (*continued*)

Command	Description
Q	Exit sed without processing any more lines.
s/*regexp*/*replacement*/	Substitute the contents of *replacement* wherever *regexp* is found. *replacement* may include the special character &, which is equivalent to the text matched by *regexp*. In addition, *replacement* may include the sequences \1 through \9, which are the contents of the corresponding subexpressions in *regexp*. For more about this, see the following discussion on back references. After the trailing slash following *replacement*, an optional flag may be specified to modify the s command's behavior.
y/*set1*/*set2*	Perform transliteration by converting characters from *set1* to the corresponding characters in *set2*. Note that unlike tr, sed requires that both sets be of the same length.

The s command is by far the most commonly used editing command. We will demonstrate just some of its power by performing an edit on our *distros.txt* file. We discussed before how the date field in *distros.txt* was not in a "computer-friendly" format. While the date is formatted MM/DD/YYYY, it would be better (for ease of sorting) if the format were YYYY-MM-DD. To perform this change on the file by hand would be both time consuming and error prone, but with sed, this change can be performed in one step:

```
[me@linuxbox ~]$ sed 's/\([0-9]\{2\}\)\/\([0-9]\{2\}\)\/\([0-9]\{4\}\)$/\3-\1
-\2/' distros.txt
SUSE        10.2    2006-12-07
Fedora      10      2008-11-25
SUSE        11.0    2008-06-19
Ubuntu      8.04    2008-04-24
Fedora      8       2007-11-08
SUSE        10.3    2007-10-04
Ubuntu      6.10    2006-10-26
Fedora      7       2007-05-31
Ubuntu      7.10    2007-10-18
Ubuntu      7.04    2007-04-19
SUSE        10.1    2006-05-11
Fedora      6       2006-10-24
Fedora      9       2008-05-13
Ubuntu      6.06    2006-06-01
Ubuntu      8.10    2008-10-30
Fedora      5       2006-03-20
```

Wow! Now that is an ugly-looking command. But it works. In just one step, we have changed the date format in our file. It is also a perfect example of why regular expressions are sometimes jokingly referred to as a "write-only" medium. We can write them, but we sometimes cannot read them. Before we are tempted to run away in terror from this command, let's look at how it was constructed. First, we know that the command will have this basic structure:

```
sed 's/regexp/replacement/' distros.txt
```

Our next step is to figure out a regular expression that will isolate the date. Since it is in MM/DD/YYYY format and appears at the end of the line, we can use an expression like this:

```
[0-9]{2}/[0-9]{2}/[0-9]{4}$
```

which matches two digits, a slash, two digits, a slash, four digits, and the end of line. So that takes care of *regexp*, but what about *replacement*? To handle that, we must introduce a new regular expression feature that appears in some applications that use BRE. This feature is called *back references* and works like this: If the sequence \n appears in *replacement* where n is a number from one to nine, the sequence will refer to the corresponding subexpression in the preceding regular expression. To create the subexpressions, we simply enclose them in parentheses like so:

```
([0-9]{2})/([0-9]{2})/([0-9]{4})$
```

We now have three subexpressions. The first contains the month, the second contains the day of the month, and the third contains the year. Now we can construct *replacement* as follows:

```
\3-\1-\2
```

which gives us the year, a dash, the month, a dash, and the day.

Now, our command looks like this:

```
sed 's/([0-9]{2})/([0-9]{2})/([0-9]{4})$/\3-\1-\2/' distros.txt
```

We have two remaining problems. The first is that the extra slashes in our regular expression will confuse sed when it tries to interpret the s command. The second is that since sed, by default, accepts only basic regular expressions, several of the characters in our regular expression will be taken as literals, rather than as metacharacters. We can solve both these problems with a liberal application of backslashes to escape the offending characters:

```
sed 's/\([0-9]\{2\}\)\/\([0-9]\{2\}\)\/\([0-9]\{4\}\)$/\3-\1-\2/' dis
tros.txt
```

And there you have it!

Another feature of the s command is the use of optional flags that may follow the replacement string. The most important of these is the g flag, which instructs sed to apply the search and replace globally to a line, not just to the first instance, which is the default.

Here is an example:

```
[me@linuxbox ~]$ echo "aaabbbccc" | sed 's/b/B/'
aaaBbbccc
```

We see that the replacement was performed but only to the first instance of the letter *b*, while the remaining instances were left unchanged. By adding the g flag, we are able to change all the instances:

```
[me@linuxbox ~]$ echo "aaabbbccc" | sed 's/b/B/g'
aaaBBBccc
```

So far, we have given sed single commands only via the command line. It is also possible to construct more complex commands in a script file using the -f option. To demonstrate, we will use sed with our *distros.txt* file to build a report. Our report will feature a title at the top, our modified dates, and all the distribution names converted to uppercase. To do this, we will need to write a script, so we'll fire up our text editor and enter the following:

```
# sed script to produce Linux distributions report

1 i\
\
Linux Distributions Report\

s/\([0-9]\{2\}\)\/\([0-9]\{2\}\)\/\([0-9]\{4\}\)$/\3-\1-\2/
y/abcdefghijklmnopqrstuvwxyz/ABCDEFGHIJKLMNOPQRSTUVWXYZ/
```

We will save our sed script as *distros.sed* and run it like this:

```
[me@linuxbox ~]$ sed -f distros.sed distros.txt

Linux Distributions Report

SUSE        10.2    2006-12-07
FEDORA      10      2008-11-25
SUSE        11.0    2008-06-19
UBUNTU      8.04    2008-04-24
FEDORA      8       2007-11-08
SUSE        10.3    2007-10-04
UBUNTU      6.10    2006-10-26
FEDORA      7       2007-05-31
UBUNTU      7.10    2007-10-18
UBUNTU      7.04    2007-04-19
SUSE        10.1    2006-05-11
FEDORA      6       2006-10-24
FEDORA      9       2008-05-13
UBUNTU      6.06    2006-06-01
UBUNTU      8.10    2008-10-30
FEDORA      5       2006-03-20
```

As we can see, our script produces the desired results, but how does it do it? Let's take another look at our script. We'll use cat to number the lines.

```
[me@linuxbox ~]$ cat -n distros.sed
     1	# sed script to produce Linux distributions report
     2
     3	1 i\
     4	\
     5	Linux Distributions Report\
     6
     7	s/\([0-9]\{2\}\)\/\([0-9]\{2\}\)\/\([0-9]\{4\}\)$/\3-\1-\2/
     8	y/abcdefghijklmnopqrstuvwxyz/ABCDEFGHIJKLMNOPQRSTUVWXYZ/
```

Line 1 of our script is a *comment*. As in many configuration files and programming languages on Linux systems, comments begin with the # character and are followed by human-readable text. Comments can be placed anywhere in the script (though not within commands themselves) and are helpful to any humans who might need to identify and/or maintain the script.

Line 2 is a blank line. Like comments, blank lines may be added to improve readability.

Many sed commands support line addresses. These are used to specify which lines of the input are to be acted upon. Line addresses may be expressed as single line numbers, line-number ranges, and the special line number $, which indicates the last line of input.

Lines 3 through 6 contain text to be inserted at the address 1, the first line of the input. The i command is followed by the sequence backslash–carriage return to produce an escaped carriage return, or what is called a *line-continuation character*. This sequence, which can be used in many circumstances including shell scripts, allows a carriage return to be embedded in a stream of text without signaling the interpreter (in this case sed) that the end of the line has been reached. The i command and the commands a (which appends text) and c (which replaces text) allow multiple lines of text, providing that each line, except the last, ends with a line-continuation character. The sixth line of our script is actually the end of our inserted text and ends with a plain carriage return rather than a line-continuation character, signaling the end of the i command.

Note: *A line-continuation character is formed by a backslash followed immediately by a carriage return. No intermediary spaces are permitted.*

Line 7 is our search-and-replace command. Since it is not preceded by an address, each line in the input stream is subject to its action.

Line 8 performs transliteration of the lowercase letters into uppercase letters. Note that unlike tr, the y command in sed does not support character ranges (for example, [a-z]), nor does it support POSIX character classes. Again, since the y command is not preceded by an address, it applies to every line in the input stream.

aspell—Interactive Spell Checker

The last tool we will look at is aspell, an interactive spellchecker. The aspell program is the successor to an earlier program named ispell, and it can be used, for the most part, as a drop-in replacement. While the aspell program is mostly used by other programs that require spellchecking capability, it can also be used very effectively as a stand-alone tool from the command line. It has the ability to intelligently check various type of text files, including HTML documents, C/C++ programs, email messages, and other kinds of specialized texts.

To spellcheck a text file containing simple prose, aspell could be used like this:

```
aspell check textfile
```

where *textfile* is the name of the file to check. As a practical example, let's create a simple text file named *foo.txt* containing some deliberate spelling errors:

```
[me@linuxbox ~]$ cat > foo.txt
The quick brown fox jimped over the laxy dog.
```

Next we'll check the file using aspell:

```
[me@linuxbox ~]$ aspell check foo.txt
```

As aspell is interactive in the check mode, we will see a screen like this:

```
The quick brown fox jimped over the laxy dog.



1) jumped                          6) wimped
2) gimped                          7) camped
```

```
3) comped                      8) humped
4) limped                      9) impede
5) pimped                      0) umped
i) Ignore                      I) Ignore all
r) Replace                     R) Replace all
a) Add                         l) Add Lower
b) Abort                       x) Exit

?
```

At the top of the display, we see our text with a suspiciously spelled word highlighted. In the middle, we see 10 spelling suggestions numbered 0 through 9, followed by a list of other possible actions. Finally, at the very bottom, we see a prompt ready to accept our choice.

If we enter 1, aspell replaces the offending word with the word *jumped* and moves on to the next misspelled word, which is *laxy*. If we select the replacement *lazy*, aspell replaces it and terminates. Once aspell has finished, we can examine our file and see that the misspellings have been corrected:

```
[me@linuxbox ~]$ cat foo.txt
The quick brown fox jumped over the lazy dog.
```

Unless told otherwise via the command-line option --dont-backup, aspell creates a backup file containing the original text by appending the extension .*bak* to the filename.

Showing off our sed editing prowess, we'll put our spelling mistakes back in so we can reuse our file:

```
[me@linuxbox ~]$ sed -i 's/lazy/laxy/; s/jumped/jimped/' foo.txt
```

The sed option -i tells sed to edit the file "in place," meaning that rather than sending the edited output to standard output, it will rewrite the file with the changes applied. We also see the ability to place more than one editing command on the line by separating them with a semicolon.

Next, we'll look at how aspell can handle different kinds of text files. Using a text editor such as vim (the adventurous may want to try sed), we will add some HTML markup to our file:

```
<html>
        <head>
                <title>Mispelled HTML file</title>
        </head>
        <body>
                <p>The quick brown fox jimped over the laxy dog.</p>
        </body>
</html>
```

Now, if we try to spellcheck our modified file, we run into a problem. If we do it this way:

```
[me@linuxbox ~]$ aspell check foo.txt
```

we'll get this:

```
<html>
        <head>
                <title>Mispelled HTML file</title>
        </head>
        <body>
                <p>The quick brown fox jimped over the laxy dog.</p>
        </body>
</html>

1) HTML                              4) Hamel
2) ht ml                             5) Hamil
3) ht-ml                             6) hotel
i) Ignore                            I) Ignore all
r) Replace                          R) Replace all
a) Add                               l) Add Lower
b) Abort                             x) Exit

?
```

aspell will see the contents of the HTML tags as misspelled. This problem can be overcome by including the -H (HTML) checking-mode option, like this:

```
[me@linuxbox ~]$ aspell -H check foo.txt
```

Our result is this:

```
<html>
        <head>
                <title>Mispelled HTML file</title>
        </head>
        <body>
                <p>The quick brown fox jimped over the laxy dog.</p>
        </body>
</html>

1) Mi spelled                        6) Misapplied
2) Mi-spelled                        7) Miscalled
3) Misspelled                        8) Respelled
4) Dispelled                         9) Misspell
5) Spelled                           0) Misled
i) Ignore                            I) Ignore all
r) Replace                          R) Replace all
a) Add                               l) Add Lower
b) Abort                             x) Exit

?
```

The HTML is ignored, and only the non-markup portions of the file are checked. In this mode, the contents of HTML tags are ignored and not checked for spelling. However, the contents of ALT tags, which benefit from checking, are checked in this mode.

Note: *By default, aspell will ignore URLs and email addresses in text. This behavior can be overridden with command-line options. It is also possible to specify which markup tags are checked and skipped. See the* aspell *man page for details.*

Final Note

In this chapter, we have looked at a few of the many command-line tools that operate on text. In the next chapter, we will look at several more. Admittedly, it may not seem immediately obvious how or why you might use some of these tools on a day-to-day basis, though we have tried to show some semipractical examples of their use. We will find in later chapters that these tools form the basis of a tool set that is used to solve a host of practical problems. This will be particularly true when we get into shell scripting, where these tools will really show their worth.

Extra Credit

There are a few more interesting text-manipulation commands worth investigating. Among these are split (split files into pieces), csplit (split files into pieces based on context), and sdiff (side-by-side merge of file differences).

21

FORMATTING OUTPUT

In this chapter, we continue our look at text-related tools, focusing on programs that are used to format text output rather than change the text itself. These tools are often used to prepare text for printing, a subject that we will cover in the next chapter. The programs that we will cover in this chapter include the following:

- nl—Number lines.
- fold—Wrap each line to a specified length.
- fmt—A simple text formatter.
- pr—Format text for printing.
- printf—Format and print data.
- groff—A document formatting system.

Simple Formatting Tools

We'll look at some of the simple formatting tools first. These are mostly single-purpose programs, and a bit unsophisticated in what they do, but they can be used for small tasks and as parts of pipelines and scripts.

nl—Number Lines

The nl program is a rather arcane tool used to perform a simple task: It numbers lines. In its simplest use, it resembles cat -n:

```
[me@linuxbox ~]$ nl distros.txt | head
     1  SUSE        10.2    12/07/2006
     2  Fedora      10      11/25/2008
     3  SUSE        11.0    06/19/2008
     4  Ubuntu      8.04    04/24/2008
     5  Fedora      8       11/08/2007
     6  SUSE        10.3    10/04/2007
     7  Ubuntu      6.10    10/26/2006
     8  Fedora      7       05/31/2007
     9  Ubuntu      7.10    10/18/2007
    10  Ubuntu      7.04    04/19/2007
```

Like cat, nl can accept either multiple filenames as command-line arguments or standard input. However, nl has a number of options and supports a primitive form of markup to allow more complex kinds of numbering.

nl supports a concept called *logical pages* when numbering. This allows nl to reset (start over) the numerical sequence when numbering. Using options, it is possible to set the starting number to a specific value and, to a limited extent, set its format. A logical page is further broken down into a header, body, and footer. Within each of these sections, line numbering may be reset and/or be assigned a different style. If nl is given multiple files, it treats them as a single stream of text. Sections in the text stream are indicated by the presence of some rather odd-looking markup added to the text, as shown in Table 21-1.

Table 21-1: nl Markup

Markup	Meaning
\:\:\:	Start of logical-page header
\:\:	Start of logical-page body
\:	Start of logical-page footer

Each of the markup elements in Table 21-1 must appear alone on its own line. After processing a markup element, nl deletes it from the text stream.

Table 21-2 lists the common options for nl.

Table 21-2: Common nl Options

Option	Meaning
-b *style*	Set body numbering to *style*, where *style* is one of the following: • **a** Number all lines. • **t** Number only non-blank lines. This is the default. • **n** None. • ***pregexp*** Number only lines matching basic regular expression *regexp*.
-f *style*	Set footer numbering to *style*. Default is n (none).
-h *style*	Set header numbering to *style*. Default is n (none).
-i *number*	Set page numbering increment to *number*. Default is 1.
-n *format*	Set numbering format to *format*, where *format* is one of the following: • **ln** Left justified, without leading zeros. • **rn** Right justified, without leading zeros. This is the default. • **rz** Right justified, with leading zeros.
-p	Do not reset page numbering at the beginning of each logical page.
-s *string*	Add *string* to the end of each line number to create a separator. Default is a single tab character.
-v *number*	Set first line number of each logical page to *number*. Default is 1.
-w *width*	Set width of the line number field to *width*. Default is 6.

Admittedly, we probably won't be numbering lines that often, but we can use nl to look at how we can combine multiple tools to perform more complex tasks. We will build on our work in the previous chapter to produce a Linux distributions report. Since we will be using nl, it will be useful to include its header/body/footer markup. To do this, we will add it to the sed script from the last chapter. Using our text editor, we will change the script as follows and save it as *distros-nl.sed*:

```
# sed script to produce Linux distributions report

1 i\
\\:\\:\\:\
\
Linux Distributions Report\
\
Name            Ver.    Released\
----            ----    --------\
\\:\\:
s/\([0-9]\{2\}\)\/\([0-9]\{2\}\)\/\([0-9]\{4\}\)$/\3-\1-\2/
```

```
$ a\
\\:\
\
End Of Report
```

The script now inserts the nl logical-page markup and adds a footer at
the end of the report. Note that we had to double up the backslashes in our
markup, because sed normally interprets them as escape characters.

Next, we'll produce our enhanced report by combining sort, sed, and nl:

```
[me@linuxbox ~]$ sort -k 1,1 -k 2n distros.txt | sed -f distros-nl.sed | nl


      Linux Distributions Report

      Name     Ver.    Released
      ----     ----    --------

   1  Fedora   5       2006-03-20
   2  Fedora   6       2006-10-24
   3  Fedora   7       2007-05-31
   4  Fedora   8       2007-11-08
   5  Fedora   9       2008-05-13
   6  Fedora   10      2008-11-25
   7  SUSE     10.1    2006-05-11
   8  SUSE     10.2    2006-12-07
   9  SUSE     10.3    2007-10-04
  10  SUSE     11.0    2008-06-19
  11  Ubuntu   6.06    2006-06-01
  12  Ubuntu   6.10    2006-10-26
  13  Ubuntu   7.04    2007-04-19
  14  Ubuntu   7.10    2007-10-18
  15  Ubuntu   8.04    2008-04-24
  16  Ubuntu   8.10    2008-10-30



      End Of Report
```

Our report is the result of our pipeline of commands. First, we sort the
list by distribution name and version (fields 1 and 2), and then we process
the results with sed, adding the report header (including the logical page
markup for nl) and footer. Finally, we process the result with nl, which, by
default, numbers only the lines of the text stream that belong to the body
section of the logical page.

We can repeat the command and experiment with different options for
nl. Some interesting ones are

```
nl -n rz
```

and

```
nl -w 3 -s ' '
```

fold—Wrap Each Line to a Specified Length

Folding is the process of breaking lines of text at a specified width. Like our other commands, fold accepts either one or more text files or standard input. If we send fold a simple stream of text, we can see how it works:

```
[me@linuxbox ~]$ echo "The quick brown fox jumped over the lazy dog." | fold
-w 12
The quick br
own fox jump
ed over the
lazy dog.
```

Here we see fold in action. The text sent by the echo command is broken into segments specified by the -w option. In this example, we specify a line width of 12 characters. If no width is specified, the default is 80 characters. Notice that the lines are broken regardless of word boundaries. The addition of the -s option will cause fold to break the line at the last available space before the line width is reached:

```
[me@linuxbox ~]$ echo "The quick brown fox jumped over the lazy dog." | fold
-w 12 -s
The quick
brown fox
jumped over
the lazy
dog.
```

fmt—A Simple Text Formatter

The fmt program also folds text, plus a lot more. It accepts either files or standard input and performs paragraph formatting on the text stream. Basically, it fills and joins lines in text while preserving blank lines and indentation.

To demonstrate, we'll need some text. Let's lift some from the fmt info page:

```
   `fmt' reads from the specified FILE arguments (or standard input if none
are given), and writes to standard output.

   By default, blank lines, spaces between words, and indentation are
preserved in the output; successive input lines with different
indentation are not joined; tabs are expanded on input and introduced on
output.

   `fmt' prefers breaking lines at the end of a sentence, and tries to avoid
line breaks after the first word of a sentence or before the last word of a
sentence. A "sentence break" is defined as either the end of a paragraph or a
word ending in any of `.?!', followed by two spaces or end of line, ignoring
any intervening parentheses or quotes. Like TeX, `fmt' reads entire
"paragraphs" before choosing line breaks; the algorithm is a variant of that
given by Donald E. Knuth and Michael F. Plass in "Breaking Paragraphs Into
Lines", `Software--Practice & Experience' 11, 11 (November 1981), 1119-1184.
```

We'll copy this text into our text editor and save the file as *fmt-info.txt.* Now, let's say we wanted to reformat this text to fit a 50-character-wide column. We could do this by processing the file with fmt and the -w option:

```
[me@linuxbox ~]$ fmt -w 50 fmt-info.txt | head
  `fmt' reads from the specified FILE arguments
  (or standard input if
none are given), and writes to standard output.

  By default, blank lines, spaces between words,
  and indentation are
preserved in the output; successive input lines
with different indentation are not joined; tabs
are expanded on input and introduced on output.
```

Well, that's an awkward result. Perhaps we should actually read this text, since it explains what's going on:

> By default, blank lines, spaces between words, and indentation are preserved in the output; successive input lines with different indentation are not joined; tabs are expanded on input and introduced on output.

So, fmt is preserving the indentation of the first line. Fortunately, fmt provides an option to correct this:

```
[me@linuxbox ~]$ fmt -cw 50 fmt-info.txt
  `fmt' reads from the specified FILE arguments
(or standard input if none are given), and writes
to standard output.

  By default, blank lines, spaces between words,
and indentation are preserved in the output;
successive input lines with different indentation
are not joined; tabs are expanded on input and
introduced on output.

  `fmt' prefers breaking lines at the end of a
sentence, and tries to avoid line breaks after
the first word of a sentence or before the
last word of a sentence. A "sentence break"
is defined as either the end of a paragraph
or a word ending in any of `.?!', followed

by two spaces or end of line, ignoring any
intervening parentheses or quotes. Like TeX,
`fmt' reads entire "paragraphs" before choosing
line breaks; the algorithm is a variant of
that given by Donald E. Knuth and Michael F.
Plass in "Breaking Paragraphs Into Lines",
`Software--Practice & Experience' 11, 11
(November 1981), 1119-1184.
```

Much better. By adding the -c option, we now have the desired result.

fmt has some interesting options, as shown in Table 21-3.

Table 21-3: fmt Options

Option	Description
-c	Operate in *crown margin* mode. This preserves the indentation of the first two lines of a paragraph. Subsequent lines are aligned with the indentation of the second line.
-p *string*	Format only those lines beginning with the prefix *string*. After formatting, the contents of *string* are prefixed to each reformatted line. This option can be used to format text in source code comments. For example, any programming language or configuration file that uses a # character to delineate a comment could be formatted by specifying -p '# ' so that only the comments will be formatted. See the example below.
-s	Split-only mode. In this mode, lines will be split only to fit the specified column width. Short lines will not be joined to fill lines. This mode is useful when formatting text, such as code, where joining is not desired.
-u	Perform uniform spacing. This will apply traditional "typewriter-style" formatting to the text. This means a single space between words and two spaces between sentences. This mode is useful for removing *justification*, that is, forced alignment to both the left and right margins.
-w *width*	Format text to fit within a column *width* characters wide. The default is 75 characters. Note: fmt actually formats lines slightly shorter than the specified width to allow for line balancing.

The -p option is particularly interesting. With it, we can format selected portions of a file, provided that the lines to be formatted all begin with the same sequence of characters. Many programming languages use the hash mark (#) to indicate the beginning of a comment and thus can be formatted using this option. Let's create a file that simulates a program that uses comments:

```
[me@linuxbox ~]$ cat > fmt-code.txt
# This file contains code with comments.

# This line is a comment.
# Followed by another comment line.
# And another.

This, on the other hand, is a line of code.
And another line of code.
And another.
```

Our sample file contains comments, which begin with the string # (a # followed by a space), and lines of "code," which do not. Now, using fmt, we can format the comments and leave the code untouched:

```
[me@linuxbox ~]$ fmt -w 50 -p '# ' fmt-code.txt
# This file contains code with comments.

# This line is a comment. Followed by another
# comment line. And another.

This, on the other hand, is a line of code.
And another line of code.
And another.
```

Notice that the adjoining comment lines are joined, while the blank lines and the lines that do not begin with the specified prefix are preserved.

pr—Format Text for Printing

The pr program is used to *paginate* text. When printing text, it is often desirable to separate the pages of output with several lines of whitespace to provide a top and bottom margin for each page. Further, this whitespace can be used to insert a header and footer on each page.

We'll demonstrate pr by formatting our *distros.txt* file into a series of very short pages (only the first two pages are shown):

```
[me@linuxbox ~]$ pr -l 15 -w 65 distros.txt


2012-12-11 18:27              distros.txt           Page 1



SUSE          10.2    12/07/2006
Fedora        10      11/25/2008
SUSE          11.0    06/19/2008
Ubuntu        8.04    04/24/2008
Fedora        8       11/08/2007



2012-12-11 18:27              distros.txt           Page 2



SUSE          10.3    10/04/2007
Ubuntu        6.10    10/26/2006
Fedora        7       05/31/2007
Ubuntu        7.10    10/18/2007
Ubuntu        7.04    04/19/2007
```

In this example, we employ the -l option (for page length) and the -w option (page width) to define a "page" that is 65 characters wide and 15 lines long. pr paginates the contents of the *distros.txt* file, separates each page with several lines of whitespace, and creates a default header containing the file modification time, filename, and page number. The pr program provides many options to control page layout. We'll take a look at more of them in Chapter 22.

printf—Format and Print Data

Unlike the other commands in this chapter, the printf command is not used for pipelines (it does not accept standard input), nor does it find frequent application directly on the command line (it's used mostly in scripts). So why is it important? Because it is so widely used.

printf (from the phrase *print formatted*) was originally developed for the C programming language and has been implemented in many programming languages, including the shell. In fact, in bash, printf is a built-in.

printf works like this:

```
printf "format" arguments
```

The command is given a string containing a format description, which is then applied to a list of arguments. The formatted result is sent to standard output. Here is a trivial example:

```
[me@linuxbox ~]$ printf "I formatted the string: %s\n" foo
I formatted the string: foo
```

The format string may contain literal text (like I formatted the string:); escape sequences (such as \n, a newline character); and sequences beginning with the % character, which are called *conversion specifications*. In the example above, the conversion specification %s is used to format the string foo and place it in the command's output. Here it is again:

```
[me@linuxbox ~]$ printf "I formatted '%s' as a string.\n" foo
I formatted 'foo' as a string.
```

As we can see, the %s conversion specification is replaced by the string foo in the command's output. The s conversion is used to format string data. There are other specifiers for other kinds of data. Table 21-4 lists the commonly used data types.

Table 21-4: Common printf Data-Type Specifiers

Specifier	Description
d	Format a number as a signed decimal integer.
f	Format and output a floating point number.

(continued)

Table 21-4 (*continued*)

Specifier	Description
o	Format an integer as an octal number.
s	Format a string.
x	Format an integer as a hexadecimal number using lowercase *a–f* where needed.
X	Same as x, but use uppercase letters.
%	Print a literal % symbol (i.e., specify "%%").

We'll demonstrate the effect each of the conversion specifiers on the string 380:

```
[me@linuxbox ~]$ printf "%d, %f, %o, %s, %x, %X\n" 380 380 380 380 380 380
380, 380.000000, 574, 380, 17c, 17C
```

Since we specified six conversion specifiers, we must also supply six arguments for printf to process. The six results show the effect of each specifier.

Several optional components may be added to the conversion specifier to adjust its output. A complete conversion specification may consist of the following:

%[*flags*][*width*][.*precision*]*conversion_specification*

Multiple optional components, when used, must appear in the order specified above to be properly interpreted. Table 21-5 describes each component.

Table 21-5: printf Conversion-Specification Components

Component	Description
flags	There are five different flags:
	• # Use the *alternate format* for output. This varies by data type. For o (octal number) conversion, the output is prefixed with 0 (zero). For x and X (hexadecimal number) conversions, the output is prefixed with 0x or 0X respectively.
	• 0 (zero) Pad the output with zeros. This means that the field will be filled with leading zeros, as in 000380.
	• - (dash) Left-align the output. By default, printf right-aligns output.
	• (space) Produce a leading space for positive numbers.
	• + (plus sign) Sign positive numbers. By default, printf signs only negative numbers.

Table 21-5 (*continued*)

Component	Description
width	A number specifying the minimum field width
.precision	For floating-point numbers, specify the number of digits of precision to be output after the decimal point. For string conversion, *precision* specifies the number of characters to output.

Table 21-6 lists some examples of different formats in action.

Table 21-6: print Conversion Specification Examples

Argument	Format	Result	Notes
380	"%d"	380	Simple formatting of an integer
380	"%#x"	0x17c	Integer formatted as a hexa-decimal number using the alternate format flag
380	"%05d"	00380	Integer formatted with leading zeros (padding) and a minimum field width of five characters
380	"%05.5f"	380.00000	Number formatted as a floating-point number with padding and 5 decimal places of precision. Since the specified minimum field width (5) is less than the actual width of the formatted number, the padding has no effect.
380	"%010.5f"	0380.00000	Increasing the minimum field width to 10 makes the padding visible.
380	"%+d"	+380	The + flag signs a positive number.
380	"%-d"	380	The - flag left-aligns the formatting.
abcdefghijk	"%5s"	abcedfghijk	A string is formatted with a minimum field width.
abcdefghijk	"%.5s"	abcde	By applying precision to a string, it is truncated.

Again, `printf` is used mostly in scripts, where it is employed to format tabular data, rather than on the command line directly. But we can still show how it can be used to solve various formatting problems. First, let's output some fields separated by tab characters:

```
[me@linuxbox ~]$ printf "%s\t%s\t%s\n" str1 str2 str3
str1    str2    str3
```

By inserting \t (the escape sequence for a tab), we achieve the desired effect. Next, some numbers with neat formatting:

```
[me@linuxbox ~]$ printf "Line: %05d %15.3f Result: %+15d\n" 1071 3.14156295
32589
Line: 01071          3.142 Result:         +32589
```

This shows the effect of minimum field width on the spacing of the fields. Or how about formatting a tiny web page?

```
[me@linuxbox ~]$ printf "<html>\n\t<head>\n\t\t<title>%s</title>\n\t</head>
\n\t<body>\n\t\t<p>%s</p>\n\t</body>\n</html>\n" "Page Title" "Page Content"
<html>
        <head>
                <title>Page Title</title>
        </head>
        <body>
                <p>Page Content</p>
        </body>
</html>
```

Document Formatting Systems

So far, we have examined the simple text-formatting tools. These are good for small, simple tasks, but what about larger jobs? One of the reasons that Unix became a popular operating system among technical and scientific users (aside from providing a powerful multitasking, multiuser environment for all kinds of software development) is that it offered tools that could be used to produce many types of documents, particularly scientific and academic publications. In fact, as the GNU documentation describes, document preparation was instrumental to the development of Unix:

> The first version of UNIX was developed on a PDP-7 which was sitting around Bell Labs. In 1971 the developers wanted to get a PDP-11 for further work on the operating system. In order to justify the cost for this system, they proposed that they would implement a document formatting system for the AT&T patents division. This first formatting program was a reimplementation of McIllroy's *roff*, written by J.F. Ossanna.

The roff Family and T_EX

Two main families of document formatters dominate the field: those descended from the original roff program, including nroff and troff, and those based on Donald Knuth's T_EX (pronounced "tek") typesetting system. And yes, the dropped "E" in the middle is part of its name.

The name *roff* is derived from the term *run off* as in, "I'll run off a copy for you." The nroff program is used to format documents for output to devices that use monospaced fonts, such as character terminals and typewriter-style printers. At the time of its introduction, this included nearly all printing devices attached to computers. The later troff program formats documents for output on *typesetters*, devices used to produce "camera-ready" type for commercial printing. Most computer printers today are able to simulate the output of typesetters. The roff family also includes some other programs that are used to prepare portions of documents. These include eqn (for mathematical equations) and tbl (for tables).

The T_EX system (in stable form) first appeared in 1989 and has, to some degree, displaced troff as the tool of choice for typesetter output. We won't be covering T_EX here, due both to its complexity (there are entire books about it) and to the fact that it is not installed by default on most modern Linux systems.

Note: *For those interested in installing T_EX, check out the* texlive *package, which can be found in most distribution repositories, and the* LyX *graphical content editor.*

groff—A Document Formatting System

groff is a suite of programs containing the GNU implementation of troff. It also includes a script that is used to emulate nroff and the rest of the roff family as well.

While roff and its descendants are used to make formatted documents, they do it in a way that is rather foreign to modern users. Most documents today are produced using word processors that are able to perform both the composition and layout of a document in a single step. Prior to the advent of the graphical word processor, documents were often produced in a two-step process involving the use of a text editor to perform composition and a processor, such as troff, to apply the formatting. Instructions for the formatting program were embedded in the composed text through the use of a markup language. The modern analog for such a process is the web page, which is composed using a text editor of some kind and then rendered by a web browser using HTML as the markup language to describe the final page layout.

We're not going to cover groff in its entirety, as many elements of its markup language deal with rather arcane details of typography. Instead we will concentrate on one of its *macro packages* that remains in wide use. These macro packages condense many of its low-level commands into a smaller set of high-level commands that make using groff much easier.

For a moment, let's consider the humble man page. It lives in the
/usr/share/man directory as a gzip-compressed text file. If we were to examine its uncompressed contents, we would see the following (the man page
for ls in section 1 is shown):

```
[me@linuxbox ~]$ zcat /usr/share/man/man1/ls.1.gz | head
.\" DO NOT MODIFY THIS FILE!  It was generated by help2man 1.35.
.TH LS "1" "April 2008" "GNU coreutils 6.10" "User Commands"
.SH NAME
ls \- list directory contents
.SH SYNOPSIS
.B ls
[\fIOPTION\fR]... [\fIFILE\fR]...
.SH DESCRIPTION
.\" Add any additional description here
.PP
```

Compared to the man page in its normal presentation, we can begin to
see a correlation between the markup language and its results:

```
[me@linuxbox ~]$ man ls | head
LS(1)                          User Commands                          LS(1)


NAME
       ls - list directory contents

SYNOPSIS
       ls [OPTION]... [FILE]...
```

This is of interest because man pages are rendered by groff, using the
mandoc macro package. In fact, we can simulate the man command with this
pipeline.

```
[me@linuxbox ~]$ zcat /usr/share/man/man1/ls.1.gz | groff -mandoc -T ascii |
head
LS(1)                          User Commands                          LS(1)



NAME
       ls - list directory contents

SYNOPSIS
       ls [OPTION]... [FILE]...
```

Here we use the groff program with the options set to specify the mandoc
macro package and the output driver for ASCII. groff can produce output
in several formats. If no format is specified, PostScript is output by default:

```
[me@linuxbox ~]$ zcat /usr/share/man/man1/ls.1.gz | groff -mandoc | head
%!PS-Adobe-3.0
%%Creator: groff version 1.18.1
%%CreationDate: Thu Feb  2 13:44:37 2012
%%DocumentNeededResources: font Times-Roman
```

```
%%+ font Times-Bold
%%+ font Times-Italic
%%DocumentSuppliedResources: procset grops 1.18 1
%%Pages: 4
%%PageOrder: Ascend
%%Orientation: Portrait
```

PostScript is a page-description language that is used to describe the contents of a printed page to a typesetter-like device. We can take the output of our command and store it to a file (assuming that we are using a graphical desktop with a *Desktop* directory):

```
[me@linuxbox ~]$ zcat /usr/share/man/man1/ls.1.gz | groff -mandoc > ~/Desktop
/foo.ps
```

An icon for the output file should appear on the desktop. By double-clicking the icon, a page viewer should start up and reveal the file in its rendered form (Figure 21-1).

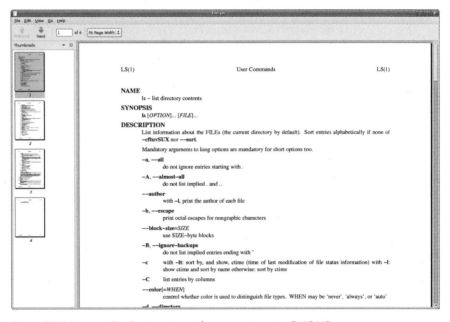

Figure 21-1: Viewing PostScript output with a page viewer in GNOME

What we see is a nicely typeset man page for ls! In fact, it's possible to convert the PostScript file into a *PDF (Portable Document Format)* file with this command:

```
[me@linuxbox ~]$ ps2pdf ~/Desktop/foo.ps ~/Desktop/ls.pdf
```

The `ps2pdf` program is part of the `ghostscript` package, which is installed on most Linux systems that support printing.

Note: *Linux systems often include many command line-programs for file-format conversion. They are often named using the convention* format2format*. Try using the command* ls /usr/bin/*[[:alpha:]]2[[:alpha:]]* *to identify them. Also try searching for programs named* formattoformat.

For our last exercise with groff, we will revisit our old friend *distros.txt.* This time, we will use the tbl program, which is used to format tables, to typeset our list of Linux distributions. To do this, we are going to use our earlier sed script to add markup to a text stream that we will feed to groff.

First, we need to modify our sed script to add the necessary requests that tbl requires. Using a text editor, we will change *distros.sed* to the following:

```
# sed script to produce Linux distributions report

1 i\
.TS\
center box;\
cb s s\
cb cb cb\
l n c.\
Linux Distributions Report\
=\
Name	Version Released\

s/\([0-9]\{2\}\)\/\([0-9]\{2\}\)\/\([0-9]\{4\}\)$/\3-\1-\2/
$ a\
.TE
```

Note that for the script to work properly, care must been taken to see that the words *Name Version Released* are separated by tabs, not spaces. We'll save the resulting file as *distros-tbl.sed.* tbl uses the .TS and .TE requests to start and end the table. The rows following the .TS request define global properties of the table, which, for our example, are centered horizontally on the page and surrounded by a box. The remaining lines of the definition describe the layout of each table row. Now, if we run our report-generating pipeline again with the new sed script, we'll get the following :

```
[me@linuxbox ~]$ sort -k 1,1 -k 2n distros.txt | sed -f distros-tbl.sed | groff
-t -T ascii 2>/dev/null
        +--------------------------------+
        | Linux Distributions Report     |
        +--------------------------------+
        | Name     Version    Released    |
        +--------------------------------+
        |Fedora      5        2006-03-20 |
        |Fedora      6        2006-10-24 |
        |Fedora      7        2007-05-31 |
        |Fedora      8        2007-11-08 |
        |Fedora      9        2008-05-13 |
        |Fedora      10       2008-11-25 |
        |SUSE        10.1     2006-05-11 |
        |SUSE        10.2     2006-12-07 |
        |SUSE        10.3     2007-10-04 |
        |SUSE        11.0     2008-06-19 |
        |Ubuntu      6.06     2006-06-01 |
```

```
|Ubuntu     6.10     2006-10-26 |
|Ubuntu     7.04     2007-04-19 |
|Ubuntu     7.10     2007-10-18 |
|Ubuntu     8.04     2008-04-24 |
|Ubuntu     8.10     2008-10-30 |
+-----------------------------+
```

Adding the -t option to groff instructs it to preprocess the text stream with tbl. Likewise, the -T option is used to output to ASCII rather than to the default output medium, PostScript.

The format of the output is the best we can expect if we are limited to the capabilities of a terminal screen or typewriter-style printer. If we specify PostScript output and graphically view the resulting output, we get a much more satisfying result (see Figure 21-2).

```
[me@linuxbox ~]$ sort -k 1,1 -k 2n distros.txt | sed -f distros-tbl.sed | groff
-t > ~/Desktop/foo.ps
```

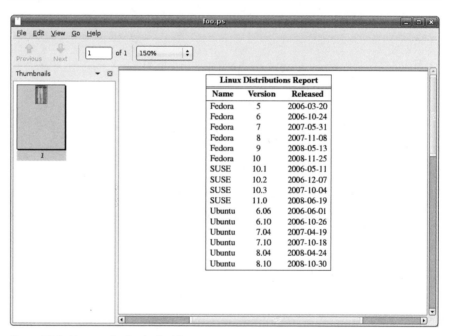

Figure 21-2: Viewing the finished table

Final Note

Given that text is so central to the character of Unix-like operating systems, it makes sense that there would be many tools that are used to manipulate and format text. As we have seen, there are! The simple formatting tools like fmt and pr will find many uses in scripts that produce short documents, while groff (and friends) can be used to write books. We may never write a technical paper using command-line tools (though many people do!), but it's good to know that we could.

22

PRINTING

After spending the last couple of chapters manipulating text, it's time to put that text on paper. In this chapter, we'll look at the command-line tools that are used to print files and control printer operation. We won't be looking at how to configure printing, as that varies from distribution to distribution and is usually set up automatically during installation. Note that we will need a working printer configuration to perform the exercises in this chapter.

We will discuss the following commands:

- pr—Convert text files for printing.
- lpr—Print files.
- lp—Print files (System V).
- a2ps—Format files for printing on a PostScript printer.
- lpstat—Show printer status information.
- lpq—Show printer queue status.
- lprm—Cancel print jobs.
- cancel—Cancel print jobs (System V).

A Brief History of Printing

To fully understand the printing features found in Unix-like operating systems, we must first learn some history. Printing on Unix-like systems goes way back to the beginning of the operating system itself. In those days, printers and how they were used were much different from how they are today.

Printing in the Dim Times

Like the computers themselves, printers in the pre-PC era tended to be large, expensive, and centralized. The typical computer user of 1980 worked at a terminal connected to a computer some distance away. The printer was located near the computer and was under the watchful eyes of the computer's operators.

When printers were expensive and centralized, as they often were in the early days of Unix, it was common practice for many users to share a printer. To identify print jobs belonging to a particular user, a *banner page* displaying the name of the user was often printed at the beginning of each print job. The computer support staff would then load up a cart containing the day's print jobs and deliver them to the individual users.

Character-Based Printers

The printer technology of the '80s was very different in two respects. First, printers of that period were almost always impact printers. *Impact printers* use a mechanical mechanism that strikes a ribbon against the paper to form character impressions on the page. Two of the popular technologies of that time were daisy-wheel printing and dot-matrix printing.

The second, and more important, characteristic of early printers was that they used a fixed set of characters that were intrinsic to the device itself. For example, a daisy-wheel printer could print only the characters actually molded into the petals of the daisy wheel. This made the printers much like high-speed typewriters. As with most typewriters, they printed using monospaced (fixed-width) fonts. This means that each character has the same width. Printing was done at fixed positions on the page, and the printable area of a page contained a fixed number of characters. Most printers printed 10 characters per inch (CPI) horizontally and 6 lines per inch (LPI) vertically. Using this scheme, a US-letter sheet of paper is 85 characters wide and 66 lines high. Taking into account a small margin on each side, 80 characters was considered the maximum width of a print line. This explains why terminal displays (and our terminal emulators) are normally 80 characters wide. It provides a *WYSIWYG (What You See Is What You Get)* view of printed output, using a monospaced font.

Data is sent to a typewriter-like printer in a simple stream of bytes containing the characters to be printed. For example, to print an *a*, the ASCII character code 97 is sent. In addition, the low-numbered ASCII control codes provided a means of moving the printer's carriage and paper, using codes for carriage return, line feed, form feed, and so on. Using the control codes, it's possible to achieve some limited font effects, such as boldface, by having the printer print a character, backspace, and print the character again to get a darker print impression on the page. We can actually witness this if we use nroff to render a man page and examine the output using cat -A:

```
[me@linuxbox ~]$ zcat /usr/share/man/man1/ls.1.gz | nroff -man | cat -A | head
LS(1)                         User Commands                         LS(1)
$
$
$
N^HNA^HAM^HME^HE$
       ls - list directory contents$
$
S^HSY^HYN^HNO^HOP^HPS^HSI^HIS^HS$
       l^Hls^Hs [_^HO_^HP_^HT_^HI_^HO_^HN]... [_^HF_^HI_^HL_^HE]...$
```

The ^H (CTRL-H) characters are the backspaces used to create the bold-face effect. Likewise, we can also see a backspace/underscore sequence used to produce underlining.

Graphical Printers

The development of GUIs led to major changes in printer technology. As computers moved to more picture-based displays, printing moved from character-based to graphical techniques. This was facilitated by the advent of the low-cost laser printer, which, instead of printing fixed characters, could print tiny dots anywhere in the printable area of the page. This made printing proportional fonts (like those used by typesetters), and even photographs and high-quality diagrams, possible.

However, moving from a character-based scheme to a graphical scheme presented a formidable technical challenge. Here's why: The number of bytes needed to fill a page using a character-based printer can be calculated this way (assuming 60 lines per page, each containing 80 characters): 60×80 = 4,800 bytes.

In comparison, a 300-dot-per-inch (DPI) laser printer (assuming an 8-by-10-inch print area per page) requires $(8 \times 300) \times (10 \times 300) \div 8$ = 900,000 bytes.

Many of the slow PC networks simply could not handle the nearly 1 megabyte of data required to print a full page on a laser printer, so it was clear that a clever invention was needed.

That invention turned out to be the page-description language. A *page-description language (PDL)* is a programming language that describes the contents of a page. Basically it says, "Go to this position, draw the character *a* in 10-point Helvetica, go to this position. . . ." until everything on the page is described. The first major PDL was PostScript from Adobe Systems, which is still in wide use today. The PostScript language is a complete programming language tailored for typography and other kinds of graphics and imaging. It includes built-in support for 35 standard, high-quality fonts, plus the ability to accept additional font definitions at runtime. At first, support for Post-Script was built into the printers themselves. This solved the data transmission problem. While the typical PostScript program was verbose in comparison to the simple byte stream of character-based printers, it was much smaller than the number of bytes required to represent the entire printed page.

A *PostScript printer* accepted a PostScript program as input. The printer contained its own processor and memory (oftentimes making the printer a more powerful computer than the computer to which it was attached) and executed a special program called a *PostScript interpreter*, which read the incoming PostScript program and rendered the results into the printer's internal memory, thus forming the pattern of bits (dots) that would be transferred to the paper. The generic name for this process of rendering something into a large bit pattern (called a *bitmap*) is *raster image processor*, or *RIP*.

As the years went by, both computers and networks became much faster. This allowed the RIP to move from the printer to the host computer, which, in turn, permitted high-quality printers to be much less expensive.

Many printers today still accept character-based streams, but many low-cost printers do not. They rely on the host computer's RIP to provide a stream of bits to print as dots. There are still some PostScript printers, too.

Printing with Linux

Modern Linux systems employ two software suites to perform and manage printing. The first, CUPS (Common Unix Printing System), provides print drivers and print-job management; the second, Ghostscript, a PostScript interpreter, acts as a RIP.

CUPS manages printers by creating and maintaining print queues. As we discussed in our brief history lesson, Unix printing was originally designed to manage a centralized printer shared by multiple users. Since printers are slow by nature, compared to the computers that are feeding them, printing systems need a way to schedule multiple print jobs and keep things organized. CUPS also has the ability to recognize different types of data (within reason) and can convert files to a printable form.

Preparing Files for Printing

As command line users, we are mostly interested in printing text, though it is certainly possible to print other data formats as well.

pr—Convert Text Files for Printing

We looked at pr a little in the previous chapter. Now we will examine some of its many options used in conjunction with printing. In our history of printing, we saw that character-based printers use monospaced fonts, resulting in fixed numbers of characters per line and lines per page. pr is used to adjust text to fit on a specific page size, with optional page headers and margins. Table 22-1 summarizes the most commonly used options.

Table 22-1: Common pr Options

Option	Description
+first[:last]	Output a range of pages starting with first and, optionally, ending with last.
-columns	Organize the content of the page into the number of columns specified by columns.
-a	By default, multicolumn output is listed vertically. By adding the -a (across) option, content is listed horizontally.
-d	Double-space output.
-D format	Format the date displayed in page headers using format. See the man page for the date command for a description of the format string.
-f	Use form feeds rather than carriage returns to separate pages.
-h header	In the center portion of the page header, use header rather the name of the file being processed.
-l length	Set page length to length. Default is 66 lines (US letter at 6 lines per inch).
-n	Number lines.
-o offset	Create a left margin offset characters wide.
-w width	Set page width to width. Default is 72 characters.

pr is often used in pipelines as a filter. In this example, we will produce a directory listing of /usr/bin and format it into paginated, three-column output using pr:

```
[me@linuxbox ~]$ ls /usr/bin' | pr -3 -w 65 | head

2012-02-18 14:00                                              Page 1
[                       apturl              bsd-write
411toppm                ar                  bsh
a2p                     arecord             btcflash
a2ps                    arecordmidi         bug-buddy
a2ps-lpr-wrapper        ark                 buildhash
```

Sending a Print Job to a Printer

The CUPS printing suite supports two methods of printing historically used on Unix-like systems. One method, called Berkeley or LPD (used in the Berkeley Software Distribution version of Unix), uses the lpr program; the other method, called SysV (from the System V version of Unix), uses the lp program. Both programs do roughly the same thing. Choosing one over the other is a matter of personal taste.

lpr—Print Files (Berkeley Style)

The lpr program can be used to send files to the printer. It may also be used in pipelines, as it accepts standard input. For example, to print the results of our multicolumn directory listing above, we could do this:

```
[me@linuxbox ~]$ ls /usr/bin | pr -3 | lpr
```

The report would be sent to the system's default printer. To send the file to a different printer, the -P option can used like this:

```
lpr -P printer_name
```

where *printer_name* is the name of the desired printer. To see a list of printers known to the system:

```
[me@linuxbox ~]$ lpstat -a
```

Note: *Many Linux distributions allow you to define a "printer" that outputs files in PDF, rather than printing on the physical printer. This is very handy for experimenting with printing commands. Check your printer configuration program to see if it supports this configuration. On some distributions, you may need to install additional packages (such as* cups-pdf*) to enable this capability.*

Table 22-2 shows some of the common options for lpr.

Table 22-2: Common lpr Options

Option	Description
-# *number*	Set number of copies to *number*.
-p	Print each page with a shaded header with the date, time, job name, and page number. This so-called "pretty print" option can be used when printing text files.
-P *printer*	Specify the name of the printer used for output. If no printer is specified, the system's default printer is used.
-r	Delete files after printing. This would be useful for programs that produce temporary printer-output files.

lp—Print Files (System V Style)

Like lpr, lp accepts either files or standard input for printing. It differs from lpr in that it supports a different (and slightly more sophisticated) option set. Table 22-3 lists the common options.

Table 22-3: Common lp Options

Option	Description
-d *printer*	Set the destination (printer) to *printer*. If no d option is specified, the system default printer is used.
-n *number*	Set the number of copies to *number*.
-o landscape	Set output to landscape orientation.
-o fitplot	Scale the file to fit the page. This is useful when printing images, such as JPEG files.
-o scaling=*number*	Scale file to *number*. The value of 100 fills the page. Values less than 100 are reduced, while values greater than 100 cause the file to be printed across multiple pages.
-o cpi=*number*	Set the output characters per inch to *number*. Default is 10.
-o lpi=*number*	Set the output lines per inch to *number*. Default is 6.
-o page-bottom=*points* -o page-left=*points* -o page-right=*points* -o page-top=*points*	Set the page margins. Values are expressed in *points*, a unit of typographic measurement. There are 72 points to an inch.
-P *pages*	Specify the list of pages. *pages* may be expressed as a comma-separated list and/or a range—for example 1,3,5,7-10.

We'll produce our directory listing again, this time printing 12 CPI and 8 LPI with a left margin of one-half inch. Note that we have to adjust the pr options to account for the new page size:

```
[me@linuxbox ~]$ ls /usr/bin | pr -4 -w 90 -l 88 | lp -o page-left=36 -o cpi=
12 -o lpi=8
```

This pipeline produces a four-column listing using smaller type than the default. The increased number of characters per inch allows us to fit more columns on the page.

Another Option: a2ps

The a2ps program is interesting. As we can surmise from its name, it's a format conversion program, but it's also much more. Its name originally meant *ASCII to PostScript*, and it was used to prepare text files for printing on PostScript printers. Over the years, however, the capabilities of the program have grown, and now its name means *Anything to PostScript*. While its name suggests a format-conversion program, it is actually a printing program. It sends its default output, rather than standard output, to the system's default printer. The program's default behavior is that of a "pretty printer," meaning that it improves the appearance of output. We can use the program to create a PostScript file on our desktop:

```
[me@linuxbox ~]$ ls /usr/bin | pr -3 -t | a2ps -o ~/Desktop/ls.ps -L 66
[stdin (plain): 11 pages on 6 sheets]
[Total: 11 pages on 6 sheets] saved into the file `/home/me/Desktop/ls.ps'
```

Here we filter the stream with pr, using the -t option (omit headers and footers) and then, with a2ps, specifying an output file (-o option) and 66 lines per page (-L option) to match the output pagination of pr. If we view the resulting file with a suitable file viewer, we will see the output shown in Figure 22-1.

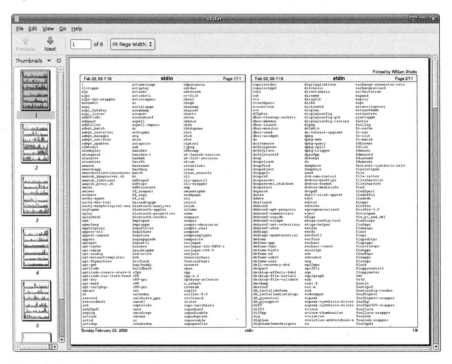

Figure 22-1: Viewing a2ps output

As we can see, the default output layout is "two up" format. This causes the contents of two pages to be printed on each sheet of paper. a2ps applies nice page headers and footers, too.

a2ps has a lot of options. Table 22-4 summarizes them.

Table 22-4: a2ps Options

Option	Description
--center-title=*text*	Set center page title to *text*.
--columns=*number*	Arrange pages into *number* columns. Default is 2.
--footer=*text*	Set page footer to *text*.
--guess	Report the types of files given as arguments. Since a2ps tries to convert and format all types of data, this option can be useful for predicting what a2ps will do when given a particular file.
--left-footer=*text*	Set left-page footer to *text*.
--left-title=*text*	Set left-page title to *text*.
--line-numbers=*interval*	Number lines of output every *interval* lines.
--list=defaults	Display default settings.
--list=*topic*	Display settings for *topic*, where *topic* is one of the following: delegations (external programs that will be used to convert data), encodings, features, variables, media (paper sizes and the like), ppd (PostScript printer descriptions), printers, prologues (portions of code that are prefixed to normal output), stylesheets, or user options.
--pages=*range*	Print pages in range.
--right-footer=*text*	Set right-page footer to *text*.
--right-title=*text*	Set right-page title to *text*.
--rows=*number*	Arrange pages into *number* rows. Default is 1.
-B	No page headers.
-b *text*	Set page header to *text*.
-f *size*	Use *size* point font.
-l *number*	Set characters per line to *number*. This and the -L option (below) can be used to make files paginated with other programs, such as pr, fit correctly on the page.

(continued)

Table 22-4 (*continued*)

Option	Description
-L *number*	Set lines per page to *number*.
-M *name*	Use media name—for example, A4.
-n *number*	Output *number* copies of each page.
-o *file*	Send output to *file*. If *file* is specified as -, use standard output.
-P *printer*	Use *printer*. If a printer is not specified, the system default printer is used.
-R	Portrait orientation
-r	Landscape orientation
-T *number*	Set tab stops to every *number* characters.
-u *text*	Underlay (watermark) pages with *text*.

This is just a summary. a2ps has several more options.

Note: *a2ps is still in active development. During my testing, I noticed different behavior on various distributions. On CentOS 4, output always went to standard output by default. On CentOS 4 and Fedora 10, output defaulted to A4 media, despite the program being configured to use letter-size media by default. I could overcome these issues by explicitly specifying the desired option. On Ubuntu 8.04, a2ps performed as documented.*

Also note that there is another output formatter that is useful for converting text into PostScript. Called enscript, *it can perform many of the same kinds of formatting and printing tricks, but unlike* a2ps, *it accepts only text input.*

Monitoring and Controlling Print Jobs

As Unix printing systems are designed to handle multiple print jobs from multiple users, CUPS is designed to do the same. Each printer is given a *print queue*, where jobs are parked until they can be *spooled* to the printer. CUPS supplies several command-line programs that are used to manage printer status and print queues. Like the lpr and lp programs, these management programs are modeled after the corresponding programs from the Berkeley and System V printing systems.

lpstat—Display Print System Status

The lpstat program is useful for determining the names and availability of printers on the system. For example, if we had a system with both a physical printer (named *printer*) and a PDF virtual printer (named *PDF*), we could check their status like this:

```
[me@linuxbox ~]$ lpstat -a
PDF accepting requests since Mon 05 Dec 2011 03:05:59 PM EST
printer accepting requests since Tue 21 Feb 2012 08:43:22 AM EST
```

Further, we could determine a more detailed description of the print system configuration this way:

```
[me@linuxbox ~]$ lpstat -s
system default destination: printer
device for PDF: cups-pdf:/
device for printer: ipp://print-server:631/printers/printer
```

In this example, we see that *printer* is the system's default printer and that it is a network printer using Internet Printing Protocol (*ipp://*) attached to a system named *print-server*.

The commonly used options are described in Table 22-5.

Table 22-5: Common lpstat Options

Option	Description
-a [*printer*...]	Display the state of the printer queue for *printer*. Note that this is the status of the printer queue's ability to accept jobs, not the status of the physical printers. If no printers are specified, all print queues are shown.
-d	Display the name of the system's default printer.
-p [*printer*...]	Display the status of the specified *printer*. If no printers are specified, all printers are shown.
-r	Display the status of the print server.
-s	Display a status summary.
-t	Display a complete status report.

lpq—Display Printer Queue Status

To see the status of a printer queue, the lpq program is used. This allows us to view the status of the queue and the print jobs it contains. Here is an example of an empty queue for a system default printer named *printer*:

```
[me@linuxbox ~]$ lpq
printer is ready
no entries
```

If we do not specify a printer (using the -P option), the system's default printer is shown. If we send a job to the printer and then look at the queue, we will see it listed:

```
[me@linuxbox ~]$ ls *.txt | pr -3 | lp
request id is printer-603 (1 file(s))
[me@linuxbox ~]$ lpq
printer is ready and printing
Rank    Owner   Job    File(s)                          Total Size
active  me      603    (stdin)                          1024 bytes
```

lprm and cancel—Cancel Print Jobs

CUPS supplies two programs used to terminate print jobs and remove them from the print queue. One is Berkeley style (lprm), and the other is System V (cancel). They differ slightly in the options they support but do basically the same thing. Using our print job above as an example, we could stop the job and remove it this way:

```
[me@linuxbox ~]$ cancel 603
[me@linuxbox ~]$ lpq
printer is ready
no entries
```

Each command has options for removing all the jobs belonging to a particular user, particular printer, and multiple job numbers. Their respective man pages have all the details.

23

COMPILING PROGRAMS

In this chapter, we will look at how to build programs
by compiling source code. The availability of source
code is the essential freedom that makes Linux possible.
The entire ecosystem of Linux development relies on
free exchange between developers. For many desktop
users, compiling is a lost art. It used to be quite common, but today, distribution providers maintain huge repositories of precompiled binaries, ready
to download and use. At the time of this writing, the Debian repository (one
of the largest of any of the distributions) contains almost 23,000 packages.

So why compile software? There are two reasons:

- **Availability.** Despite the number of precompiled programs in distribution repositories, some distributions may not include all the desired
  applications. In this case, the only way to get the desired program is
  to compile it from source.

- **Timeliness.** While some distributions specialize in cutting-edge versions of programs, many do not. This means that in order to have the
  very latest version of a program, compiling is necessary.

Compiling software from source code can become very complex and technical, well beyond the reach of many users. However, many compiling tasks are quite easy and involve only a few steps. It all depends on the package. We will look at a very simple case in order to provide an overview of the process and as a starting point for those who wish to undertake further study.

We will introduce one new command:

- make—Utility to maintain programs.

What Is Compiling?

Simply put, compiling is the process of translating *source code* (the human-readable description of a program written by a programmer) into the native language of the computer's processor.

The computer's processor (or *CPU*) works at a very elemental level, executing programs in what is called *machine language*. This is a numeric code that describes very small operations, such as "add this byte," "point to this location in memory," or "copy this byte." Each of these instructions is expressed in binary (ones and zeros). The earliest computer programs were written using this numeric code, which may explain why programmers who wrote it were said to smoke a lot, drink gallons of coffee, and wear thick glasses.

This problem was overcome by the advent of *assembly language*, which replaced the numeric codes with (slightly) easier to use character *mnemonics* such as CPY (for copy) and MOV (for move). Programs written in assembly language are processed into machine language by a program called an *assembler*. Assembly language is still used today for certain specialized programming tasks, such as *device drivers* and *embedded systems*.

We next come to what are called *high-level programming languages*. They are called this because they allow the programmer to be less concerned with the details of what the processor is doing and more with solving the problem at hand. The early ones (developed during the 1950s) included *FORTRAN* (designed for scientific and technical tasks) and *COBOL* (designed for business applications). Both are still in limited use today.

While there are many popular programming languages, two predominate. Most programs written for modern systems are written in either C or C++. In the examples to follow, we will be compiling a C program.

Programs written in high-level programming languages are converted into machine language by processing them with another program, called a *compiler*. Some compilers translate high-level instructions into assembly language and then use an assembler to perform the final stage of translation into machine language.

A process often used in conjunction with compiling is called *linking*. Programs perform many common tasks. Take, for instance, opening a file.

Many programs perform this task, but it would be wasteful to have each program implement its own routine to open files. It makes more sense to have a single piece of programming that knows how to open files and to allow all programs that need it to share it. Providing support for common tasks is accomplished by what are called *libraries*. They contain multiple *routines*, each performing some common task that multiple programs can share. If we look in the */lib* and */usr/lib* directories, we can see where many of them live. A program called a *linker* is used to form the connections between the output of the compiler and the libraries that the compiled program requires. The final result of this process is the *executable program file*, ready for use.

Are All Programs Compiled?

No. As we have seen, some programs, such as shell scripts, do not require compiling but are executed directly. These are written in what are known as *scripting* or *interpreted* languages. These languages, which have grown in popularity in recent years, include Perl, Python, PHP, Ruby, and many others.

Scripted languages are executed by a special program called an *interpreter*. An interpreter inputs the program file and reads and executes each instruction contained within it. In general, interpreted programs execute much more slowly than compiled programs. This is because each source code instruction in an interpreted program is translated every time it is carried out, whereas with a compiled program, a source code instruction is translated only once, and this translation is permanently recorded in the final executable file.

So why are interpreted languages so popular? For many programming chores, the results are "fast enough," but the real advantage is that it is generally faster and easier to develop interpreted programs than compiled programs. Programs are usually developed in a repeating cycle of code, compile, test. As a program grows in size, the compilation phase of the cycle can become quite long. Interpreted languages remove the compilation step and thus speed up program development.

Compiling a C Program

Let's compile something. Before we do that, however, we're going to need some tools like the compiler, the linker, and make. The C compiler used almost universally in the Linux environment is called gcc (GNU C Compiler), originally written by Richard Stallman. Most distributions do not install gcc by default. We can check to see if the compiler is present like this:

```
[me@linuxbox ~]$ which gcc
/usr/bin/gcc
```

The results in this example indicate that the compiler is installed.

Note: *Your distribution may have a metapackage (a collection of packages) for software development. If so, consider installing it if you intend to compile programs on your system. If your system does not provide a metapackage, try installing the gcc and make packages. On many distributions, they are sufficient to carry out the exercise below.*

Obtaining the Source Code

For our compiling exercise, we are going to compile a program from the GNU Project called diction. This handy little program checks text files for writing quality and style. As programs go, it is fairly small and easy to build.

Following convention, we're first going to create a directory for our source code named *src* and then download the source code into it using ftp:

```
[me@linuxbox ~]$ mkdir src
[me@linuxbox ~]$ cd src
[me@linuxbox src]$ ftp ftp.gnu.org
Connected to ftp.gnu.org.
220 GNU FTP server ready.
Name (ftp.gnu.org:me): anonymous
230 Login successful.
Remote system type is UNIX.
Using binary mode to transfer files.
ftp> cd gnu/diction
250 Directory successfully changed.
ftp> ls
200 PORT command successful. Consider using PASV.
150 Here comes the directory listing.
-rw-r--r--    1 1003    65534    68940 Aug 28  1998 diction-0.7.tar.gz
-rw-r--r--    1 1003    65534    90957 Mar 04  2002 diction-1.02.tar.gz
-rw-r--r--    1 1003    65534   141062 Sep 17  2007 diction-1.11.tar.gz
226 Directory send OK.
ftp> get diction-1.11.tar.gz
local: diction-1.11.tar.gz remote: diction-1.11.tar.gz
200 PORT command successful. Consider using PASV.
150 Opening BINARY mode data connection for diction-1.11.tar.gz (141062
bytes).
226 File send OK.
141062 bytes received in 0.16 secs (847.4 kB/s)
ftp> bye
221 Goodbye.
[me@linuxbox src]$ ls
diction-1.11.tar.gz
```

Note: *Since we are the maintainer of this source code while we compile it, we will keep it in ~/src. Source code installed by your distribution will be installed in /usr/src, while source code intended for use by multiple users is usually installed in /usr/local/src.*

As we can see, source code is usually supplied in the form of a compressed tar file. Sometimes called a *tarball,* this file contains the *source tree,* or hierarchy of directories and files that compose the source code. After arriving at the FTP site, we examine the list of tar files available and select the newest version for download. Using the get command within ftp, we copy the file from the FTP server to the local machine.

Once the tar file is downloaded, it must be unpacked. This is done with the tar program:

```
[me@linuxbox src]$ tar xzf diction-1.11.tar.gz
[me@linuxbox src]$ ls
diction-1.11        diction-1.11.tar.gz
```

Note: *The* diction *program, like all GNU Project software, follows certain standards for source code packaging. Most other source code available in the Linux ecosystem also follows this standard. One element of the standard is that when the source code tar file is unpacked, a directory will be created that contains the source tree and that this directory will be named* project-x.xx, *thus containing both the project's name and its version number. This scheme allows easy installation of multiple versions of the same program. However, it is often a good idea to examine the layout of the tree before unpacking it. Some projects will not create the directory but instead will deliver the files directly into the current directory. This will make a mess in your otherwise well-organized* src *directory. To avoid this, use the following command to examine the contents of the tar file:*

```
tar tzvf tarfile | head
```

Examining the Source Tree

Unpacking the tar file results in the creation of a new directory, named *diction-1.11*. This directory contains the source tree. Let's look inside:

```
[me@linuxbox src]$ cd diction-1.11
[me@linuxbox diction-1.11]$ ls
config.guess   diction.c        getopt.c       nl
config.h.in    diction.pot      getopt.h       nl.po
config.sub     diction.spec     getopt_int.h   README
configure      diction.spec.in  INSTALL        sentence.c
configure.in   diction.texi.in  install-sh     sentence.h
COPYING        en               Makefile.in    style.1.in
de             en_GB            misc.c         style.c
de.po          en_GB.po         misc.h         test
diction.1.in   getopt1.c        NEWS
```

In it, we see a number of files. Programs belonging to the GNU Project, as well as many others, will supply the documentation files *README, INSTALL, NEWS,* and *COPYING.* These files contain the description of the program, information on how to build and install it, and its licensing terms. It is always a good idea to carefully read the *README* and *INSTALL* files before attempting to build the program.

The other interesting files in this directory are the ones ending with *.c* and *.h*:

```
[me@linuxbox diction-1.11]$ ls *.c
diction.c getopt1.c getopt.c misc.c sentence.c style.c
[me@linuxbox diction-1.11]$ ls *.h
getopt.h getopt_int.h misc.h sentence.h
```

The .*c* files contain the two C programs supplied by the package (*style* and *diction*), divided into modules. It is common practice for large programs to be broken into smaller, easier-to-manage pieces. The source code files are ordinary text and can be examined with less:

```
[me@linuxbox diction-1.11]$ less diction.c
```

The .*h* files are known as *header files*. These, too, are ordinary text. Header files contain descriptions of the routines included in a source code file or library. In order for the compiler to connect the modules, it must receive a description of all the modules needed to complete the entire program. Near the beginning of the *diction.c* file, we see this line:

```
#include "getopt.h"
```

This instructs the compiler to read the file *getopt.h* as it reads the source code in *diction.c* in order to "know" what's in *getopt.c*. The *getopt.c* file supplies routines that are shared by both the style and diction programs.

Above the include statement for *getopt.h*, we see some other include statements such as these:

```
#include <regex.h>
#include <stdio.h>
#include <stdlib.h>
#include <string.h>
#include <unistd.h>
```

These also refer to header files, but they refer to header files that live outside the current source tree. They are supplied by the system to support the compilation of every program. If we look in */usr/include*, we can see them:

```
[me@linuxbox diction-1.11]$ ls /usr/include
```

The header files in this directory were installed when we installed the compiler.

Building the Program

Most programs build with a simple, two-command sequence:

```
./configure
make
```

The configure program is a shell script that is supplied with the source tree. Its job is to analyze the build environment. Most source code is designed to be *portable*. That is, it is designed to build on more than one kind of Unix-like system. But in order to do that, the source code may need to undergo slight adjustments during the build to accommodate differences between systems. configure also checks to see that necessary external tools and components are installed.

Let's run `configure`. Since `configure` is not located where the shell normally expects programs to be located, we must explicitly tell the shell its location by prefixing the command with `./`. This indicates that the program is located in the current working directory:

```
[me@linuxbox diction-1.11]$ ./configure
```

`configure` will output a lot of messages as it tests and configures the build. When it finishes, the output will look something like this:

```
checking libintl.h presence... yes
checking for libintl.h... yes
checking for library containing gettext... none required
configure: creating ./config.status
config.status: creating Makefile
config.status: creating diction.1
config.status: creating diction.texi
config.status: creating diction.spec
config.status: creating style.1
config.status: creating test/rundiction
config.status: creating config.h
[me@linuxbox diction-1.11]$
```

What's important here is that there are no error messages. If there were, the configuration would have failed, and the program would not build until the errors are corrected.

We see `configure` created several new files in our source directory. The most important one is *Makefile*. *Makefile* is a configuration file that instructs the `make` program exactly how to build the program. Without it, `make` will refuse to run. *Makefile* is an ordinary text file, so we can view it:

```
[me@linuxbox diction-1.11]$ less Makefile
```

The `make` program takes as input a *makefile* (which is normally named *Makefile*), which describes the relationships and dependencies among the components that compose the finished program.

The first part of the makefile defines variables that are substituted in later sections of the makefile. For example, we see the line

```
CC=            gcc
```

which defines the C compiler to be `gcc`. Later in the makefile, we see one instance where it gets used:

```
diction:       diction.o sentence.o misc.o getopt.o getopt1.o
               $(CC) -o $@ $(LDFLAGS) diction.o sentence.o misc.o \
               getopt.o getopt1.o $(LIBS)
```

A substitution is performed here, and the value `$(CC)` is replaced by `gcc` at runtime.

Most of the makefile consists of lines, which define a *target*—in this case the executable file *diction*—and the files on which it is dependent. The remaining lines describe the command(s) needed to create the target from its components. We see in this example that the executable file *diction* (one of the final end products) depends on the existence of *diction.o*, *sentence.o*, *misc.o*, *getopt.o*, and *getopt1.o*. Later on, in the makefile, we see definitions of each of these as targets.

```
diction.o:      diction.c config.h getopt.h misc.h sentence.h
getopt.o:       getopt.c getopt.h getopt_int.h
getopt1.o:      getopt1.c getopt.h getopt_int.h
misc.o:         misc.c config.h misc.h
sentence.o:     sentence.c config.h misc.h sentence.h
style.o:        style.c config.h getopt.h misc.h sentence.h
```

However, we don't see any command specified for them. This is handled by a general target, earlier in the file, that describes the command used to compile any *.c* file into a *.o* file:

```
.c.o:
                $(CC) -c $(CPPFLAGS) $(CFLAGS) $<
```

This all seems very complicated. Why not simply list all the steps to compile the parts and be done with it? The answer will become clear in a moment. In the meantime, let's run make and build our programs:

```
[me@linuxbox diction-1.11]$ make
```

The make program will run, using the contents of *Makefile* to guide its actions. It will produce a lot of messages.

When it finishes, we will see that all the targets are now present in our directory:

```
[me@linuxbox diction-1.11]$ ls
config.guess    de.po           en              install-sh      sentence.c
config.h        diction         en_GB           Makefile        sentence.h
config.h.in     diction.1       en_GB.mo        Makefile.in     sentence.o
config.log      diction.1.in    en_GB.po        misc.c          style
config.status   diction.c       getopt1.c       misc.h          style.1
config.sub      diction.o       getopt1.o       misc.o          style.1.in
configure       diction.pot     getopt.c        NEWS            style.c
configure.in    diction.spec    getopt.h        nl              style.o
COPYING         diction.spec.in getopt_int.h    nl.mo           test
de              diction.texi    getopt.o        nl.po
de.mo           diction.texi.in INSTALL         README
```

Among the files, we see diction and style, the programs that we set out to build. Congratulations are in order! We just compiled our first programs from source code!

But just out of curiosity, let's run make again:

```
[me@linuxbox diction-1.11]$ make
make: Nothing to be done for `all'.
```

It produces only this strange message. What's going on? Why didn't it build the program again? Ah, this is the magic of make. Rather than simply build everything again, make builds only what needs building. With all of the targets present, make determined that there was nothing to do. We can demonstrate this by deleting one of the targets and running make again to see what it does.

```
[me@linuxbox diction-1.11]$ rm getopt.o
[me@linuxbox diction-1.11]$ make
```

We see that make rebuilds *getopt.o* and relinks the diction and style programs, since they depend on the missing module. This behavior also points out another important feature of make: It keeps targets up-to-date. make insists that targets be newer than their dependencies. This makes perfect sense, as a programmer will often update a bit of source code and then use make to build a new version of the finished product. make ensures that everything that needs building based on the updated code is built. If we use the touch program to "update" one of the source code files, we can see this happen:

```
[me@linuxbox diction-1.11]$ ls -l diction getopt.c
-rwxr-xr-x 1 me       me        37164 2009-03-05 06:14 diction
-rw-r--r-- 1 me       me        33125 2007-03-30 17:45 getopt.c
[me@linuxbox diction-1.11]$ touch getopt.c
[me@linuxbox diction-1.11]$ ls -l diction getopt.c
-rwxr-xr-x 1 me       me        37164 2009-03-05 06:14 diction
-rw-r--r-- 1 me       me        33125 2009-03-05 06:23 getopt.c
[me@linuxbox diction-1.11]$ make
```

After make runs, we see that it has restored the target to being newer than the dependency:

```
[me@linuxbox diction-1.11]$ ls -l diction getopt.c
-rwxr-xr-x 1 me       me        37164 2009-03-05 06:24 diction
-rw-r--r-- 1 me       me        33125 2009-03-05 06:23 getopt.c
```

The ability of make to intelligently build only what needs building is a great benefit to programmers. While the time savings may not be apparent with our small project, it is significant with larger projects. Remember, the Linux kernel (a program that undergoes continuous modification and improvement) contains several *million* lines of code.

Installing the Program

Well-packaged source code often includes a special make target called install. This target will install the final product in a system directory for use. Usually, this directory is */usr/local/bin*, the traditional location for locally built software. However, this directory is not normally writable by ordinary users, so we must become the superuser to perform the installation:

```
[me@linuxbox diction-1.11]$ sudo make install
```

After we perform the installation, we can check that the program is ready to go:

```
[me@linuxbox diction-1.11]$ which diction
/usr/local/bin/diction
[me@linuxbox diction-1.11]$ man diction
```

And there we have it!

Final Note

In this chapter, we have seen how three simple commands—`./configure`, `make`, `make install`—can be used to build many source code packages. We have also seen the important role that `make` plays in the maintenance of programs. The `make` program can be used for any task that needs to maintain a target/dependency relationship, not just for compiling source code.

PART 4

WRITING SHELL SCRIPTS

24

WRITING YOUR FIRST SCRIPT

In the preceding chapters, we have assembled an arsenal of command-line tools. While these tools can solve many kinds of computing problems, we are still limited to manually using them one by one on the command line. Wouldn't it be great if we could get the shell to do more of the work? We can. By joining our tools together into programs of our own design, the shell can carry out complex sequences of tasks all by itself. We enable it to do this by writing *shell scripts*.

What Are Shell Scripts?

In the simplest terms, a shell script is a file containing a series of commands. The shell reads this file and carries out the commands as though they have been entered directly on the command line.

The shell is distinctive, in that it is both a powerful command-line interface to the system and a scripting language interpreter. As we will see, most of the things that can be done on the command line can be done in scripts, and most of the things that can be done in scripts can be done on the command line.

We have covered many shell features, but we have focused on those features most often used directly on the command line. The shell also provides a set of features usually (but not always) used when writing programs.

How to Write a Shell Script

To successfully create and run a shell script, we need to do three things:

1. **Write a script.** Shell scripts are ordinary text files. So we need a text editor to write them. The best text editors will provide *syntax highlighting*, allowing us to see a color-coded view of the elements of the script. Syntax highlighting will help us spot certain kinds of common errors. vim, gedit, kate, and many other editors are good candidates for writing scripts.

2. **Make the script executable.** The system is fussy about not letting any old text file be treated as a program, and for good reason! We need to set the script file's permissions to allow execution.

3. **Put the script somewhere the shell can find it.** The shell automatically searches certain directories for executable files when no explicit pathname is specified. For maximum convenience, we will place our scripts in these directories.

Script File Format

In keeping with programming tradition, we'll create a "hello world" program to demonstrate an extremely simple script. So let's fire up our text editors and enter the following script:

```
#!/bin/bash

# This is our first script.

echo 'Hello World!'
```

The last line of our script is pretty familiar, just an echo command with a string argument. The second line is also familiar. It looks like a comment that we have seen in many of the configuration files we have examined and edited. One thing about comments in shell scripts is that they may also appear at the ends of lines, like so:

```
echo 'Hello World!' # This is a comment too
```

Everything from the # symbol onward on the line is ignored.
Like many things, this works on the command line, too:

```
[me@linuxbox ~]$ echo 'Hello World!' # This is a comment too
Hello World!
```

Though comments are of little use on the command line, they will work.

The first line of our script is a little mysterious. It looks as if it should be a comment, since it starts with #, but it looks too purposeful to be just that. The #! character sequence is, in fact, a special construct called a *shebang*. The shebang is used to tell the system the name of the interpreter that should be used to execute the script that follows. Every shell script should include this as its first line.

Let's save our script file as *hello_world*.

Executable Permissions

The next thing we have to do is make our script executable. This is easily done using chmod:

```
[me@linuxbox ~]$ ls -l hello_world
-rw-r--r-- 1 me         me        63 2012-03-07 10:10 hello_world
[me@linuxbox ~]$ chmod 755 hello_world
[me@linuxbox ~]$ ls -l hello_world
-rwxr-xr-x 1 me         me        63 2012-03-07 10:10 hello_world
```

There are two common permission settings for scripts: 755 for scripts that everyone can execute and 700 for scripts that only the owner can execute. Note that scripts must be readable in order to be executed.

Script File Location

With the permissions set, we can now execute our script:

```
[me@linuxbox ~]$ ./hello_world
Hello World!
```

In order for the script to run, we must precede the script name with an explicit path. If we don't, we get this:

```
[me@linuxbox ~]$ hello_world
bash: hello_world: command not found
```

Why is this? What makes our script different from other programs? As it turns out, nothing. Our script is fine. Its location is the problem. Back in Chapter 11, we discussed the PATH environment variable and its effect on how the system searches for executable programs. To recap, the system searches a list of directories each time it needs to find an executable program, if no explicit path is specified. This is how the system knows to execute */bin/ls* when we type ls at the command line. The */bin* directory is one of the directories that the system automatically searches. The list of directories is held within an environment variable named PATH. The PATH variable contains a colon-separated list of directories to be searched. We can view the contents of PATH:

```
[me@linuxbox ~]$ echo $PATH
/home/me/bin:/usr/local/sbin:/usr/local/bin:/usr/sbin:/usr/bin:/sbin:/bin:/usr
/games
```

Here we see our list of directories. If our script were located in any of the directories in the list, our problem would be solved. Notice the first directory in the list, */home/me/bin*. Most Linux distributions configure the PATH variable to contain a *bin* directory in the user's home directory to allow users to execute their own programs. So if we create the *bin* directory and place our script within it, it should start to work like other programs:

```
[me@linuxbox ~]$ mkdir bin
[me@linuxbox ~]$ mv hello_world bin
[me@linuxbox ~]$ hello_world
Hello World!
```

If the PATH variable does not contain the directory, we can easily add it by including this line in our *.bashrc* file:

```
export PATH=~/bin:"$PATH"
```

After this change is made, it will take effect in each new terminal session. To apply the change to the current terminal session, we must have the shell reread the *.bashrc* file. This can be done by "sourcing" it:

```
[me@linuxbox ~]$ . .bashrc
```

The dot (.) command is a synonym for the source command, a shell builtin that reads a specified file of shell commands and treats it like input from the keyboard.

Note: *Ubuntu automatically adds the ~/*bin *directory to the* PATH *variable if the ~/*bin *directory exists when the user's* .bashrc *file is executed. So, on Ubuntu systems, if we create the ~/*bin *directory and then log out and log in again, everything works.*

Good Locations for Scripts

The *~/bin* directory is a good place to put scripts intended for personal use. If we write a script that everyone on a system is allowed to use, the traditional location is */usr/local/bin*. Scripts intended for use by the system administrator are often located in */usr/local/sbin*. In most cases, locally supplied software, whether scripts or compiled programs, should be placed in the */usr/local* hierarchy and not in */bin* or */usr/bin*. These directories are specified by the Linux Filesystem Hierarchy Standard to contain only files supplied and maintained by the Linux distributor.

More Formatting Tricks

One of the key goals of serious script writing is ease of *maintenance*; that is, the ease with which a script may be modified by its author or others to be adapted to changing needs. Making a script easy to read and understand is one way to facilitate easy maintenance.

Long Option Names

Many of the commands we have studied feature both short and long option names. For instance, the ls command has many options that can be expressed in either short or long form. For example:

```
[me@linuxbox ~]$ ls -ad
```

and

```
[me@linuxbox ~]$ ls --all --directory
```

are equivalent commands. In the interests of reduced typing, short options are preferred when entering options on the command line, but when writing scripts, long options can improve readability.

Indentation and Line Continuation

When employing long commands, readability can be enhanced by spreading the command over several lines. In Chapter 17, we looked at a particularly long example of the find command:

```
[me@linuxbox ~]$ find playground \( -type f -not -perm 0600 -exec chmod 0600
'{}' ';' \) -or \( -type d -not -perm 0700 -exec chmod 0700 '{}' ';' \)
```

This command is a little hard to figure out at first glance. In a script, this command might be easier to understand if written this way:

```
find playground \
        \( \
                -type f \
                -not -perm 0600 \
                -exec chmod 0600 '{}' ';' \
        \) \
        -or \
        \( \
                -type d \
                -not -perm 0700 \
                -exec chmod 0700 '{}' ';' \
        \)
```

Through the use of line continuations (backslash-linefeed sequences) and indentation, the logic of this complex command is more clearly described to the reader. This technique works on the command line, too, though it is seldom used as it is very awkward to type and edit. One difference between a script and the command line is that a script may employ tab characters to achieve indentation, whereas the command line cannot because tabs are used to activate completion.

CONFIGURING VIM FOR SCRIPT WRITING

The vim text editor has many, many configuration settings. Several common options can facilitate script writing.

:syntax on turns on syntax highlighting. With this setting, different elements of shell syntax will be displayed in different colors when viewing a script. This is helpful for identifying certain kinds of programming errors. It looks cool, too. Note that for this feature to work, you must have a complete version of vim installed, and the file you are editing must have a shebang indicating the file is a shell script. If you have difficulty with :syntax on, try :set syntax=sh instead.

:set hlsearch turns on the option to highlight search results. Say we search for the word *echo*. With this option on, each instance of the word will be highlighted.

:set tabstop=4 sets the number of columns occupied by a tab character. The default is eight columns. Setting the value to 4 (which is a common practice) allows long lines to fit more easily on the screen.

:set autoindent turns on the auto indent feature. This causes vim to indent a new line the same amount as the line just typed. This speeds up typing on many kinds of programming constructs. To stop indentation, type CTRL-D.

These changes can be made permanent by adding these commands (without the leading colon characters) to your ~/.vimrc file.

Final Note

In this first chapter about scripting, we have looked at how scripts are written and made to easily execute on our system. We also saw how we can use various formatting techniques to improve the readability (and thus, the maintainability) of our scripts. In future chapters, ease of maintenance will come up again and again as a central principle in good script writing.

25

STARTING A PROJECT

Starting with this chapter, we will begin to build a program. The purpose of this project is to see how various shell features are used to create programs and, more importantly, create *good* programs.

The program we will write is a *report generator*. It will present various statistics about our system and its status, and it will produce this report in HTML format so we can view it with a web browser.

Programs are usually built up in a series of stages, with each stage adding features and capabilities. The first stage of our program will produce a very minimal HTML page that contains no system information. That will come later.

First Stage: Minimal Document

The first thing we need to know is the format of a well-formed HTML document. It looks like this:

```
<HTML>
        <HEAD>
                <TITLE>Page Title</TITLE>
```

```
        </HEAD>
        <BODY>
                Page body.
        </BODY>
</HTML>
```

If we enter this into our text editor and save the file as *foo.html*, we can use the following URL in Firefox to view the file: *file:///home/username/foo.html*.

The first stage of our program will be able to output this HTML file to standard output. We can write a program to do this pretty easily. Let's start our text editor and create a new file named *~/bin/sys_info_page*.

```
[me@linuxbox ~]$ vim ~/bin/sys_info_page
```

And we'll enter the following program:

```
#!/bin/bash

# Program to output a system information page

echo "<HTML>"
echo "    <HEAD>"
echo "            <TITLE>Page Title</TITLE>"
echo "    </HEAD>"
echo "    <BODY>"
echo "            Page body."
echo "    </BODY>"
echo "</HTML>"
```

Our first attempt at this problem contains a shebang; a comment (always a good idea); and a sequence of echo commands, one for each line of output. After saving the file, we'll make it executable and attempt to run it:

```
[me@linuxbox ~]$ chmod 755 ~/bin/sys_info_page
[me@linuxbox ~]$ sys_info_page
```

When the program runs, we should see the text of the HTML document displayed on the screen, because the echo commands in the script send their output to standard output. We'll run the program again and redirect the output of the program to the file *sys_info_page.html*, so that we can view the result with a web browser:

```
[me@linuxbox ~]$ sys_info_page > sys_info_page.html
[me@linuxbox ~]$ firefox sys_info_page.html
```

So far, so good.

When writing programs, it's always a good idea to strive for simplicity and clarity. Maintenance is easier when a program is easy to read and understand, not to mention that the program is easier to write when we reduce the amount of typing. Our current version of the program works fine, but it could be simpler. We could combine all the echo commands into one, which would certainly make it easier to add more lines to the program's output. So, let's change our program to this:

```
#!/bin/bash

# Program to output a system information page

echo "<HTML>
        <HEAD>
                <TITLE>Page Title</TITLE>
        </HEAD>
        <BODY>
                Page body.
        </BODY>
</HTML>"
```

A quoted string may include newlines and, therefore, contain multiple lines of text. The shell will keep reading the text until it encounters the closing quotation mark. It works this way on the command line, too:

```
[me@linuxbox ~]$ echo "<HTML>
>         <HEAD>
>                 <TITLE>Page Title</TITLE>
>         </HEAD>
>         <BODY>
>                 Page body.
>         </BODY>
> </HTML>"
```

The leading > character is the shell prompt contained in the PS2 shell variable. It appears whenever we type a multiline statement into the shell. This feature is a little obscure right now, but later, when we cover multiline programming statements, it will turn out to be quite handy.

Second Stage: Adding a Little Data

Now that our program can generate a minimal document, let's put some data in the report. To do this, we will make the following changes:

```
#!/bin/bash

# Program to output a system information page

echo "<HTML>
        <HEAD>
                <TITLE>System Information Report</TITLE>
        </HEAD>

        <BODY>
                <H1>System Information Report</H1>
        </BODY>
</HTML>"
```

We added a page title and a heading to the body of the report.

Variables and Constants

There is an issue with our script, however. Notice how the string System Information Report is repeated? With our tiny script it's not a problem, but let's imagine that our script was really long and we had multiple instances of this string. If we wanted to change the title to something else, we would have to change it in multiple places, which could be a lot of work. What if we could arrange the script so that the string appeared only once and not multiple times? That would make future maintenance of the script much easier. Here's how we could do that:

```
#!/bin/bash

# Program to output a system information page

title="System Information Report"

echo "<HTML>
        <HEAD>
                <TITLE>$title</TITLE>
        </HEAD>
        <BODY>
                <H1>$title</H1>
        </BODY>
</HTML>"
```

By creating a variable named title and assigning it the value System Information Report, we can take advantage of parameter expansion and place the string in multiple locations.

Creating Variables and Constants

So, how do we create a variable? Simple, we just use it. When the shell encounters a variable, it automatically creates it. This differs from many programming languages in which variables must be explicitly *declared* or defined before use. The shell is very lax about this, which can lead to some problems. For example, consider this scenario played out on the command line:

```
[me@linuxbox ~]$ foo="yes"
[me@linuxbox ~]$ echo $foo
yes
[me@linuxbox ~]$ echo $fool

[me@linuxbox ~]$
```

We first assign the value yes to the variable foo and then display its value with echo. Next we display the value of the variable name misspelled as fool and get a blank result. This is because the shell happily created the variable fool when it encountered it and then gave it the default value of nothing, or empty. From this, we learn that we must pay close attention to our spelling! It's also important to understand what really happened in this example. From our previous look at how the shell performs expansions, we know that the command

```
[me@linuxbox ~]$ echo $foo
```

undergoes parameter expansion and results in

```
[me@linuxbox ~]$ echo yes
```

On the other hand, the command

```
[me@linuxbox ~]$ echo $fool
```

expands into

```
[me@linuxbox ~]$ echo
```

The empty variable expands into nothing! This can play havoc with commands that require arguments. Here's an example:

```
[me@linuxbox ~]$ foo=foo.txt
[me@linuxbox ~]$ foo1=foo1.txt
[me@linuxbox ~]$ cp $foo $fool
cp: missing destination file operand after `foo.txt'
Try `cp --help' for more information.
```

We assign values to two variables, foo and foo1. We then perform a cp but misspell the name of the second argument. After expansion, the cp command is sent only one argument, though it requires two.

There are some rules about variable names:

- Variable names may consist of alphanumeric characters (letters and numbers) and underscore characters.

- The first character of a variable name must be either a letter or an underscore.

- Spaces and punctuation symbols are not allowed.

The word *variable* implies a value that changes, and in many applications, variables are used this way. However, the variable in our application, title, is used as a *constant*. A constant is just like a variable in that it has a name and contains a value. The difference is that the value of a constant does not change. In an application that performs geometric calculations, we might define PI as a constant and assign it the value of 3.1415, instead of using the number literally throughout our program. The shell makes no distinction between variables and constants; these terms are mostly for the programmer's convenience. A common convention is to use uppercase letters to designate constants and lowercase letters for true variables. We will modify our script to comply with this convention:

```
#!/bin/bash

# Program to output a system information page

TITLE="System Information Report For $HOSTNAME"

echo "<HTML>
        <HEAD>
                <TITLE>$TITLE</TITLE>
        </HEAD>
        <BODY>
                <H1>$TITLE</H1>
        </BODY>
</HTML>"
```

We also took the opportunity to jazz up our title by adding the value of the shell variable HOSTNAME. This is the network name of the machine.

Note: *The shell actually does provide a way to enforce the immutability of constants, through the use of the declare built-in command with the -r (read-only) option. Had we assigned TITLE this way:*

```
declare -r TITLE="Page Title"
```

the shell would prevent any subsequent assignment to TITLE. This feature is rarely used, but it exists for very formal scripts.

Assigning Values to Variables and Constants

Here is where our knowledge of expansion really starts to pay off. As we have seen, variables are assigned values this way:

```
variable=value
```

where *variable* is the name of the variable and *value* is a string. Unlike some other programming languages, the shell does not care about the type of data assigned to a variable; it treats them all as strings. You can force the shell to restrict the assignment to integers by using the declare command with the -i option, but, like setting variables as read-only, this is rarely done.

Note that in an assignment, there must be no spaces between the variable name, the equal sign, and the value. So what can the value consist of? Anything that we can expand into a string.

```
a=z                    # Assign the string "z" to variable a.
b="a string"           # Embedded spaces must be within quotes.
c="a string and $b"    # Other expansions such as variables can be
                       # expanded into the assignment.
d=$(ls -l foo.txt)     # Results of a command.
```

```
e=$((5 * 7))              # Arithmetic expansion.
f="\t\ta string\n"        # Escape sequences such as tabs and newlines.
```

Multiple variable assignments may be done on a single line:

```
a=5 b="a string"
```

During expansion, variable names may be surrounded by optional curly braces {}. This is useful in cases where a variable name becomes ambiguous due to its surrounding context. Here, we try to change the name of a file from *myfile* to *myfile1*, using a variable:

```
[me@linuxbox ~]$ filename="myfile"
[me@linuxbox ~]$ touch $filename
[me@linuxbox ~]$ mv $filename $filename1
mv: missing destination file operand after `myfile'
Try `mv --help' for more information.
```

This attempt fails because the shell interprets the second argument of the mv command as a new (and empty) variable. The problem can be overcome this way:

```
[me@linuxbox ~]$ mv $filename ${filename}1
```

By adding the surrounding braces, we ensure that the shell no longer interprets the trailing 1 as part of the variable name.

We'll take this opportunity to add some data to our report, namely the date and time the report was created and the username of the creator:

```
#!/bin/bash

# Program to output a system information page

TITLE="System Information Report For $HOSTNAME"
CURRENT_TIME=$(date +"%x %r %Z")
TIME_STAMP="Generated $CURRENT_TIME, by $USER"

echo "<HTML>
        <HEAD>
                <TITLE>$TITLE</TITLE>
        </HEAD>
        <BODY>
                <H1>$TITLE</H1>
                <P>$TIME_STAMP</P>
        </BODY>
</HTML>"
```

Here Documents

We've looked at two different methods of outputting our text, both using the echo command. There is a third way called a *here document* or *here script*. A here document is an additional form of I/O redirection in which we embed a body of text into our script and feed it into the standard input of a command. It works like this:

```
command << token
text
token
```

where *command* is the name of a command that accepts standard input and *token* is a string used to indicate the end of the embedded text. We'll modify our script to use a here document:

```
#!/bin/bash

# Program to output a system information page

TITLE="System Information Report For $HOSTNAME"
CURRENT_TIME=$(date +"%x %r %Z")
TIME_STAMP="Generated $CURRENT_TIME, by $USER"

cat << _EOF_
<HTML>
        <HEAD>
                <TITLE>$TITLE</TITLE>
        </HEAD>
        <BODY>
                <H1>$TITLE</H1>
                <P>$TIME_STAMP</P>
        </BODY>
</HTML>
_EOF_
```

Instead of using echo, our script now uses cat and a here document. The string _EOF_ (meaning *end-of-file*, a common convention) was selected as the token and marks the end of the embedded text. Note that the token must appear alone and that there must not be trailing spaces on the line.

So what's the advantage of using a here document? It's mostly the same as echo, except that, by default, single and double quotes within here documents lose their special meaning to the shell. Here is a command-line example:

```
[me@linuxbox ~]$ foo="some text"
[me@linuxbox ~]$ cat << _EOF_
> $foo
> "$foo"
> '$foo'
> \$foo
> _EOF_
some text
"some text"
'some text'
$foo
```

As we can see, the shell pays no attention to the quotation marks. It treats them as ordinary characters. This allows us to embed quotes freely within a here document. This could turn out to be handy for our report program.

Here documents can be used with any command that accepts standard input. In this example, we use a here document to pass a series of commands to the ftp program in order to retrieve a file from a remote FTP server:

```
#!/bin/bash

# Script to retrieve a file via FTP

FTP_SERVER=ftp.nl.debian.org
FTP_PATH=/debian/dists/lenny/main/installer-i386/current/images/cdrom
REMOTE_FILE=debian-cd_info.tar.gz

ftp -n << _EOF_
open $FTP_SERVER
user anonymous me@linuxbox
cd $FTP_PATH
hash
get $REMOTE_FILE
bye
_EOF_
ls -l $REMOTE_FILE
```

If we change the redirection operator from << to <<-, the shell will ignore leading tab characters in the here document. This allows a here document to be indented, which can improve readability:

```
#!/bin/bash

# Script to retrieve a file via FTP

FTP_SERVER=ftp.nl.debian.org
FTP_PATH=/debian/dists/lenny/main/installer-i386/current/images/cdrom
REMOTE_FILE=debian-cd_info.tar.gz

ftp -n <<- _EOF_
        open $FTP_SERVER
        user anonymous me@linuxbox
        cd $FTP_PATH
        hash
        get $REMOTE_FILE
        bye
        _EOF_

ls -l $REMOTE_FILE
```

Final Note

In this chapter, we started a project that will carry us through the process of building a successful script. We introduced the concept of variables and constants and how they can be employed. They are the first of many applications we will find for parameter expansion. We also looked at how to produce output from our script and various methods for embedding blocks of text.

26

TOP-DOWN DESIGN

As programs get larger and more complex, they become more difficult to design, code, and maintain. As with any large project, it is often a good idea to break large, complex tasks into a series of small, simple tasks.

Let's imagine that we are trying to describe a common, everyday task—going to the market to buy food—to a person from Mars. We might describe the overall process as the following series of steps:

1. Get in car.
2. Drive to market.
3. Park car.
4. Enter market.
5. Purchase food.
6. Return to car.
7. Drive home.
8. Park car.
9. Enter house.

However, a person from Mars is likely to need more detail. We could further break down the subtask "Park car" into another series of steps.

1. Find parking space.
2. Drive car into space.
3. Turn off motor.
4. Set parking brake.
5. Exit car.
6. Lock car.

The "Turn off motor" subtask could further be broken down into steps including "Turn off ignition," "Remove ignition key," and so on, until every step of the entire process of going to the market has been fully defined.

This process of identifying the top-level steps and developing increasingly detailed views of those steps is called *top-down design*. This technique allows us to break large, complex tasks into many small, simple tasks. Top-down design is a common method of designing programs and one that is well suited to shell programming in particular.

In this chapter, we will use top-down design to further develop our report-generator script.

Shell Functions

Our script currently performs the following steps to generate the HTML document:

1. Open page.
2. Open page header.
3. Set page title.
4. Close page header.
5. Open page body.
6. Output page heading.
7. Output timestamp.
8. Close page body.
9. Close page.

For our next stage of development, we will add some tasks between steps 7 and 8. These will include:

- **System uptime and load.** This is the amount of time since the last shutdown or reboot and the average number of tasks currently running on the processor over several time intervals.

- **Disk space.** The overall use of space on the system's storage devices.

- **Home space.** The amount of storage space being used by each user.

If we had a command for each of these tasks, we could add them to our script simply through command substitution:

```
#!/bin/bash

# Program to output a system information page

TITLE="System Information Report For $HOSTNAME"
```

```
CURRENT_TIME=$(date +"%x %r %Z")
TIME_STAMP="Generated $CURRENT_TIME, by $USER"

cat << _EOF_
<HTML>
        <HEAD>
                <TITLE>$TITLE</TITLE>
        </HEAD>
        <BODY>
                <H1>$TITLE</H1>
                <P>$TIME_STAMP</P>
                $(report_uptime)
                $(report_disk_space)
                $(report_home_space)
        </BODY>
</HTML>
_EOF_
```

We could create these additional commands two ways. We could write three separate scripts and place them in a directory listed in our PATH, or we could embed the scripts within our program as *shell functions*. As we have mentioned before, shell functions are "miniscripts" that are located inside other scripts and can act as autonomous programs. Shell functions have two syntactic forms. The first looks like this:

```
function name {
        commands
        return
}
```

where *name* is the name of the function and *commands* is a series of commands contained within the function. The second looks like this:

```
name () {
        commands
        return
}
```

Both forms are equivalent and may be used interchangeably. Below we see a script that demonstrates the use of a shell function:

```
 1      #!/bin/bash
 2
 3      # Shell function demo
 4
 5      function funct {
 6              echo "Step 2"
 7              return
 8      }
 9
10      # Main program starts here
11
12      echo "Step 1"
13      funct
14      echo "Step 3"
```

As the shell reads the script, it passes over lines 1 through 11, as those lines consist of comments and the function definition. Execution begins at line 12, with an echo command. Line 13 *calls* the shell function funct, and the shell executes the function just as it would any other command. Program control then moves to line 6, and the second echo command is executed. Line 7 is executed next. Its return command terminates the function and returns control to the program at the line following the function call (line 14), and the final echo command is executed. Note that in order for function calls to be recognized as shell functions and not interpreted as the names of external programs, shell function definitions must appear in the script before they are called.

We'll add minimal shell function definitions to our script:

```
#!/bin/bash

# Program to output a system information page

TITLE="System Information Report For $HOSTNAME"
CURRENT_TIME=$(date +"%x %r %Z")
TIME_STAMP="Generated $CURRENT_TIME, by $USER"

report_uptime () {
        return
}

report_disk_space () {
        return
}

report_home_space () {
        return
}

cat << _EOF_
<HTML>
        <HEAD>
                <TITLE>$TITLE</TITLE>
        </HEAD>
        <BODY>
                <H1>$TITLE</H1>
                <P>$TIME_STAMP</P>
                $(report_uptime)
                $(report_disk_space)
                $(report_home_space)
        </BODY>
</HTML>
_EOF_
```

Shell-function names follow the same rules as variables. A function must contain at least one command. The return command (which is optional) satisfies the requirement.

Local Variables

In the scripts we have written so far, all the variables (including constants) have been *global variables*. Global variables maintain their existence throughout the program. This is fine for many things, but it can sometimes complicate the use of shell functions. Inside shell functions, it is often desirable to have *local variables.* Local variables are accessible only within the shell function in which they are defined, and they cease to exist once the shell function terminates.

Having local variables allows the programmer to use variables with names that may already exist, either in the script globally or in other shell functions, without having to worry about potential name conflicts.

Here is an example script that demonstrates how local variables are defined and used:

```
#!/bin/bash

# local-vars: script to demonstrate local variables

foo=0    # global variable foo

funct_1 () {

        local foo        # variable foo local to funct_1

        foo=1
        echo "funct_1: foo = $foo"
}

funct_2 () {

        local foo        # variable foo local to funct_2

        foo=2
        echo "funct_2: foo = $foo"
}

echo "global:  foo = $foo"
funct_1
echo "global:  foo = $foo"
funct_2
echo "global:  foo = $foo"
```

As we can see, local variables are defined by preceding the variable name with the word local. This creates a variable that is local to the shell function in which it is defined. Once the script is outside the shell function, the variable no longer exists. When we run this script, we see the results:

```
[me@linuxbox ~]$ local-vars
global:  foo = 0
funct_1: foo = 1
global:  foo = 0
funct_2: foo = 2
global:  foo = 0
```

We see that the assignment of values to the local variable foo within both shell functions has no effect on the value of foo defined outside the functions.

This feature allows shell functions to be written so that they remain independent of each other and of the script in which they appear. This is very valuable, as it helps prevent one part of a program from interfering with another. It also allows shell functions to be written so that they can be portable. That is, they may be cut and pasted from script to script, as needed.

Keep Scripts Running

While developing our program, it is useful to keep the program in a runnable state. By doing this, and testing frequently, we can detect errors early in the development process. This will make debugging problems much easier. For example, if we run the program, make a small change, run the program again, and find a problem, it's very likely that the most recent change is the source of the problem. By adding empty functions, called *stubs* in programmer-speak, we can verify the logical flow of our program at an early stage. When constructing a stub, it's a good idea to include something that provides feedback to the programmer that shows the logical flow is being carried out. If we look at the output of our script now, we see that there are some blank lines in our output after the timestamp, but we can't be sure of the cause.

```
[me@linuxbox ~]$ sys_info_page
<HTML>
        <HEAD>
                <TITLE>System Information Report For twin2</TITLE>
        </HEAD>
        <BODY>
                <H1>System Information Report For linuxbox</H1>
                <P>Generated 03/19/2012 04:02:10 PM EDT, by me</P>


        </BODY>
</HTML>
```

We can change the functions to include some feedback:

```
report_uptime () {
        echo "Function report_uptime executed."
        return
}

report_disk_space () {
        echo "Function report_disk_space executed."
        return
}

report_home_space () {
        echo "Function report_home_space executed."
        return
}
```

And then we run the script again:

```
[me@linuxbox ~]$ sys_info_page
<HTML>
        <HEAD>
                <TITLE>System Information Report For linuxbox</TITLE>
        </HEAD>
        <BODY>
                <H1>System Information Report For linuxbox</H1>
                <P>Generated 03/20/2012 05:17:26 AM EDT, by me</P>
                Function report_uptime executed.
                Function report_disk_space executed.
                Function report_home_space executed.
        </BODY>
</HTML>
```

We now see that, in fact, our three functions are being executed.

With our function framework in place and working, it's time to flesh out some of the function code. First, the report_uptime function:

```
report_uptime () {
        cat <<- _EOF_
                <H2>System Uptime</H2>
                <PRE>$(uptime)</PRE>
                _EOF_
        return
}
```

It's pretty straightforward. We use a here document to output a section header and the output of the uptime command, surrounded by <PRE> tags to preserve the formatting of the command. The report_disk_space function is similar:

```
report_disk_space () {
        cat <<- _EOF_
                <H2>Disk Space Utilization</H2>
                <PRE>$(df -h)</PRE>
                _EOF_
        return
}
```

This function uses the df -h command to determine the amount of disk space. Lastly, we'll build the report_home_space function:

```
report_home_space () {
        cat <<- _EOF_
                <H2>Home Space Utilization</H2>
                <PRE>$(du -sh /home/*)</PRE>
                _EOF_
        return
}
```

We use the du command with the -sh options to perform this task. This, however, is not a complete solution to the problem. While it will work on some systems (Ubuntu, for example), it will not work on others. The reason is that many systems set the permissions of home directories to prevent them from being world readable, which is a reasonable security measure. On these systems, the report_home_space function, as written, will work only if our script is run with superuser privileges. A better solution would be to have the script adjust its behavior according to the privileges of the user. We will take this up in Chapter 27.

SHELL FUNCTIONS IN YOUR .BASHRC FILE

Shell functions make excellent replacements for aliases, and they are actually the preferred method of creating small commands for personal use. Aliases are very limited in the kind of commands and shell features they support, whereas shell functions allow anything that can be scripted. For example, if we liked the report_disk_space shell function that we developed for our script, we could create a similar function named ds for our *.bashrc* file:

```
ds () {
        echo "Disk Space Utilization For $HOSTNAME"
        df -h
}
```

Final Note

In this chapter, we have introduced a common method of program design called top-down design, and we have seen how shell functions are used to build the stepwise refinement that it requires. We have also seen how local variables can be used to make shell functions independent from one another and from the program in which they are placed. This makes it possible for shell functions to be written in a portable manner and to be reusable by allowing them to be placed in multiple programs—a great time saver.

27

FLOW CONTROL: BRANCHING WITH IF

In the last chapter, we were presented with a problem. How can we make our report-generator script adapt to the privileges of the user running the script? The solution to this problem will require us to find a way to "change directions" within our script, based on the results of a test. In programming terms, we need the program to *branch*.

Let's consider a simple example of logic expressed in *pseudocode*, a simulation of a computer language intended for human consumption:

```
X = 5
If X = 5, then:
        Say "X equals 5."
Otherwise:
        Say "X is not equal to 5."
```

This is an example of a branch. Based on the condition "Does X = 5?" do one thing: "Say 'X equals 5.'" Otherwise do another thing: "Say 'X is not equal to 5.'"

Using if

Using the shell, we can code the logic above as follows:

```
x=5

if [ $x = 5 ]; then
        echo "x equals 5."
else
        echo "x does not equal 5."
fi
```

Or we can enter it directly at the command line (slightly shortened):

```
[me@linuxbox ~]$ x=5
[me@linuxbox ~]$ if [ $x = 5 ]; then echo "equals 5"; else echo "does not equal
5"; fi
equals 5
[me@linuxbox ~]$ x=0
[me@linuxbox ~]$ if [ $x = 5 ]; then echo "equals 5"; else echo "does not equal
5"; fi
does not equal 5
```

In this example, we execute the command twice. Once, with the value of x set to 5, which results in the string equals 5 being output, and the second time with the value of x set to 0, which results in the string does not equal 5 being output.

The if statement has the following syntax:

```
if commands; then
        commands
[elif commands; then
        commands...]
[else
        commands]
fi
```

where commands is a list of commands. This is a little confusing at first glance. But before we can clear this up, we have to look at how the shell evaluates the success or failure of a command.

Exit Status

Commands (including the scripts and shell functions we write) issue a value to the system when they terminate, called an *exit status*. This value, which is an integer in the range of 0 to 255, indicates the success or failure of the command's execution. By convention, a value of 0 indicates success, and any other value indicates failure. The shell provides a parameter that we can use to examine the exit status. Here we see it in action:

```
[me@linuxbox ~]$ ls -d /usr/bin
/usr/bin
[me@linuxbox ~]$ echo $?
0
[me@linuxbox ~]$ ls -d /bin/usr
ls: cannot access /bin/usr: No such file or directory
[me@linuxbox ~]$ echo $?
2
```

In this example, we execute the ls command twice. The first time, the command executes successfully. If we display the value of the parameter $?, we see that it is 0. We execute the ls command a second time, producing an error, and examine the parameter $? again. This time it contains a 2, indicating that the command encountered an error. Some commands use different exit-status values to provide diagnostics for errors, while many commands simply exit with a value of 1 when they fail. Man pages often include a section entitled "Exit Status," which describes what codes are used. However, a 0 always indicates success.

The shell provides two extremely simple built-in commands that do nothing except terminate with either a 0 or 1 exit status. The true command always executes successfully, and the false command always executes unsuccessfully:

```
[me@linuxbox ~]$ true
[me@linuxbox ~]$ echo $?
0
[me@linuxbox ~]$ false
[me@linuxbox ~]$ echo $?
1
```

We can use these commands to see how the if statement works. What the if statement really does is evaluate the success or failure of commands:

```
[me@linuxbox ~]$ if true; then echo "It's true."; fi
It's true.
[me@linuxbox ~]$ if false; then echo "It's true."; fi
[me@linuxbox ~]$
```

The command echo "It's true." is executed when the command following if executes successfully, and it is not executed when the command following if does not execute successfully. If a list of commands follows if, the last command in the list is evaluated:

```
[me@linuxbox ~]$ if false; true; then echo "It's true."; fi
It's true.
[me@linuxbox ~]$ if true; false; then echo "It's true."; fi
[me@linuxbox ~]$
```

Using test

By far, the command used most frequently with if is test. The test command performs a variety of checks and comparisons. It has two equivalent forms:

> test *expression*

and the more popular

> [*expression*]

where *expression* is an expression that is evaluated as either true or false. The test command returns an exit status of 0 when the expression is true and a status of 1 when the expression is false.

File Expressions

The expressions in Table 27-1 are used to evaluate the status of files.

Table 27-1: test File Expressions

Expression	Is true if . . .
file1 -ef *file2*	*file1* and *file2* have the same inode numbers (the two filenames refer to the same file by hard linking).
file1 -nt *file2*	*file1* is newer than *file2*.
file1 -ot *file2*	*file1* is older than *file2*.
-b *file*	*file* exists and is a block-special (device) file.
-c *file*	*file* exists and is a character-special (device) file.
-d *file*	*file* exists and is a directory.
-e *file*	*file* exists.
-f *file*	*file* exists and is a regular file.
-g *file*	*file* exists and is set-group-ID.
-G *file*	*file* exists and is owned by the effective group ID.
-k *file*	*file* exists and has its "sticky bit" set.
-L *file*	*file* exists and is a symbolic link.
-O *file*	*file* exists and is owned by the effective user ID.
-p *file*	*file* exists and is a named pipe.
-r *file*	*file* exists and is readable (has readable permission for the effective user).
-s *file*	*file* exists and has a length greater than zero.

Table 27-1 (*continued*)

Expression	Is true if . . .
-S *file*	*file* exists and is a network socket.
-t *fd*	*fd* is a file descriptor directed to/from the terminal. This can be used to determine whether standard input/output/error is being redirected.
-u *file*	*file* exists and is setuid.
-w *file*	*file* exists and is writable (has write permission for the effective user).
-x *file*	*file* exists and is executable (has execute/search permission for the effective user).

Here we have a script that demonstrates some of the file expressions:

```
#!/bin/bash

# test-file: Evaluate the status of a file

FILE=~/.bashrc

if [ -e "$FILE" ]; then
        if [ -f "$FILE" ]; then
                echo "$FILE is a regular file."
        fi
        if [ -d "$FILE" ]; then
                echo "$FILE is a directory."
        fi
        if [ -r "$FILE" ]; then
                echo "$FILE is readable."
        fi
        if [ -w "$FILE" ]; then
                echo "$FILE is writable."
        fi
        if [ -x "$FILE" ]; then
                echo "$FILE is executable/searchable."
        fi
else
        echo "$FILE does not exist"
        exit 1
fi

exit
```

The script evaluates the file assigned to the constant FILE and displays its results as the evaluation is performed. There are two interesting things to note about this script. First, notice how the parameter $FILE is quoted within the expressions. This is not required, but it is a defense against the parameter being empty. If the parameter expansion of $FILE were to result in an empty value, it would cause an error (the operators would be interpreted as non-null strings rather than operators). Using the quotes around the parameter ensures that the operator is always followed by a string, even if the string is empty. Second, notice the presence of the exit commands near the end of the script. The exit command accepts a single, optional argument, which becomes the script's exit status. When no argument is passed, the exit status defaults to 0. Using exit in this way allows the script to indicate failure if $FILE expands to the name of a nonexistent file. The exit command appearing on the last line of the script is there as a formality. When a script *runs off the end* (reaches end-of-file), it terminates with an exit status of 0 by default, anyway.

Similarly, shell functions can return an exit status by including an integer argument to the return command. If we were to convert the script above to a shell function to include it in a larger program, we could replace the exit commands with return statements and get the desired behavior:

```
test_file () {

        # test-file: Evaluate the status of a file

        FILE=~/.bashrc

        if [ -e "$FILE" ]; then
                if [ -f "$FILE" ]; then
                        echo "$FILE is a regular file."
                fi
                if [ -d "$FILE" ]; then
                        echo "$FILE is a directory."
                fi
                if [ -r "$FILE" ]; then
                        echo "$FILE is readable."
                fi
                if [ -w "$FILE" ]; then
                        echo "$FILE is writable."
                fi
                if [ -x "$FILE" ]; then
                        echo "$FILE is executable/searchable."
                fi
        else
                echo "$FILE does not exist"
                return 1
        fi

}
```

String Expressions

The expressions in Table 27-2 are used to evaluate strings.

Table 27-2: test String Expressions

Expression	Is true if . . .
string	*string* is not null.
-n *string*	The length of *string* is greater than zero.

Table 27-2 (*continued*)

Expression	Is true if . . .
-z *string*	The length of *string* is zero.
string1 = *string2* *string1* == *string2*	*string1* and *string2* are equal. Single or double equal signs may be used, but the use of double equal signs is greatly preferred.
string1 != *string2*	*string1* and *string2* are not equal.
string1 > *string2*	*string1* sorts after *string2*.
string1 < *string2*	*string1* sorts before *string2*.

Warning: *The > and < expression operators must be quoted (or escaped with a backslash) when used with* test. *If they are not, they will be interpreted by the shell as redirection operators, with potentially destructive results. Also note that while the* bash *documentation states that the sorting order conforms to the collation order of the current locale, it does not. ASCII (POSIX) order is used in versions of* bash *up to and including 4.0.*

Here is a script that incorporates string expressions:

```
#!/bin/bash

# test-string: evaluate the value of a string

ANSWER=maybe

if [ -z "$ANSWER" ]; then
        echo "There is no answer." >&2
        exit 1
fi

if [ "$ANSWER" = "yes" ]; then
        echo "The answer is YES."
elif [ "$ANSWER" = "no" ]; then
        echo "The answer is NO."
elif [ "$ANSWER" = "maybe" ]; then
        echo "The answer is MAYBE."
else
        echo "The answer is UNKNOWN."
fi
```

In this script, we evaluate the constant ANSWER. We first determine if the string is empty. If it is, we terminate the script and set the exit status to 1. Notice the redirection that is applied to the echo command. This redirects the error message "There is no answer." to standard error, which is the "proper" thing to do with error messages. If the string is not empty, we evaluate the value of the string to see if it is equal to either "yes," "no," or "maybe." We do this by using elif, which is short for *else if.* By using elif, we are able to construct a more complex logical test.

Integer Expressions

The expressions in Table 27-3 are used with integers.

Table 27-3: test Integer Expressions

Expression	Is true if . . .
integer1 -eq *integer2*	*integer1* is equal to *integer2*.
integer1 -ne *integer2*	*integer1* is not equal to *integer2*.
integer1 -le *integer2*	*integer1* is less than or equal to *integer2*.
integer1 -lt *integer2*	*integer1* is less than *integer2*.
integer1 -ge *integer2*	*integer1* is greater than or equal to *integer2*.
integer1 -gt *integer2*	*integer1* is greater than *integer2*.

Here is a script that demonstrates them:

```
#!/bin/bash

# test-integer: evaluate the value of an integer.

INT=-5

if [ -z "$INT" ]; then
        echo "INT is empty." >&2
        exit 1
fi

if [ $INT -eq 0 ]; then
        echo "INT is zero."
else
        if [ $INT -lt 0 ]; then
                echo "INT is negative."
        else
                echo "INT is positive."
        fi
        if [ $((INT % 2)) -eq 0 ]; then
                echo "INT is even."
        else
                echo "INT is odd."
        fi
fi
```

The interesting part of the script is how it determines whether an integer is even or odd. By performing a modulo 2 operation on the number, which divides the number by 2 and returns the remainder, it can tell if the number is odd or even.

A More Modern Version of test

Recent versions of bash include a compound command that acts as an enhanced replacement for test. It uses the following syntax:

[[*expression*]]

where *expression* is an expression that evaluates to either a true or false result. The [[ ]] command is very similar to test (it supports all of its expressions) but adds an important new string expression:

string1 =~ *regex*

which returns true if *string1* is matched by the extended regular expression *regex*. This opens up a lot of possibilities for performing such tasks as data validation. In our earlier example of the integer expressions, the script would fail if the constant INT contained anything except an integer. The script needs a way to verify that the constant contains an integer. Using [[ ]] with the =~ string expression operator, we could improve the script this way:

```
#!/bin/bash

# test-integer2: evaluate the value of an integer.

INT=-5

if [[ "$INT" =~ ^-?[0-9]+$ ]]; then
        if [ $INT -eq 0 ]; then
                echo "INT is zero."
        else
                if [ $INT -lt 0 ]; then
                        echo "INT is negative."
                else
                        echo "INT is positive."
                fi
                if [ $((INT % 2)) -eq 0 ]; then
                        echo "INT is even."
                else
                        echo "INT is odd."
                fi
        fi
else
        echo "INT is not an integer." >&2
        exit 1
fi
```

By applying the regular expression, we are able to limit the value of INT to only strings that begin with an optional minus sign, followed by one or more numerals. This expression also eliminates the possibility of empty values.

Another added feature of [[ ]] is that the == operator supports pattern matching the same way pathname expansion does. For example:

```
[me@linuxbox ~]$ FILE=foo.bar
[me@linuxbox ~]$ if [[ $FILE == foo.* ]]; then
> echo "$FILE matches pattern 'foo.*'"
> fi
foo.bar matches pattern 'foo.*'
```

This makes [[ ]] useful for evaluating file- and pathnames.

(( ))—Designed for Integers

In addition to the [[ ]] compound command, bash also provides the (( )) compound command, which is useful for operating on integers. It supports a full set of arithmetic evaluations, a subject we will cover fully in Chapter 34.

(( )) is used to perform *arithmetic truth tests*. An arithmetic truth test results in true if the result of the arithmetic evaluation is non-zero.

```
[me@linuxbox ~]$ if ((1)); then echo "It is true."; fi
It is true.
[me@linuxbox ~]$ if ((0)); then echo "It is true."; fi
[me@linuxbox ~]$
```

Using (( )), we can slightly simplify the test-integer2 script like this:

```
#!/bin/bash

# test-integer2a: evaluate the value of an integer.

INT=-5

if [[ "$INT" =~ ^-?[0-9]+$ ]]; then
        if ((INT == 0)); then
                echo "INT is zero."
        else
                if ((INT < 0)); then
                        echo "INT is negative."
                else
                        echo "INT is positive."
                fi
                if (( ((INT % 2)) == 0)); then
                        echo "INT is even."
                else
                        echo "INT is odd."
                fi
        fi
else
        echo "INT is not an integer." >&2
        exit 1
fi
```

Notice that we use less-than and greater-than signs and that == is used to test for equivalence. This is a more natural-looking syntax for working with integers. Notice too, that because the compound command (( )) is part of the shell syntax rather than an ordinary command, and it deals only with integers, it is able to recognize variables by name and does not require expansion to be performed.

Combining Expressions

It's also possible to combine expressions to create more complex evaluations. Expressions are combined by using logical operators. We saw these in Chapter 17, when we learned about the find command. There are three logical operations for test and [[ ]]. They are AND, OR, and NOT. test and [[ ]] use different operators to represent these operations, as shown in Table 27-4.

Table 27-4: Logical Operators

Operation	test	[[ ]] and (( ))
AND	-a	&&
OR	-o	||
NOT	!	!

Here's an example of an AND operation. The following script determines if an integer is within a range of values:

```bash
#!/bin/bash

# test-integer3: determine if an integer is within a
# specified range of values.

MIN_VAL=1
MAX_VAL=100

INT=50

if [[ "$INT" =~ ^-?[0-9]+$ ]]; then
        if [[ INT -ge MIN_VAL && INT -le MAX_VAL ]]; then
                echo "$INT is within $MIN_VAL to $MAX_VAL."
        else
                echo "$INT is out of range."
        fi
else
        echo "INT is not an integer." >&2
        exit 1
fi
```

In this script, we determine if the value of integer INT lies between the values of MIN_VAL and MAX_VAL. This is performed by a single use of [[ ]], which includes two expressions separated by the && operator. We could have also coded this using test:

```
if [ $INT -ge $MIN_VAL -a $INT -le $MAX_VAL ]; then
        echo "$INT is within $MIN_VAL to $MAX_VAL."
else
        echo "$INT is out of range."
fi
```

The ! negation operator reverses the outcome of an expression. It returns true if an expression is false, and it returns false if an expression is true. In the following script, we modify the logic of our evaluation to find values of INT that are outside the specified range:

```
#!/bin/bash

# test-integer4: determine if an integer is outside a
# specified range of values.

MIN_VAL=1
MAX_VAL=100

INT=50

if [[ "$INT" =~ ^-?[0-9]+$ ]]; then
        if [[ ! (INT -ge MIN_VAL && INT -le MAX_VAL) ]]; then
                echo "$INT is outside $MIN_VAL to $MAX_VAL."
        else
                echo "$INT is in range."
        fi
else
        echo "INT is not an integer." >&2
        exit 1
fi
```

We also include parentheses around the expression for grouping. If these were not included, the negation would apply to only the first expression and not the combination of the two. Coding this with test would be done this way:

```
if [ ! \( $INT -ge $MIN_VAL -a $INT -le $MAX_VAL \) ]; then
        echo "$INT is outside $MIN_VAL to $MAX_VAL."
else
        echo "$INT is in range."
fi
```

Since all expressions and operators used by test are treated as command arguments by the shell (unlike [[ ]] and (( ))), characters that have special meaning to bash, such as <, >, (, and), must be quoted or escaped.

Seeing that test and [[ ]] do roughly the same thing, which is preferable? test is traditional (and part of POSIX), whereas [[ ]] is specific to bash. It's important to know how to use test, since it is very widely used, but [[ ]] is clearly more useful and is easier to code.

PORTABILITY IS THE HOBGOBLIN OF LITTLE MINDS

If you talk to "real" Unix people, you quickly discover that many of them don't like Linux very much. They regard it as impure and unclean. One tenet of Unix followers is that everything should be *portable*. This means that any script you write should be able to run, unchanged, on any Unix-like system.

Unix people have good reason to believe this. Having seen what proprietary extensions to commands and shells did to the Unix world before POSIX, they are naturally wary of the effect of Linux on their beloved OS.

But portability has a serious downside. It prevents progress. It requires that things are always done using "lowest common denominator" techniques. In the case of shell programming, it means making everything compatible with sh, the original Bourne shell.

This downside is the excuse that proprietary vendors use to justify their proprietary extensions, only they call them "innovations." But they are really just lock-in devices for their customers.

The GNU tools, such as bash, have no such restrictions. They encourage portability by supporting standards and by being universally available. You can install bash and the other GNU tools on almost any kind of system, even Windows, without cost. So feel free to use all the features of bash. It's *really* portable.

Control Operators: Another Way to Branch

bash provides two control operators that can perform branching. The && (AND) and || (OR) operators work like the logical operators in the [[ ]] compound command. This is the syntax:

    command1 && command2

and

    command1 || command2

It is important to understand the behavior of these. With the && operator, *command1* is executed and *command2* is executed if, and only if, *command1* is successful. With the || operator, *command1* is executed and *command2* is executed if, and only if, *command1* is unsuccessful.

In practical terms, it means that we can do something like this:

```
[me@linuxbox ~]$ mkdir temp && cd temp
```

This will create a directory named *temp*, and if it succeeds, the current working directory will be changed to *temp*. The second command is attempted only if the mkdir command is successful. Likewise, a command like

```
[me@linuxbox ~]$ [ -d temp ] || mkdir temp
```

will test for the existence of the directory *temp*, and only if the test fails will the directory be created. This type of construct is very handy for handling errors in scripts, a subject we will discuss more in later chapters. For example, we could do this in a script:

```
[ -d temp ] || exit 1
```

If the script requires the directory *temp*, and it does not exist, then the script will terminate with an exit status of 1.

Final Note

We started this chapter with a question. How could we make our sys_info_page script detect whether or not the user had permission to read all the home directories? With our knowledge of if, we can solve the problem by adding this code to the report_home_space function:

```
report_home_space () {
        if [[ $(id -u) -eq 0 ]]; then
                cat <<- _EOF_
                        <H2>Home Space Utilization (All Users)</H2>
                        <PRE>$(du -sh /home/*)</PRE>
                        _EOF_
        else
                cat <<- _EOF_
                        <H2>Home Space Utilization ($USER)</H2>
                        <PRE>$(du -sh $HOME)</PRE>
                        _EOF_
        fi
        return
}
```

We evaluate the output of the id command. With the -u option, id outputs the numeric user ID number of the effective user. The superuser is always zero, and every other user is a number greater than zero. Knowing this, we can construct two different here documents, one taking advantage of superuser privileges and the other restricted to the user's own home directory.

We are going to take a break from the sys_info_page program, but don't worry. It will be back. In the meantime, we'll cover some topics that we'll need when we resume our work.

28

READING KEYBOARD INPUT

The scripts we have written so far lack a feature common to most computer programs—*interactivity*, the ability of the program to interact with the user. While many programs don't need to be interactive, some programs benefit from being able to accept input directly from the user. Take, for example, this script from the previous chapter:

```
#!/bin/bash

# test-integer2: evaluate the value of an integer.

INT=-5

if [[ "$INT" =~ ^-?[0-9]+$ ]]; then
        if [ $INT -eq 0 ]; then
                echo "INT is zero."
        else
                if [ $INT -lt 0 ]; then
                        echo "INT is negative."
```

```
        else
                echo "INT is positive."
        fi
        if [ $((INT % 2)) -eq 0 ]; then
                echo "INT is even."
        else
                echo "INT is odd."
        fi
    fi
else
    echo "INT is not an integer." >&2
    exit 1
fi
```

Each time we want to change the value of INT, we have to edit the script. The script would be much more useful if it could ask the user for a value. In this chapter, we will begin to look at how we can add interactivity to our programs.

read—Read Values from Standard Input

The read built-in command is used to read a single line of standard input. This command can be used to read keyboard input or, when redirection is employed, a line of data from a file. The command has the following syntax:

read [-*options*] [*variable...*]

where *options* is one or more of the available options listed in Table 28-1 and *variable* is the name of one or more variables used to hold the input value. If no variable name is supplied, the shell variable REPLY contains the line of data.

Table 28-1: read Options

Option	Description
-a *array*	Assign the input to *array*, starting with index zero. We will cover arrays in Chapter 35.
-d *delimiter*	The first character in the string *delimiter* is used to indicate end of input, rather than a newline character.
-e	Use Readline to handle input. This permits input editing in the same manner as the command line.
-n *num*	Read *num* characters of input, rather than an entire line.
-p *prompt*	Display a prompt for input using the string *prompt*.
-r	Raw mode. Do not interpret backslash characters as escapes.

Table 28-1 (*continued*)

Option	Description
-s	Silent mode. Do not echo characters to the display as they are typed. This is useful when inputting passwords and other confidential information.
-t *seconds*	Timeout. Terminate input after *seconds*. read returns a non-zero exit status if an input times out.
-u *fd*	Use input from file descriptor *fd*, rather than standard input.

Basically, read assigns fields from standard input to the specified variables. If we modify our integer evaluation script to use read, it might look like this:

```
#!/bin/bash

# read-integer: evaluate the value of an integer.

echo -n "Please enter an integer -> "
read int

if [[ "$int" =~ ^-?[0-9]+$ ]]; then
        if [ $int -eq 0 ]; then
                echo "$int is zero."
        else
                if [ $int -lt 0 ]; then
                        echo "$int is negative."
                else
                        echo "$int is positive."
                fi
                if [ $((int % 2)) -eq 0 ]; then
                        echo "$int is even."
                else
                        echo "$int is odd."
                fi

        fi
else
        echo "Input value is not an integer." >&2
        exit 1
fi
```

We use echo with the -n option (which suppresses the trailing newline on output) to display a prompt and then use read to input a value for the variable int. Running this script results in this:

```
[me@linuxbox ~]$ read-integer
Please enter an integer -> 5
5 is positive.
5 is odd.
```

read can assign input to multiple variables, as shown in this script:

```
#!/bin/bash

# read-multiple: read multiple values from keyboard

echo -n "Enter one or more values > "
read var1 var2 var3 var4 var5

echo "var1 = '$var1'"
echo "var2 = '$var2'"
echo "var3 = '$var3'"
echo "var4 = '$var4'"
echo "var5 = '$var5'"
```

In this script, we assign and display up to five values. Notice how read behaves when given different numbers of values:

```
[me@linuxbox ~]$ read-multiple
Enter one or more values > a b c d e
var1 = 'a'
var2 = 'b'
var3 = 'c'
var4 = 'd'
var5 = 'e'
[me@linuxbox ~]$ read-multiple
Enter one or more values > a
var1 = 'a'
var2 = ''
var3 = ''
var4 = ''
var5 = ''
[me@linuxbox ~]$ read-multiple
Enter one or more values > a b c d e f g
var1 = 'a'
var2 = 'b'
var3 = 'c'
var4 = 'd'
var5 = 'e f g'
```

If read receives fewer than the expected number, the extra variables are empty, while an excessive amount of input results in the final variable containing all of the extra input.

If no variables are listed after the read command, a shell variable, REPLY, will be assigned all the input:

```
#!/bin/bash

# read-single: read multiple values into default variable

echo -n "Enter one or more values > "
read

echo "REPLY = '$REPLY'"
```

Running this script results in this:

```
[me@linuxbox ~]$ read-single
Enter one or more values > a b c d
REPLY = 'a b c d'
```

Options

read supports the options shown previously in Table 28-1.

Using the various options, we can do interesting things with read. For example, with the -p option, we can provide a prompt string:

```
#!/bin/bash

# read-single: read multiple values into default variable

read -p "Enter one or more values > "

echo "REPLY = '$REPLY'"
```

With the -t and -s options we can write a script that reads "secret" input and times out if the input is not completed in a specified time:

```
#!/bin/bash

# read-secret: input a secret passphrase

if read -t 10 -sp "Enter secret passphrase > " secret_pass; then
        echo -e "\nSecret passphrase = '$secret_pass'"
else
        echo -e "\nInput timed out" >&2
        exit 1
fi
```

The script prompts the user for a secret passphrase and waits 10 seconds for input. If the entry is not completed within the specified time, the script exits with an error. Since the -s option is included, the characters of the passphrase are not echoed to the display as they are typed.

Separating Input Fields with IFS

Normally, the shell performs word splitting on the input provided to read. As we have seen, this means that multiple words separated by one or more spaces become separate items on the input line and are assigned to separate variables by read. This behavior is configured by a shell variable named IFS (for Internal Field Separator). The default value of IFS contains a space, a tab, and a newline character, each of which will separate items from one another.

We can adjust the value of IFS to control the separation of fields input to read. For example, the */etc/passwd* file contains lines of data that use the colon character as a field separator. By changing the value of IFS to a single colon,

we can use read to input the contents of */etc/passwd* and successfully separate
fields into different variables. Here we have a script that does just that:

```
#!/bin/bash

# read-ifs: read fields from a file

FILE=/etc/passwd

read -p "Enter a username > " user_name

file_info=$(grep "^$user_name:" $FILE)  ❶

if [ -n "$file_info" ]; then
        IFS=":" read user pw uid gid name home shell <<< "$file_info"  ❷
        echo "User =        '$user'"
        echo "UID =         '$uid'"
        echo "GID =         '$gid'"
        echo "Full Name = '$name'"
        echo "Home Dir. = '$home'"
        echo "Shell =       '$shell'"
else
        echo "No such user '$user_name'" >&2
        exit 1
fi
```

This script prompts the user to enter the username of an account on
the system and then displays the different fields found in the user's record
in the */etc/passwd* file. The script contains two interesting lines. The first,
at ❶, assigns the results of a grep command to the variable file_info. The
regular expression used by grep ensures that the username will match only
a single line in the */etc/passwd* file.

The second interesting line, at ❷, consists of three parts: a variable
assignment, a read command with a list of variable names as arguments, and
a strange new redirection operator. We'll look at the variable assignment
first.

The shell allows one or more variable assignments to take place immediately before a command. These assignments alter the environment for
the command that follows. The effect of the assignment is temporary, only
changing the environment for the duration of the command. In our case,
the value of IFS is changed to a colon character. Alternatively, we could have
coded it this way:

```
OLD_IFS="$IFS"
IFS=":"
read user pw uid gid name home shell <<< "$file_info"
IFS="$OLD_IFS"
```

where we store the value of IFS, assign a new value, perform the read command, and then restore IFS to its original value. Clearly, placing the variable
assignment in front of the command is a more concise way of doing the
same thing.

The <<< operator indicates a here string. A *here string* is like a here document, only shorter, consisting of a single string. In our example, the line of data from the */etc/passwd* file is fed to the standard input of the read command. We might wonder why this rather oblique method was chosen rather than

```
echo "$file_info" | IFS=":" read user pw uid gid name home shell
```

Well, there's a reason . . .

Validating Input

With our new ability to have keyboard input comes an additional programming challenge: validating input. Very often the difference between a well-written program and a poorly written one lies in the program's ability to deal with the unexpected. Frequently, the unexpected appears in the form of bad input. We did a little of this with our evaluation programs in the previous chapter, where we checked the values of integers and screened out empty values and non-numeric characters. It is important to perform these kinds of programming checks every time a program receives input to guard against invalid data. This is especially important for programs that are shared by multiple users. Omitting these safeguards in the interests of economy might be excused if a program is to be used once and only by the author to perform some special task. Even then, if the program performs dangerous tasks such as deleting files, it would be wise to include data validation, just in case.

Here we have an example program that validates various kinds of input:

```
#!/bin/bash

# read-validate: validate input


invalid_input () {
        echo "Invalid input '$REPLY'" >&2
        exit 1
}

read -p "Enter a single item > "

# input is empty (invalid)
[[ -z $REPLY ]] && invalid_input

# input is multiple items (invalid)
(( $(echo $REPLY | wc -w) > 1 )) && invalid_input

# is input a valid filename?
if [[ $REPLY =~ ^[-[:alnum:]\._]+$ ]]; then
        echo "'$REPLY' is a valid filename."
        if [[ -e $REPLY ]]; then
                echo "And file '$REPLY' exists."
        else
                echo "However, file '$REPLY' does not exist."
        fi

        # is input a floating point number?
        if [[ $REPLY =~ ^-?[[:digit:]]*\.[[:digit:]]+$ ]]; then
                echo "'$REPLY' is a floating point number."
        else
                echo "'$REPLY' is not a floating point number."
        fi

        # is input an integer?
        if [[ $REPLY =~ ^-?[[:digit:]]+$ ]]; then
                echo "'$REPLY' is an integer."
        else
                echo "'$REPLY' is not an integer."
        fi
else
        echo "The string '$REPLY' is not a valid filename."
fi
```

This script prompts the user to enter an item. The item is subsequently analyzed to determine its contents. As we can see, the script makes use of many of the concepts that we have covered thus far, including shell functions, [[ ]], (( )), the control operator &&, and if, as well as a healthy dose of regular expressions.

Menus

A common type of interactivity is called *menu driven*. In menu-driven programs, the user is presented with a list of choices and is asked to choose one. For example, we could imagine a program that presented the following:

```
Please Select:

1. Display System Information
2. Display Disk Space
3. Display Home Space Utilization
0. Quit

Enter selection [0-3] >
```

Using what we learned from writing our sys_info_page program, we can construct a menu-driven program to perform the tasks on the above menu:

```
#!/bin/bash

# read-menu: a menu driven system information program

clear
echo "
Please Select:

1. Display System Information
2. Display Disk Space
3. Display Home Space Utilization
0. Quit
"
read -p "Enter selection [0-3] > "

if [[ $REPLY =~ ^[0-3]$ ]]; then
        if [[ $REPLY == 0 ]]; then
                echo "Program terminated."
                exit
        fi
        if [[ $REPLY == 1 ]]; then
                echo "Hostname: $HOSTNAME"
                uptime
                exit
        fi
        if [[ $REPLY == 2 ]]; then
                df -h
                exit
        fi
        if [[ $REPLY == 3 ]]; then
                if [[ $(id -u) -eq 0 ]]; then
                        echo "Home Space Utilization (All Users)"
                        du -sh /home/*
                else
                        echo "Home Space Utilization ($USER)"
                        du -sh $HOME
                fi
                exit
        fi
```

```
else
        echo "Invalid entry." >&2
        exit 1
fi
```

This script is logically divided into two parts. The first part displays the menu and inputs the response from the user. The second part identifies the response and carries out the selected action. Notice the use of the exit command in this script. It is used here to prevent the script from executing unnecessary code after an action has been carried out. The presence of multiple exit points in a program is generally a bad idea (it makes program logic harder to understand), but it works in this script.

Final Note

In this chapter, we took our first steps toward interactivity, allowing users to input data into our programs via the keyboard. Using the techniques presented thus far, it is possible to write many useful programs, such as specialized calculation programs and easy-to-use frontends for arcane command-line tools. In the next chapter, we will build on the menu-driven program concept to make it even better.

Extra Credit

It is important to study the programs in this chapter carefully and have a complete understanding of the way they are logically structured, as the programs to come will be increasingly complex. As an exercise, rewrite the programs in this chapter using the test command rather than the [[ ]] compound command. Hint: Use grep to evaluate the regular expressions, and then evaluate its exit status. This will be good practice.

29

FLOW CONTROL: LOOPING
WITH WHILE AND UNTIL

In the previous chapter, we developed a menu-driven
program to produce various kinds of system information. The program works, but it still has a significant
usability problem. It executes only a single choice
and then terminates. Even worse, if an invalid selection is made, the program terminates with an error, without giving the user an opportunity to try
again. It would be better if we could somehow construct the program so that
it could repeat the menu display and selection over and over, until the user
chooses to exit the program.

In this chapter, we will look at a programming concept called *looping*,
which can be used to make portions of programs repeat. The shell provides
three compound commands for looping. We will look at two of them in this
chapter and the third in Chapter 33.

Looping

Daily life is full of repeated activities. Going to work each day, walking the dog, and slicing a carrot are all tasks that involve repeating a series of steps. Let's consider slicing a carrot. If we express this activity in pseudocode, it might look something like this:

1. Get cutting board.

2. Get knife.

3. Place carrot on cutting board.

4. Lift knife.

5. Advance carrot.

6. Slice carrot.

7. If entire carrot sliced, then quit, else go to step 4.

Steps 4 through 7 form a *loop*. The actions within the loop are repeated until the condition, "entire carrot sliced," is reached.

while

bash can express a similar idea. Let's say we wanted to display five numbers in sequential order from 1 to 5. A bash script could be constructed as follows:

```
#!/bin/bash

# while-count: display a series of numbers

count=1

while [ $count -le 5 ]; do
        echo $count
        count=$((count + 1))
done
echo "Finished."
```

When executed, this script displays the following:

```
[me@linuxbox ~]$ while-count
1
2
3
4
5
Finished.
```

The syntax of the while command is:

```
while commands; do commands; done
```

Like if, while evaluates the exit status of a list of commands. As long as the exit status is 0, it performs the commands inside the loop. In the script above, the variable count is created and assigned an initial value of 1. The while command evaluates the exit status of the test command. As long as the test command returns an exit status of 0, the commands within the loop are executed. At the end of each cycle, the test command is repeated. After five iterations of the loop, the value of count has increased to 6, the test command no longer returns an exit status of 0, and the loop terminates. The program continues with the next statement following the loop.

We can use a *while loop* to improve the read-menu program from Chapter 28:

```
#!/bin/bash

# while-menu: a menu driven system information program

DELAY=3 # Number of seconds to display results

while [[ $REPLY != 0 ]]; do
        clear
        cat <<- _EOF_
                Please Select:

                1. Display System Information
                2. Display Disk Space
                3. Display Home Space Utilization
                0. Quit

        _EOF_
        read -p "Enter selection [0-3] > "

        if [[ $REPLY =~ ^[0-3]$ ]]; then
                if [[ $REPLY == 1 ]]; then
                        echo "Hostname: $HOSTNAME"
                        uptime
                        sleep $DELAY
                fi
                if [[ $REPLY == 2 ]]; then
                        df -h
                        sleep $DELAY
                fi
                if [[ $REPLY == 3 ]]; then
                        if [[ $(id -u) -eq 0 ]]; then
                                echo "Home Space Utilization (All Users)"
                                du -sh /home/*
                        else
                                echo "Home Space Utilization ($USER)"
                                du -sh $HOME
                        fi
                        sleep $DELAY
                fi
        else
                echo "Invalid entry."
                sleep $DELAY
        fi
done
echo "Program terminated."
```

By enclosing the menu in a while loop, we are able to have the program repeat the menu display after each selection. The loop continues as long as REPLY is not equal to 0 and the menu is displayed again, giving the user the opportunity to make another selection. At the end of each action, a sleep command is executed so the program will pause for a few seconds to allow the results of the selection to be seen before the screen is cleared and the menu is redisplayed. Once REPLY is equal to 0, indicating the "quit" selection, the loop terminates and execution continues with the line following done.

Breaking out of a Loop

bash provides two built-in commands that can be used to control program flow inside loops. The break command immediately terminates a loop, and program control resumes with the next statement following the loop. The continue command causes the remainder of the loop to be skipped, and program control resumes with the next iteration of the loop. Here we see a version of the while-menu program incorporating both break and continue:

```bash
#!/bin/bash

# while-menu2: a menu driven system information program

DELAY=3 # Number of seconds to display results

while true; do
        clear
        cat <<- _EOF_
                Please Select:

                1. Display System Information
                2. Display Disk Space
                3. Display Home Space Utilization
                0. Quit

        _EOF_
        read -p "Enter selection [0-3] > "

        if [[ $REPLY =~ ^[0-3]$ ]]; then
                if [[ $REPLY == 1 ]]; then
                        echo "Hostname: $HOSTNAME"
                        uptime
                        sleep $DELAY
                        continue
                fi
                if [[ $REPLY == 2 ]]; then
                        df -h
                        sleep $DELAY
                        continue
                fi
                if [[ $REPLY == 3 ]]; then
                        if [[ $(id -u) -eq 0 ]]; then
                                echo "Home Space Utilization (All Users)"
                                du -sh /home/*
```

```
                else
                              echo "Home Space Utilization ($USER)"
                              du -sh $HOME
                fi
                sleep $DELAY
                continue
        fi
        if [[ $REPLY == 0 ]]; then
                break
        fi
    else
            echo "Invalid entry."
            sleep $DELAY
    fi
done
echo "Program terminated."
```

In this version of the script, we set up an *endless loop* (one that never terminates on its own) by using the true command to supply an exit status to while. Since true will always exit with a exit status of 0, the loop will never end. This is a surprisingly common scripting technique. Since the loop will never end on its own, it's up to the programmer to provide some way to break out of the loop when the time is right. In this script, the break command is used to exit the loop when the 0 selection is chosen. The continue command has been included at the end of the other script choices to allow for more efficient execution. By using continue, the script will skip over code that is not needed when a selection is identified. For example, if the 1 selection is chosen and identified, there is no reason to test for the other selections.

until

The until command is much like while, except instead of exiting a loop when a non-zero exit status is encountered, it does the opposite. An *until loop* continues until it receives a 0 exit status. In our while-count script, we continued the loop as long as the value of the count variable was less than or equal to 5. We could get the same result by coding the script with until:

```
#!/bin/bash

# until-count: display a series of numbers

count=1

until [ $count -gt 5 ]; do
        echo $count
        count=$((count + 1))
done
echo "Finished."
```

By changing the test expression to $count -gt 5, until will terminate the loop at the correct time. Deciding whether to use the while or until loop is usually a matter of choosing the one that allows the clearest test to be written.

Reading Files with Loops

while and until can process standard input. This allows files to be processed with while and until loops. In the following example, we will display the contents of the *distros.txt* file used in earlier chapters:

```
#!/bin/bash

# while-read: read lines from a file

while read distro version release; do
        printf "Distro: %s\tVersion: %s\tReleased: %s\n" \
                $distro \
                $version \
                $release
done < distros.txt
```

To redirect a file to the loop, we place the redirection operator after the done statement. The loop will use read to input the fields from the redirected file. The read command will exit after each line is read, with a 0 exit status until the end-of-file is reached. At that point, it will exit with a non-zero exit status, thereby terminating the loop. It is also possible to pipe standard input into a loop:

```
#!/bin/bash

# while-read2: read lines from a file

sort -k 1,1 -k 2n distros.txt | while read distro version release; do
        printf "Distro: %s\tVersion: %s\tReleased: %s\n" \
                $distro \
                $version \
                $release
done
```

Here we take the output of the sort command and display the stream of text. However, it is important to remember that since a pipe will execute the loop in a subshell, any variables created or assigned within the loop will be lost when the loop terminates.

Final Note

With the introduction of loops and our previous encounters with branching, subroutines, and sequences, we have covered the major types of flow control used in programs. bash has some more tricks up its sleeve, but they are refinements on these basic concepts.

30

TROUBLESHOOTING

As our scripts become more complex, it's time to take
a look at what happens when things go wrong and they
don't do what we want. In this chapter, we'll look at
some of the common kinds of errors that occur in
scripts and describe a few techniques that can be used
to track down and eradicate problems.

Syntactic Errors

One general class of errors is *syntactic*. Syntactic errors involve mistyping
some element of shell syntax. In most cases, these kinds of errors will lead
to the shell refusing to execute the script.

In the following discussions, we will use this script to demonstrate common types of errors:

```
#!/bin/bash

# trouble: script to demonstrate common errors
```

```
number=1

if [ $number = 1 ]; then
        echo "Number is equal to 1."
else
        echo "Number is not equal to 1."
fi
```

As written, this script runs successfully:

```
[me@linuxbox ~]$ trouble
Number is equal to 1.
```

Missing Quotes

Let's edit our script and remove the trailing quote from the argument following the first echo command:

```
#!/bin/bash

# trouble: script to demonstrate common errors

number=1

if [ $number = 1 ]; then
        echo "Number is equal to 1.
else
        echo "Number is not equal to 1."
fi
```

Watch what happens:

```
[me@linuxbox ~]$ trouble
/home/me/bin/trouble: line 10: unexpected EOF while looking for matching `"'
/home/me/bin/trouble: line 13: syntax error: unexpected end of file
```

It generates two errors. Interestingly, the line numbers reported are not where the missing quote was removed but rather much later in the program. We can see why if we follow the program after the missing quote. bash will continue looking for the closing quote until it finds one, which it does immediately after the second echo command. bash becomes very confused after that, and the syntax of the if command is broken because the fi statement is now inside a quoted (but open) string.

In long scripts, this kind of error can be quite hard to find. Using an editor with syntax highlighting will help. If a complete version of vim is installed, syntax highlighting can be enabled by entering the command:

```
:syntax on
```

Missing or Unexpected Tokens

Another common mistake is forgetting to complete a compound command, such as if or while. Let's look at what happens if we remove the semicolon after the test in the if command.

```
#!/bin/bash

# trouble: script to demonstrate common errors

number=1

if [ $number = 1 ] then
        echo "Number is equal to 1."
else
        echo "Number is not equal to 1."
fi
```

The result is this:

```
[me@linuxbox ~]$ trouble
/home/me/bin/trouble: line 9: syntax error near unexpected token `else'
/home/me/bin/trouble: line 9: `else'
```

Again, the error message points to a error that occurs later than the actual problem. What happens is really pretty interesting. As we recall, if accepts a list of commands and evaluates the exit code of the last command in the list. In our program, we intend this list to consist of a single command, [, a synonym for test. The [command takes what follows it as a list of arguments—in our case, four arguments: $number, =, 1, and]. With the semicolon removed, the word then is added to the list of arguments, which is syntactically legal. The following echo command is legal, too. It's interpreted as another command in the list of commands that if will evaluate for an exit code. The else is encountered next, but it's out of place, since the shell recognizes it as a *reserved word* (a word that has special meaning to the shell) and not the name of a command. Hence the error message.

Unanticipated Expansions

It's possible to have errors that occur only intermittently in a script. Sometimes the script will run fine, and other times it will fail because of the results of an expansion. If we return our missing semicolon and change the value of number to an empty variable, we can demonstrate:

```
#!/bin/bash

# trouble: script to demonstrate common errors

number=
```

```
if [ $number = 1 ]; then
        echo "Number is equal to 1."
else
        echo "Number is not equal to 1."
fi
```

Running the script with this change results in the output:

```
[me@linuxbox ~]$ trouble
/home/me/bin/trouble: line 7: [: =: unary operator expected
 Number is not equal to 1.
```

We get this rather cryptic error message, followed by the output of the second echo command. The problem is the expansion of the number variable within the test command. When the command

```
[ $number = 1 ]
```

undergoes expansion with number being empty, the result is this:

```
[  = 1 ]
```

which is invalid, and the error is generated. The = operator is a binary operator (it requires a value on each side), but the first value is missing, so the test command expects a unary operator (such as -z) instead. Further, since the test failed (because of the error), the if command receives a non-zero exit code and acts accordingly, and the second echo command is executed.

This problem can be corrected by adding quotes around the first argument in the test command:

```
[ "$number" = 1 ]
```

Then when expansion occurs, the result will be this:

```
[ "" = 1 ]
```

which yields the correct number of arguments. In addition to being used with empty strings, quotes should be used in cases where a value could expand into multiword strings, as with filenames containing embedded spaces.

Logical Errors

Unlike syntactic errors, *logical errors* do not prevent a script from running. The script will run, but it will not produce the desired result due to a problem with its logic. There are countless numbers of possible logical errors, but here are a few of the most common kinds found in scripts:

- **Incorrect conditional expressions.** It's easy to incorrectly code an if/then/else statement and have the wrong logic carried out. Sometimes the logic will be reversed, or it will be incomplete.

- **"Off by one" errors.** When coding loops that employ counters, it is possible to overlook that the loop may require that the counting start with 0, rather than 1, for the count to conclude at the correct point. These kinds of errors result in either a loop "going off the end" by counting too far, or else missing the last iteration of the loop by terminating one iteration too soon.

- **Unanticipated situations.** Most logical errors result from a program encountering data or situations that were unforeseen by the programmer. These can also include unanticipated expansions, such as a filename that contains embedded spaces that expands into multiple command arguments rather than a single filename.

Defensive Programming

It is important to verify assumptions when programming. This means a careful evaluation of the exit status of programs and commands that are used by a script. Here is an example, based on a true story. An unfortunate system administrator wrote a script to perform a maintenance task on an important server. The script contained the following two lines of code:

```
cd $dir_name
rm *
```

There is nothing intrinsically wrong with these two lines, as long as the directory named in the variable, dir_name, exists. But what happens if it does not? In that case, the cd command fails, and the script continues to the next line and deletes the files in the current working directory. Not the desired outcome at all! The hapless administrator destroyed an important part of the server because of this design decision.

Let's look at some ways this design could be improved. First, it might be wise to make the execution of rm contingent on the success of cd:

```
cd $dir_name && rm *
```

This way, if the cd command fails, the rm command is not carried out. This is better, but it still leaves open the possibility that the variable, dir_name, is unset or empty, which would result in the files in the user's home directory being deleted. This could also be avoided by checking to see that dir_name actually contains the name of an existing directory:

```
[[ -d $dir_name ]] && cd $dir_name && rm *
```

Often, it is best to terminate the script with an error when an situation such as the one above occurs:

```
if [[ -d $dir_name ]]; then
        if cd $dir_name; then
                rm *
```

```
        else
                echo "cannot cd to '$dir_name'" >&2
                exit 1
        fi
else
        echo "no such directory: '$dir_name'" >&2
        exit 1
fi
```

Here, we check both the name, to see that it is that of an existing directory, and the success of the cd command. If either fails, a descriptive error message is sent to standard error, and the script terminates with an exit status of 1 to indicate a failure.

Verifying Input

A general rule of good programming is that if a program accepts input, it must be able to deal with anything it receives. This usually means that input must be carefully screened to ensure that only valid input is accepted for further processing. We saw an example of this in the previous chapter when we studied the read command. One script contained the following test to verify a menu selection:

```
[[ $REPLY =~ ^[0-3]$ ]]
```

This test is very specific. It will return a 0 exit status only if the string returned by the user is a numeral in the range of 0 to 3. Nothing else will be accepted. Sometimes these sorts of tests can be very challenging to write, but the effort is necessary to produce a high-quality script.

DESIGN IS A FUNCTION OF TIME

When I was a college student studying industrial design, a wise professor stated that the degree of design on a project was determined by the amount of time given to the designer. If you were given 5 minutes to design a device that kills flies, you designed a flyswatter. If you were given 5 months, you might come up with a laser-guided "anti-fly system" instead.

The same principle applies to programming. Sometimes a "quick-and-dirty" script will do if it's going to be used only once and only by the programmer. That kind of script is common and should be developed quickly to make the effort economical. Such scripts don't need a lot of comments and defensive checks. On the other hand, if a script is intended for *production use,* that is, a script that will be used over and over for an important task or by multiple users, it needs much more careful development.

Testing

Testing is an important step in every kind of software development, including scripts. There is a saying in the open source world, "release early, release often," that reflects this fact. By releasing early and often, software gets more exposure to use and testing. Experience has shown that bugs are much easier to find, and much less expensive to fix, if they are found early in the development cycle.

Stubs

In a previous discussion, we saw how stubs can be used to verify program flow. From the earliest stages of script development, they are a valuable technique to check the progress of our work.

Let's look at the previous file-deletion problem and see how this could be coded for easy testing. Testing the original fragment of code would be dangerous, since its purpose is to delete files, but we could modify the code to make the test safe:

```
if [[ -d $dir_name ]]; then
        if cd $dir_name; then
                echo rm * # TESTING
        else
                echo "cannot cd to '$dir_name'" >&2
                exit 1
        fi
else
        echo "no such directory: '$dir_name'" >&2
        exit 1
fi
exit # TESTING
```

Since the error conditions already output useful messages, we don't have to add any. The most important change is placing an echo command just before the rm command to allow the command and its expanded argument list to be displayed, rather than executed. This change allows safe execution of the code. At the end of the code fragment, we place an exit command to conclude the test and prevent any other part of the script from being carried out. The need for this will vary according to the design of the script.

We also include some comments that act as "markers" for our test-related changes. These can be used to help find and remove the changes when testing is complete.

Test Cases

To perform useful testing, it's important to develop and apply good *test cases*. This is done by carefully choosing input data or operating conditions that reflect *edge* and *corner* cases. In our code fragment (which is very simple), we want to know how the code performs under three specific conditions:

- dir_name contains the name of an existing directory.

- dir_name contains the name of a nonexistent directory.

- dir_name is empty.

By performing the test with each of these conditions, good *test coverage* is achieved.

Just as with design, testing is a function of time, as well. Not every script feature needs to be extensively tested. It's really a matter of determining what is most important. Since it could be very destructive if it malfunctioned, our code fragment deserves careful consideration during both its design and its testing.

Debugging

If testing reveals a problem with a script, the next step is debugging. "A problem" usually means that the script is, in some way, not performing to the programmer's expectations. If this is the case, we need to carefully determine exactly what the script is actually doing and why. Finding bugs can sometimes involve a lot of detective work.

A well-designed script will try to help. It should be programmed defensively to detect abnormal conditions and provide useful feedback to the user. Sometimes, however, problems are strange and unexpected, and more involved techniques are required.

Finding the Problem Area

In some scripts, particularly long ones, it is sometimes useful to isolate the area of the script that is related to the problem. This won't always be the actual error, but isolation will often provide insights into the actual cause. One technique that can be used to isolate code is "commenting out" sections of a script. For example, our file-deletion fragment could be modified to determine if the removed section was related to an error:

```
if [[ -d $dir_name ]]; then
        if cd $dir_name; then
                rm *
        else
                echo "cannot cd to '$dir_name'" >&2
                exit 1
        fi
# else
#       echo "no such directory: '$dir_name'" >&2
#       exit 1
fi
```

By placing comment symbols at the beginning of each line in a logical section of a script, we prevent that section from being executed. Testing can then be performed again to see if the removal of the code has any impact on the behavior of the bug.

Tracing

Bugs are often cases of unexpected logical flow within a script. That is, portions of the script are either never executed or are executed in the wrong order or at the wrong time. To view the actual flow of the program, we use a technique called *tracing*.

One tracing method involves placing informative messages in a script that display the location of execution. We can add messages to our code fragment:

```
echo "preparing to delete files" >&2
if [[ -d $dir_name ]]; then
        if cd $dir_name; then
echo "deleting files" >&2
                rm *
        else
                echo "cannot cd to '$dir_name'" >&2
                exit 1
        fi
else
        echo "no such directory: '$dir_name'" >&2
        exit 1
fi
echo "file deletion complete" >&2
```

We send the messages to standard error to separate them from normal output. We also do not indent the lines containing the messages, so it is easier to find when it's time to remove them.

Now when the script is executed, it's possible to see that the file deletion has been performed:

```
[me@linuxbox ~]$ deletion-script
preparing to delete files
deleting files
file deletion complete
[me@linuxbox ~]$
```

bash also provides a method of tracing, implemented by the -x option and the set command with the -x option. Using our earlier trouble script, we can activate tracing for the entire script by adding the -x option to the first line:

```
#!/bin/bash -x

# trouble: script to demonstrate common errors

number=1
```

```
if [ $number = 1 ]; then
        echo "Number is equal to 1."
else
        echo "Number is not equal to 1."
fi
```

When executed, the results look like this:

```
[me@linuxbox ~]$ trouble
+ number=1
+ '[' 1 = 1 ']'
+ echo 'Number is equal to 1.'
Number is equal to 1.
```

With tracing enabled, we see the commands performed with expansions applied. The leading plus signs indicate the display of the trace to distinguish them from lines of regular output. The plus sign is the default character for trace output. It is contained in the PS4 (prompt string 4) shell variable. The contents of this variable can be adjusted to make the prompt more useful. Here, we modify it to include the current line number in the script where the trace is performed. Note that single quotes are required to prevent expansion until the prompt is actually used:

```
[me@linuxbox ~]$ export PS4='$LINENO + '
[me@linuxbox ~]$ trouble
5 + number=1
7 + '[' 1 = 1 ']'
8 + echo 'Number is equal to 1.'
Number is equal to 1.
```

To perform a trace on a selected portion of a script, rather than the entire script, we can use the set command with the -x option:

```
#!/bin/bash

# trouble: script to demonstrate common errors

number=1

set -x # Turn on tracing
if [ $number = 1 ]; then
        echo "Number is equal to 1."
else
        echo "Number is not equal to 1."
fi
set +x # Turn off tracing
```

We use the set command with the -x option to activate tracing and the +x option to deactivate tracing. This technique can be used to examine multiple portions of a troublesome script.

Examining Values During Execution

It is often useful, along with tracing, to display the content of variables to see the internal workings of a script while it is being executed. Applying additional echo statements will usually do the trick:

```bash
#!/bin/bash

# trouble: script to demonstrate common errors

number=1

echo "number=$number" # DEBUG
set -x # Turn on tracing
if [ $number = 1 ]; then
        echo "Number is equal to 1."
else
        echo "Number is not equal to 1."
fi
set +x # Turn off tracing
```

In this trivial example, we simply display the value of the variable number and mark the added line with a comment to facilitate its later identification and removal. This technique is particularly useful when watching the behavior of loops and arithmetic within scripts.

Final Note

In this chapter, we looked at just a few of the problems that can crop up during script development. Of course, there are many more. The techniques described here will enable finding most common bugs. Debugging is an art that can be developed through experience, both in avoiding bugs (testing constantly throughout development) and in finding bugs (effective use of tracing).

31

FLOW CONTROL: BRANCHING WITH CASE

In this chapter, we will continue to look at flow control. In Chapter 28, we constructed some simple menus and built the logic used to act on a user's selection. To do this, we used a series of `if` commands to identify which of the possible choices had been selected. This type of construct appears frequently in programs, so much so that many programming languages (including the shell) provide a flow-control mechanism for multiple-choice decisions.

case

The bash multiple-choice compound command is called case. It has the following syntax:

```
case word in
        [pattern [| pattern]...) commands ;;]...
esac
```

If we look at the read-menu program from Chapter 28, we see the logic used to act on a user's selection:

```
#!/bin/bash

# read-menu: a menu driven system information program

clear
echo "
Please Select:

1. Display System Information
2. Display Disk Space
3. Display Home Space Utilization
0. Quit
"
read -p "Enter selection [0-3] > "

if [[ $REPLY =~ ^[0-3]$ ]]; then
        if [[ $REPLY == 0 ]]; then
                echo "Program terminated."
                exit
        fi
        if [[ $REPLY == 1 ]]; then
                echo "Hostname: $HOSTNAME"
                uptime
                exit
        fi
        if [[ $REPLY == 2 ]]; then
                df -h
                exit
        fi
        if [[ $REPLY == 3 ]]; then
                if [[ $(id -u) -eq 0 ]]; then
                        echo "Home Space Utilization (All Users)"
                        du -sh /home/*
                else
                        echo "Home Space Utilization ($USER)"
                        du -sh $HOME
                fi
                exit
        fi
else
        echo "Invalid entry." >&2
        exit 1
fi
```

Using case, we can replace this logic with something simpler:

```
#!/bin/bash

# case-menu: a menu driven system information program

clear
echo "
Please Select:

1. Display System Information
2. Display Disk Space
3. Display Home Space Utilization
0. Quit
"
read -p "Enter selection [0-3] > "

case $REPLY in
        0)      echo "Program terminated."
                exit
                ;;
        1)      echo "Hostname: $HOSTNAME"
                uptime
                ;;
        2)      df -h
                ;;
        3)      if [[ $(id -u) -eq 0 ]]; then
                        echo "Home Space Utilization (All Users)"
                        du -sh /home/*
                else
                        echo "Home Space Utilization ($USER)"
                        du -sh $HOME
                fi
                ;;
        *)      echo "Invalid entry" >&2
                exit 1
                ;;
esac
```

The case command looks at the value of *word*—in our example, the value of the REPLY variable—and then attempts to match it against one of the specified *patterns*. When a match is found, the *commands* associated with the specified pattern are executed. After a match is found, no further matches are attempted.

Patterns

The patterns used by case are the same as those used by pathname expansion. Patterns are terminated with a) character. Table 31-1 shows some valid patterns.

Table31-1: case Pattern Examples

Pattern	Description
a)	Matches if *word* equals *a*.
[[:alpha:]])	Matches if *word* is a single alphabetic character.
???)	Matches if *word* is exactly three characters long.
*.txt)	Matches if *word* ends with the characters *.txt*.
*)	Matches any value of *word*. It is good practice to include this as the last pattern in a case command to catch any values of *word* that did not match a previous pattern; that is, to catch any possible invalid values.

Here is an example of patterns at work:

```
#!/bin/bash

read -p "enter word > "

case $REPLY in
        [[:alpha:]])    echo "is a single alphabetic character." ;;
        [ABC][0-9])     echo "is A, B, or C followed by a digit." ;;
        ???)            echo "is three characters long." ;;
        *.txt)          echo "is a word ending in '.txt'" ;;
        *)              echo "is something else." ;;
esac
```

Combining Multiple Patterns

It is also possible to combine multiple patterns using the vertical pipe character as a separator. This creates an "or" conditional pattern. This is useful for such things as handling both upper- and lowercase characters. For example:

```
#!/bin/bash

# case-menu: a menu driven system information program

clear
echo "
Please Select:

A. Display System Information
B. Display Disk Space
C. Display Home Space Utilization
Q. Quit
"
read -p "Enter selection [A, B, C or Q] > "

case $REPLY in
        q|Q)    echo "Program terminated."
                exit
                ;;
```

```
        a|A)    echo "Hostname: $HOSTNAME"
                uptime
                ;;
        b|B)    df -h
                ;;
        c|C)    if [[ $(id -u) -eq 0 ]]; then
                        echo "Home Space Utilization (All Users)"
                        du -sh /home/*
                else
                        echo "Home Space Utilization ($USER)"
                        du -sh $HOME
                fi
                ;;
        *)      echo "Invalid entry" >&2
                exit 1
                ;;
esac
```

Here, we modify the case-menu program to use letters instead of digits for menu selection. Notice that the new patterns allow for entry of both upper- and lowercase letters.

Final Note

The case command is a handy addition to our bag of programming tricks. As we will see in the next chapter, it's the perfect tool for handling certain types of problems.

32

POSITIONAL PARAMETERS

One feature that has been missing from our programs is the ability to accept and process command-line options and arguments. In this chapter, we will examine the shell features that allow our programs to get access to the contents of the command line.

Accessing the Command Line

The shell provides a set of variables called *positional parameters* that contain the individual words on the command line. The variables are named 0 through 9. They can be demonstrated this way:

```
#!/bin/bash

# posit-param: script to view command line parameters

echo "
\$0 = $0
\$1 = $1
\$2 = $2
```

```
\$3 = $3
\$4 = $4
\$5 = $5
\$6 = $6
\$7 = $7
\$8 = $8
\$9 = $9
"
```

This very simple script displays the values of the variables $0 through $9. When executed with no command-line arguments:

```
[me@linuxbox ~]$ posit-param

$0 = /home/me/bin/posit-param
$1 =
$2 =
$3 =
$4 =
$5 =
$6 =
$7 =
$8 =
$9 =
```

Even when no arguments are provided, $0 will always contain the first item appearing on the command line, which is the pathname of the program being executed. When arguments are provided, we see the results:

```
[me@linuxbox ~]$ posit-param a b c d

$0 = /home/me/bin/posit-param
$1 = a
$2 = b
$3 = c
$4 = d
$5 =
$6 =
$7 =
$8 =
$9 =
```

Note: *You can actually access more than nine parameters using parameter expansion. To specify a number greater than nine, surround the number in braces; for example, ${10}, ${55}, ${211}, and so on.*

Determining the Number of Arguments

The shell also provides a variable, $#, that yields the number of arguments on the command line:

```
#!/bin/bash

# posit-param: script to view command line parameters
```

```
echo "
Number of arguments: $#
\$0 = $0
\$1 = $1
\$2 = $2
\$3 = $3
\$4 = $4
\$5 = $5
\$6 = $6
\$7 = $7
\$8 = $8
\$9 = $9
"
```

The result:

```
[me@linuxbox ~]$ posit-param a b c d

Number of arguments: 4
$0 = /home/me/bin/posit-param
$1 = a
$2 = b
$3 = c
$4 = d
$5 =
$6 =
$7 =
$8 =
$9 =
```

shift—Getting Access to Many Arguments

But what happens when we give the program a large number of arguments such as this:

```
[me@linuxbox ~]$ posit-param *

Number of arguments: 82
$0 = /home/me/bin/posit-param
$1 = addresses.ldif
$2 = bin
$3 = bookmarks.html
$4 = debian-500-i386-netinst.iso
$5 = debian-500-i386-netinst.jigdo
$6 = debian-500-i386-netinst.template
$7 = debian-cd_info.tar.gz
$8 = Desktop
$9 = dirlist-bin.txt
```

On this example system, the wildcard * expands into 82 arguments. How can we process that many? The shell provides a method, albeit a clumsy one, to do this. The shift command causes each parameter to "move down one" each time it is executed. In fact, by using shift, it is possible to get by with only one parameter (in addition to $0, which never changes).

```
#!/bin/bash

# posit-param2: script to display all arguments

count=1

while [[ $# -gt 0 ]]; do
        echo "Argument $count = $1"
        count=$((count + 1))
        shift
done
```

Each time shift is executed, the value of $2 is moved to $1, the value of
$3 is moved to $2, and so on. The value of $# is also reduced by 1.

In the posit-param2 program, we create a loop that evaluates the number
of arguments remaining and continues as long as there is at least one. We
display the current argument, increment the variable count with each iteration of the loop to provide a running count of the number of arguments
processed, and, finally, execute a shift to load $1 with the next argument.
Here is the program at work:

```
[me@linuxbox ~]$ posit-param2 a b c d
Argument 1 = a
Argument 2 = b
Argument 3 = c
Argument 4 = d
```

Simple Applications

Even without shift, it's possible to write useful applications using positional
parameters. By way of example, here is a simple file-information program:

```
#!/bin/bash

# file_info: simple file information program

PROGNAME=$(basename $0)

if [[ -e $1 ]]; then
        echo -e "\nFile Type:"
        file $1
        echo -e "\nFile Status:"
        stat $1
else
        echo "$PROGNAME: usage: $PROGNAME file" >&2
        exit 1
fi
```

This program displays the file type (determined by the file command)
and the file status (from the stat command) of a specified file. One interesting feature of this program is the PROGNAME variable. It is given the value that
results from the basename $0 command. The basename command removes the

leading portion of a pathname, leaving only the base name of a file. In our example, basename removes the leading portion of the pathname contained in the $0 parameter, the full pathname of our example program. This value is useful when constructing messages such as the usage message at the end of the program. When it's coded this way, the script can be renamed, and the message automatically adjusts to contain the name of the program.

Using Positional Parameters with Shell Functions

Just as positional parameters are used to pass arguments to shell scripts, they can also be used to pass arguments to shell functions. To demonstrate, we will convert the file_info script into a shell function:

```
file_info () {

        # file_info: function to display file information

        if [[ -e $1 ]]; then
                echo -e "\nFile Type:"
                file $1
                echo -e "\nFile Status:"
                stat $1
        else
                echo "$FUNCNAME: usage: $FUNCNAME file" >&2
                return 1
        fi
}
```

Now, if a script that incorporates the file_info shell function calls the function with a filename argument, the argument will be passed to the function.

With this capability, we can write many useful shell functions that can be used not only in scripts but also within the *.bashrc* file.

Notice that the PROGNAME variable was changed to the shell variable FUNCNAME. The shell automatically updates this variable to keep track of the currently executed shell function. Note that $0 always contains the full pathname of the first item on the command line (i.e., the name of the program) and does not contain the name of the shell function as we might expect.

Handling Positional Parameters En Masse

It is sometimes useful to manage all the positional parameters as a group. For example, we might want to write a *wrapper* around another program. This means that we create a script or shell function that simplifies the execution of another program. The wrapper supplies a list of arcane command-line options and then passes a list of arguments to the lower-level program.

The shell provides two special parameters for this purpose. They both expand into the complete list of positional parameters but differ in rather subtle ways. Table 32-1 describes these parameters.

Table 32-1: The * and @ Special Parameters

Parameter	Description
$*	Expands into the list of positional parameters, starting with 1. When surrounded by double quotes, it expands into a double-quoted string containing all the positional parameters, each separated by the first character of the IFS shell variable (by default a space character).
$@	Expands into the list of positional parameters, starting with 1. When surrounded by double quotes, it expands each positional parameter into a separate word surrounded by double quotes.

Here is a script that shows these special parameters in action:

```
#!/bin/bash

# posit-params3 : script to demonstrate $* and $@

print_params () {
        echo "\$1 = $1"
        echo "\$2 = $2"
        echo "\$3 = $3"
        echo "\$4 = $4"
}

pass_params () {
        echo -e "\n" '$* :';    print_params $*
        echo -e "\n" '"$*"' :'; print_params "$*"
        echo -e "\n" '$@ :';    print_params $@
        echo -e "\n" '"$@"' :'; print_params "$@"
}

pass_params "word" "words with spaces"
```

In this rather convoluted program, we create two arguments, word and words with spaces, and pass them to the pass_params function. That function, in turn, passes them on to the print_params function, using each of the four methods available with the special parameters $* and $@. When executed, the script reveals the differences:

```
[me@linuxbox ~]$ posit-param3

 $* :
$1 = word
$2 = words
$3 = with
$4 = spaces

 "$*" :
$1 = word words with spaces
$2 =
```

```
$3 =
$4 =

 $@ :
$1 = word
$2 = words
$3 = with
$4 = spaces

 "$@" :
$1 = word
$2 = words with spaces
$3 =
$4 =
```

With our arguments, both $* and $@ produce a four-word result: word, words, with, and spaces. "$*" produces a one-word result: word words with spaces. "$@" produces a two-word result: word and words with spaces.

This matches our actual intent. The lesson to take from this is that even though the shell provides four different ways of getting the list of positional parameters, "$@" is by far the most useful for most situations, because it preserves the integrity of each positional parameter.

A More Complete Application

After a long hiatus, we are going to resume work on our sys_info_page program. Our next addition will add several command-line options to the program as follows:

- **Output file.** We will add an option to specify a name for a file to contain the program's output. It will be specified as either -f *file* or --file *file*.

- **Interactive mode.** This option will prompt the user for an output filename and will determine if the specified file already exists. If it does, the user will be prompted before the existing file is overwritten. This option will be specified by either -i or --interactive.

- **Help.** Either -h or --help may be specified to cause the program to output an informative usage message.

Here is the code needed to implement the command-line processing:

```
usage () {
        echo "$PROGNAME: usage: $PROGNAME [-f file | -i]"
        return
}

# process command line options

interactive=
filename=

while [[ -n $1 ]]; do
        case $1 in
```

```
                    -f | --file)            shift
                                            filename=$1
                                            ;;
                    -i | --interactive)     interactive=1
                                            ;;
                    -h | --help)            usage
                                            exit
                                            ;;
                    *)                      usage >&2
                                            exit 1
                                            ;;
            esac
            shift
done
```

First, we add a shell function called usage to display a message when the help option is invoked or an unknown option is attempted.

Next, we begin the processing loop. This loop continues while the positional parameter $1 is not empty. At the bottom of the loop, we have a shift command to advance the positional parameters to ensure that the loop will eventually terminate.

Within the loop, we have a case statement that examines the current positional parameter to see if it matches any of the supported choices. If a supported parameter is found, it is acted upon. If not, the usage message is displayed, and the script terminates with an error.

The -f parameter is handled in an interesting way. When detected, it causes an additional shift to occur, which advances the positional parameter $1 to the filename argument supplied to the -f option.

We next add the code to implement the interactive mode:

```
# interactive mode

if [[ -n $interactive ]]; then
        while true; do
                read -p "Enter name of output file: " filename
                if [[ -e $filename ]]; then
                        read -p "'$filename' exists. Overwrite? [y/n/q] > "
                        case $REPLY in
                                Y|y)    break
                                        ;;
                                Q|q)    echo "Program terminated."
                                        exit
                                        ;;
                                *)      continue
                                        ;;
                        esac
                elif [[ -z $filename ]]; then
                        continue
                else
                        break
                fi
        done
fi
```

If the interactive variable is not empty, an endless loop is started, which contains the filename prompt and subsequent existing file-handling code. If the desired output file already exists, the user is prompted to overwrite, choose another filename, or quit the program. If the user chooses to overwrite an existing file, a break is executed to terminate the loop. Notice that the case statement detects only if the user chooses to overwrite or quit. Any other choice causes the loop to continue and prompts the user again.

In order to implement the output filename feature, we must first convert the existing page-writing code into a shell function, for reasons that will become clear in a moment:

```
write_html_page () {
        cat <<- _EOF_
        <HTML>
                <HEAD>
                        <TITLE>$TITLE</TITLE>
                </HEAD>
                <BODY>
                        <H1>$TITLE</H1>
                        <P>$TIME_STAMP</P>
                        $(report_uptime)
                        $(report_disk_space)
                        $(report_home_space)
                </BODY>
        </HTML>
        _EOF_
        return
}

# output html page

if [[ -n $filename ]]; then
        if touch $filename && [[ -f $filename ]]; then
                write_html_page > $filename
        else
                echo "$PROGNAME: Cannot write file '$filename'" >&2
                exit 1
        fi
else
        write_html_page
fi
```

The code that handles the logic of the -f option appears at the end of the listing shown above. In it, we test for the existence of a filename, and, if one is found, a test is performed to see if the file is indeed writable. To do this, a touch is performed, followed by a test to determine if the resulting file is a regular file. These two tests take care of situations where an invalid pathname is input (touch will fail), and, if the file already exists, that it's a regular file.

As we can see, the write_html_page function is called to perform the actual generation of the page. Its output is either directed to standard output (if the variable filename is empty) or redirected to the specified file.

Final Note

With the addition of positional parameters, we can now write fairly functional scripts. For simple, repetitive tasks, positional parameters make it possible to write very useful shell functions that can be placed in a user's *.bashrc* file.

Our sys_info_page program has grown in complexity and sophistication. Here is a complete listing, with the most recent changes highlighted:

```
#!/bin/bash

# sys_info_page: program to output a system information page

PROGNAME=$(basename $0)
TITLE="System Information Report For $HOSTNAME"
CURRENT_TIME=$(date +"%x %r %Z")
TIME_STAMP="Generated $CURRENT_TIME, by $USER"

report_uptime () {
        cat <<- _EOF_
                <H2>System Uptime</H2>
                <PRE>$(uptime)</PRE>
                _EOF_
        return
}

report_disk_space () {
        cat <<- _EOF_
                <H2>Disk Space Utilization</H2>
                <PRE>$(df -h)</PRE>
                _EOF_
        return
}

report_home_space () {
        if [[ $(id -u) -eq 0 ]]; then
                cat <<- _EOF_
                        <H2>Home Space Utilization (All Users)</H2>
                        <PRE>$(du -sh /home/*)</PRE>
                        _EOF_
        else
                cat <<- _EOF_
                        <H2>Home Space Utilization ($USER)</H2>
                        <PRE>$(du -sh $HOME)</PRE>
                        _EOF_
        fi
        return
}

usage () {
        echo "$PROGNAME: usage: $PROGNAME [-f file | -i]"
        return
}

write_html_page () {
        cat <<- _EOF_
        <HTML>
                <HEAD>
```

```bash
                                <TITLE>$TITLE</TITLE>
                </HEAD>
                <BODY>
                                <H1>$TITLE</H1>
                                <P>$TIME_STAMP</P>
                                $(report_uptime)
                                $(report_disk_space)
                                $(report_home_space)
                </BODY>
        </HTML>
        _EOF_
        return
}

# process command line options

interactive=
filename=

while [[ -n $1 ]]; do
        case $1 in
                -f | --file)                    shift
                                                filename=$1
                                                ;;
                -i | --interactive)             interactive=1
                                                ;;
                -h | --help)                    usage
                                                exit
                                                ;;
                *)                              usage >&2
                                                exit 1
                                                ;;
        esac
        shift
done

# interactive mode

if [[ -n $interactive ]]; then
        while true; do
                read -p "Enter name of output file: " filename
                if [[ -e $filename ]]; then
                        read -p "'$filename' exists. Overwrite? [y/n/q] > "
                        case $REPLY in
                                Y|y)    break
                                        ;;
                                Q|q)    echo "Program terminated."
                                        exit
                                        ;;
                                *)      continue
                                        ;;
                        esac
                elif [[ -z $filename ]]; then
                        continue
                else
                        break
                fi
        done
fi
```

```
# output html page

if [[ -n $filename ]]; then
        if touch $filename && [[ -f $filename ]]; then
                write_html_page > $filename
        else
                echo "$PROGNAME: Cannot write file '$filename'" >&2
                exit 1
        fi
else
        write_html_page
fi
```

Our script is pretty good now, but we're not quite done. In the next chapter, we will add one last improvement to our script.

33

FLOW CONTROL: LOOPING WITH FOR

In this final chapter on flow control, we will look at another of the shell's looping constructs. The *for loop* differs from the while and until loops in that it provides a means of processing sequences during a loop. This turns out to be very useful when programming. Accordingly, the for loop is a very popular construct in bash scripting.

A for loop is implemented, naturally enough, with the for command. In modern versions of bash, for is available in two forms.

for: Traditional Shell Form

The original for command's syntax is as follows:

```
for variable [in words]; do
        commands
done
```

where *variable* is the name of a variable that will increment during the execution of the loop, *words* is an optional list of items that will be sequentially assigned to *variable*, and *commands* are the commands that are to be executed on each iteration of the loop.

The for command is useful on the command line. We can easily demonstrate how it works:

```
[me@linuxbox ~]$ for i in A B C D; do echo $i; done
A
B
C
D
```

In this example, for is given a list of four words: *A*, *B*, *C*, and *D*. With a list of four words, the loop is executed four times. Each time the loop is executed, a word is assigned to the variable i. Inside the loop, we have an echo command that displays the value of i to show the assignment. As with the while and until loops, the done keyword closes the loop.

The really powerful feature of for is the number of interesting ways we can create the list of words. For example, we can use brace expansion:

```
[me@linuxbox ~]$ for i in {A..D}; do echo $i; done
A
B
C
D
```

or pathname expansion:

```
[me@linuxbox ~]$ for i in distros*.txt; do echo $i; done
distros-by-date.txt
distros-dates.txt
distros-key-names.txt
distros-key-vernums.txt
distros-names.txt
distros.txt
distros-vernums.txt
distros-versions.txt
```

or command substitution:

```
#!/bin/bash

# longest-word : find longest string in a file

while [[ -n $1 ]]; do
        if [[ -r $1 ]]; then
                max_word=
                max_len=0
                for i in $(strings $1); do
                        len=$(echo -n $i | wc -c)
                        if (( len > max_len )); then
                                max_len=$len
                                max_word=$i
                        fi
```

```
            done
            echo "$1: '$max_word' ($max_len characters)"
        fi
        shift
done
```

In this example, we look for the longest string found within a file. When given one or more filenames on the command line, this program uses the strings program (which is included in the GNU binutils package) to generate a list of readable text "words" in each file. The for loop processes each word in turn and determines if the current word is the longest found so far. When the loop concludes, the longest word is displayed.

If the optional in *words* portion of the for command is omitted, for defaults to processing the positional parameters. We will modify our longest-word script to use this method:

```
#!/bin/bash

# longest-word2 : find longest string in a file

for i; do
        if [[ -r $i ]]; then
                max_word=
                max_len=0
                for j in $(strings $i); do
                        len=$(echo -n $j | wc -c)
                        if (( len > max_len )); then
                                max_len=$len
                                max_word=$j
                        fi
                done
                echo "$i: '$max_word' ($max_len characters)"
        fi
done
```

As we can see, we have changed the outermost loop to use for in place of while. Because we omitted the list of words in the for command, the positional parameters are used instead. Inside the loop, previous instances of the variable i have been changed to the variable j. The use of shift has also been eliminated.

WHY I?

You may have noticed that the variable i was chosen for each of the for loop examples above. Why? No specific reason actually, besides tradition. The variable used with for can be any valid variable, but i is the most common, followed by j and k.

The basis of this tradition comes from the Fortran programming language. In Fortran, undeclared variables starting with the letters *I, J, K, L,* and *M* are automatically typed as integers, while variables beginning with any other letter are typed as real (numbers with decimal fractions). This behavior led programmers to use the variables I, J, and K for loop variables, since it was less work to use them when a temporary variable (as a loop variable often was) was needed.

It also led to the following Fortran-based witticism: "GOD is real, unless declared integer."

for: C Language Form

Recent versions of bash have added a second form of for-command syntax, one that resembles the form found in the C programming language. Many other languages support this form, as well.

```
for (( expression1; expression2; expression3 )); do
        commands
done
```

where *expression1*, *expression2*, and *expression3* are arithmetic expressions and *commands* are the commands to be performed during each iteration of the loop.

In terms of behavior, this form is equivalent to the following construct:

```
(( expression1 ))
while (( expression2 )); do
        commands
        (( expression3 ))
done
```

expression1 is used to initialize conditions for the loop, *expression2* is used to determine when the loop is finished, and *expression3* is carried out at the end of each iteration of the loop.

Here is a typical application:

```
#!/bin/bash

# simple_counter : demo of C style for command

for (( i=0; i<5; i=i+1 )); do
        echo $i
done
```

When executed, it produces the following output:

```
[me@linuxbox ~]$ simple_counter
0
1
2
3
4
```

In this example, *expression1* initializes the variable i with the value of 0, *expression2* allows the loop to continue as long as the value of i remains less than 5, and *expression3* increments the value of i by 1 each time the loop repeats.

The C-language form of for is useful anytime a numeric sequence is needed. We will see several applications of this in the next two chapters.

Final Note

With our knowledge of the for command, we will now apply the final improvements to our sys_info_page script. Currently, the report_home_space function looks like this:

```
report_home_space () {
    if [[ $(id -u) -eq 0 ]]; then
        cat <<- _EOF_
            <H2>Home Space Utilization (All Users)</H2>
            <PRE>$(du -sh /home/*)</PRE>
            _EOF_
    else
        cat <<- _EOF_
            <H2>Home Space Utilization ($USER)</H2>
            <PRE>$(du -sh $HOME)</PRE>
            _EOF_
    fi
    return
}
```

Next, we will rewrite it to provide more detail for each user's home directory and include the total number of files and subdirectories in each:

```
report_home_space () {

    local format="%8s%10s%10s\n"
    local i dir_list total_files total_dirs total_size user_name

    if [[ $(id -u) -eq 0 ]]; then
        dir_list=/home/*
        user_name="All Users"
    else
        dir_list=$HOME
        user_name=$USER
    fi

    echo "<H2>Home Space Utilization ($user_name)</H2>"

    for i in $dir_list; do

        total_files=$(find $i -type f | wc -l)
        total_dirs=$(find $i -type d | wc -l)
        total_size=$(du -sh $i | cut -f 1)
        echo "<H3>$i</H3>"
        echo "<PRE>"
        printf "$format" "Dirs" "Files" "Size"
        printf "$format" "----" "-----" "----"
        printf "$format" $total_dirs $total_files $total_size
        echo "</PRE>"
    done
    return
}
```

This rewrite applies much of what we have learned so far. We still test for the superuser, but instead of performing the complete set of actions as part of the `if`, we set some variables used later in a for loop. We have added several local variables to the function and made use of `printf` to format some of the output.

34

STRINGS AND NUMBERS

Computer programs are all about working with data.
In past chapters, we have focused on processing data
at the file level. However, many programming problems need to be solved using smaller units of data
such as strings and numbers.

In this chapter, we will look at several shell features that are used to
manipulate strings and numbers. The shell provides a variety of parameter
expansions that perform string operations. In addition to arithmetic expansion (which we touched upon in Chapter 7), there is a common command-
line program called bc, which performs higher-level math.

Parameter Expansion

Though parameter expansion came up in Chapter 7, we did not cover it in
detail because most parameter expansions are used in scripts rather than on
the command line. We have already worked with some forms of parameter
expansion; for example, shell variables. The shell provides many more.

Basic Parameters

The simplest form of parameter expansion is reflected in the ordinary use of variables. For example, $a, when expanded, becomes whatever the variable a contains. Simple parameters may also be surrounded by braces, such as ${a}. This has no effect on the expansion, but it is required if the variable is adjacent to other text, which may confuse the shell. In this example, we attempt to create a filename by appending the string _file to the contents of the variable a.

```
[me@linuxbox ~]$ a="foo"
[me@linuxbox ~]$ echo "$a_file"
```

If we perform this sequence, the result will be nothing, because the shell will try to expand a variable named a_file rather than a. This problem can be solved by adding braces:

```
[me@linuxbox ~]$ echo "${a}_file"
foo_file
```

We have also seen that positional parameters greater than 9 can be accessed by surrounding the number in braces. For example, to access the 11th positional parameter, we can do this: ${11}.

Expansions to Manage Empty Variables

Several parameter expansions deal with nonexistent and empty variables. These expansions are handy for handling missing positional parameters and assigning default values to parameters. Here is one such expansion:

> ${parameter:-word}

If *parameter* is unset (i.e., does not exist) or is empty, this expansion results in the value of *word*. If *parameter* is not empty, the expansion results in the value of *parameter*.

```
[me@linuxbox ~]$ foo=
[me@linuxbox ~]$ echo ${foo:-"substitute value if unset"}
substitute value if unset
[me@linuxbox ~]$ echo $foo

[me@linuxbox ~]$ foo=bar
[me@linuxbox ~]$ echo ${foo:-"substitute value if unset"}
bar
[me@linuxbox ~]$ echo $foo
bar
```

Here is another expansion, in which we use the equal sign instead of a dash:

> ${parameter:=word}

If *parameter* is unset or empty, this expansion results in the value of *word*. In addition, the value of *word* is assigned to *parameter*. If *parameter* is not empty, the expansion results in the value of *parameter*.

```
[me@linuxbox ~]$ foo=
[me@linuxbox ~]$ echo ${foo:="default value if unset"}
default value if unset
[me@linuxbox ~]$ echo $foo
default value if unset
[me@linuxbox ~]$ foo=bar
[me@linuxbox ~]$ echo ${foo:="default value if unset"}
bar
[me@linuxbox ~]$ echo $foo
bar
```

Note: *Positional and other special parameters cannot be assigned this way.*

Here we use a question mark:

> ${*parameter*:?*word*}

If *parameter* is unset or empty, this expansion causes the script to exit with an error, and the contents of *word* are sent to standard error. If *parameter* is not empty, the expansion results in the value of *parameter*.

```
[me@linuxbox ~]$ foo=
[me@linuxbox ~]$ echo ${foo:?"parameter is empty"}
bash: foo: parameter is empty
[me@linuxbox ~]$ echo $?
1
[me@linuxbox ~]$ foo=bar
[me@linuxbox ~]$ echo ${foo:?"parameter is empty"}
bar
[me@linuxbox ~]$ echo $?
0
```

Here we use a plus sign:

> ${*parameter*:+*word*}

If *parameter* is unset or empty, the expansion results in nothing. If *parameter* is not empty, the value of *word* is substituted for *parameter*; however, the value of *parameter* is not changed.

```
[me@linuxbox ~]$ foo=
[me@linuxbox ~]$ echo ${foo:+"substitute value if set"}

[me@linuxbox ~]$ foo=bar
[me@linuxbox ~]$ echo ${foo:+"substitute value if set"}
substitute value if set
```

Expansions That Return Variable Names

The shell has the ability to return the names of variables. This feature is used in some rather exotic situations.

```
${!prefix*}
${!prefix@}
```

This expansion returns the names of existing variables with names beginning with *prefix*. According to the bash documentation, both forms of the expansion perform identically. Here, we list all the variables in the environment with names that begin with BASH:

```
[me@linuxbox ~]$ echo ${!BASH*}
BASH BASH_ARGC BASH_ARGV BASH_COMMAND BASH_COMPLETION BASH_COMPLETION_DIR
BASH_LINENO BASH_SOURCE BASH_SUBSHELL BASH_VERSINFO BASH_VERSION
```

String Operations

There is a large set of expansions that can be used to operate on strings. Many of these expansions are particularly well suited for operations on pathnames. The expansion

$${#parameter}$$

expands into the length of the string contained by *parameter*. Normally, *parameter* is a string; however, if *parameter* is either @ or *, then the expansion results in the number of positional parameters.

```
[me@linuxbox ~]$ foo="This string is long."
[me@linuxbox ~]$ echo "'$foo' is ${#foo} characters long."
'This string is long.' is 20 characters long.
```

```
${parameter:offset}
${parameter:offset:length}
```

This expansion is used to extract a portion of the string contained in *parameter*. The extraction begins at *offset* characters from the beginning of the string and continues until the end of the string, unless the *length* is specified.

```
[me@linuxbox ~]$ foo="This string is long."
[me@linuxbox ~]$ echo ${foo:5}
string is long.
[me@linuxbox ~]$ echo ${foo:5:6}
string
```

If the value of *offset* is negative, it is taken to mean it starts from the end of the string rather than the beginning. Note that negative values must be preceded by a space to prevent confusion with the ${parameter:-word} expansion. *length*, if present, must not be less than 0.

If *parameter* is @, the result of the expansion is *length* positional parameters, starting at *offset*.

```
[me@linuxbox ~]$ foo="This string is long."
[me@linuxbox ~]$ echo ${foo: -5}
long.
[me@linuxbox ~]$ echo ${foo: -5:2}
lo
```

```
${parameter#pattern}
${parameter##pattern}
```

These expansions remove a leading portion of the string contained in *parameter* defined by *pattern*. *pattern* is a wildcard pattern like those used in pathname expansion. The difference in the two forms is that the # form removes the shortest match, while the ## form removes the longest match.

```
[me@linuxbox ~]$ foo=file.txt.zip
[me@linuxbox ~]$ echo ${foo#*.}
txt.zip
[me@linuxbox ~]$ echo ${foo##*.}
zip
```

```
${parameter%pattern}
${parameter%%pattern}
```

These expansions are the same as the # and ## expansions above, except they remove text from the end of the string contained in *parameter* rather than from the beginning.

```
[me@linuxbox ~]$ foo=file.txt.zip
[me@linuxbox ~]$ echo ${foo%.*}
file.txt
[me@linuxbox ~]$ echo ${foo%%.*}
file
```

```
${parameter/pattern/string}
${parameter//pattern/string}
${parameter/#pattern/string}
${parameter/%pattern/string}
```

This expansion performs a search and replace upon the contents of *parameter*. If text is found matching wildcard *pattern*, it is replaced with the contents of *string*. In the normal form, only the first occurrence of *pattern* is replaced. In the // form, all occurrences are replaced. The /# form requires that the match occur at the beginning of the string, and the /% form requires the match to occur at the end of the string. /*string* may be omitted, which causes the text matched by *pattern* to be deleted.

```
[me@linuxbox ~]$ foo=JPG.JPG
[me@linuxbox ~]$ echo ${foo/JPG/jpg}
jpg.JPG
[me@linuxbox ~]$ echo ${foo//JPG/jpg}
jpg.jpg
[me@linuxbox ~]$ echo ${foo/#JPG/jpg}
jpg.JPG
[me@linuxbox ~]$ echo ${foo/%JPG/jpg}
JPG.jpg
```

Parameter expansion is a good thing to know. The string-manipulation expansions can be used as substitutes for other common commands such as sed and cut. Expansions improve the efficiency of scripts by eliminating the use of external programs. As an example, we will modify the longest-word program discussed in the previous chapter to use the parameter expansion

${#j} in place of the command substitution $(echo $j | wc -c) and its result-
ing subshell, like so:

```
#!/bin/bash

# longest-word3 : find longest string in a file

for i; do
        if [[ -r $i ]]; then
                max_word=
                max_len=0
                for j in $(strings $i); do
                        len=${#j}
                        if (( len > max_len )); then
                                max_len=$len
                                max_word=$j
                        fi
                done
                echo "$i: '$max_word' ($max_len characters)"
        fi
done
```

Next, we will compare the efficiency of the two versions by using the
time command:

```
[me@linuxbox ~]$ time longest-word2 dirlist-usr-bin.txt
dirlist-usr-bin.txt: 'scrollkeeper-get-extended-content-list' (38 characters)

real    0m3.618s
user    0m1.544s
sys     0m1.768s
[me@linuxbox ~]$ time longest-word3 dirlist-usr-bin.txt
dirlist-usr-bin.txt: 'scrollkeeper-get-extended-content-list' (38 characters)

real    0m0.060s
user    0m0.056s
sys     0m0.008s
```

The original version of the script takes 3.618 seconds to scan the
text file, while the new version, using parameter expansion, takes only
0.06 seconds—a very significant improvement.

Arithmetic Evaluation and Expansion

We looked at arithmetic expansion in Chapter 7. It is used to perform various arithmetic operations on integers. Its basic form is

$((expression))$

where *expression* is a valid arithmetic expression.

This is related to the compound command (( )) used for arithmetic
evaluation (truth tests) we encountered in Chapter 27.

In previous chapters, we saw some of the common types of expressions
and operators. Here, we will look at a more complete list.

Number Bases

Back in Chapter 9, we got a look at octal (base 8) and hexadecimal (base 16) numbers. In arithmetic expressions, the shell supports integer constants in any base. Table 34-1 shows the notations used to specify the bases.

Table 34-1: Specifying Different Number Bases

Notation	Description
Number	By default, numbers without any notation are treated as decimal (base 10) integers.
0*number*	In arithmetic expressions, numbers with a leading zero are considered octal.
0x*number*	Hexadecimal notation
base#number	*number* is in *base*.

Some examples:

```
[me@linuxbox ~]$ echo $((0xff))
255
[me@linuxbox ~]$ echo $((2#11111111))
255
```

In these examples, we print the value of the hexadecimal number ff (the largest two-digit number) and the largest eight-digit binary (base 2) number.

Unary Operators

There are two unary operators, the + and the -, which are used to indicate if a number is positive or negative, respectively.

Simple Arithmetic

The ordinary arithmetic operators are listed in Table 34-2.

Table 34-2: Arithmetic Operators

Operator	Description
+	Addition
-	Subtraction
*	Multiplication
/	Integer division
**	Exponentiation
%	Modulo (remainder)

Most of these are self-explanatory, but integer division and modulo require further discussion.

Since the shell's arithmetic operates on only integers, the results of division are always whole numbers:

```
[me@linuxbox ~]$ echo $(( 5 / 2 ))
2
```

This makes the determination of a remainder in a division operation more important:

```
[me@linuxbox ~]$ echo $(( 5 % 2 ))
1
```

By using the division and modulo operators, we can determine that 5 divided by 2 results in 2, with a remainder of 1.

Calculating the remainder is useful in loops. It allows an operation to be performed at specified intervals during the loop's execution. In the example below, we display a line of numbers, highlighting each multiple of 5:

```
#!/bin/bash

# modulo : demonstrate the modulo operator

for ((i = 0; i <= 20; i = i + 1)); do
        remainder=$((i % 5))
        if (( remainder == 0 )); then
                printf "<%d> " $i
        else
                printf "%d " $i
        fi
done
printf "\n"
```

When executed, the results look like this:

```
[me@linuxbox ~]$ modulo
<0> 1 2 3 4 <5> 6 7 8 9 <10> 11 12 13 14 <15> 16 17 18 19 <20>
```

Assignment

Although its uses may not be immediately apparent, arithmetic expressions may perform assignment. We have performed assignment many times, though in a different context. Each time we give a variable a value, we are performing assignment. We can also do it within arithmetic expressions:

```
[me@linuxbox ~]$ foo=
[me@linuxbox ~]$ echo $foo

[me@linuxbox ~]$ if (( foo = 5 ));then echo "It is true."; fi
It is true.
[me@linuxbox ~]$ echo $foo
5
```

In the example above, we first assign an empty value to the variable foo and verify that it is indeed empty. Next, we perform an if with the compound command ((foo = 5)). This process does two interesting things: (1) it assigns the value of 5 to the variable foo, and (2) it evaluates to true because the assignment was successful.

Note: *It is important to remember the exact meaning of the = in the expression above. A single = performs assignment: foo = 5 says, "Make foo equal to 5." A double == evaluates equivalence: foo == 5 says, "Does foo equal 5?" This can be very confusing because the* test *command accepts a single = for string equivalence. This is yet another reason to use the more modern [[ ]] and (( )) compound commands in place of* test.

In addition to =, the shell provides notations that perform some very useful assignments, as shown in Table 34-3.

Table 34-3: Assignment Operators

Notation	Description
parameter = *value*	Simple assignment. Assigns *value* to *parameter*.
parameter += *value*	Addition. Equivalent to *parameter* = *parameter* + *value*.
parameter -= *value*	Subtraction. Equivalent to *parameter* = *parameter* – *value*.
parameter *= *value*	Multiplication. Equivalent to *parameter* = *parameter* × *value*.
parameter /= *value*	Integer division. Equivalent to *parameter* = *parameter* ÷ *value*.
parameter %= *value*	Modulo. Equivalent to *parameter* = *parameter* % *value*.
parameter++	Variable post-increment. Equivalent to *parameter* = *parameter* + 1. (However, see the following discussion.)
parameter--	Variable post-decrement. Equivalent to *parameter* = *parameter* - 1.
++*parameter*	Variable pre-increment. Equivalent to *parameter* = *parameter* + 1.
--*parameter*	Variable pre-decrement. Equivalent to *parameter* = *parameter* - 1.

These assignment operators provide a convenient shorthand for many common arithmetic tasks. Of special interest are the increment (++) and decrement (--) operators, which increase or decrease the value of their parameters by 1. This style of notation is taken from the C programming language and has been incorporated by several other programming languages, including bash.

The operators may appear either at the front of a parameter or at the end. While they both either increment or decrement the parameter by 1, the two placements have a subtle difference. If placed at the front of the parameter, the parameter is incremented (or decremented) before the parameter is returned. If placed after, the operation is performed *after* the parameter is returned. This is rather strange, but it is the intended behavior. Here is a demonstration:

```
[me@linuxbox ~]$ foo=1
[me@linuxbox ~]$ echo $((foo++))
1
[me@linuxbox ~]$ echo $foo
2
```

If we assign the value of 1 to the variable foo and then increment it with the ++ operator placed after the parameter name, foo is returned with the value of 1. However, if we look at the value of the variable a second time, we see the incremented value. If we place the ++ operator in front of the parameter, we get this more expected behavior:

```
[me@linuxbox ~]$ foo=1
[me@linuxbox ~]$ echo $((++foo))
2
[me@linuxbox ~]$ echo $foo
2
```

For most shell applications, prefixing the operator will be the most useful.

The ++ and -- operators are often used in conjunction with loops. We will make some improvements to our modulo script to tighten it up a bit:

```
#!/bin/bash

# modulo2 : demonstrate the modulo operator

for ((i = 0; i <= 20; ++i )); do
        if (((i % 5) == 0 )); then
                printf "<%d> " $i
        else
                printf "%d " $i
        fi
done
printf "\n"
```

Bit Operations

One class of operators manipulates numbers in an unusual way. These operators work at the bit level. They are used for certain kinds of low-level tasks, often involving setting or reading bit flags. Table 34-4 lists the bit operators.

Table 34-4: Bit Operators

Operator	Description
~	Bitwise negation. Negate all the bits in a number.
<<	Left bitwise shift. Shift all the bits in a number to the left.
>>	Right bitwise shift. Shift all the bits in a number to the right.
&	Bitwise AND. Perform an AND operation on all the bits in two numbers.
|	Bitwise OR. Perform an OR operation on all the bits in two numbers.
^	Bitwise XOR. Perform an exclusive OR operation on all the bits in two numbers.

Note that there are also corresponding assignment operators (for example, <<=) for all but bitwise negation.

Here we will demonstrate producing a list of powers of 2, using the left bitwise shift operator:

```
[me@linuxbox ~]$ for ((i=0;i<8;++i)); do echo $((1<<i)); done
1
2
4
8
16
32
64
128
```

Logic

As we discovered in Chapter 27, the (( )) compound command supports a variety of comparison operators. There are a few more that can be used to evaluate logic. Table 34-5 shows the complete list.

Table 34-5: Comparison Operators

Operator	Description
<=	Less than or equal to
>=	Greater than or equal to
<	Less than
>	Greater than
==	Equal to

(continued)

Table 34-5 (continued)

Operator	Description
!=	Not equal to
&&	Logical AND
||	Logical OR
expr1?expr2:expr3	Comparison (ternary) operator. If expression *expr1* evaluates to be non-zero (arithmetic true) then *expr2*, else *expr3*.

When used for logical operations, expressions follow the rules of arithmetic logic; that is, expressions that evaluate as 0 are considered false, while non-zero expressions are considered true. The (( )) compound command maps the results into the shell's normal exit codes:

```
[me@linuxbox ~]$ if ((1)); then echo "true"; else echo "false"; fi
true
[me@linuxbox ~]$ if ((0)); then echo "true"; else echo "false"; fi
false
```

The strangest of the logical operators is the *ternary operator*. This operator (which is modeled after the one in the C programming language) performs a standalone logical test. It can be used as a kind of if/then/else statement. It acts on three arithmetic expressions (strings won't work), and if the first expression is true (or non-zero), the second expression is performed. Otherwise, the third expression is performed. We can try this on the command line.

```
[me@linuxbox ~]$ a=0
[me@linuxbox ~]$ ((a<1?++a:--a))
[me@linuxbox ~]$ echo $a
1
[me@linuxbox ~]$ ((a<1?++a:--a))

[me@linuxbox ~]$ echo $a
0
```

Here we see a ternary operator in action. This example implements a toggle. Each time the operator is performed, the value of the variable a switches from 0 to 1 or vice versa.

Please note that performing assignment within the expressions is not straightforward. When this is attempted, bash will declare an error:

```
[me@linuxbox ~]$ a=0
[me@linuxbox ~]$ ((a<1?a+=1:a-=1))
bash: ((: a<1?a+=1:a-=1: attempted assignment to non-variable (error token is
"-=1")
```

This problem can be mitigated by surrounding the assignment expression with parentheses:

```
[me@linuxbox ~]$ ((a<1?(a+=1):(a-=1)))
```

Next, we see a more comprehensive example of using arithmetic operators in a script that produces a simple table of numbers:

```
#!/bin/bash

# arith-loop: script to demonstrate arithmetic operators

finished=0
a=0
printf "a\ta**2\ta**3\n"
printf "=\t====\t====\n"

until ((finished)); do
        b=$((a**2))
        c=$((a**3))
        printf "%d\t%d\t%d\n" $a $b $c
        ((a<10?++a:(finished=1)))
done
```

In this script, we implement an until loop based on the value of the finished variable. Initially, the variable is set to 0 (arithmetic false), and we continue the loop until it becomes non-zero. Within the loop, we calculate the square and cube of the counter variable a. At the end of the loop, the value of the counter variable is evaluated. If it is less than 10 (the maximum number of iterations), it is incremented by 1, else the variable finished is given the value of 1, making finished arithmetically true and thereby terminating the loop. Running the script gives this result:

```
[me@linuxbox ~]$ arith-loop
a         a**2    a**3
=         ====    ====
0         0       0
1         1       1
2         4       8
3         9       27
4         16      64
5         25      125
6         36      216
7         49      343
8         64      512
9         81      729
10        100     1000
```

bc—An Arbitrary-Precision Calculator Language

We have seen that the shell can handle all types of integer arithmetic, but what if we need to perform higher math or even just use floating-point numbers? The answer is, we can't. At least not directly with the shell. To do this, we need to use an external program. There are several approaches we can take. Embedding Perl or AWK programs is one possible solution but, unfortunately, outside the scope of this book.

Another approach is to use a specialized calculator program. One such program found on most Linux systems is called bc.

The bc program reads a file written in its own C-like language and executes it. A bc script may be a separate file, or it may be read from standard input. The bc language supports quite a few features, including variables, loops, and programmer-defined functions. We won't cover bc entirely here, just enough to get a taste. bc is well documented by its man page.

Let's start with a simple example. We'll write a bc script to add 2 plus 2:

```
/* A very simple bc script */

2 + 2
```

The first line of the script is a comment. bc uses the same syntax for comments as the C programming language. Comments, which may span multiple lines, begin with /* and end with */.

Using bc

If we save the bc script above as *foo.bc*, we can run it this way:

```
[me@linuxbox ~]$ bc foo.bc
bc 1.06.94

Copyright 1991-1994, 1997, 1998, 2000, 2004, 2006 Free Software Foundation,
Inc.
This is free software with ABSOLUTELY NO WARRANTY.
For details type `warranty'.
4
```

If we look carefully, we can see the result at the very bottom, after the copyright message. This message can be suppressed with the -q (quiet) option.

bc can also be used interactively:

```
[me@linuxbox ~]$ bc -q
2 + 2
4
quit
```

When using bc interactively, we simply type the calculations we wish to perform, and the results are immediately displayed. The bc command quit ends the interactive session.

It is also possible to pass a script to bc via standard input:

```
[me@linuxbox ~]$ bc < foo.bc
4
```

The ability to take standard input means that we can use here documents, here strings, and pipes to pass scripts. This is a here string example:

```
[me@linuxbox ~]$ bc <<< "2+2"
4
```

An Example Script

As a real-world example, we will construct a script that performs a common calculation, monthly loan payments. In the script below, we use a here document to pass a script to bc:

```
#!/bin/bash

# loan-calc : script to calculate monthly loan payments

PROGNAME=$(basename $0)

usage () {
        cat <<- EOF
        Usage: $PROGNAME PRINCIPAL INTEREST MONTHS

        Where:

        PRINCIPAL is the amount of the loan.
        INTEREST is the APR as a number (7% = 0.07).
        MONTHS is the length of the loan's term.

        EOF
}

if (($# != 3)); then
        usage
        exit 1
fi

principal=$1
interest=$2
months=$3

bc <<- EOF
        scale = 10
        i = $interest / 12
        p = $principal
        n = $months
        a = p * ((i * ((1 + i) ^ n)) / (((1 + i) ^ n) - 1))
        print a, "\n"
EOF
```

When executed, the results look like this:

```
[me@linuxbox ~]$ loan-calc 135000 0.0775 180
1270.7222490000
```

This example calculates the monthly payment for a $135,000 loan at 7.75% APR for 180 months (15 years). Notice the precision of the answer. This is determined by the value given to the special scale variable in the bc script. A full description of the bc scripting language is provided by the bc man page. While its mathematical notation is slightly different from that of the shell (bc more closely resembles C), most of it will be quite familiar, based on what we have learned so far.

Final Note

In this chapter, we have learned about many of the little things that can be used to get the "real work" done in scripts. As our experience with scripting grows, the ability to effectively manipulate strings and numbers will prove extremely valuable. Our loan-calc script demonstrates that even simple scripts can do some really useful things.

Extra Credit

While the basic functionality of the loan-calc script is in place, the script is far from complete. For extra credit, try improving the loan-calc script with the following features:

- Full verification of the command-line arguments
- A command-line option to implement an "interactive" mode that will prompt the user to input the principal, interest rate, and term of the loan
- A better format for the output

35

ARRAYS

In the last chapter, we looked at how the shell can manipulate strings and numbers. The data types we have looked at so far are known in computer science circles as *scalar variables,* that is, variables that contain a single value.

In this chapter, we will look at another kind of data structure called an *array,* which holds multiple values. Arrays are a feature of virtually every programming language. The shell supports them, too, though in a rather limited fashion. Even so, they can be very useful for solving programming problems.

What Are Arrays?

Arrays are variables that hold more than one value at a time. Arrays are organized like a table. Let's consider a spreadsheet as an example. A spreadsheet acts like a *two-dimensional array.* It has both rows and columns, and an individual cell in the spreadsheet can be located according to its row and column address. An array behaves the same way. An array has cells, which are called *elements*, and each element contains data. An individual array element is accessed using an address called an *index* or *subscript*.

Most programming languages support *multidimensional arrays*. A spreadsheet is an example of a multidimensional array with two dimensions, width and height. Many languages support arrays with an arbitrary number of dimensions, though two- and three-dimensional arrays are probably the most commonly used.

Arrays in bash are limited to a single dimension. We can think of them as a spreadsheet with a single column. Even with this limitation, there are many applications for them. Array support first appeared in bash version 2. The original Unix shell program, sh, did not support arrays at all.

Creating an Array

Array variables are named just like other bash variables and are created automatically when they are accessed. Here is an example:

```
[me@linuxbox ~]$ a[1]=foo
[me@linuxbox ~]$ echo ${a[1]}
foo
```

Here we see an example of both the assignment and access of an array element. With the first command, element 1 of array a is assigned the value foo. The second command displays the stored value of element 1. The use of braces in the second command is required to prevent the shell from attempting pathname expansion on the name of the array element.

An array can also be created with the declare command:

```
[me@linuxbox ~]$ declare -a a
```

Using the -a option, this example of declare creates the array a.

Assigning Values to an Array

Values may be assigned in one of two ways. Single values may be assigned using the following syntax:

```
name[subscript]=value
```

where *name* is the name of the array and *subscript* is an integer (or arithmetic expression) greater than or equal to 0. Note that the first element of an array is subscript 0, not 1. *value* is a string or integer assigned to the array element.

Multiple values may be assigned using the following syntax:

```
name=(value1 value2 ...)
```

where *name* is the name of the array and *value1 value2 ...* are values assigned sequentially to elements of the array, starting with element 0. For example, if we wanted to assign abbreviated days of the week to the array days, we could do this:

```
[me@linuxbox ~]$ days=(Sun Mon Tue Wed Thu Fri Sat)
```

It is also possible to assign values to a specific element by specifying a subscript for each value:

```
[me@linuxbox ~]$ days=([0]=Sun [1]=Mon [2]=Tue [3]=Wed [4]=Thu [5]=Fri [6]=Sat)
```

Accessing Array Elements

So what are arrays good for? Just as many data-management tasks can be performed with a spreadsheet program, many programming tasks can be performed with arrays.

Let's consider a simple data-gathering and presentation example. We will construct a script that examines the modification times of the files in a specified directory. From this data, our script will output a table showing at what hour of the day the files were last modified. Such a script could be used to determine when a system is most active. This script, called hours, produces this result:

```
[me@linuxbox ~]$ hours .
Hour    Files   Hour    Files
----    -----   ----    -----
00      0       12      11
01      1       13      7
02      0       14      1
03      0       15      7
04      1       16      6
05      1       17      5
06      6       18      4
07      3       19      4
08      1       20      1
09      14      21      0
10      2       22      0
11      5       23      0

Total files = 80
```

We execute the hours program, specifying the current directory as the target. It produces a table showing, for each hour of the day (0–23), how many files were last modified. The code to produce this is as follows:

```
#!/bin/bash

# hours : script to count files by modification time

usage () {
        echo "usage: $(basename $0) directory" >&2
}
```

```
# Check that argument is a directory
if [[ ! -d $1 ]]; then
        usage
        exit 1
fi

# Initialize array
for i in {0..23}; do hours[i]=0; done

# Collect data
for i in $(stat -c %y "$1"/* | cut -c 12-13); do
        j=${i/#0}
        ((++hours[j]))
        ((++count))
done

# Display data
echo -e "Hour\tFiles\tHour\tFiles"
echo -e "----\t-----\t----\t-----"
for i in {0..11}; do
        j=$((i + 12))
        printf "%02d\t%d\t%02d\t%d\n" $i ${hours[i]} $j ${hours[j]}
done
printf "\nTotal files = %d\n" $count
```

The script consists of one function (usage) and a main body with four sections. In the first section, we check that there is a command-line argument and that it is a directory. If it is not, we display the usage message and exit.

The second section initializes the array hours. It does this by assigning each element a value of 0. There is no special requirement to prepare arrays prior to use, but our script needs to ensure that no element is empty. Note the interesting way the loop is constructed. By employing brace expansion ({0..23}), we are able to easily generate a sequence of words for the for command.

The next section gathers the data by running the stat program on each file in the directory. We use cut to extract the two-digit hour from the result. Inside the loop, we need to remove leading zeros from the hour field, since the shell will try (and ultimately fail) to interpret values 00 through 09 as octal numbers (see Table 34-2). Next, we increment the value of the array element corresponding with the hour of the day. Finally, we increment a counter (count) to track the total number of files in the directory.

The last section of the script displays the contents of the array. We first output a couple of header lines and then enter a loop that produces four columns of output. Lastly, we output the final tally of files.

Array Operations

There are many common array operations. Such things as deleting arrays, determining their size, sorting, and so on have many applications in scripting.

Outputting the Entire Contents of an Array

The subscripts * and @ can be used to access every element in an array. As with positional parameters, the @ notation is the more useful of the two. Here is a demonstration:

```
[me@linuxbox ~]$ animals=("a dog" "a cat" "a fish")
[me@linuxbox ~]$ for i in ${animals[*]}; do echo $i; done
a
dog
a
cat
a
fish
[me@linuxbox ~]$ for i in ${animals[@]}; do echo $i; done
a
dog
a
cat
a
fish
[me@linuxbox ~]$ for i in "${animals[*]}"; do echo $i; done
a dog a cat a fish
[me@linuxbox ~]$ for i in "${animals[@]}"; do echo $i; done
a dog
a cat
a fish
```

We create the array animals and assign it three two-word strings. We then execute four loops to see the effect of word-splitting on the array contents. The behavior of notations ${animals[*]} and ${animals[@]} is identical until they are quoted. The * notation results in a single word containing the array's contents, while the @ notation results in three words, which matches the array's "real" contents.

Determining the Number of Array Elements

Using parameter expansion, we can determine the number of elements in an array in much the same way as finding the length of a string. Here is an example:

```
[me@linuxbox ~]$ a[100]=foo
[me@linuxbox ~]$ echo ${#a[@]}  # number of array elements
1
[me@linuxbox ~]$ echo ${#a[100]}  # length of element 100
3
```

We create array a and assign the string foo to element 100. Next, we use parameter expansion to examine the length of the array, using the @ notation. Finally, we look at the length of element 100, which contains the string foo. It is interesting to note that while we assigned our string to element 100, bash reports only one element in the array. This differs from the behavior of some other languages, in which the unused elements of the array (elements 0–99) would be initialized with empty values and counted.

Finding the Subscripts Used by an Array

As bash allows arrays to contain "gaps" in the assignment of subscripts, it is sometimes useful to determine which elements actually exist. This can be done with a parameter expansion using the following forms:

$${!array[*]}$$
$${!array[@]}$$

where *array* is the name of an array variable. Like the other expansions that use * and @, the @ form enclosed in quotes is the most useful, as it expands into separate words:

```
[me@linuxbox ~]$ foo=([2]=a [4]=b [6]=c)
[me@linuxbox ~]$ for i in "${foo[@]}"; do echo $i; done
a
b
c
[me@linuxbox ~]$ for i in "${!foo[@]}"; do echo $i; done
2
4
6
```

Adding Elements to the End of an Array

Knowing the number of elements in an array is no help if we need to append values to the end of an array, since the values returned by the * and @ notations do not tell us the maximum array index in use. Fortunately, the shell provides us with a solution. By using the += assignment operator, we can automatically append values to the end of an array. Here, we assign three values to the array foo, and then append three more.

```
[me@linuxbox ~]$ foo=(a b c)
[me@linuxbox ~]$ echo ${foo[@]}
a b c
[me@linuxbox ~]$ foo+=(d e f)
[me@linuxbox ~]$ echo ${foo[@]}
a b c d e f
```

Sorting an Array

Just as with spreadsheets, it is often necessary to sort the values in a column of data. The shell has no direct way of doing this, but it's not hard to do with a little coding:

```
#!/bin/bash

# array-sort : Sort an array

a=(f e d c b a)
echo "Original array: ${a[@]}"
a_sorted=($(for i in "${a[@]}"; do echo $i; done | sort))
echo "Sorted array:   ${a_sorted[@]}"
```

When executed, the script produces this:

```
[me@linuxbox ~]$ array-sort
Original array: f e d c b a
Sorted array:   a b c d e f
```

The script operates by copying the contents of the original array (a) into a second array (a_sorted) with a tricky piece of command substitution. This basic technique can be used to perform many kinds of operations on the array by changing the design of the pipeline.

Deleting an Array

To delete an array, use the unset command:

```
[me@linuxbox ~]$ foo=(a b c d e f)
[me@linuxbox ~]$ echo ${foo[@]}
a b c d e f
[me@linuxbox ~]$ unset foo
[me@linuxbox ~]$ echo ${foo[@]}

[me@linuxbox ~]$
```

unset may also be used to delete single array elements:

```
[me@linuxbox ~]$ foo=(a b c d e f)
[me@linuxbox ~]$ echo ${foo[@]}
a b c d e f
[me@linuxbox ~]$ unset 'foo[2]'
[me@linuxbox ~]$ echo ${foo[@]}
a b d e f
```

In this example, we delete the third element of the array, subscript 2. Remember, arrays start with subscript 0, not 1! Notice also that the array element must be quoted to prevent the shell from performing pathname expansion.

Interestingly, the assignment of an empty value to an array does not empty its contents:

```
[me@linuxbox ~]$ foo=(a b c d e f)
[me@linuxbox ~]$ foo=
[me@linuxbox ~]$ echo ${foo[@]}
b c d e f
```

Any reference to an array variable without a subscript refers to element 0 of the array:

```
[me@linuxbox ~]$ foo=(a b c d e f)
[me@linuxbox ~]$ echo ${foo[@]}
a b c d e f
[me@linuxbox ~]$ foo=A
[me@linuxbox ~]$ echo ${foo[@]}
A b c d e f
```

Final Note

If we search the bash man page for the word *array*, we find many instances in which bash makes use of array variables. Most of these are rather obscure, but they may provide occasional utility in some special circumstances. In fact, the entire topic of arrays is rather underutilized in shell programming, largely because the traditional Unix shell programs (such as sh) lacked any support for arrays. This lack of popularity is unfortunate, because arrays are widely used in other programming languages and provide a powerful tool for solving many kinds of programming problems.

Arrays and loops have a natural affinity and are often used together. The following form of loop is particularly well suited to calculating array subscripts:

```
for ((expr1; expr2; expr3))
```

36

EXOTICA

In this, the final chapter of our journey, we will look at some odds and ends. While we have certainly covered a lot of ground in the previous chapters, there are many bash features that we have not covered. Most are fairly obscure and useful mainly to those integrating bash into a Linux distribution. However, there are a few that, while not in common use, are helpful for certain programming problems. We will cover them here.

Group Commands and Subshells

bash allows commands to be grouped together. This can be done in one of two ways: either with a *group command* or with a *subshell*. Here are examples of the syntax of each.

Group command:

```
{ command1; command2; [command3; ...] }
```

Subshell:

```
(command1; command2; [command3;...])
```

The two forms differ in that a group command surrounds its commands with braces and a subshell uses parentheses. It is important to note that, due to the way bash implements group commands, the braces must be separated from the commands by a space and the last command must be terminated with either a semicolon or a newline prior to the closing brace.

Performing Redirections

So what are group commands and subshells good for? While they have an important difference (which we will get to in a moment), they are both used to manage redirection. Let's consider a script segment that performs redirections on multiple commands:

```
ls -l > output.txt
echo "Listing of foo.txt" >> output.txt
cat foo.txt >> output.txt
```

This is pretty straightforward: three commands with their output redirected to a file named *output.txt*. Using a group command, we could code this as follows:

```
{ ls -l; echo "Listing of foo.txt"; cat foo.txt; } > output.txt
```

Using a subshell is similar:

```
(ls -l; echo "Listing of foo.txt"; cat foo.txt) > output.txt
```

Using this technique, we have saved ourselves some typing, but where a group command or subshell really shines is with pipelines. When constructing a pipeline of commands, it is often useful to combine the results of several commands into a single stream. Group commands and subshells make this easy:

```
{ ls -l; echo "Listing of foo.txt"; cat foo.txt; } | lpr
```

Here we have combined the output of our three commands and piped them into the input of lpr to produce a printed report.

Process Substitution

While they look similar and can both be used to combine streams for redirection, there is an important difference between group commands and subshells. Whereas a group command executes all of its commands in the current shell, a subshell (as the name suggests) executes its commands in a child copy of the current shell. This means that the environment is copied and given to a new instance of the shell. When the subshell exits, the copy of the environment is lost, so any changes made to the subshell's environment (including variable assignment) are lost as well.

Therefore, in most cases, unless a script requires a subshell, group commands are preferable to subshells. Group commands are both faster and require less memory.

We saw an example of the subshell environment problem in Chapter 28, when we discovered that a read command in a pipeline does not work as we might intuitively expect. To recap, when we construct a pipeline like this:

```
echo "foo" | read
echo $REPLY
```

the content of the REPLY variable is always empty, because the read command is executed in a subshell and its copy of REPLY is destroyed when the subshell terminates.

Because commands in pipelines are always executed in subshells, any command that assigns variables will encounter this issue. Fortunately, the shell provides an exotic form of expansion called *process substitution* that can be used to work around this problem.

Process substitution is expressed in two ways: for processes that produce standard output:

> <(*list*)

or for processes that intake standard input:

> >(*list*)

where *list* is a list of commands.

To solve our problem with read, we can employ process substitution like this:

```
read < <(echo "foo")
echo $REPLY
```

Process substitution allows us to treat the output of a subshell as an ordinary file for purposes of redirection. In fact, since it is a form of expansion, we can examine its real value:

```
[me@linuxbox ~]$ echo <(echo "foo")
/dev/fd/63
```

By using echo to view the result of the expansion, we see that the output of the subshell is being provided by a file named */dev/fd/63*.

Process substitution is often used with loops containing read. Here is an example of a read loop that processes the contents of a directory listing created by a subshell:

```
#!/bin/bash

# pro-sub : demo of process substitution

while read attr links owner group size date time filename; do
```

```
        cat <<- EOF
                Filename:   $filename
                Size:       $size
                Owner:      $owner
                Group:      $group
                Modified:   $date $time
                Links:      $links
                Attributes: $attr

        EOF
done < <(ls -l | tail -n +2)
```

The loop executes read for each line of a directory listing. The listing itself is produced on the final line of the script. This line redirects the output of the process substitution into the standard input of the loop. The tail command is included in the process substitution pipeline to eliminate the first line of the listing, which is not needed.

When executed, the script produces output like this:

```
[me@linuxbox ~]$ pro-sub | head -n 20
Filename:   addresses.ldif
Size:       14540
Owner:      me
Group:      me
Modified:   2012-04-02 11:12
Links:      1
Attributes: -rw-r--r--

Filename:   bin
Size:       4096
Owner:      me
Group:      me
Modified:   2012-07-10 07:31
Links:      2
Attributes: drwxr-xr-x

Filename:   bookmarks.html
Size:       394213
Owner:      me
Group:      me
```

Traps

In Chapter 10, we saw how programs can respond to signals. We can add this capability to our scripts, too. While the scripts we have written so far have not needed this capability (because they have very short execution times and do not create temporary files), larger and more complicated scripts may benefit from having a signal-handling routine.

When we design a large, complicated script, it is important to consider what happens if the user logs off or shuts down the computer while the script is running. When such an event occurs, a signal will be sent to all affected processes. In turn, the programs representing those processes can perform actions to ensure a proper and orderly termination of the program. Let's say, for example, that we wrote a script that created a temporary file during its execution. In the course of good design, we would have the script delete the file when the script finishes its work. It would also be smart to have the script delete the file if a signal is received indicating that the program was going to be terminated prematurely.

bash provides a mechanism for this purpose known as a *trap*. Traps are implemented with the appropriately named built-in command trap. trap uses the following syntax:

trap *argument signal* [*signal...*]

where *argument* is a string that will be read and treated as a command, and *signal* is the specification of a signal that will trigger the execution of the interpreted command.

Here is a simple example:

```
#!/bin/bash

# trap-demo : simple signal handling demo

trap "echo 'I am ignoring you.'" SIGINT SIGTERM

for i in {1..5}; do
        echo "Iteration $i of 5"
        sleep 5
done
```

This script defines a trap that will execute an echo command each time either the SIGINT or SIGTERM signal is received while the script is running. Execution of the program looks like this when the user attempts to stop the script by pressing CTRL-C:

```
[me@linuxbox ~]$ trap-demo
Iteration 1 of 5
Iteration 2 of 5
I am ignoring you.
Iteration 3 of 5
I am ignoring you.
Iteration 4 of 5
Iteration 5 of 5
```

As we can see, each time the user attempts to interrupt the program, the message is printed instead.

Constructing a string to form a useful sequence of commands can be awkward, so it is common practice to specify a shell function as the command. In this example, a separate shell function is specified for each signal to be handled:

```
#!/bin/bash

# trap-demo2 : simple signal handling demo

exit_on_signal_SIGINT () {
        echo "Script interrupted." 2>&1
        exit 0
}
```

```
exit_on_signal_SIGTERM () {
        echo "Script terminated." 2>&1
        exit 0
}

trap exit_on_signal_SIGINT SIGINT
trap exit_on_signal_SIGTERM SIGTERM

for i in {1..5}; do
        echo "Iteration $i of 5"
        sleep 5
done
```

This script features two trap commands, one for each signal. Each trap, in turn, specifies a shell function to be executed when the particular signal is received. Note the inclusion of an exit command in each of the signal-handling functions. Without an exit, the script would continue after completing the function.

When the user presses CTRL-C during the execution of this script, the results look like this:

```
[me@linuxbox ~]$ trap-demo2
Iteration 1 of 5
Iteration 2 of 5
Script interrupted.
```

TEMPORARY FILES

One reason signal handlers are included in scripts is to remove temporary files that the script may create to hold intermediate results during execution. There is something of an art to naming temporary files. Traditionally, programs on Unix-like systems create their temporary files in the */tmp* directory, a shared directory intended for such files. However, since the directory is shared, this poses certain security concerns, particularly for programs running with superuser privileges. Aside from the obvious step of setting proper permissions for files exposed to all users of the system, it is important to give temporary files non-predictable filenames. This avoids an exploit known as a *temp race attack*. One way to create a non-predictable (but still descriptive) name is to do something like this:

```
tempfile=/tmp/$(basename $0).$$.$RANDOM
```

This will create a filename consisting of the program's name, followed by its process ID (PID), followed by a random integer. Note, however, that the $RANDOM shell variable returns a value only in the range of 1 to 32767, which is not a very large range in computer terms, so a single instance of the variable is not sufficient to overcome a determined attacker.

A better way is to use the mktemp program (not to be confused with the mktemp standard library function) to both name and create the temporary file.

The mktemp program accepts a template as an argument that is used to build the filename. The template should include a series of X characters, which are replaced by a corresponding number of random letters and numbers. The longer the series of X characters, the longer the series of random characters. Here is an example:

```
tempfile=$(mktemp /tmp/foobar.$$.XXXXXXXXXX)
```

This creates a temporary file and assigns its name to the variable tempfile. The X characters in the template are replaced with random letters and numbers so that the final filename (which, in this example, also includes the expanded value of the special parameter $$ to obtain the PID) might be something like

```
/tmp/foobar.6593.UOZuvM6654
```

While the mktemp man page states that mktemp makes a temporary filename, mktemp also creates the file as well.

For scripts that are executed by regular users, it may be wise to avoid the use of the */tmp* directory and create a directory for temporary files within the user's home directory, with a line of code such as this:

```
[[ -d $HOME/tmp ]] || mkdir $HOME/tmp
```

Asynchronous Execution

It is sometimes desirable to perform more than one task at the same time. We have seen that all modern operating systems are at least multitasking if not multiuser as well. Scripts can be constructed to behave in a multitasking fashion.

Usually this involves launching a script that, in turn, launches one or more child scripts that perform an additional task while the parent script continues to run. However, when a series of scripts runs this way, there can be problems keeping the parent and child coordinated. That is, what if the parent or child is dependent on the other, and one script must wait for the other to finish its task before finishing its own?

bash has a built-in command to help manage *asynchronous execution* such as this. The wait command causes a parent script to pause until a specified process (i.e., the child script) finishes.

wait

We will demonstrate the wait command first. To do this, we will need two scripts. Here is the parent script:

```
#!/bin/bash

# async-parent : Asynchronous execution demo (parent)

echo "Parent: starting..."
```

```
echo "Parent: launching child script..."
async-child &
pid=$!
echo "Parent: child (PID= $pid) launched."

echo "Parent: continuing..."
sleep 2

echo "Parent: pausing to wait for child to finish..."
wait $pid

echo "Parent: child is finished. Continuing..."
echo "Parent: parent is done. Exiting."
```

And here is the child script:

```
#!/bin/bash

# async-child : Asynchronous execution demo (child)

echo "Child: child is running..."
sleep 5
echo "Child: child is done. Exiting."
```

In this example, we see that the child script is very simple. The real action is being performed by the parent. In the parent script, the child script is launched and put into the background. The process ID of the child script is recorded by assigning the pid variable with the value of the $! shell parameter, which will always contain the process ID of the last job put into the background.

The parent script continues and then executes a wait command with the PID of the child process. This causes the parent script to pause until the child script exits, at which point the parent script concludes.

When executed, the parent and child scripts produce the following output:

```
[me@linuxbox ~]$ async-parent
Parent: starting...
Parent: launching child script...
Parent: child (PID= 6741) launched.
Parent: continuing...
Child: child is running...
Parent: pausing to wait for child to finish...
Child: child is done. Exiting.
Parent: child is finished. Continuing...
Parent: parent is done. Exiting.
```

Named Pipes

In most Unix-like systems, it is possible to create a special type of file called a named pipe. *Named pipes* are used to create a connection between two processes and can be used just like other types of files. They are not that popular, but they're good to know about.

There is a common programming architecture called *client/server*, which can make use of a communication method such as named pipes, as well as other kinds of *interprocess communication* such as network connections.

The most widely used type of client/server system is, of course, a web browser communicating with a web server. The web browser acts as the client, making requests to the server, and the server responds to the browser with web pages.

Named pipes behave like files but actually form first-in, first-out (FIFO) buffers. As with ordinary (unnamed) pipes, data goes in one end and emerges out the other. With named pipes, it is possible to set up something like this:

    process1 > named_pipe

and

    process2 < named_pipe

and it will behave as if

    process1 | process2

Setting Up a Named Pipe

First, we must create a named pipe. This is done using the mkfifo command:

```
[me@linuxbox ~]$ mkfifo pipe1
[me@linuxbox ~]$ ls -l pipe1
prw-r--r-- 1 me    me     0 2012-07-17 06:41 pipe1
```

Here we use mkfifo to create a named pipe called pipe1. Using ls, we examine the file and see that the first letter in the attributes field is *p*, indicating that it is a named pipe.

Using Named Pipes

To demonstrate how the named pipe works, we will need two terminal windows (or, alternatively, two virtual consoles). In the first terminal, we enter a simple command and redirect its output to the named pipe:

```
[me@linuxbox ~]$ ls -l > pipe1
```

After we press ENTER, the command will appear to hang. This is because there is nothing receiving data from the other end of the pipe yet. When this occurs, it is said that the pipe is *blocked*. This condition will clear once we attach a process to the other end and it begins to read input from the pipe. Using the second terminal window, we enter this command:

```
[me@linuxbox ~]$ cat < pipe1
```

The directory listing produced from the first terminal window appears in the second terminal as the output from the cat command. The ls command in the first terminal successfully completes once it is no longer blocked.

Final Note

Well, we have completed our journey. The only thing left to do now is practice, practice, practice. Even though we covered a lot of ground in our trek, we barely scratched the surface as far as the command line goes. There are still thousands of command-line programs left to be discovered and enjoyed. Start digging around in */usr/bin* and you'll see!

INDEX

displaying control characters, 235
DOS format, 236
EDITOR variable, 111
expanding tabs, 246
files, 17
filtering, 55
folding, 271
formatting, 268
formatting for typesetters, 279
formatting tables, 282
joining, 247
linefeed character, 236
lowercase to uppercase
    conversion, 254
numbering lines, 236, 268
paginating, 274
pasting, 246
preparing for printing, 288
removing duplicate lines, 55
rendering in PostScript, 280
ROT13 encoded, 255
searching for patterns, 56
sorting, 55, 236
spell checking, 263
substituting, 259
substituting tabs for spaces, 246
tab delimited, 245
transliterating characters, 254
Unix format, 236
viewing with less, 17, 55
text editors, 115, 234, 254
    emacs, 116
    gedit, 115, 310
    interactive, 254
    kate, 115, 310
    kedit, 115
    kwrite, 115
    line, 122
    nano, 115, 122
    pico, 115
    stream, 256
    syntax highlighting, 310, 314
    vi, 115
    vim, 115, 310, 314
    visual, 122
    for writing shell scripts, 310

tilde expansion, 61, 65
tload command, 106
top command, 98
top-down design, 326
Torvalds, Linus, xxv
touch command, 198–199, 213,
    305, 389
tr command, 254
traceroute command, 177
tracing, 371
transliterating characters, 254
traps, 427
troff command, 279
true command, 335
TTY (field), 96
type command, 40
typesetters, 279, 287
TZ variable, 112

U

Ubuntu, 79, 89, 149, 222, 312
umask command, 84, 92
umount command, 163
unalias command, 47
unary operator expected (error
    message), 366
unary operators, 405
unexpand command, 246
unexpected tokens, 365
uniq command, 55, 242
Unix, xxvi
Unix System V, 290
unix2dos command, 236
unset command, 421
until compound command, 361
until loop, 361
unzip command, 210
updatedb command, 189
upstream providers, 151
uptime, 326
uptime command, 331
USB flash drives, 159, 171
Usenet, 255
USER variable, 110, 112

The Electronic Frontier Foundation (EFF) is the leading organization defending civil liberties in the digital world. We defend free speech on the Internet, fight illegal surveillance, promote the rights of innovators to develop new digital technologies, and work to ensure that the rights and freedoms we enjoy are enhanced — rather than eroded — as our use of technology grows.

EFF.ORG

ELECTRONIC FRONTIER FOUNDATION

Protecting Rights and Promoting Freedom on the Electronic Frontier

The Linux Command Line was written using OpenOffice.org Writer on a Dell Inspiron 530N, factory configured with Ubuntu 8.04. The fonts used in this book are New Baskerville, Futura, TheSansMono Condensed, and Dogma. The book was typeset in LibreOffice Writer.

This book was printed and bound at Sheridan Books, Inc. in Chelsea, Michigan. The paper is 60# Finch Offset, which is certified by the Forest Stewardship Council (FSC).

The book uses a layflat binding, in which the pages are bound together with a cold-set, flexible glue and the first and last pages of the resulting book block are attached to the cover. The cover is not actually glued to the book's spine, and when open, the book lies flat and the spine doesn't crack.